Economic ideology and Japanese industrial policy

Economic ideology and Japanese industrial policy

Developmentalism from 1931 to 1965

BAI GAO
Duke University

CAMBRIDGE
UNIVERSITY PRESS

PUBLISHED BY THE PRESS SYNDICATE OF THE UNIVERSITY OF CAMBRIDGE
The Pitt Building, Trumpington Street, Cambridge CB2 1RP, United Kingdom

CAMBRIDGE UNIVERSITY PRESS
The Edinburgh Building, Cambridge CB2 2RU, United Kingdom
40 West 20th Street, New York, NY 10011-4211, USA
10 Stamford Road, Oakleigh, Melbourne 3166, Australia

First published 1997

Printed in the United States of America

Typeset in Sabon

Library of Congress Cataloguing-in-Publication Data
Gao, Bai, 1955–
Economic ideology and Japanese industrial policy :
developmentalism from 1931 to 1965 / Bai Gao.
p.   cm.
Includes bibliographical references and index.
ISBN 0-521-58240-7 (hardbound)
1. Japan – Economic conditions – 1918–1945.   2. Japan – Economic
conditions – 1945–1989.   3. Japan – Economic policy – 1945–1989.
4. Industry and state – Japan.   I. Title.
HC462.9.G34   1997
338.951'09045 – dc20   96-36770
                                                               CIP

*A catalog record for this book is available from
the British Library.*

ISBN 0 521 58240 7 hardback

To my parents

Contents

Acknowledgments

In the course of six years of working on this project, I have received inspiration, advice, and support from many people. I am most grateful to four members on my Ph.D dissertation committee at Princeton University: Paul DiMaggio, Frank Dobbin, Marius Jansen, and Gilbert Rozman. Each of them helped me greatly, not only in different ways but also at different stages of this journey. After I chose this topic for my dissertation, Marius Jansen immediately recognized the potential value of the topic to the field of Japanese studies. From then on, he has given me constant intellectual encouragement and moral support. Gilbert Rozman has been very supportive since I went to Princeton in 1987. His suggestion, based on his rich fieldwork experiences in foreign countries, of not spending too much time in Japan polishing a proposal but focusing on collecting firsthand materials turned out to be a valuable one. It enabled me not only to become familiar with my research subject, but also to collect enough empirical data. Both Jansen and Rozman helped me greatly in ensuring the funding that made this project possible. When I worked on the analytical framework of this dissertation, Frank Dobbin guided me into the literature of economic sociology. The reading lists he gave me often helped me to solve problems. He has also made constant efforts to improve my analytical skill. Paul DiMaggio came to Princeton when my dissertation was at the critical stage. He not only helped me to clarify several important concepts and offered substantial comments based on his broad interdisciplinary knowledge, but also advised me on how to structure the dissertation for future publication. Both Rozman and DiMaggio provided detailed editorial comments. The experience of precepting Sheldon Garon's course in the fall of 1992 at Princeton also provided me with an opportunity to learn more about modern Japanese history.

Andrew Gordon, Chalmers Johnson, Meg McKean, John Meyer, Kenneth Pyle, Richard Samuels, Kozo Yamamura, and Viviana Zelizer either read chapters from different versions of this manuscript or reviewed the papers generated from this research. I have benefited greatly from their comments. I also wish to thank four anonymous reviewers, two at Cambridge University Press and two at Cornell University Press, for their helpful comments.

No fieldwork, especially in a foreign country, can be done without help from scholars and friends in that country. I wish to thank Takemae Eiji of Tokyo Keizai University and Harada Sumitaka of the University of Tokyo for their generous support as my advisors in Japan during the fieldwork for my dissertation. I also thank Amakawa Akira of Yokohama National University and Nakamura Masanori of Hitotsubashi University for their support as my advisors when I revised parts of this manuscript while working on my new project on Japanese antimonopoly policy. I am grateful to the Institute of Social Science at the University of Tokyo, the School of International Business and Law at Yokohama National University, and the Faculty of Economics at Hitotsubashi University for hosting me as visiting scholar and providing research facilities and access to libraries. Mitsuda Akimasa of the Japan Foundation, Sakai Ken of the Ministry of Finance, Yuasa Hiroshi of the Washington Bureau of Sankei Shinbun, and Hua Dongming of Tokyo Keizai University arranged several meetings with Japanese scholars and government economists for me. Yoshikawa Jun and Oshio Takashi of the Economic Planning Agency provided the data concerning government economists. Ōkita Saburō, one of my research subjects in this study, not only provided time for my interview, but also helped me in getting data from other agencies and introducing me to other scholars. Hara Akira, Ide Yoshinori, Okazaki Tetsuji, and Tachi Ryūichirō, of the University of Tokyo; Kanamori Hisao of the Japan Economic Research Center; Amakawa Akira, Kisugi Shin, and Miyazaki Yoshikazu, of Yokohama National University; and Tomizuka Fumitarō of Tokyo Keizai University spent time talking to me and providing many insights into the Japanese politics and economy that greatly enriched my understanding of Japan. Sakai Saburō, the former staff at the Showa Research Association, provided important information about activities of that organization and the role played by several intellectuals in these activities. Abe Kyōko of the Industrial Bank of Japan collected the data concerning Shimomura Osamu. I also obtained many insights into Japanese politics and economics from my year-long weekly discussions with Itō Yoshizō, a former bureaucrat who had served in all major Japanese economic bureaucracies. When I worked on the final version of this manuscript, I benefited greatly from frequent discussions with Nakamura Masanori, one of the major figures in the debate on the origin of the contemporary Japanese economic system. Needless to say, none of these individuals is responsible for the views I presented in the book.

Parts of this manuscript have been presented at the meeting of the Japanese Association of Postwar Occupation History, the 1995 annual meeting of the Social Science History Association in Chicago, the 1995 annual meeting of the American Sociological Association in Washington D.C., the School of International Business and Law, Yokohama National University, Tokyo Keizai University, the Yokohama Research Association of the History of Postwar Occupation, the Center for International Studies at Duke University, the international conference on Japanese studies at Kyoto, the 1994 annual meeting of the American Sociological Association in Los Angeles, the 1994 annual conference of the Chinese Scholars of Political Science and International Studies at the East-West Center in Hawaii, the 1994 annual meeting of the American Association for Asian Studies in Boston, the Council for Regional Studies at Princeton University, the 1991 annual conference of the International Conference of Orientalists in Japan, and the Woodrow Wilson Society of Fellows. I wish to thank these audiences for their comments.

This project was financially supported by a three-year University Fellowship between 1987 and 1990 from the Graduate School of Princeton University, a dissertation fellowship from the Japan Foundation between July 1990 and August 1991, and a two-year fellowship from the Woodrow Wilson Society of Fellows at Princeton University between 1991 and 1993. A one-month pilot research trip to Japan in late 1989 was supported by the Center for International Studies and the Council for Regional Studies at Princeton University, and two minor research grants from the Asian/Pacific Studies Institute and the Art and Science Council, both at Duke University, covered part of the research cost during the revision. Finally, I wish to thank my colleagues at the Department of Sociology at Duke University, especially Kenneth Land, the chair of the department, for reducing my teaching load as a new junior faculty member in my first year, which gave me the time to complete the project.

I am grateful to Elizabeth Neal, the editor of social sciences at Cambridge University Press, for her support and confidence in this manuscript. Helen Greenberg, the copyeditor, improved my expression of ideas greatly. Finally, Louise Calabro, the production editor, smoothed the process of publication. Raphael Allen and Danna Zeller provided editorial help with early drafts of the first two chapters of this manuscript as a Ph.D dissertation. Their friendship gave my life at Princeton a warm memory.

I am indebted to the Society for Japanese Studies for permission to reproduce and adapt portions from my article "Arisawa Hiromi and His Theory for a Managed Economy," *Journal of Japanese Studies*, vol. 20, No. 1 (Winter 1994), pp. 115–53.

Finally, I wish to thank my wife, Hongqiu Yang. A sociologist herself, she has always been the first reader of my work, providing incisive commentary. More than anything else, her moral support for my academic career has been one of the major forces allowing me to overcome all the difficulties I have confronted in doing this study. In a broader sense, this dissertation is a product of the happy years we spent together in China, the United States, and Japan. My son Michael had competed with the completion of the final revision of this manuscript for who would come first. Eventually, he won. The final revision of the manuscript was completed when he was one month old.

Abbreviations

CMC	Council of Management Consultation
CPA	Cabinet Planning Agency
CPB	Cabinet Planning Board
CRB	Cabinet Resource Bureau
CSB	Cabinet Survey Bureau
EPA	Economic Planning Agency
ESB	Economic Stabilization Board
ESS	Economic and Scientific Section
GATT	General Agreement on Tariffs and Trade
GHQ	General Headquarters
ICIS	Investigation Committee on Industrial Structure
IMF	International Monetary Fund
JCED	Japan Committee of Economic Development
LDP	Liberal Democratic Party
MCI	Ministry of Commerce and Industry
MITI	Ministry of International Trade and Industry
NIDP	National Income Doubling Plan
NPRA	National Policy Research Association
RFB	Reconstruction Finance Bank
SCAP	Supreme Commander for Allied Powers
SIS	Subcommittee on Industrial System
SRA	Shōwa Research Association
SSCMA	The Special Survey Committee at the Ministry of Foreign Affairs

Note on Japanese usage

Japanese names in text appear according to Japanese custom, the surname preceding the personal name. Japanese authors use surname-first order for Japanese language publication. When their English language publications are cited, however, their names appear surname-last.

1. Introduction

It has been a half-century since the end of World War II, the war that changed the course of modern history. How did this war affect our present life? This question was repeatedly raised and answered in Japan during the war's 50th anniversary. "With regard to the Japanese economy," writes economist Noguchi Yukio (1995), "the war never ended." Even today, after 50 years, the Japanese economy still operates, both institutionally and ideologically, by the "1940 system," a wartime establishment that was alien (*ishitsu*) to prewar Japan. This system, which overemphasizes production while rejecting competition, has resulted in "institutional exhaustion" – a major symptom of the "Japanese disease" that has made the nation's economy crumble. Senior bureaucrat Sakakibara Eisuke (1995) disagrees, however. He argues that present-day Japanese capitalism should be regarded not as alien but as parallel to developments in Europe and the United States – one of the three distinctive patterns of modern capitalism that evolved from a great transformation in the period between the late 1920s and the early 1950s. After World War I, the Communist Revolution, as exemplified in the Soviet Union, was not the only alternative to traditional capitalism. Capitalism in all major industrialized countries transcended the stage of laissez-faire and entered a new era of state intervention. From this process emerged democratic socialism, practiced in France and Britain; state socialism, practiced in Germany, Italy, and Japan; and the New Deal, practiced in the United States. Today's economic institutions in these countries still reflect the transformation that occurred decades ago. For this reason, says Sakakibara, one cannot judge whether Japanese capitalism is alien according to neoclassical assertions such as "consumer rights" or "perfect competition." Instead one should analyze this historical transformation from a comparative perspective.

Both Noguchi and Sakakibara have a point. It is true that the institutions and ideologies that originated in 1931–45 and helped to create one of the world's strongest economies are now stifling rather than supporting the Japanese economy. It is also true that the wartime legacies have put Japanese capitalism on a totally different track in the postwar era and have made it a competing model to Anglo-Saxon capitalism, though the difference between Japan and its Western counterparts was deliberately denied during the Cold War. Many questions, however, remain: What kinds of institutional and ideological changes occurred in the Japanese economy in 1931–45? Why have the wartime legacies continued in postwar Japan? When we talk about these continuities, how should we count the impact of democratic reforms introduced by the occupation authority in the late 1940s and the changes in social and economic structures brought by high growth? In other words, is present-day Japanese capitalism simply a heritage of wartime or has it absorbed new elements in the postwar era? If the latter, what are these new elements?

This book addresses these issues directly and portrays the emergence of Japanese developmentalism – a distinctive set of economic ideas and ideologies on how to create wealth for a late-developed nation – in the period between the Great Depression and the end of World War II and discusses its postwar evolution. From a broad historical perspective, this book shows how the policy innovations of the state and the institutional reforms of the economy in 1931–45, governed by these ideas and ideologies, caused Japanese capitalism to depart considerably from pre-1930 practice (I will discuss why the changes in 1931–1945 can be regarded as a departure in Chapter 3). Moreover, many wartime ideologies and institutions survived the postwar democratic reforms and were reinforced to combat the economic crisis in the late 1940s; they adapted well to the Cold War situation and the global technological revolution in the 1950s; and they were further upgraded in the liberalization of trade and capital investment in the 1960s.

The continuities of the wartime institutions and ideologies in the postwar era have been sustained by three important factors. First, as a country heavily dependent on trade, Japan encountered great pressure to respond as a nation-state to the changes in the world system. The perceived external threats, such as the Cold War and the liberalization of trade and capital investment, often revived the wartime practice of national mobilization, though for different purpose. Second, the various versions of nationalism that rose and fell from 1931 to 1965 often promoted the legitimacy of policy goals in terms of collective survival and downplayed the value of individuals. Popular ideology not only influenced public judgment on economic ideas; it also changed the way economists perceived the situation. As a result, many problems in today's Japanese economy were created and enforced in the name of the "national interest." Third, the vested interests in the state and in state–business relations often constrained the selection of means for industrial policy. Although certain new economic ideas changed the ways political actors perceived interests and formulated strategies, they alone could not influence policy outcome. They had to gain policy-making power by generating support from political and business elites.

Although the questions of how Japanese capitalism differs from Anglo-Saxon capitalism and what the origin of the difference is are as old as the field of Japanese studies, they have never been addressed as seriously in the past as today. Before communism collapsed in the former Soviet Union and the Eastern European countries, the ideological pressure to keep the Western bloc united remained strong. "During the Cold War," states Chalmers Johnson (1993:54), "there was only one capitalist god and He lived in the United States, even though there was growing awareness of very promising national churches in Germany and Japan." For this reason, Japanese studies in the United States had long been perceived as irrelevant to the mainstream of American economic, political, and intellectual life. Even when the sudden "loss of irrelevance" (Steinhoff 1993) of Japanese studies, due to the rapid expansion of Japan's economic power in the international market, posed a great intellectual challenge to Western social sciences in the 1980s, studies that focused on political and economic differences between Japan and the United States were still labeled either *revisionist* or *Japan bashing*. By the end of the 1980s, according to Johnson (1988), none of the major schools of Western economic theory, including neoclassical, Keynesian, and Marxist, had succeeded in explaining the Japanese achievement in economic development; the field of Japanese political economy was suffering "a crisis in theory." Speaking of the seriousness of this failure, Alan Blinder (1990:21) wrote that "all in all, economists weaned on Western economic thought must conclude that Japan does almost everything wrong. Such a litany of errors should cost them dearly. Yet Japan's economy is a dynamo. How do they do it? American capitalism rests on a grand theory began by Adam Smith. There is no comparable theory of Japanese capitalism, but we need one if we are to formulate an intelligent economic policy toward Japan. The Japanese themselves seem less concerned with conceptualizations than with results. So, we may have to produce that theory ourselves."

Since that time, however, the serious academic efforts to build theory on Japanese capitalism have been shaken and divided by a succession of striking changes in the world, which make some people believe that this task has become less significant. First of all, communism collapsed in the former Soviet Union and the Eastern European countries, one of the most important historical events of the twentieth century. Predicting the impact of this great transformation on our future, Francis Fukuyama (1989:3–4) states that

> the ultimate triumph of Western liberal democracy seems at its close to be returning full circle to where it started. . . . What we may be witnessing is not just the end of the Cold War, or the passing of a particular period of postwar history, but the end of history as such: that is, the end point of mankind's ideological evolution and the universalization of Western liberal democracy as the final form of human development.

Fukuyama's argument suggests that there no longer exists any ideology to compete with the orthodox view of economic liberalism and democratic politics now that both fascism and communism, not to mention the Japanese variant of capitalism, have disappeared from the historical arena.

Second, in the past few years, Japan's seemingly irresistible competitiveness has declined suddenly as a result of the breakdown of Japan's bubble economy in the worst economic stagnation since World War II. Many Japanese firms have lost their edge in international competition in several strategic industries, notably automobiles, computers, and software, where American firms are demonstrating a comeback. In addition, the widely praised practices of lifetime employment and the seniority-based wage system have become problematic; many prominent Japanese companies have begun to lay off their employees under the pressure of recession. The reaction in the West verges on sensationalism. The prominent British business magazine *The Economist* (1994) issued a special edition titled "Oriental Renaissance," in which it argued that "Japan's working practices and institutions were successful only at times of very high growth. Many had built-in obsolescence." Success has made this system outmoded, declared *The*

Economist, even among those who once preached it, and Japan is converging with the West.

The reality, however, is much harsher than assumed by Fukuyama and *The Economist.* More than at any time in history, the conflicts among countries' institutionalized beliefs about how the economy works may challenge the order of the international economy. Capitalism, both its institutions and its ideologies, never has been homogeneous and probably never will be. "With their common enemy consigned to history, capitalist countries are starting to skirmish over the relative merits of their systems" (Neff 1993). Comparative capitalism is replacing comparative communism, emerging as a leading research agenda in this post–Cold War era. In the 1980s, Japanese government officials tended to avoid involvement in direct intellectual confrontation with Western countries, especially the United States, for various political reasons. In the 1990s, however, they have become very outspoken, strongly defending the legitimacy of Japan's economic institutions. Eisuke Sakakibara (1993:v) argues that "a neo-classical, or neo-American, view of capitalism, which dominated the world in the decade of the 1980s, seems to have passed its peak. . . . The post-socialist age may also become a post laissez-faire age." What does this change of attitude mean? According to Japan's former prime minister Nakasone Yasuhiro and his three advisors, Anglo-Saxon capitalism can no longer claim universality because developmentalism, which is based on the market economy but admits active intervention by the state, is spreading out in East Asia. Whether these two types of market economies can compromise with each other will determine the international order in the future (Nakasone, Murakami, Satō, and Nishibe 1992:168). It is argued that because capitalism differs across national borders as a result of various historical and cultural backgrounds, and will continue to do so, the countries "will have to accommodate each other in certain ways. In some instances, these accommodations may take the form of modification of the principle of laissez-faire" (Sakakibara 1993:vi). In this sense, asserts David Williams (1994:xiv), "history will not end until Japan, and much of East Asia with her, is made to conform to this new consensus. Until this happens, the world will stand beyond the end of history regardless of what has happened in Eastern Europe." Samuel Huntington (1993) warned that the fundamental source of international conflict in the post–Cold War era will be

primarily cultural because the conflicts between deeply institutionalized beliefs and value systems in different civilizations through hun-
dreds or even thousands of years of history will not disappear easily. As
the interactions between peoples of different cultures increase, cultural
consciousness will be intensified; eventually the result may be the
"clash of civilizations."

The challenge to international economic order created by the differences in economic ideologies is heightened by the fact that many former socialist economies and developing countries are attracted by the
Japanese model of economic development. At the beginning of the
transition from a planned economy to a market economy, the former
Soviet Union and the Eastern European countries embraced the doctrine of neoclassical economics and attempted to turn a planned economy into a market economy through *shock therapy*. As this program
has failed to deliver what it promised, many government officials and
intellectuals in the former socialist countries perceive the Japanese experience of managing the economy as a valuable lesson. In addition, the
Japanese developmental strategy has been regarded as the secret of
economic success in many newly industrialized countries in East Asia
and developing countries in Latin America. Moreover, as *Business
Week* (1994 Special Issue:32) reports in a special issue entitled "21st
Century Capitalism: How Nations and Industries Will Compete in the
Emerging Global Economy," dozens of Japanese

> from ministries, think tanks, and universities have spread out through
> Eastern Europe and Southeast Asia to proselytize Japanese-style eco-
> nomics to governments eager for advice. This missionary work goes
> largely unnoticed by the Western press, but in the next decade it could
> have a profound effect on global capitalism. . . . A likely outcome of
> this quiet counsel: Many nations will absorb at least some of the
> lessons of Japanese industrial policy, which include protection of in-
> fant industries and emphasis on exports. As a result, the world proba-
> bly won't embrace wholesale neoclassical, American-style capitalism,
> which largely trusts markets over state intervention.

Because the Japanese type of capitalism has been, is, and will be
practiced by many countries in an increasingly interdependent international economy, the intellectual foundation of Japanese industrial policy and business strategy deserves serious study. It is not only an academic research agenda, but also has important implications for the
international political economy. Deliberately neglecting the differences
because we do not like them will simply keep us from making serious

yet realistic efforts to build a better framework for the international economy in the future. To replace the objective examination of what exists with ideological assertions of what should be is the major barrier to such an effort.

This book aims to contribute to the existing literature on Japanese political economy in the following ways.

First, it shifts the focus of analysis on Japanese industrial policy from the conventional, actor-centered approach, which focuses on who won the battle in policy making, to an institutional perspective that emphasizes the impact of industrial policy on the transformation of the governance of the Japanese economy.

Since Chalmers Johnson presented the theory of the *developmental state* in his classic study on the Ministry of International Trade and Industry (MITI) in 1982, many studies on Japanese industrial policy have emphasized whether the state policy has been influenced or resisted by the private sector. Among the state, nonmarket governance structures, and the market, the focus of dichotomy in the debate has been located between the state and the other two, but whether the private sector was regarded as the personalized nonmarket structures or the personalized market is often unclear. These studies have certainly enriched our understanding of the important role played by the private sector in both the policy-making process and economic growth. Nevertheless, as David Williams (1994:194) points out, developmental state is a *macro theory* in which the nation-state is the unit of analysis. This theory is based in part on a comparison with Anglo-Saxon capitalism. Thus, micro-level analyses, which focus on the conflicts within Japan's policy community, cannot replace discussions of the institutional differences between Japanese capitalism and its Western counterparts at the national level.

In this book, I shift the focus of dichotomy from the state to the market. I argue that the most important distinction between developmentalism and liberal capitalism is not how the state is constrained by the private sector, but how the market is organized by both the state and nonmarket governance structures. As economic growth strengthened the power of the private sector in domestic politics and foreign countries, especially the United States, often pressured Japan to eliminate the barriers between foreign companies and Japanese markets, nonmarket governance structures in many cases have replaced direct bureaucratic control. In history, however, the development of these structures had been driven primarily by the industrial policy practiced by the Japanese state. *Governance structure* refers to the mechanisms that interdependent economic actors adopt to organize their business transactions and to solve their problems in order for economic activity to continue. In this matrix of social relationships, the market is simply one type of governance structure, and its weight varies considerably among different capitalist economies. The obligational network, hierarchy, monitoring, the promotional network, and trade associations also play a very important role in organizing economic life (Lindberg, Campbell, and Hollingsworth 1991:5–6). These mechanisms, as alternatives to the market, constitute "the vast area of social regulation – the social arrangements that condition and shape microeconomic choices . . . [and] encompasses all of the divers ways in which individual economic behavior is embedded in a broader social framework" (Block 1990:42). The state, moreover, plays a very important role in developing nonmarket governance structures of the economy. According to Leon N. Lindberg and John L. Campbell (1991), the state affects the governance of the economy not only through direct control of resource allocation, but also through defining the range of organizational forms by establishing the rules within which economic activity takes place and by facilitating the development of more multilaterally and formally organized governance mechanisms to achieve its goal in economic development. As Alfred Stepan (1978:xii) points out, the state attempts "not only to structure relationships between civil society and public authority in a polity but also to structure many crucial relationships within civil society as well."

In the Japanese case, I further argue, the development of nonmarket governance structures resulted directly from the politics of industrial policy, whereby the state often attempted to constrain the market forces through bureaucratic control, while the private sector fought hard to protect its own interest. As a political compromise, nonmarket governance structures prevailed. They served as a tool not only for the private sector to resist direct bureaucratic control, but also for the state to constrain the market forces in order to achieve its policy objective. Rather than focusing on who beat whom in policy making, I emphasize the mutual impact both sides had on each other on the institutional evolution of the governance of the Japanese economy. The private sector indeed often conflicted with the state, but it did not always reject the idea of organizing the market. What it cared about was whether it could organize the market by itself and what kind of mechanism could protect its interest best. Thus, the real point at issue regarding the conflicts between the state and the private sector in developmental politics is often *how* to organize the market in economic development rather than *whether* the market should be organized.

Second, this book stresses the role played by ideas and ideologies in formulating state industrial policy and shaping the direction of the institutional evolution of the Japanese economic system.

Ideas and ideologies are important to modern politics. According to Peter Hall (1989:383), policy making occurs in the context of a prevailing set of ideas:

> These include shared conceptions about the nature of society and the economy, various ideas about the appropriate role of government, a number of common political ideals, and collective memories of past policy experiences. Together, such ideas constitute the political discourse of a nation. They provide a language in which policy can be described within the political arena and the terms in which policies are judged there.

Although ideas and ideologies are not the only forces driving modern politics, they are indispensable to understanding the political process of state policy making because "beliefs about causal connections between interests and policies are at least as important as the nature of the interests themselves" (Goldstein 1993:237). Atul Kohli (1994) remarks that studies of developmental states so far have focused more on a state's capacity to implement its policy goals than on the origins of those goals, and believes that future research on developmental states should focus explicitly on "the politics of how developmental goals emerge as a priority." Taking this perspective seriously, I give economic ideas the central place in the analysis of Japanese industrial policy. By doing so, I change the developmental state from an independent variable to the dependent variable, examining how the developmental programs adopted by the Japanese state were shaped by modern politics and what role ideas and ideologies played in the policy making.

Ideas and ideologies not only shape policy outcomes, they also express the meaning contained in the institutions that evolved in the politics of industrial policy. On the one hand, these ideas and ideologies are subjective. They are neither a collection of analytic abstractions and transcriptions of an already given reality nor a set of principles for purely utilitarian calculations. Rather, they are a symbolic instrument, a "cultural tool," and a "construction of the world" by which economic actors discover, elaborate, and express the meaning of their life in an effort to create an order for this temporal world (Block 1990; Gudeman 1986; Swidler 1986). On the other hand, the rational meaning (an institutionalized rule in its infant state) is real and concrete. It reflects the realistic reasoning of actors concerning how to handle their relationship in economic activities effectively rather than an outcome of ceremonial conformity to any existing rules of culture. Only after they are accepted by all parties concerned through a political process do rational meanings become institutionalized rules. As the meaning contained in these ideas and ideologies does not have much ritual power in comparison with its later state as "highly rationalized myth" (Meyer and Rowan 1977), it is an important indicator of the power structure that shapes institutional creations and reproductions, as well as the rationale that economic actors decided to accept certain practice as their agreed pattern of "industrial culture" (Dobbin 1994; Dyson 1983).

For these reasons, I do not analyze the Japanese experience by applying Western economic theories; instead, I emphasize *how the Japanese themselves thought about economic development.* John Hicks (1969:6) once pointed out that "the way in which the economist develops his hypotheses is by asking himself the question: 'What should I do if I were in that position?' It is a question that must always be qualified by adding: 'if I were that kind of person.' . . . It is only by getting a feel of what people were like that one can begin to guess." Joseph A. Schumpeter addressed the same issue. He argued that the application of an analyst's own model in studies of the economic behavior of others

> does not in itself say anything about reality or about anybody's actual behavior or rationality. It is of particular importance to note that even if the model should fit anyone's behavior this does not mean that the individual in question consciously aims at the result and still less that he arrives at it by processes at all similar to the analytic procedure. . . . Beyond very simple cases which we may hope hail from an almost universal pattern of human behavior, understanding an end and judging rationality of means often requires that the analyst 'put himself' into places very far distant from his time and social location. Sometimes he has to transplant himself into another cultural world. (Swedberg 1991b:321, 325)

I argue that the ways in which the Japanese perceived the situation, formulated their strategies, fought for legitimacy, and confronted each other and structural change at each turning point of economic development have strongly influenced the kinds of goals that were set for industrial policy and the kinds of economic institutions that were derived from the implementation of industrial policy. Therefore, they can best reveal the economic rationale underlying Japanese industrial policy and the nature of Japan's economic institutions.

Third, this book intends to highlight the importance of history in understanding the dynamics in the evolution of modern economic institutions.

Peter Berger and Thomas Luckmann (1966:54–5) point out that "institutions always have a history, of which they are products. It is impossible to understand an institution adequately without an understanding of the historical process in which it was produced." For this reason, both Paul DiMaggio (1988) and Stephan Krasner (1984) argue that the causal arguments appropriate for periods after the institution is established may not be appropriate for periods of crisis when institutions are first created or are undergoing dramatic changes. Thus, "only a dynamic analysis can handle the problem of institution formation in the economy" (Swedberg and Granovetter 1992b:19). Institutions, moreover, do not evolve in an incremental pattern, but rather in the form of *punctuated equilibrium* (Krasner 1984). A new practice is often institutionalized as a response to rapid structural changes as actors urgently seek new solutions when the established practice is discredited by crisis (Dobbin 1994; Krasner 1984; Weir and Skocpol 1985). As Okazaki Tetsuji (1993:97–8) argues, the economic system, as an equilibrium of multiple institutions that complement each other, lives on path dependence. When a crisis in history creates changes in these institutions simultaneously, it will shift to a new equilibrium that is different in nature from the previous one. Even after the great shock that stimulated the institutional recomposition disappears in history, the repatterned economic system will continue irreversibly on its own inertia.

Embracing the neo-Weberian position that "one can only hope to find and explain historically specific patterns and sequences of transformation" (Lindberg, Campbell, and Hollingsworth 1991:4), I re-elaborate Karl Polanyi's ([1944] 1957) perspective, which regards fascism, socialism, and the New Deal as three distinctive patterns with which industrialized countries responded to the failure of the self-regulated market indicated by the Great Depression and the disorder of the international economy and military confrontations among nation-states. According to Polanyi, the power and dynamism of fascist movements were not a function of their capacity to recruit supporters but rather a result of their ability to provide an alternative solution to the impasse of liberal capitalism. Despite the fact that Germany, Italy, and Japan were confronted by conjunctural problems common to all industrialized countries in the between-wars period, they inherited structural problems peculiar to their own countries. As a result, "the economic policies of Italy, Germany and Japan differed notably from those of the capitalist countries in the 1930s" (Woolf 1968:142). Fascism was not only a political system, it also had enormous economic implications. Economically, fascism was not only a system of war mobilization, but also a major revision of many basic principles of liberal capitalism. It was this latter facet of the wartime system that distinguished Japanese capitalism from liberal capitalism in 1931–45 and transformed the Japanese economy into an alternative model of development in the postwar environment. This is not to say that the Japanese economic system is still fascist, but that without taking the impact of fascism into account, we cannot explain fully the irreversible departure of the Japanese economy in 1931–45 from its pre-1930 practice, both institutionally and ideologically.

Fascism has been regarded as an inadequate concept with which to interpret Japanese politics in 1931–45 (Duus and Okimoto 1979). Our present concern with comparative capitalism, however, has bestowed on this concept new significance. The 1930s can be viewed as an intersection of history at which the patterns of policy innovations and institutional reforms shared by Germany, Italy, and Japan not only reflected the tensions and contradictions generated in their singular paths to industrialization, but also represented a major revision of liberal capitalism that considerably shaped the track of these economies in the years that followed. As an analytical category, fascism demonstrates one distinctive pattern of the institutional recomposition of capitalist economies in the 1930s that led to further development of the diverse forms of capitalism in the postwar era. Rather than using fascism as a holistic concept to label the entire Japanese economy in 1931–45, I treat fascism as one of the important variables that led to a renaissance of the Japanese economic system with a strong developmental orientation. Instead of using the conventional definition of fascism, which emphasizes primarily politics, I confine the discussion of this concept to its basic economic principles.

Although the rise of Japanese developmentalism in 1931–45 was influenced by fascism, its postwar evolution was shaped by liberal capitalism in the form of the Pax Americana in three different ways. First, the land reform, new labor legislation, the *zaibatsu* dissolution, and the new constitution that prevented Japan from declaring war democratized the Japanese economy and eliminated its military components. Second, the implementation in 1949 of the Dodge plan, which reconnected the Japanese economy with the international market, and the liberalization of trade and capital investment in the 1960s, which forced Japan to open its domestic markets, changed Japanese developmentalism from an inward-oriented economic system characterized by strong bureaucratic control to an externally oriented economic system characterized by both strong leadership of the state and entrepreneurship of the private sector in international competition. Third, the U.S. policy of using Japan to contain communism during the Cold War also helped preserve many wartime institutions, such as the state bureaucracy and the main bank system. As a whole, the Pax Americana has not turned the Japanese economy toward the Anglo-Saxon type of liberal capitalism. Instead, it made various developmental elements of the wartime economic system, which were first derived from fascism, compatible with a new, democratic political institution and a free trade regime. In other words, the Japanese economic system was forced to make great adaptations, but it has been able to retain its developmental nature. Barrington Moore (1966) argues that fascism as a political system could coexist with capitalism as an economic system before the end of World War II. I argue the opposite way: that the policy innovations and institutional developments influenced by fascism during 1931–45 as an economic system, after certain adaptations, could coexist with democracy as a political system in the postwar era. As an alternative model of industrialization, moreover, this economic system has demonstrated great strength in international competition in peace.

Fourth, this book advances the research agenda of comparative capitalism by exploring the institutionalized beliefs of developmentalism reflected in Japanese industrial policy and economic institutions. The book shows that despite changes, sometimes substantial, in its leading propositions, Japanese developmentalism possesses certain continuities. I demonstrate that the ideology of Japanese developmentalism differed significantly from the orthodoxy of liberal capitalism, not only in the unit of analysis, the preference, and the instrumental means, but also in some essential assumptions about economics. Japanese developmentalism addressed the issue of industrialization at the level of the nation-state and considered how to strengthen national production as the top priority of industrial policy. To work toward this goal, Japanese developmentalism declared three general principles, and each of them was sustained by some distinctive instrumental means. The first principle consisted of viewing the economy strategically. By building an optimal industrial structure (*sangyō kōzō*) through government planning and industrial policy, this principle attempted to position the economy in a way that could maximize Japan's gain from international trade. The second principle was to restrain excessive competition (*kado kyōsō*). Sustained by state regulations and various nonmarket governance structures, this principle aimed at concentrating resources effectively in strategic industries, and maintaining order in economic growth. The third principle was to reject the profit motive in management. Supported by the Japanese management system, this principle was designed to mobilize human resources by trading companies' short-term profits for labor's cooperation in promoting productivity (*seisansei*). These principles were first institutionalized in the Japanese economic system in 1931–45 under the influence of the fascist ideology. Despite the postwar changes in Japan's economic institutions and national purpose, they remained fundamental to Japanese industrial policy, though with new implications.

As an economic ideology, Japanese developmentalism was never purely Japanese. From the 1930s to the 1960s, certain Western economic ideas exerted a strong impact on Japanese industrial policy. Besides the German theory of total war, the ideas of Karl Marx's *production force,* Joseph A. Schumpeter's *innovation,* and John M. Keynes's *demand management* were borrowed selectively, with considerable adjustment to local conditions. These ideas prescribed three distinctive paradigms successively in modern Japanese industrial policy: the paradigm of the managed economy in 1931–49, of promoting exports in the 1950s, and of high growth and liberalization in the 1960s. As modern Japanese history indicates, there is nothing in traditional Japanese culture that made Western individualist economics impossible, nor has there been a continuous, progressive erosion of national culture or values. Under certain circumstances, both Western economic theories and indigenous Japanese values exerted a strong influence on modern economic ideology. Once these circumstances disappeared, however, no set of ideas could be held forever.

The ideological difference between Japanese capitalism and its Anglo-Saxon counterpart, moreover, is not permanent. Japanese developmentalism has evolved in a dynamic process involving a constant redefinition of what is rational for the nation's economy. Although the wartime legacy provided the general principles for the Japanese postwar economy, the policy innovations and institutional reforms in the postwar era were no less important. They upgraded or even transcended the wartime system in many important ways and transformed Japanese developmentalism from the military version in war to the trade version in peace. Moreover, Japanese developmentalism abstracts only one particular setting of human experience, and it is constrained by the time and space of modern Japanese history. Each choice made has side effects and social costs. Because structural conditions and the international environment have changed rapidly, the elements that worked well in the 1950s and 1960s have become major barriers to today's Japanese economy and are under strong pressure to change.

Chalmers Johnson (1988:112) once commented that "the study of Japanese industrial policy is as much an exercise in intellectual history as in economic 'science'. There are lessons to be learned from the history of Japanese industrial policy, but they must first be isolated and abstracted from their intellectual and historical context." Modern Japanese economic ideology is rich and complicated. To reveal this ideology, I concentrate on a succession of political debates on major policy issues in 1931–65 involving Japanese economists, statesmen, business leaders, and the general public, which originally appeared in academic journals, business magazines, newspapers, official documents, and books. This study focuses on the 1931–65 period because this period was crucial to the institutional development of Japanese capitalism. Japanese developmentalism, which emerged in response to the Great Depression and World War II, was challenged by the postwar democratic reforms. Driven by the pressure to promote exports in the 1950s and the liberalization of trade and capital investment in the 1960s, however, the wartime legacies were upgraded to adapt to new environments. Although the strength of this system was not widely recognized by Western academia until the end of the 1970s, the transformation of Japanese developmentalism from the military version to the trade version was largely accomplished by the end of the 1960s. At the macro level, the state emerged as a major actor in the economic arena, with a strong capacity to sustain economic growth, in sharp contrast to the role played by the market in Anglo-Saxon capitalist economies. At the micro level, Japanese management, which emphasized cooperative labor relations, diverged markedly from its Western counterparts, which were characterized by conflicts between workers and managers. At the middle level, the prewar *zaibatsu* were reorganized into *keiretsu* after the temporary dissolution during the democratic reforms sponsored by the Occupation Authority; business groups emerged as a powerful weapon in market competition.

The book is organized both horizontally and vertically. Horizontally, I first portray the general historical background of each period covered by each chapter. This is followed by a description of the dependent variable to be explained – the major institutional evolution of Japanese developmentalism, as reflected in state industrial policy in that period. Then I analyze how the dependent variable can be traced back to the Japanese worldview, the characteristics of the Japanese nationalist ideology, the leading economic ideas in policy-making circles, and the present structures of the state and state–business relations. Vertically, I pay attention to the evolutionary linkages across different periods. By reading relevant sections in each empirical chapter, readers can gain a sense about how one particular angle in this study has evolved overtime.

I confine my study to explaining how the ideology of developmentalism influenced industrial policy and the institutional evolution of the Japanese economy. I do not consider, for example, whether the Japanese miracle was caused by these ideas, or whether Japanese developmentalism was more *rational* than neoclassical economics. In my view, Japanese developmentalism is simply a competing ideology with Anglo-Saxon economics. When I describe what was believed to be rational, I do not apply a set of criteria other than those applied by the Japanese themselves.

In Chapter 2, I discuss both static and dynamic characteristics of the ideology of Japanese developmentalism. In Chapters 3 to 6, the empirical chapters, I chronicle the evolution of this ideology between the 1930s and the 1960s, around three distinctive paradigms in Japanese industrial policy focusing on four different programs; each of these programs provides the format for an empirical chapter.

Chapters 3 and 4 demonstrate the policy paradigm of the managed economy in Japanese industrial policy in 1931–45 and 1946–9. By analyzing the emergence of the managed economy as the leading paradigm in Japanese industrial policy, Chapter 3 deals primarily with two questions: In what kind of historical environment did Japanese developmentalism emerge as a competing model to liberal capitalism? What was the nature of this military version of Japanese developmentalism? Chapter 4 explains how democratic reforms instituted by the occupation authority changed the Japanese economic system in some ways, while other components of the wartime legacies survived.

In Chapter 5, I discuss how Japanese developmentalism began to transform itself from the military version to the trade version under the policy paradigm of promoting exports in the 1950s. I explain why the focus of Japanese industrial policy shifted from the effectiveness of state control over the distribution of materials at the macro level to the productive efficiency of private firms at the micro level. I also show that the wartime legacies of business organization and labor relations, which had been interrupted during the postwar occupation, began to revive for the new national goal.

In Chapter 6, I argue further that the Japanese emphasis on the national power of production was expanded from the industry level to the entire economy under the paradigm of high growth and liberalization in the 1960s, and I also show that the contemporary governance structure of the Japanese economy was formed by the end of the 1960s.

In Chapter 7, I discuss the significance of the Japanese case to social science in general.

The Epilogue deals briefly with how history sheds new light on these debates differently, considering the fate of Japanese developmentalism after the 1960s. The discussion consists of two parts. Part one is about the triumph it achieved in dealing with the two oil shocks in the 1970s and the yen appreciation resulting from the Plaza Agreement in the 1980s, as indicated by worldwide appraisal. Part two reveals the dark side of Japanese developmentalism by discussing the breakdown of the bubble economy and the challenge the Japanese economy is facing today.

2. The ideology of Japanese developmentalism

Until very recently, the economic ideology that inspired Japanese industrial policy has been largely neglected in social science discussions in English-speaking countries (but see Pyle 1974). It was widely believed that the Japanese experience of economic development had little intellectual foundation. Not only does every educated person in North America know that Western mainstream economics is largely irrelevant to the study of Japanese-type economies, even specialists in Japanese studies believe that neither academic nor government economists played a major role in Japan's high-growth strategy. Academia in general has long indulged in what Saitō Seiichirō (1981:298) calls "a fallacious contrast between the prosperity of the Japanese economy and the desolation of Japanese economics."

These perceptions may be correct in the sense that neoclassical economics has not exerted any notable influence on Japanese development. Academicians, however, have neglected the fact that a group of Japanese economists represented by Arisawa Hiromi (1896–1988), Nakayama Ichirō (1898–1980), and Tōbata Seiichi (1899–1983), who belonged to the generation educated before World War II, played a very important role in the state's policy making. These economists helped the nation to establish an urgent agenda, to identify the future direction of economic development, and to build a theoretical framework for Japan's industrial policy in the context of international pressures and domestic turmoil from the 1930s to the 1960s. Their major propositions, reflected in successive state policies, constituted the core of what Japanese economist Kanamori Hisao (1985:127) calls "*Jissen-ha* economics" (the economics of actual fighting) – the logic of Japanese industrial policy. With such a character, *Jissen-ha* economics distinguishes itself from two major factions in Japanese academic economics: *marukei* (Marxist economics) and *kinkei* (modern economics, including all non-Marxist economics developed since the "marginal revolution" except the German historical school and institutional economics)

18

(Hayasaka, Masamura, Takeyama, Hamaguchi, Shibata, and Hoshino 1974:14–15). To a large extent, *Jissen-ha* economics represents the major propositions of Japanese developmentalism. The core members of *Jissen-ha* economists were a group of Japanese academic elites. Arisawa Hiromi was the president of the Academy of Japan; both Nakayama Ichirō and Tsuru Shigeto served as president of Hitotsubashi University. They are recognized more widely, however, for their close connections with high politics and their prominent role in state policy making. Arisawa, Nakayama, and Tōbata have been called *Gosanke* in postwar Japan. In Japanese history, *Gosanke* refers to the three branch families of the Tokugawa house, who were major supporters of the central *bakufu* (Japan's feudal government). The term *Gosanke* here illustrates the importance of these three economists to state policies. It implies that these three men, more than any others, served in multiple positions as heads of important advisory committees to the Japanese state, providing intellectual leadership in designing economic policy.

Some economists even worked directly in state bureaucracies. Tsuru Shigeto, an academician, served as the deputy director of the Economic Stabilization Board in the late 1940s; Ishibashi Tanzan, an economic critic, became a career politician and served as minister of finance, minister of MITI, and eventually prime minister, gaining an opportunity to put the economists' theories into practice. Another group of economists who receive special attention in this study are the *kanchō* economists (government economists), represented by Ōkita Saburō, who became Japan's minister of foreign affairs in the late 1970s; Inaba Hidezō in his early years; Gotō Yonosuke; and Shimomura Osamu, who was the chief economic advisor to Prime Minister Ikeda Shigeto in the late 1950s and early 1960s. Their regular duties as government economists included conducting economic surveys and making long-term plans, which to a large extent are highly routinized bureaucratic tasks. Their vision, intelligence, and determination, however, sustained by special structural conditions, enabled them to act like modern *shishi* (a samurai with high spirit), exerting strong influence on Japan's economic development (Komiya and Yamamura 1981; Ōkita 1990).

These economists' contribution to the nation are so important that one cannot easily separate their names from the overall history of the postwar Japanese economy. For example, no one can discuss Japan's postwar economic recovery in the late 1940s without acknowledging the *priority production program* and its designer, Arisawa Hiromi. Any book on postwar labor relations in Japan must take note of the Head-quarters of Productivity and the Central Committee of Labor. Naka-yama Ichirō served as the vice-president of the former and the president of the latter for many years and established the famous three principles for the productivity movement, which was crucial to the stabilization of Japanese labor relations and the institutionalization of Japanese management. Without Shimomura Osamu, the father of the high-growth thesis, the Japanese might never have known the significance of the high-growth policy to the Japanese economy. As leading Japanese economist Ryūtarō Komiya (1986:22) points out, "until about 1965, Japan's industrial policy, implemented primarily by the Ministry of International Trade and Industry, was based on the ideological ground-work laid by this generation." To acknowledge their great contribu-tions, the Japanese government conferred on each of the *Gosanke* the Order of the Rising Sun, First Class, with Star and Ribbon, as the era of high growth in Japan was drawing to an end in the early 1970s. This is the highest honor possible for a Japanese civilian; only those who have reached age 70 are eligible for consideration. Very few Japanese re-ceived this honor. This meaningful event, unfortunately, seems to have drawn no attention from Japan specialists in the West. No one has even thought to ask why the Japanese state has shown such great respect to these three economists.

The paradigms of industrial policy

The impact of *Jissen-ha* economists on the Japanese economy is re-flected largely in their contributions to the development of three succes-sive paradigms of Japanese industrial policy between the 1930s and the 1960s.

The paradigm of industrial policy is an important category in analyz-ing Japanese developmentalism for two reasons. First, it represents an authoritative or even a dominant view in the political discourse con-cerning industrial policies. As pointed out in the famous National In-come Doubling Plan (Keizai Kikakuchō 1960:171), "Economic plan-ning in Japan is based on a system of free-enterprise and free market. It does not have detailed goals for each field of the economy and then realize them by cohesion. It simply presents the general principles of economic operation." The general principles reflected in policy paradigms, however, are more important. As Sawa Takamitsu (1984) says, they are virtually the framework by which Japanese politicians, businessmen, and the general public comprehend the economy and the basis on which these economic actors form their expectations. Through the paradigms of industrial policy, the Japanese state not only provides individual Japanese with a "way of seeing things," it also blinds them. In other words, the state not only shapes the way in which economic actors perceive the world, it also deprives them of the power of independent judgment. By persuading economic actors to accept a "definition of the situation," the state gains some control over the outcomes because "how a problem is defined determines the nature of the solution" (Jacobsen 1995:292). As a result, these paradigms reflect both the wisdom and the cognitive constraints of the developmental state in each era, which reveal the historical nature of Japanese developmentalism. As this book shows, the power of the Japanese state has often been reflected in its ability to set the agenda for the Japanese economy through its industrial policy. The original policy formulations of the state were often altered, and many policies were not carried out as expected due to political resistance. Nevertheless, these policy paradigms succeeded in leading the institutional buildup of the Japanese economy to strengthen national competitiveness.

Second, policy paradigm links ideology directly to industrial policy and institutional development. By definition, it involves both economic institutions and ideas about how the economy and politics are interrelated (Samuels 1994). Frank Dobbin (1994:19) points out that "policy paradigms consist of both practices, in the form of policies, and means–ends designations, in the form of the tenets of governmental action. They reinforce industrial cultures by creating and sustaining particular behavior patterns among economic actors, and by symbolizing those patterns as efficient." By emphasizing policy paradigm, we can discover how Japanese developmentalism differs from its Anglo-Saxon counterparts, not only institutionally but also intellectually. This intellectual difference, I contend, is more fundamental: Ideas may not always materialize into policies, and not every policy can be explained by policy paradigms. Nevertheless, they always supply the theoretical foundation and the major dynamics for every policy innovation and institutional development. For these reasons, I emphasize those general principles that have inspired and guided Japanese industrial policy, at the risk of neglecting detailed variations among individual policies.

A study that emphasizes the paradigms of Japanese industrial policy is different from the studies that focus on economic reality in periodization. For example, although the Japanese economy experienced high growth in the 1950s, high growth itself did not become the state policy paradigm until the 1960s. Similarly, the effort to stabilize labor relations began in 1955 under the paradigm of promoting exports and technological innovation, but its impact on Japanese management did not become apparent to many analysts until the late 1970s. In this sense, the policy paradigm reflects the time when economic actors changed their rationale. There is a time lag between the policy change and its effect on materialized economic reality.

A scrutiny of Japanese debates on the general principles of industrial policy from the 1930s to the 1960s reveals three distinctive policy paradigms: the managed economy, which lasted from the beginning of the 1930s to the end of World War II in 1945, and then from 1946 to 1949; promoting exports, which dominated in the 1950s; and high growth and liberalization, which occupied the center of Japanese economic policy in the 1960s.

The managed economy

The paradigm of the managed economy in 1931–45 represented a military version of developmentalism in Japanese industrial policy. The managed economy was a watershed in the history of Japanese capitalism, marking a major departure from the pre-1930 practice. When the Great Depression intensified the conflicts of interest among the great powers in Asia, Japan responded with militarism as a solution. In 1931 it engaged in the military occupation of Manchuria, the northeastern region of China; in 1937, in the full-scale invasion of China; and in 1941, in direct confrontation with the United States. In the military version of developmentalism, the economy was perceived as the foundation of national defense. During this process, a drastic institutional recomposition occurred in Japanese capitalism. Influenced by the German theory of total war, the ideology of the managed economy resembled the orthodox doctrine of mercantilism, which regards wealth as the essential means of acquiring military power and views military power as an important means of acquiring wealth (Williams 1994).

The rise of the Japanese managed economy occurred at a turning point of history when states in all the industrialized countries strengthened their intervention in order to counter the Great Depression. Thus, its historical significance needs to be understood in a broader context. According to Karl Polanyi ([1944] 1957:132), the evolution of capitalism was driven by two opposing movements:

> One was the principle of economic liberalism, aiming at the establishment of a self-regulating market, relying on the support of the trading classes, and using largely laissez-faire and free trade as its methods; the other was the principle of social protection aiming at the conservation of man and nature as well as productive organization, relying on the varying support of those most immediately affected by the deleterious action of the market – primarily, but not exclusively, the working and the landed classes – and using protective legislation, restrictive associations, and other instruments of intervention as its methods.

Polanyi believed that "the protective countermovement was not external; rather, it was essential for the vitality of a capitalist order" (Block 1990:39). The state became the major player in the 1930s' countermovement. This had a deep historical reason. In the history of capitalism the state played an important role, first in the emergence of the market society from mercantilism and then in the collapse of the market society into fascism and world war. According to Polanyi, the rise of the self-regulated market did not result from a natural evolution, but rather from deliberate mercantilist state policy as a by-product of a state-building strategy. Although the countermovement was spontaneous and unplanned, and came from all sectors of society in response to the devastating impact of the market, the states in all industrialized countries passed interventionist legislation concerning public health, factory conditions, social insurance, trade associations, and public utilities in the late nineteenth century, though they differed considerably in ideology. In addition to the fact that the success of this countermovement impaired the effectiveness of the market, it also resulted in even deeper economic disorders in the twentieth century that stimulated a stronger countermovement to protect society. This eventually led to the rise of fascism (Polanyi [1944] 1957).

Although all industrialized countries witnessed the protective countermovement in the 1930s when the market stopped functioning, "the emerging regimes of fascism, socialism, and the New Deal were similar only in discarding laissez-faire principles" (Polanyi [1944] 1957:224). State intervention reflected an epochal dynamic of the 1930s, which was shared by all industrialized countries. What was singular in fascism? I argue that the impact of fascism on the Japanese managed economy in 1931–45 can be identified in three areas of ideology, which shaped the institutional transformation of Japanese capitalism.

First, the economy was endowed with strategic significance. As Polanyi pointed out, the failure of the self-regulated market in the 1930s did more than result in the rise of state intervention. The collapse of the gold standard had a direct implication for international politics because "the balance of power system could not ensure peace once the world economy on which it rested had failed" ([1944] 1957:4). Like the Germans and Italians, the Japanese believed that the collapse of the order in international economy after World War I would inevitably lead to military conflicts. The total war theory argued that "In modern war victory or defeat is determined directly not only by the fighting strength on the battlefield, but mainly by the strength of industries that made weapons . . . [the state must] utilize every economic instrument, to devote all available materials, and to fight to the last minute in order to survive" (Arisawa 1934:18, 80–1). This theory changed Japanese economic thinking profoundly. In the ideology of the managed economy, the end of the economy was derived not from the economic perspective but from the political perspective. In other words, the economy was no longer the end itself but an means of the nation-state in international politics (Tōa Keizai Chōsakyoku 1935:23). In contrast to the state intervention practiced by liberal capitalism in the United States and Britain in the 1930s, which aimed primarily at combating the Great Depression, state intervention in Japan, similar to that in Germany and Italy, from early on was a strategic measure to prepare for imminent war. These three countries paid special attention to the development of heavy-chemical industries in order to ensure munitions production.

The strategic view of the economy changed the role of the state. Chalmers Johnson (1982:33) points out that

> It is true that industrial policy in one form or another goes back to the Meiji era, but it is also true that after the turn of the century the government moved progressively away from its former policies of interference in the domestic economy (if not in those of the colonies or dependencies), and that for about thirty years an approximation of laissez faire was in vogue.

Driven by the pressure of the Great Depression and war mobilization, the Japanese state emerged as the "economic general staff." It not only started making long-term plans to promote production and upgrade the industrial structure of the economy, it also exercised tight control of resource allocations, adopting a discriminatory policy to ensure the supply of materials and capital to the munitions industries. The General National Mobilization Law enacted in 1938 gave the state bureaucracy unprecedented power to shape the managed economy by using administrative decrees. From then on, the state bureaucracy could issue orders directly to the private sector without consulting with the Diet. This has had a long-lasting impact on the postwar Japanese economy. A number of new studies published in Japan in the 1990s reconfirm that "the steersman of the Japanese economy has been bureaucrats at the Ministry of Finance and MITI, rather than individual companies" (Kobayashi, Okazaki, Yonekura, and NHK 1995:3; also see Kobayashi 1995; Nakamura [1978] 1993; Noguchi 1995; Okazaki and Okuno 1993b).

Second, although both liberal capitalism and fascism tried to constrain the market forces in the 1930s, the ideology of the Japanese managed economy, shared with its German and Italian counterparts, had a strong anticapitalist orientation that was sustained by nationalist ideology. It rejected the assumption of economic man. The freedom of individuals and the property right of private ownership were challenged by the claim for the national interest, which referred to "economic strength, independence in the world, [and] military power" (Woolf 1968:128). Ideologically, fascism aimed at

> creating a social order that modulated the profit-seeking impulses of the capitalists and the wage-seeking impulses of the proletariat by simplifying the social structure, and by eliminating the market mechanism as the principal means for the allocation and distribution of social goods. They wished to achieve social harmony and consensus with institutional reforms that contained and redirected individual materialistic motives in the name of higher collective purposes rather than through appeals to traditional "collectivist' values. (Duus and Okimoto 1979:69–70)

As Nathaniel S. Preston (1967:210) points out,

> fascism's control over the economic order proved ultimately to be for a noneconomic purpose, even an anti-economic purpose. Communist effort has been consistently geared to economic development, with military power as an important concomitant objective but deemed a

temporary necessity rather than a goal in itself. Fascism placed military preparedness at the forefront of its objectives from at least 1935 on.

To restrain the market forces, the state encouraged the development of nonmarket governance structures, such as cartels, control associations, and the main bank system. Before the Great Depression, cartels had not fully developed in Japan (Haley 1991; Takahashi 1933); control associations did not exist; indirect financing constituted only about 30% of the total capital supply, in contrast to 90% at present (Okazaki 1993). During the Great Depression, the Japanese state started a program of industrial rationalization. Cartels were established in each industry to control production in order to ease economic hardship by preventing private companies from bankruptcy. The state enacted the Important Industry Law in 1931. According to this law, when two-thirds of the companies in one industry joined a cartel, the state had the authority to force the rest of the companies to follow the agreement set by the cartel. If a cartel agreement contradicted the "public interest," the state could change or eliminate it. In the 1930s, the state also enacted a series of industry laws that made every element of business activity in that industry subject to state licensing. This marked the beginning of intensive government regulations that have lasted up to the present day. On the eve of the Pacific war, the Japanese state promulgated the Important Industry Association Ordinance, which resulted in the establishment of control associations in more than 20 industries. These associations were entrusted by the state with administrative power but were operated by the private sector. They had the authority to decide not only the amount, varieties, and methods of production, but also terms, prices, partners, and timing of transactions. They also had the power to determine profits, dividends, and bonuses (Nakamura 1974a:97–101, 128–33). In order to ensure the capital supply to the munitions industries, the main bank system evolved. By the end of World War II, this practice had spread to the nonmunitions industries as well (Okazaki 1993; Teranishi 1993a). The development of these nonmarket governance structures indicates that the Japanese state not only intervened directly in the economy, it also encouraged the development of nonstate institutions that constrained the market forces and placed them under its control. The private sector, under the pressure of nationalism during the war, had to compromise with the state, accepting the state's supervision in order to protect itself from more serious state intervention.

To oppose the profit principle, the state exerted strong pressure on private companies. Before the development of the managed economy, according to Okazaki Tetsuji (in Kobayashi, Okazaki, Yonekura, and NHK 1995:18–19), Japan's economic system "was very different from its present form . . . [the] job was separated from permanent employment. There was a high priority toward capital return to shareholders and reward to managers. The present practice of keeping profits within the company for investing in equipment almost did not exist." As the state strengthened its control over business activities during the war, the profit principle was strongly challenged. State control was achieved not only by directing the flow of capital into the munitions industries, but also by constraining the property right of shareholders in private companies. The increased indirect financing and the bureaucratic control over dividends gave managers great autonomy. Through a series of administrative orders by the state after the China war broke out, the job transfer of individual workers was no longer allowed; the starting salary of employees was under the control of the state, and all employees' salaries were raised together once a year (Kobayashi et al. 1995; Naguchi 1995; Otaka 1993). Meanwhile, the industrial patriotic association was established in all companies. Unlike the pre-1937 era, when white-collar and blue-collar workers belonged to different unions, these industrial patriotic associations included both groups as their members. As S. J. Woolf (1968:137) notes, "the attempted elimination of the opposed interests of capital and labor [was] unique to fascism, a deliberate contrast to the class concept accepted by both capitalism and communist Russia."

Third, the ideology of the Japanese managed economy, shared with Japan's German and Italian counterparts, also had a strong anticommunist orientation. As an alternative protective countermovement to liberal capitalism, fascism represented "a revolutionary tendency directed as much against conservatism as against the competing revolutionary force of socialism." It was both "counterrevolution and nationalist revisionism." Woolf (1968:129, 136) points out that

> Despite the sporadic protests of the fascist left wings against big capital and absentee landowners, the regimes rapidly abandoned any attempt radically to change the existing structure of economic power,

> and endeavored instead to turn this structure to the service of their
> politically motivated economic aims . . . the governments in Italy,
> Germany and Japan had little desire to nationalize industries, for
> ideological as well as political reasons. . . . The policy of the regimes
> was rather to leave the industrial sector in private hands and ensure
> that it acted in accordance with national 'needs."

This character in the Japanese case resulted from the politics of practicing industrial policy. Direct control was asserted and pursued by segments of the state. Due to the constraints of the economic situation and resistance of the private sector, however, many policy measures were altered or even failed. The rise of Japanese developmentalism in 1931–45 did not occur peacefully; the process of transformation was full of resistance and conflicts (Hara 1995c). As a result, in comparison with the socialist program adopted by the Soviet Union, the control of the Japanese state over the economy did not take the form of nationalizing property; the operation of the managed economy was still based on private ownership. In comparison with the New Deal, however, the Japanese state established much stronger control over the economy through both direct bureaucratic intervention and nonmarket governance structures, no matter how incomplete it might be. This character of Japanese developmentalism in 1931–45 has some important contemporary implications.

Promoting exports

In many ways, the paradigm of promoting exports in Japanese industrial policy during the 1950s represented the beginning of the transition of Japanese developmentalism from the military version to the trade version. Various elements of the wartime system began to reconsolidate within the constraints of the new social structure, political institution, and international environment defined by liberal capitalism through a series of democratic reforms, and the visions of the trade version of developmentalism emerged. Nevertheless, they were not widely accepted in domestic politics and still conflicted with competing political agendas. Unlike the managed economy, which had a strong inward orientation, the paradigm of promoting exports was aggressively outward. This outward orientation, however, was not cosmopolitan, but nationalistic. It aimed to strengthen the nation's power by engaging in international competition with a grand strategy.

First, the strategic view of the economy still dominated Japanese industrial policy, though serving a new national purpose.

The new constitution, whose Article Nine prohibits Japan from having the right to declare war, changed the goal of the Japanese economy. As Miwa Ryōichi (Hara and Miwa 1992:422–3) points out, although the development of heavy-chemical industries characterized the industrial structure of the Japanese economy in both the wartime and postwar periods, it was centered on the production of weapons in the former and on the production of civilian commercial products in the latter. The peacetime constitution changed Japan's national goal from "rich nation, strong army" to "rich nation without a strong army," and the foundation of national power was shifted from military forces to wealth (see also Yamamura 1967).

Nevertheless, the economy was still viewed strategically. Although Japan lost World War II, Prime Minister Yoshida Shigeru held that "A defeated nation, by analyzing and exploiting the shifting relations among world powers, could contain the damage incurred in defeat and instead could win the peace" (Pyle 1992:21). The fallout between liberal capitalism and communist Russia, the ally in World War II against fascism, provided Japan with a great opportunity to maneuver. Facing the Cold War environment, Yoshida designed a grand strategy for Japan: Take the U.S. side politically and militarily in exchange for economic aid and military protection, and in the meantime concentrate Japan's resources on economic growth while minimizing spending on national defense. This economic nationalist strategy, however, was challenged by both the conservatives, who promoted rearmament and the amendment of the constitution, and the progressives, who advocated remaining distant from the United States.

In the 1950s, the development of heavy-chemical industries remained the top priority in Japanese industrial policy. Although these industries were no longer centered on the production of weapons, they were still regarded as the foundation or the strategic components in the industrial structure of the economy, which would maximize Japan's gain in international trade. As the slogan "export or die" indicates, in the 1950s the promotion of exports was directly related to national survival. Japanese economic ideology revised the classical definition of *comparative advantage*: This term no longer meant rich resources or cheap labor that had been given naturally to an economy, but rather production technology that would add value to products and thus generate more benefits for the nation in international trade. Even Japan did not have this comparative advantage at the time; it had to be obtained by human effort. Production technology was perceived as Japan's only alternative in the 1950s to military force in building the nation's power. Although technology had always had strategic implications for Japan's national security, it was of central importance in Japanese economic ideology in the 1950s because, after learning about the achievements of technological development in the United States, many Japanese concluded that their defeat in World War II was a result of losing the competition in technology.

In this policy paradigm, the state changed its method of intervention. During the war, the ultimate goal of Japanese industrial policy was to support the military. The state directly controlled the distribution of materials and prices. The function of the market in resource allocation was largely replaced by bureaucratic control and nonmarket governance mechanisms. This trend was further strengthened in the occupation period to combat the economic crisis. After the implementation of the Dodge Plan in 1949, in contrast, the state still controlled, but by organizing market competition. It abolished the control over material distribution and prices, and changed the control over credit from direct to indirect. As a result, the market resumed its function, and private companies, which had been heavily protected by the state in the managed economy, were forced to enter the market and had to ensure the supply of capital, materials, and marketing channels by themselves (Kobayashi 1995:238). Beginning in 1950, the principle of rejecting competition was changed to restraining "excessive competition."

Second, the anticapitalist orientation, marked by restraint of market competition and the profit principle, began to reemerge in new forms after they were strongly challenged during the occupation. Although the Japanese economy in the 1950s is often called a *free economy* (*Juyū keizai*), in contrast to the managed economy, it was considerably different from the Anglo-Saxon type of liberal capitalism.

The dissolution of *zaibatsu* and the enactment of the antimonopoly law in the late 1940s encouraged market competition. To promote exports, however, the state revised the antimonopoly law twice, providing legitimacy for business reorganization. As a result of democratic reforms, the prewar type of holding companies, which had the power to control the capital and personnel of their subordinates, did not come back, and in comparison with the prewar period, the order of market competition was more unstable in the postwar period (Hara 1995c:91). Nevertheless, cross-shareholding and the exchange of personnel, which had been prohibited in the 1947 antimonopoly law, became legal again. Former *zaibatsu* companies, represented by Mitsubishi and Mitsui, began to reorganize themselves into *keiretsu* after temporary dissolution during the occupation. These *keiretsu* networks, centered on large commercial banks, provided manufacturers with reliable financing in pursuing technological transfers and investments in production equipment. At the same time, the Japanese state restrained market competition in strategic industries through intensive government regulations. To nurture the competitiveness of Japanese companies in strategic industries, the state continued to restrain imports of foreign products to Japan. To promote exports, the state also controlled foreign exchange. Finally, cartels, which had been a critical instrument in Japanese industrial policy since the Great Depression, were again allowed to combat economic recession and to promote rationalization after being outlawed since 1947. In the managed economy, the function of these nonmarket mechanisms was to counter the Great Depression and to prevent market forces from disrupting the nation's goal of ensuring the production of munitions industries. In the 1950s, their function was to prevent market forces from scattering the capital supply, to nurture the competitiveness of Japanese companies, and to maintain industrial order with rapid economic growth.

The profit principle was rejected again in the management of Japanese companies. This principle influenced business strategy in the rationalization movement of the early 1950s, in which Japanese companies made massive layoffs in an effort to reduce production cost. In the mid-1950s, progressive business leaders who gathered at the Japan Committee of Economic Development (Nihon Keizai Dōyūkai) initiated the productivity movement with the support of the state, aiming to include labor unions in their program of promoting exports. In order to pursue comparative advantage in production technology, some large companies made a historical trade-off. They started giving up allocative efficiency, as measured in short-term cost–benefit analyses; this had been their primary concern in the early 1950s. In exchange they wanted to gain labor's cooperation in technological innovation and quality control; to do this, they were required by labor unions to provide job security and to increase salaries. During this process, the traditional value of harmony was strategically advocated by business leaders to smoothe the relationship between management and labor, which had been a source of constant confrontation for a decade. Labor's response was divided. The majority of labor unions still remained skeptical, but one-third of them decided to cooperate with management. The so-called Takano Minoru line of the labor movement, which had advocated political confrontation with management, was replaced by the Futoda Kaoru–Iwai Akira line, which emphasized gaining economic benefits through spring strikes (Nakamura 1995a:37–8). This solution to the labor conflicts was not widely accepted until the mid-1960s. As the Miike strike of 1960 indicates, a major labor dispute at the national level was to come soon. Nevertheless, the productivity movement had marked the beginning of the effort to stabilize labor relations.

According to Okazaki Tetsuji (Kobayashi et al. 1995:126), the rejection of the profit principle was supported in part by a side effect of democratic reforms. At the end of the war, there was a possibility that Japanese management would return to the prewar tradition. Nevertheless, the *zaibatsu* dissolution destroyed the core of the prewar corporate system. When the members of *zaibatsu* families were removed from managerial posts, management was finally separated from ownership. As a result, those who fought hard with the state to protect profits were replaced by a new generation of managers, and employee sovereignty was established. Supported by the main bank system, these managers obtained much greater autonomy. They aggressively engaged in competition in long-term investment. In addition, after the land reform and labor reform democratized Japanese society, equality became a widespread ideal. Under such circumstances, the wartime practice of ensuring job security and annual wage increases was regarded as desirable (Sakakibara 1990).

Third, even the anticommunist orientation continued in the 1950s. The postwar democratic reforms did not touch the state bureaucracy. As all of the major political competitors of bureaucrats disappeared, the occupation authority had to depend on the Japanese government to carry out administration. In addition, because the unprecedented economic crisis caused by hyperinflation and the shortage of materials demanded strong leadership, state capacity was enhanced greatly in the late 1940s. Nevertheless, in the 1950s the Japanese state ended bureaucratic control over the distribution of materials and prices, and shifted the focus of industrial policy to promoting the competitiveness of Japanese companies. The state did not reject the market, but it intended to keep competition at a certain level. This is a very important facet of Japanese developmentalism. Without taking this into account, one cannot interpret precisely the strength of the Japanese economy.

In the 1930s, Japan, similar to Germany and Italy, tried to snap the links between its national economy and the world, aiming to insulate the national economy and domestic prices from cyclical movements in an effort to reduce its vulnerability to external disturbance (Woolf 1968). This inward orientation resulted in a tendency to depend on control, through both state bureaucracy and nonmarket governance structures, to allocate resources. After the Japanese economy was reconnected with the international market by implementation of the Dodge Plan, however, its survival would be ultimately determined by the competitiveness of Japanese products in the international market. To promote competitiveness, the Japanese state had to use the function of the market. Bureaucrats' power in the economy remained strong until the end of the 1960s. Beginning in 1950, however, the Japanese state had already changed its strategy from largely replacing the market to organizing the market.

High growth and liberalization

The paradigm of high growth and liberalization in Japanese industrial policy of the 1960s indicates another major adaptation of Japanese developmentalism to the emerging free-trade regime that changed the environment of the Japanese economy from a closed domestic market to an opened domestic market.

During the first decade's postwar reconstruction, Japan and many Western European countries suffered from a shortage of dollars. They all adopted a protectionist policy to guard their domestic markets in order to balance their international payments. Beginning in the second half of the 1950s, the United States began to push for the liberalization of trade. A new regime of free trade was emerging in the international economy, sustained by the hegemony of the Pax Americana. As Japan joined the International Monetary Fund (IMF) and the General Agreement on Tariffs and Trade (GATT), it was required to liberalize its imports and foreign currency exchange.

Under this policy paradigm, Japanese developmentalism finally accomplished the transformation to a trade version.

First, the strategic view of the economy was raised to a new level. In the 1950s, Yoshida's economic nationalist strategy failed to unify the country. The issues of rearmament and the revision of the constitution dominated national attention, which eventually led to a clash between the conservatives and the progressives on the issue of extending the Japan–U.S. security treaty in 1960. After Ikeda Hayato became prime minister, he adopted the slogan of "shifting from the political season to the economic season." The state, led by the conservative Liberal Democratic Party, adopted the policy paradigm of high growth and liberalization of trade in an effort to shift the attention of the general public away from these sensitive political issues. This program effectively demobilized the progressive forces, and the developmental agenda obtained wide political support.

In the 1950s, the state emphasized the promotion of competitiveness of Japanese companies in strategic industries. In the 1960s, in contrast, the interpretation of the national power of production was further extended to the high growth rate in the entire economy. It aimed not simply at sustaining economic growth or adjusting for market fluctuations, but at achieving economic growth at a much quicker pace than other countries. In this policy paradigm, macro financial policy was directly tied to industrial policy. Government planning and public spending were regarded as important means to sustain economic growth. The state increased public spending aggressively in an effort to promote infrastructure, human capital, social welfare, and science and technology, and to upgrade the industrial structure of the Japanese economy by moving quickly toward the heavy-chemical industries. The high-growth policy distinguished Japanese developmentalism from liberal capitalism. After World War II, Keynesian economics became influential in state policy in most industrialized countries. Although the application of this form of economics had often gone beyond the short-term adjustment of market fluctuations, the policy objectives in Western industrialized countries were basically full employment, a welfare state, or economic growth in general. In the Japanese case, however, macro financial policy was directly applied to sustain the high growth, upgrade the industrial structure of the economy, and strengthen the national competitiveness in international trade. These differences suggest that when Western economic ideas were diffused throughout Japanese policy making, they were often applied in a "developmental" way.

The strategic view of the economy was further reflected in the state's effort to incorporate the whole country into the *new industrial system* (*shinsangyō taisei*). By pressuring Japan to liberalize trade and capital investment, liberal capitalism once again defined the rule of the international economy, which Japan had no power to refuse but was able to adapt. When Japan's domestic markets were open to foreign companies, it also stimulated a new wave of nationalism in Japanese economic ideology. Since the 1930s, the importation of foreign products had been controlled by the Japanese state. Although the paradigm of promoting exports had already demonstrated an aggressive outward orientation, it concentrated on exporting Japanese products to the international market rather than allowing foreign products to compete in Japan's domestic market. The liberalization of trade and capital investment was regarded as the "second black ship coming"[1] at the time, an external threat greater than any except that which resulted in the Meiji Restoration in the 1860s. Many Japanese were unsure whether Japanese companies could survive the imminent competition with foreign companies in their backyard. To meet this challenge, MITI's bureaucrats explicitly called for a new national mobilization, reviving the wartime legacies.

Second, the industrial reorganization served to restrain market competition in order to increase the economy of scale. It was argued that foreign companies could reduce prices, as their advantage in capital enhanced their economies of scale. In order to compete with them, Japanese companies had to be organized into an industrial system that would not only coordinate capital investment and organize each industry's distribution system, but also encourage mergers among large Japanese companies in order to increase the economy of scale. All these measures conflicted with the antimonopoly law. Supported by the state, however, they were carried out anyway. As a result, *keiretsu* witnessed a new wave of development and became the major player in the international competition. The practice of relational contracting, as later history indicates, considerably restrained the market competition. It especially limited the access of foreign companies to Japanese markets.

In the meantime, the Japanese management system, characterized by

---

[1] In 1853, Commodore Matthew C. Perry of the United States headed four warships (black in color) to Japan, demanding the access of American ships to Japanese ports. This event created a domestic crisis in Japan and it eventually led to the Meiji Restoration. Today *black ship* is often used as a metaphor of a major external challenge, especially in the form of a foreign demand to open the Japanese markets.

permanent employment, the seniority-based wage system, and the company-based labor union, was eventually institutionalized in large Japanese companies. In the 1950s, despite the fact that some Japanese business leaders started to stabilize labor relations through the productivity movement, the impact of the confrontational strategy adopted by both management and labor still remained strong, and there were still considerable resistance and doubts about this initiative on both sides. A major confrontation eventually took place between the two sides at the national level during the Miike strike in 1960 when the Mitsui Company intended to lay off more than 6,000 workers in the Miike coal mine, as the coal industry had become a sunset industry. The Miike dispute became a turning point in postwar Japanese labor relations. Although this dispute ended with labor's failure, it forced the state, business leaders, and labor unions to reexamine the confrontational strategies they had adopted. Labor unions realized that national-level and industry-level confrontations could not effectively protect their interests; they decided to participate fully in the productivity movement. Management also clearly recognized the huge cost of the confrontational strategy. As the labor market became favorable to the supply side for the first time in 1963, management also lost its leverage over labor unions. In order to ensure the supply of labor, permanent employment became widely institutionalized. The state once regarded labor disputes as an issue of public security. Now it realized that in order to sustain rapid economic growth without serious social disturbance, it had to treat labor relations as an issue of social policy.

Third, under this policy paradigm, the Japanese economy witnessed the increasing importance of private ordering and the declining power of state bureaucracy. The settlement of the private ordering in the governance of the Japanese economy reflected the continuity not only of the anticapitalist orientation of restraining market competition, but also of the anticommunist orientation, which rejected direct control by the state. This development directly resulted from the politics of building the new industrial system. At this time, MITI proposed *state–private sector coordination,* which would give the state the power to supervise all loans made by commercial banks (Calder 1994). MITI's proposal was perceived as reviving direct bureaucratic control and was strongly resisted by the big commercial banks. Resisting MITI's bureaucratic control, the private sector came up with a proposal of *independent adjustment.* Eventually, MITI's efforts to enact the "Special

Measures Law for the Promotion of Designated Industries" were blocked, and the independent adjustment proposed by the private sector through nonmarket and nonstate institutions became the major instrument in meeting the challenge of liberalizing trade and capital investment.

This development has a strong contemporary implication. With this settlement, the division of labor between the state and the private sector was redefined. Beginning at that time, the Japanese state began to depend more strongly on administrative guidance in its economic intervention. At the same time, the state relaxed its antimonopoly law; in the late 1960s, it encouraged further industrial reorganization among big companies through mergers in order to strengthen the competitiveness of Japanese companies. Supported by the state, the industrial reorganization under the policy paradigm of liberalization resulted in the further development of nonmarket governance mechanisms, which privatized the protection of Japan's domestic markets. As a result, not only did *keiretsu* emerge as the major player in the international competition, various social regulations of the market, such as trade associations and *dangō*,[2] also helped to block access of foreign companies to Japanese markets. Although Japan's domestic markets were opened, they were still tightly protected by both vertical and horizontal business alliances that practiced relational contracting.

By the end of the 1960s, the transformation of Japanese developmentalism from the military version to the trade version was largely accomplished. Even though many original components of the wartime economic system had changed in appearance, the general principles established in 1931–45 remained. Amaya Naohiro, a young MITI bureaucrat, commented in the early 1960s (Amaya, Komiya, and Sakamoto, 1962:71–2) that

> The United States and Europe replaced their wartime practices in the postwar period with the social and economic continuities that originated in the nineteenth century. The operation of their postwar economies simply took the form of returning to the prewar tradition. Japan, in contrast, never returned to its prewar tradition. Something new, yet quite different, was born, which was strongly influenced by the wartime economy. Although the economy as a whole admitted the ideology of free economy, the market was vertically divided. . . . Unlike the markets in the U.S. and Europe, which have high horizontal

---

[2] *Dango* refers to the practice of price fixing by competitors before bids are submitted for government construction projects.

mobility, the Japanese market is vertically divided into several markets and each of them is topped by a commercial bank. . . . Based on these social conditions, the government intervened in various ways.

Amaya's statement may need some qualifications, as World War II also left the United States with many legacies, such as the social security program, government subsidies to agriculture, the military–industry complex, and the national science policy. Nevertheless, in comparison with the Japanese case, the basic economic principles and institutions that governed the American economy were not seriously affected by the war to that degree.

The economics of industrialization

As stated earlier, the industrial policy practiced by the Japanese state competes with the Anglo-Saxon experience. Murakami Yasusuke (1992), in his splendid analysis of developmentalism, stated that Western mainstream economic theories are virtually the "economics of capitalism," which emphasize the equilibrium of the market. These theories regard industrialization as an extension of capitalism and Japanese industrial policy as a variant of liberal capitalism. In contrast, Japanese developmentalism represents the "economics of industrialization," which focuses on how a latecomer country to industrialization can create wealth in a dynamic process. Ideologically, Japanese developmentalism advocates an economic system based on private ownership and a market economy. This system, however, has a goal: the industrialization of the nation (the continuous growth of per capita production). To achieve this goal, this ideology not only admits state intervention in the market from a long-term point of view (this practice distinguishes Japanese developmentalism from Keynesian economics, which focuses on short-term intervention), but also encourages the development of nonmarket governance structures in the economy, such as industrial associations and business groups, to restrain market forces.

According to Murakami (1992), Japanese developmentalism and neoclassical economics are deeply divided on the assumption of marginal cost. Neoclassical economics is based on the assumption of increasing marginal cost. In theory, the market can efficiently allocate resources and achieve equilibrium only when the marginal cost increases. This assumption is indispensable for mathematical modeling. The postwar reality, however, is characterized by decreasing marginal cost, which has been sustained not only by the economy of scale (before production reaches the level where capital and equipment are at full capacity), but also by technological innovation. As a result, how to build institutions to trigger economic growth created by decreasing marginal cost is a crucial question for every country. Decreasing marginal cost was recognized earlier by Alfred Marshall and Joan Robinson, but it was ignored by neoclassical economists in the postwar period until the mid-1980s when Paul Romer raised this question again. In contrast, the major purpose of Japanese industrial policy since the 1950s has been to trigger economic growth by decreasing marginal cost through various institutions. Given this difference in economic thinking, Murakami concluded, it is not at all surprising that developmentalism beat liberal capitalism in the postwar international competition (Nakasone, et al. 1992:204–6). This is a major characteristic of developmentalism not only in Japan but also in other East Asian countries. To stimulate growth, the state has often intervened in the economy. In many cases, this was achieved through nonstate institutions.

Another fundamental difference between Western mainstream economic theories and Japanese developmentalism involves the relationship between the economy and politics. In Western mainstream economic thinking, the economy is treated as separate from politics, and the operation of the economy has little to do with political ideology. Japanese developmentalism, in contrast, directly acknowledges the inseparability of industrialization and nationalism, not only because industrialization, as the foundation of both wealth and power, has been a national goal in Japan since the Meiji Restoration (Samuels 1994), but also because the goal of industrialization has been supported by grand political strategies derived from nationalism during the Cold War (Pyle 1992). Friedrich List ([1841] 1985:119, 126) once made a distinction between Anglo-Saxon economic thinking and the German historical school. He argued that in the former, the economy does not have a national boundary. As a "science which teaches how the entire human race may attain prosperity," List said, classical economics was based on the assumption that "a state of things which has yet to come into existence is actually in existence." In contrast, the German historical school presented "a science which limits its teaching to inquiring how a *given nation* can obtain (under the existing conditions of the world) prosperity, civilization, and power, by means of agriculture, industry, and commerce." In this sense, as Murakami (1992:6) pointed out, Japanese developmentalism is an extension of mercantilism and of the German historical school. Japanese developmentalism regards the nation-state as the basic unit of the political economy; this view often places certain constraints on parliamentary democracy. Because of this nationalistic character, Japanese economic ideology is certainly not a "pure science" that "studies human behavior as a relationship between ends and scarce means which have alternative uses" (Robbins 1935); rather, it is integral, or a mixture of what Thomas Rohlen (1974) calls the "logic of business" and the "ideology of community."

The nation-state as the unit of analysis

The unit of analysis in Japanese economic ideology was the nation-state, and methodological individualism was rejected in Japanese developmentalism.

According to Arisawa Hiromi, Tōbata Seiichi, and Nakayama Ichirō (1960), the economy is not given by nature but is operated by human beings. Human beings, moreover, do not operate the economy as individual firms or households, but rather as a collection of large-scale groups such as nation-states. By "perceiving the economy as a natural given [, which] precludes the concept of subjective entity," Western economics has downplayed the role of the state. It includes no concept of an entity that deals with the economy as a collective actor, equivalent to the concept of the individual. Even when the collective actor is considered, the conceptualization in Western economics tends to be very abstract. Many countries engaged in economic planning between the two world wars. These plans were governed by neither the "absolute god" nor the "invisible hand," but rather by a group of human beings working under the name of the state. Without understanding the role of the state, one cannot interpret the operation of the modern economy. Morozumi Yoshihiko, a former deputy minister of MITI, once argued that "industrial policy has to be considered according to the availability of resources within the unit of the sovereign state. Issues in industrial policy such as national security and promotion of international competitiveness cannot be considered without the precondition of the coexistence of sovereign states" (1966:17). Chalmers Johnson reminded us of this trait of Japanese industrial policy in the early

1980s. Elaborating on Robert Ozaki's argument, Johnson (1982:26) pointed out that Japanese industrial policy is "a reflection of economic nationalism, with nationalism understood to mean giving priority to the interests of one's own nation." Although the nationalistic dimension of Japanese industrial policy received little attention in the 1980s, it began to receive great attention in the 1990s and has generated a number of important studies. Kenneth Pyle (1992) reveals the foundation of Japanese economic nationalism through an analysis of Japan's grand strategy in diplomacy. Richard Samuels (1994), in his study of the Japanese defense industry, portrays the "techno-nationalism" that has guided Japanese industrial policy. David Williams (1994) states directly that Japanese industrial policy is a practice of "neomercantilism."

Unlike Anglo-Saxon capitalism, which was nurtured in the cultural environment of individualism that emerged in the Enlightenment, Japanese industrialization was a radical response to the national crisis imposed by the Western threat in the mid-nineteenth century. From the very beginning, Japanese industrialization was driven to achieve three collective goals: to "increase production and develop industry" (*shokusan kōgyō*), to build up "a rich country and a strong army" (*fukoku kyōhei*), and to pursue "enlightenment and civilization" (*bunmei kaika*). Japanese industrialization was motivated not by the wish to improve individual economic well-being but by the desire to strengthen the nation's power in international competition. In the Japanese context, industrialization was a transplant or an imitation, which did not include the laissez-faire mindset. Even when Western ideas of individualism and civil society were introduced to Japan after the Meiji Restoration, the diffusion of these ideas was often constrained by the structure of Japanese society, and they were often separated from their original cultural contexts and modified according to the Japanese environment. Although the Japanese could distinguish clearly between the state and the individual and between society and the individual, they felt ambivalent about the distinction between the state and society, or, in Japanese, between the *kan* (official) and the *min* (the people). Not only was the government inconsistent in its definition of the *min;* even young intellectuals in the 1880s were often confused, "mixing Napoleon with Abraham Lincoln, or generals and bureaucrats with fiery parliamentarians" (Gluck 1985:63). When the concept of society was first introduced to Japan, it was translated as "group of fellows" and was often explained further as "government." Despite the fact that the original Western socialism accepted individualism in its ideology, socialism became an alternative theory to individualism when it was introduced to Japan after the Meiji Restoration. To the Japanese, *society* sounded very familiar because it was a collective entity, whereas *individual* sounded too radical because *individualistic* was often perceived as equivalent to *selfish*. In such a social environment, the Western idea of free competition asserted by classical economics was often confused with the social Darwinists' "competition for survival" (Arisawa and Tamanoi 1973).

This nationalist orientation in Japanese economic ideology encountered a great challenge during the period of "Taishō democracy." After the Sino-Japanese War of 1894–5 and the Russo-Japanese War of 1904–5, Japan underwent rapid industrialization. By the end of World War I, Japan had become one of the major powers in the Far East. As the power of the private sector and its political representatives, the political parties, reached a peak, the ideologies of Western individualism and laissez-faire economics also spread widely and grew quite influential. Although they did not completely prevail over other perspectives in the 1920s because of the strong influence of Marxism, declarations favoring individual shareholders' profits and the laissez-faire economy were more influential in political discourse than before or after that time.

The rise of fascism in Japan resulted in the adoption of the nation-state as the unit of analysis in modern Japanese economic ideology for two reasons. First, as Simon Reich (1990:40) points out, "Fascist states have a comprehensive ideology that, unlike communist regimes, is specifically nationalistic in tone and substance." This ideology reinterpreted the relationship among different social classes in terms of shared history and blood ties; all Japanese were members of a big family, with the emperor at the top. In fascist economic ideology, the economy has a national boundary. The state discriminated between foreign-owned and domestic-owned companies. Within the nation, it was argued, people should work for the public interest, maximizing munitions production; meanwhile, the pursuit of individual interests must be suppressed. This ideology aimed at generating what Francis Fukuyama (1995) calls *high trust* that binds the people in one nation closely together while keeping outsiders at a distance. Second, the nation-state was the basic unit for war mobilization. In the managed economy, the importance of the nation-state was derived directly from the theory of the "defense state" (*Kokubō kokka*). According to Iijima Banshi (1941:202–3), "The defense state is the state which could carry out total war. In case of emergency, the state could mobilize the nation's politics, economy, and culture for the purpose of defense, and fight as long as its strength allows. Even in peacetime, the state should organize the civilian forces, which are usually driven by the needs of daily life, in a way that can shift these forces whenever necessary for the purpose of war."

Even after the war ended, this mentality persisted. "During the wartime," Sahashi Shigeru (cited by Tsūsanshō, Vol. 10 1990:52), then director of the Enterprise Bureau at MITI, argued on the eve of liberalization of trade that

> there was the National General Mobilization Law, the state was bestowed with great power to mobilize everything for the purpose of war by coercion and in the form of top-down. In order to make Japan the first class country among the first class countries, the national general mobilization is still needed today, though its format may differ from the wartime. Without the national general mobilization to consolidate the intelligence and power of the whole nation, people will assert and do whatever as they like and consequently Japan can accomplish nothing.

Although the foundation of national power changed from military force to wealth, the nation-state remained the basic unit of analysis in Japanese industrial policy. In 1967, in the debate on liberalization of capital investment, Arisawa Hiromi wrote that "without economic independence, Japan will not have political and diplomatic independence. When we consider the happiness and peace of the Japanese people, we must have a foundation on which we can make independent judgment" (Arisawa 1967:270). Morozumi Yoshihiko, a MITI official in charge of drafting the policy proposal regarding Japan's strategy for meeting the challenge of liberalization at that time, stated that MITI's efforts to build the new industrial system "may be criticized as 'nationalistic which violates the ideal of international community.' This proposition, however, is not hypothetical but realistic, because we live in a world which is preconditioned by the coexistence of sovereign nation-states" (1966:7–8). As a result, writes Richard Samuels (1994:340), "national systems of innovation can be integrated in the global economy without sacrificing their integrity. Japanese scientific and technological networks have long been linked internationally in ways that actually reinforce nationalism. International networks neither obviate the relevance of national systems nor dilute techno-national incentives."

The production orientation

A strong production orientation is a distinctive characteristic of Japanese developmentalism. Western mainstream economic theory is based on the assumption of utility maximization, which is measured at the micro level by profits for shareholders and by wages, leisure, and other economic benefits for individual employees, and at the macro level by the interests of consumers in modern capitalist economies. Moreover, utility presumably is maximized in a short time span. In the Japanese case, however, these measures of the utility maximization principle have been constantly overshadowed by other priorities in state policy and business strategy. In short, the Japanese preference for national power of production reflected an extreme position to solve the dilemma of economic development described by Albert Hirschman (1958:10): "to achieve higher per capita incomes, current consumption must be reduced; to make available more leisure time, work must be more rigorously scheduled. . . . The tension of development is therefore not so much between known benefits and costs as between the goal and the ignorance and misconceptions about the road to that goal."

In the managed economy, maximizing production for war mobilization was regarded as the public interest, whereas private firms' pursuit of profit and consumption by individual civilians were perceived as selfish. A similar argument was made during the early postwar period, when maximizing production was believed to be the only way for the nation to survive the economic crisis. This goal was given priority over the profits of companies and the equal distribution of economic welfare to labor. In the early 1950s, the profit principle made a brief comeback, but it soon was replaced by a preference for production technology. In the 1960s the preference for production was extended to high growth at the macro level, which prevailed over other concerns, such as environmental protection and consumers' interests. According to the conventional understanding, the incentive driving both an individual and a nation to make money is to spend money, and a country's production level will determine its consumption level. In Japan, however, the consumption level and the production level are widely disparate. Even in the 1990s, Japanese consumers suffer from much higher domestic prices than do consumers in any other major industrialized country. Japanese workers still work longer than their counterparts elsewhere. In view of Japan's wealth today, the overemphasis on production can no longer be interpreted as a reflection of poverty or late development, but rather as the result of a different economic rationale – what Lester Thurow (1991:118) calls *producer economics.*

Unlike consumer-oriented economic theories, which regard consumption as the ultimate good, producer economics reflects "a universal human desire to build, to belong to an empire, to conquer neighboring empires, and to become the world's leading economic power" (Thurow 1991:118). In this system, the economic man is replaced by the political man, whose incentive for economic activity is not individualistic but collective. This kind of economic thinking can be traced back at least to the developmental argument made by the German historical school. According to Friedrich List, the production and consumption of wealth conflict with each other. Production is the foundation of a nation's power; consumption can only weaken this power. List pointed out ([1841] 1985:133, 144–5) that

> the causes of wealth are something totally different from wealth itself. A person may possess wealth, i.e. exchangeable value; if, however, he does not possess the power of producing objects of more value than he consumes, he will become poorer. A person may be poor; if he, however, possesses the power of producing a larger amount of valuable articles than he consumes, he becomes rich. The power of producing wealth is therefore infinitely more important than wealth itself; it insures not only the possession and the increase of what has been gained, but also the replacement of what has been lost. This is still more the case with entire nations (who cannot live out of mere rentals) than with private individuals . . . the nation must sacrifice and give up a measure of material property in order to gain culture, skill, and powers of united production; it must sacrifice some present advantages in order to insure to itself future ones. . . . If . . . a sacrifice of value is caused by protective duties, it is made good by the gain of power of production, which not only secures to the nation an infinitely greater amount of material goods, but also industrial independence in case of war. Through industrial independence and the

internal prosperity derived from it the nation obtains the means for successfully carrying on foreign trade and for extending its mercantile marine; it increases its civilization, perfects its institutions internally, and strengthens its external power.

What made the Japanese adopt producer economics? Richard Samuels (1994:ix) believes that a feeling of "insecurity" – "pervasive anxiety" – motivates millions of Japanese every day. I argue further that this "pervasive anxiety" was greatly increased by the Japanese perception of national crisis and external threat during the 1931–45 war, which fundamentally changed the Japanese preference of end in economic goals. Since the Meiji Restoration, the Japanese have been subject to the pressure of the need to catch up with the industrialized West. Nevertheless, even though the German historical school strongly influenced Japanese economic ideology from the beginning, the orientation toward production did not become an exclusive priority of Japanese developmentalism until the 1930s. The feeling of insecurity in Japanese economic ideology implies a national boundary; it cannot be understood and interpreted properly without reference to the international environment. When the Japanese were driven by the pressure to survive total war with other nation-states, the unit of analysis in economic ideology changed from the individual and the social class to the nation-state; in addition, the preference of end also shifted from consumption by individuals and profits for shareholders to national power of production.

The practice of the managed economy shook the foundation of orthodox laissez-faire and individualism in Japanese economic ideology. In the general mobilization for war, private firms encountered strong pressure from the state to adhere to a new *economic ethic*. According to this ethic, the profit principle should be replaced by the *public interest principle,* and private firms should regard their role in supporting the nation's munitions production as the top priority (Ryū 1939). In the ideology of the managed economy, the general mobilization for munitions production was perceived as a matter of national survival in total war. Therefore "all munitions needs should be fulfilled as the military commander asks, and all civilian needs should be limited to a minimum" (Arisawa 1934:80–1). Consumption had to be suppressed so that compulsory saving could be achieved. In munitions production, moreover, production itself was the top priority; production costs were a secondary issue.

This preference of end was not purely economic but also political. As explained in a document prepared by the Showa Research Association for Prime Minister Konoe's "new order," "The promotion of production is an urgent goal during the war and it should be achieved internally by economic means. A laissez-faire economy based on the profit principle, however, cannot integrate economic laws with ethics. Therefore the profit principle of the laissez-faire economy must be suppressed in order to make internal integration possible" (see Sakai 1979:346). This new economic ethic "regards the public interest as more important than individual interest, and forbids the practice of treating profit and individual interest as the first priority in economic activity" (Arisawa 1937b:8–9). This orientation was stressed again in the priority production program of the early postwar period, when Japan suffered from hyperinflation and a severe shortage of materials.

The Japanese insecurity or pervasive anxiety did not disappear even after the war. The perception of national crisis was constantly present in postwar Japanese economic ideology, as exemplified by the slogan "export or die" in the 1950s and by the perception of the second black ship coming during the liberalization of trade and capital investment in the 1960s. In the face of these perceived crises, the wartime legacy of sacrificing other needs to strengthen the national power of production for collective survival was perpetuated, and governed the Japanese economy for several decades.

In the paradigm of promoting exports of the 1950s, the Japanese industrial focus on national power of production shifted from the goal to the means – that is, from quantity of production to quality and technology. Because the products of the heavy-chemical industries were value-added in international trade, Japanese firms invested aggressively in production equipment and technological transfer, disregarding the significance of short-term profit to business operations. They believed that the development of know-how, production technology, and new products in heavy-chemical industries required time and energy, and that the comparative advantage of production technology in these industries in international competition could be realized only after economy of scale had been achieved by reducing production costs in mass production (Itō, Kiyono, Okuno, and Suzumura 1988:104–5).

The external pressure for liberalizing trade and capital investment in the 1960s was perceived as a great threat to the Japanese economy. Under such circumstances, the paradigm of high growth extended the

Japanese understanding of national power of production from the industry level to the level of the entire economy. The National Income Doubling Plan of 1961 demonstrated that Japanese industrial policy in the 1950s had aimed basically to promote national competitiveness through big companies in several strategic industries. By 1960, however, technological innovation had reached Japan's medium-sized and small firms. To compete with foreign products in its domestic markets, Japan had to improve its infrastructure, upgrade the industrial structure by moving further toward heavy-chemical industries, promote trade, and develop human capital, science, and technology. As Shimomura Osamu (1962) remarked, high growth in Japan did not simply mean economic growth at a high rate. Rather, it implied the real promotion of productivity by rationalizing the production process and investing in production equipment. Once the industrial structure had been upgraded, Japan would be able to strengthen its export capacity and reduce its dependence on imports.

The strategic view of the economy

To promote the national power of production, Japanese developmentalism established three general principles. Each of them was sustained by distinctive instrumental means.

The first is the strategic view of the economy. Neoclassical economics views the economy as a natural system that is controlled by the invisible hand of the market, and assumes that an equilibrium between supply and demand will be reached automatically. Japanese developmentalism, in contrast, regards the economy as an open system; human beings can intervene in its operation or can even manipulate it. Industrialization is a program of *social engineering* – a purposeful collective effort to catch up with the West, which can be planned and sustained (Fallows 1994). This view of the economy is exemplified by the concept of *upgrading industrial structure (sangyō kōzō no kōdoka)*. According to Chalmers Johnson, industrial structure has been one of the "basic components" of Japanese industrial policy, which concerns the "proportion of agriculture, mining, manufacturing, and services in the nation's total production; and within manufacturing it concerns the percentages of light and heavy industries and of labor-intensive and knowledge-intensive industries" (1982:28). This concept represents the will of the Japanese state to maximize Japan's gains from international trade through strategic intervention in the economy.

The 1949 White Paper on International Trade and Industry described the logic of industrial structure. It argued that the Japanese economy was "incomplete" within its national territory because Japan, as a country with few national resources, would not be able to sustain its economy for even a single day without imports. For this reason, Japan had to export in order to raise funds to make these imports possible; the production cycle of the Japanese economy could not be completed without going overseas. "In the absence of foreign trade," it said, "domestic production and employment will shrink, leading to an extremely short economic cycle. As a result, maintenance of a reasonable national standard of living will become impossible." In contrast to classical economic theory, which emphasizes the increase in economic welfare caused by free trade, according to Itō Monoshige and his colleagues, Japanese industrial policy focuses on the increase in economic welfare created by the change in industrial structure. Because international trade is indispensable in the operation of the Japanese economy, "the extent of economic benefits for Japan from its trade with other nations is determined by the structure of trade between Japan and its trading partners, that is, by the type and amount of Japanese exports and imports. The structure of trade, in turn, is determined by Japan's industrial structure, which depends on technology, production facilities, and endowment of productive factors." An optimal industrial structure does not exist at present, but it is desired and pursued (Itō et al. 1988:34–5).

Industrial structure as a leading concept in Japanese industrial policy was a product of the Great Depression and war mobilization in the early Showa period. It became a key issue in the discussion of the relationship between the economy and national defense. The national mobilization by major industrialized countries during World War I greatly extended the Japanese understanding of modern war. The total war theory, which dominated the Japanese economic ideology in the 1930s, stressed the close relationship between war and the economy. *Kōgi kokubō* (broadly defined as "national security") was its major proposition. In the face of imminent military conflicts with other countries, the transition of the economy from peace to war became the top priority. To mobilize the entire economy for war, the state in both Germany and Japan categorized industries and companies into a hierarchical order according to their importance to munitions production, and then advocated a discriminatory policy in resource allocation in favor of companies and industries that were strategic to national defense. In this sense, the concept of industrial structure prescribed how to position the economy strategically in order to ensure national security.

From the very beginning, the concept of industrial structure has two major implications. First, it asserts the development of heavy-chemical industries. The saying "There is no longer any munitions industry, only munitions production" indicates that World War II organized the whole Japanese national economy into a munitions production system that centered on heavy-chemical industries. The conversion of civilian production to munitions production had already occurred during World War I as a natural process. During World War II the conversion was enforced through government planning. It was argued at the time that

> without heavy-mechanical, automobile, tractor and modern chemical industries, without the advanced technology of metal production and training in precision manufacturing, a country's economy simply will not have the foundation to produce advanced weapons . . . the organization of Japan's munitions production system cannot be accomplished without rapidly upgrading industrial structure. (Arisawa 1937b:72)

Second, the concept of industrial structure advocates a strategic intervention by the state. Driven by the pressure of war mobilization, the Japanese had no time to wait for market forces to respond to the nation's urgent need to move the economy toward heavy-chemical industries. To conduct the managed economy, the state had to control the distribution of materials by coercion. As Arisawa Hiromi (1937c:1–2) pointed out at the time, in the national emergency

> it is no longer possible to realize the goal by simply depending upon entrepreneurs' initiative. Nowadays, the state has to exercise its power and directly assume its leadership in economic activities. In a semi-war situation, an economy led by the state has to be coercive. This is the genuine nature of the managed economy.

The wartime practice of promoting industrial structure left a rich legacy to the postwar Japanese economy. Arisawa Hiromi (1949c:85–6) remarked:

> The promotion of industrial structure [during the war] was driven by the need for technological independence in an isolated economy[;] it

has to be adjusted according to comparative cost [in the postwar period]. Nevertheless, the factory equipment, the learned technologies, and the trained labor acquired in the promotion of industrial structure will not disappear and they can be further upgraded. In this sense, the promotion of industrial structure can be regarded as the only plus in the war legacy.

In the postwar era, despite the belief that the foundation of national power had shifted from the military to trade, the strategic view of the economy underlying the concept of industrial structure remained influential. First, because Japan's capital was limited in the 1950s and 1960s, a discriminatory policy was still considered highly necessary for concentrating financial resources in the development of strategic industries. Second, even in peacetime, heavy-chemical industries remained strategically important to the Japanese economy. They assumed new significance because they were more value-added in international trade than other industries. The wartime production capacity in the mechanical, chemical, and transportation industries left the Japanese economy with a strong foundation for further development of heavy-chemical industries in the postwar period. Third, the state capacity in economic intervention built up during the war continued to be a powerful instrument guiding economic development, though the form of state intervention changed over time. After the 1960s, the private sector gained more power in determining the direction of the Japanese economy. Although analysts in the United States vary in their assessments of the role of the state in the Japanese economy, they agree that the Japanese practice of promoting industrial structure is different from that of the laissez-faire economies, whether it is called *plan rational* (Johnson 1982), *techno-nationalism* (Samuels 1994), or *strategic capitalism* (Calder 1994). That is, no matter who is most important in the policy-making process, economic actors in Japan still practice strategic and purposeful intervention for the sake of international competition, which aims at maximizing Japan's economic gains from trade. The economy still is not regarded as a natural given, but instead as an object of social engineering.

Organized competition

The second principle of Japanese developmentalism is to prevent excessive competition (*kado kyōsō no haijo*) or to organize competition. According to orthodox or liberal capitalism, "competition is by definition good, because it kills off the overpriced producers. Killing them off is, in its turn, good, because more efficient suppliers will give the consumer a better deal" (Fallows 1994:183–4). The Japanese, however, view competition differently. When it becomes excessive, argues Morozumi Yoshihiko (1966:61), "the losses to the national economy [may] exceed the gains that arise from that competition." When numerous small companies compete with each other in the market, he states, their profits will decline, and the capital return may become negative throughout the industry. More important, excessive competition will cause capital and labor to be concentrated in one industry more than is necessary; in the end, competition may not create the most efficient production system for the Japanese economy. The concept of excessive competition is self-contradictory to Western mainstream economists because, although competition inevitably creates friction and waste, these social costs are necessary to eliminate inefficient firms from the market and to shift resources from the industries that have become uncompetitive (Itō et al. 1988). In Japanese developmentalism, however, production technology is perceived as the most important factor in making Japanese companies competitive in the international market, and Japan must enlarge the size of companies in heavy-chemical industries. Because the development of heavy-chemical industries requires huge amounts of capital, moreover, the state must strengthen the integration of companies in research and development, investment, and cooperation in order to create companies that can compete internationally in strategic industries with the proper economy of scale. Therefore, the concept of preventing excessive competition reflects the will of the state to allocate resources more effectively within the boundary of the national economy to promote industrial structure and national competitiveness. This concept involves a value judgment: Market competition may often exceed the level preferred by economic actors and thus must be restrained.

The principle of restraining competition emerged in 1931–45 when the Japanese struggled to survive the Great Depression. According to Yoshino Shinji, a senior bureaucrat at the Ministry of Commerce and Industry, although competition stimulated the development of modern industries, "various evils are gradually becoming apparent. . . . Holding to absolute freedom will not rescue the industrial world from its present disturbances. Industry needs a plan of comprehensive development and a measure of control" (cited in Johnson 1982:108). When the

Japanese state replaced cartels with control associations after the Pacific war broke out, it was argued that

> cartels in the past were agencies established for promoting the common interests of their members. Therefore they resisted sacrificing their own interests for the national interest or for achieving the national goal. . . . Besides, being a union in nature, they often operated according to the principles of collective decision, equal opportunity, and merit. [They could] not conduct the managed economy according to the national priority. For these reasons, the control associations had to adopt the principle of leadership. (Shōkō Gyōsei kenkyūkai 1942:20).

In postwar Japan, countermeasures to excessive competition adopted by the Japanese state have resulted in two institutional fixtures in the Japanese economy: government regulations and nonmarket governance structures.

The meaning of *state regulation* here is very different from Chalmers Johnson's meaning of *regulatory state;* he uses that term in contrast to *developmental state.* In a regulatory state such as the United States, regulations emphasize the rules of competition. In contrast, in the developmental state, regulations determine how much competition is allowed; the term *excessive competition* is used in conjunction with demands to lessen competition in all sorts of industries. Bureaucrats regard the situation as ideal when "an industry is composed of only a few firms whose market shares are stable and whose rankings in terms of sales, profits, and number of employees are unchanging" (Komiya 1988:11). As a result, by the early 1990s, more than 11,000 regulations were at work in the Japanese economy. The widespread use of state regulations, as Komiya Ryōtarō points out, resulted in the *Genkyōku system,* whereby "the ministerial bureau, division, or section under whose jurisdiction a given industry falls, wants its industry to be orderly and organized, and no disruptions of any kind to exist" (1988:11).

There are several types of nonmarket mechanisms governing the economy. *Keiretsu* refers to business networks or "clans," which, according to Ronald Dore (1987), comprise two types of relational contracting. Major manufacturers and their suppliers share the losses of bad times and the gains of good times; they recognize the hierarchical nature of the relationship and distribute benefits and risks accordingly; and they forbid the stronger side from using its bargaining superiority and the competition among workers during recessions to reduce their orders as much as possible. Big companies compete only in the consumer market and in developing new consumer products. By contrast, in the production goods market, they are to maintain a "stable," "obligated," cooperative relationship (Dore 1987:175–8). In these relational contracts, values and sentiments sustain obligations, and transactions may not reflect the price signal of the market. In the Japanese economy, cartels are a legitimate and common practice at the cost of consumer interests, and various trade associations play an important role in price adjustment, industrywide price formulas, refusals to deal, market versus big-buyer prices, and preferences for products from Japanese-owned plants overseas (Tilton 1996). These nonmarket mechanisms, according to the Weberian approach, are "an effective regulation of conduct depending . . . upon the strong common purpose of the group," excluding "outsiders" in an effort to reduce uncertainty in economic exchange (Bendix 1960:65). Thus, a cool "logic of business" is at work behind the cultural appearance of trust among trading partners, and the Japanese who seem to have arrived at a selfless state are achieving rational ends quite thoroughly (Ouchi 1981:85). As a result of excessive state regulation and *keiretsu,* the absence of competition in many sectors of the Japanese economy has resulted in high consumer prices and great difficulties for foreign firms seeking to enter the Japanese markets. Deregulation and antitrust have become the central issues in the 1990s.

It is wrong, however, to assume that there is no competition in the Japanese economy. On the contrary, competition among Japanese companies is intense (often becoming excessive, as the concept itself suggests), and entrepreneurship has been a driving force in Japanese competitiveness. The competition in Japan, however, is never laissez-faire. The principle of preventing excessive competition means that in the Japanese economy private companies compete within the scope defined by the state. Within this scope, competition is certainly driven by market forces. After the Japanese state identified the strategic industries, what it did in the initial stage was to prevent foreign competition by enacting tariffs and restrictions on imports and by providing Japanese companies with low-interest loans. As a result, competition became intense among Japanese companies since all of them intended to gain a share in the industries that had a high potential for growth (Murakami 1992). This resulted in excessive competition. Under such circumstances, the state intervened by restraining the pattern and degree of competition in each industry through regulations and administrative guidance. These mechanisms usually did not allow medium-sized and small companies to compete horizontally with big companies; instead, they organized these companies into a hierarchy in which smaller companies would work for larger ones as supportive rather than competing forces. Organizing the market, either by reducing the number of competitors to prevent excessive competition or by providing some competitors with favorable treatment through a discriminatory policy in resource allocation, rather than replacing the market, has been a distinctive characteristic of Japanese industrial policy since 1950. This distinguish Japanese developmentalism from both socialism and liberal capitalism.

Restrained competition had a direct implication for foreign companies. Morozumi Yoshihiko (1966:115) once argued that "in order to protect our national interest, we need to enact the anti-dumping tariffs to prevent the practice of dumping by foreign monopolies. We also need countermeasures to international economic policies adopted by other countries." In the ideology of Japanese developmentalism, foreign investment was perceived as a potential threat to Japan's national security. It was argued that the danger to national security in peacetime no longer was related only to national defense and munitions. It could also mean that "foreign capitals impose unfavorable terms in economic transactions by employing their dominant power over the market, and take initiatives that will harm the interest of the Japanese economy" (Morozumi 1966:135). Although the liberalization of capital investment was perceived as inevitable, it was believed that Japan had to protect itself from the danger that foreign capital would take over the industries that had great growth potential and were the most profitable. If the nation failed to do so, the result might be a colonial economy in which most profits would be drawn to foreign countries, and Japan would not be able to industrialize independently (Arisawa 1967).

According to Western mainstream economic theory, the practice of restraining competition is not only inefficient in resource allocation but also unfair because the constraint on market competition may result in monopoly. Japanese developmentalism, however, perceived this issue in relation to the promotion of industrial structure and national competitiveness. Arisawa Hiromi once justified the conflicts between the national power of production and the interests of consumers: He admitted that big business and monopoly capital always pursued their interests in the name of national interest. The irony, he argued, was that as long as the state policy fit the interest of monopoly capital, it also fit Japan's national interest. Certainly, the effort to build the national power of production was often made at the expense of consumers' interests. In a capitalist economy, however, not only national interest but any fair policy would be a double-edged sword to the Japanese economy. To unconditionally stress a fair policy, such as a strict anti-monopoly policy, would cause the nation to lose its international competitiveness (1967:274).

To many analysts, this pro–big business policy produces economic inequality by sustaining the dual structure of the economy (*nijū kōzō*) – the coexistence of large firms representing modern industries and medium-sized and small companies representing premodern industries. In Japanese developmentalism, however, this dual structure was both a barrier and an advantage to industrialization. On the one hand, the dual structure could intensify the competition for capital and resources between the large companies and the medium-sized and small firms. This situation would reduce the economy of scale and weaken Japan's international competitiveness. On the other hand, this structure could enable Japanese firms to compete with foreign rivals by combining the technological and capital strength of big corporations with the cheap labor and flexibility of medium-sized and small firms, and at the same time could bring the fruits of economic development to various social strata by integrating them into the international competition.

Rejecting the profit principle

The third principle of developmentalism is the rejection of profit in management. This is reflected in the concept of *promoting productivity* (*seisansei no kōjō*). According to Nakayama Ichirō, one of the leading authorities on this topic in Japan, productivity refers to an efficient relationship between input and output, but it emphasizes labor. In the long run, productivity can be attributed directly to innovation: the development of new products, the adoption of new production technology, the discovery of new resources and markets, and the rationalization of companies. The promotion of production will stimulate economic growth and upgrade industrial structure. In the short term, however, productivity can be influenced directly by labor because productivity is related closely to prices, wages, and distribution ([1956] 1972 vol. 14:270–319). Japanese management, characterized by permanent employment, seniority-based salary, and firm-based labor unions, is an institution to promote productivity by defining who owns the firm and how the rights, responsibilities, benefits, risks, and information are distributed among parties affiliated with the firm (Ozaki 1988:834).

In Anglo-Saxon capitalism, the financial market functions as the major means by which individual shareholders generate profits, whereas the labor market enables individual employees to improve their incomes and other economic welfare. In Japanese capitalism, in contrast, both markets play a marginal role: The financial market provides less opportunity for shareholders to maximize profits (Aoki 1989; Dore 1973, 1987; Thurow 1992); meanwhile, the labor market does little to promote social mobility, though there are some new trends recently (Dore 1973, 1987; Ouchi 1981; Vogel 1979). Lester Thurow (1991:125) points out that in Anglo-Saxon capitalism, the order of priority is that shareholders are served first, customers next, and employees last. In Japanese capitalism the order is reversed. The Anglo-Saxon enterprise system is perceived as irrational because

> it gives disproportionate power to capitalists to control the destiny of the entire corporation they own even if they may be few in number relative to the total number of people working at the corporation, are typically outsiders who do not participate in productive activities at the firm, and often hold shares of the stock whose value is only a fraction of the value of total assets of the corporation. (Ozaki 1988:834)

Employment is perceived as very important to the promotion of productivity because the modern economy always involves tension between the promotion of productivity and employment. The efficient organization of materials and labor means that the same output can be produced by less input, and the same input can create more output. In other words, the adoption of advanced production technology will drive some workers out of the production process and thus create the problem of unemployment. Japanese management, however, has achieved both goals simultaneously by practicing permanent employment.

The concept of productivity evolved in the war mobilization in the late 1930s and was institutionalized in the productivity movement of the late 1950s, after a disruption by the rising labor movements sponsored by the democratic reformers in the late 1940s. All three institutions that constitute contemporary Japanese management – lifetime employment, the seniority-based wage, and the firm-based labor union – existed on a large scale during the war. The "control over human resources" occupied seven articles in the National General Mobilization Law. In October 1941, all Japanese men aged 16 to 40 and all unmarried women aged 16 to 25 were required to register their "occupational ability" with the state. Because the rapidly increasing munitions production suffered from a shortage of skilled workers, the state sponsored various training programs. To ensure the allocation of labor for the war mobilization, the state controlled employment and prohibited workers from moving between companies. This greatly encouraged permanent employment. To control inflation and the production cost of munitions industries, as Andrew Gordon (1985:275) points out, the state also began to adopt the so-called livelihood wage, "which in theory would meet the basic material needs of a worker and his family by rising automatically with age, seniority, and greater family responsibility." At the same time, all activities of labor unions were banned by the state, and all unions were forced to join the firm-based *Sangyō Hōkoku Renmei* (the industrial patriotic associations). The central mission of the SHR after the Pacific war broke out was to promote productivity.

This process was sustained ideologically by the combination of a version of the Marxist theory of production force articulated by Ōkōchi Kazuo, a professor of economics at the Imperial University of Tokyo, and the fascist ideology that asserted what was called *compulsory equality*. This version of the Marxist theory of production force argued that "in order to promote the production power of the nation, a reform that rationalizes the social structure is highly necessary" (Takabatake 1960:204). To mobilize Japanese workers into the state program of the managed economy, the working conditions of labor must be improved. Without a social policy to protect and train the labor force, capital would not be able to sustain the cycle of reproduction. This was not a political declaration for the working class but an intrinsic logic of the economy. Ōkōchi regarded the profit principle of private firms in their business operations as the major barrier to war mobilization because it suggested that firms paid workers as little as possible to reduce production costs. Yamanouchi Yasushi addressed the same issue from a slightly different angle. He argued that in mobilizing all human resources for the total war, the existence of unprivileged social groups was the biggest political barrier. Therefore, fascist movements in both Japan and Germany intended to make these social groups assume their political responsibility in the war between their countries and other nation-states by achieving equality through the compulsion of the state (Yamanouchi 1995a:11–2).

In the postwar era, the Japanese perception of the concept of productivity was closely related to the agenda of building a comparative advantage in production technology. Although the wartime legacies were challenged strongly in the first decade after World War II, as labor movements arose during the democratic reforms and management conducted massive layoffs in the rationalization movement at the end of the 1940s, they revived and began to be institutionalized in Japanese management in the mid-1950s. In contrast to the wartime version of productivity, which interpreted productivity as a necessity of general mobilization for war, the new version emphasized the importance of labor in absorbing new production technology and promoting the industrial structure when the Japanese economy was under strong pressure to promote exports. At that time, Japanese companies were confronted with what Charles Sabel (1994:137) calls "the central dilemma of growth" between *learning* – "acquiring the knowledge to make things valued in markets" – and *monitoring* – "the determination by the transacting parties that the gains from learning be distributed according to the standards agreed to between them, as interpreted by each." Without providing job security to workers and increasing their salaries, Japanese companies could not gain labor's cooperation in technological innovation and quality control.

How did Japanese companies overcome the conflict between learning and monitoring? They accepted the three principles of the productivity movement proposed by Nakayama Ichirō, then vice-president of the Headquarters of Productivity. First, the ultimate purpose of promoting productivity was to increase employment. Government and business must make every effort to prevent unemployment. Second, management must consult with labor on how to promote productivity according to the actual conditions at each firm. Third, the benefits created by the promotion of productivity must be distributed fairly between management and labor (Nakayama [1956] 1972). Although these three principles implied better labor relations, they were not a ritual confirmation of the traditional value of harmony but a realistic rationalization of the relationship between management and workers. By adopting these principles, Japanese companies were able to externalize the domestic conflicts between management and labor by sharing the benefits created by the promotion of production technology, and they transformed the competing "distributional coalitions" (Olson 1982) within the company to a cooperative production coalition in competition with outsiders. In this sense, permanent employment and the seniority-based wage system have helped Japanese companies to distribute economic welfare between the firms and the workers "in ways that augment the creation of values" (Lazonick 1991:70). As a result, the comparative advantage of Japanese companies in production technology was strengthened enormously. Murakami Yasusuke addressed this issue in a broader framework. He argued that in developmentalism the state must have a broadly defined income policy to supplement its industrial policy. The reason is that the competition among private companies may not necessarily bring harmonious equilibrium to the market. Developmentalism will produce social tensions. In order to sustain the developmental program, it is necessary to create institutions to soften these social tensions. Otherwise, the developmental program may be destroyed by political instability. In this regard, income equality and job security are two major issues (Murakami 1994:183, 196–200).

The intellectual roots of Japanese developmentalism

The intellectual roots of Japanese developmentalism can be traced to the German historical school. As economics came into being as an academic discipline in Japan after the Meiji Restoration, the German historical school became the first institutionalized perspective; it dominated both Japanese academia and state policy making for several decades (Pyle 1974).

The emergence of economics as an academic discipline in Japan was a product of the Meiji Restoration. According to Sugihara Shirō (1990:10–11, 16), a prominent historian of Japanese economics, few books concerning economics came to Japan before 1868. The major topics in *Rangaku* (Dutch studies) were military science, medical science, astronomy, and other natural sciences. After the Meiji Restoration, the program of economic development sponsored by the state created a boom of importing Western economic theories. During the "People's Rights movement" in the 1870s, many English books of the classical school were translated. By 1882, there were about 2,200 books concerning economics in Japanese institutions of higher learning and state bureaucracies. Most of those books were about British economic theories. In terms of volume, books written by Henry Fawcett, who was influenced by John Stuart Mill, were rated number one. In the 1880s, Sugihara continues, after the Japanese state decided to build its political institutions according to the German model, "German economics, as the cornerstone of German social sciences, was forcibly imported. Meanwhile, the influence of British economics declined, along with all British conservative social sciences."

In 1897 the Social Party Association was established. This first nationwide academic association for economics became the major representative of the German historical school in Japan. In their opening declaration, the economists who belonged to this association expressed their ideological stand:

> We oppose laissez-faire capitalism because the extremely selfish motivation and the excessive free competition will deepen the gap between the rich and the poor. We also oppose socialism because its proposal to destroy existing economic institutions and to eliminate the capitalist class will disturb the course of national development. Our doctrine is to sustain the economic system of private ownership, and we will try within this framework to avoid class conflict and to pursue societal harmony by the efforts of individuals and the power of the state. (Sumitani 1986:115)

From the time of the mid-Meiji period and throughout the Taishō period, the German historical school remained the dominant perspective in both the state and academia (Pyle 1974).

In 1931–45, as Chapter 3 shows, the German theory of total war was the leading perspective in Japanese industrial policy. This theory may not appear in any textbook concerning the history of economic thought today. Its impact on the rise of the managed economy, however, is probably greater than that of any economic theory.

From the 1930s to the 1960s, as indicated by the three successive paradigms of industrial policy, Japanese developmentalism was inspired intellectually by three great thinkers in Western economics: Karl Marx, Joseph A. Schumpeter, and John M. Keynes. Roughly speaking, the Marxian theory of production force and the concept of the planned economy, together with the German theory of total war, served as the intellectual basis for the managed economy during the 1930s and 1940s; Schumpeter's ideas of innovation and entrepreneurship provided the major agendas for the managerial reforms in the 1950s; and the Keynesian idea of demand management laid the theoretical foundation for the high-growth policy in the 1960s.

In addition to the detailed analyses in the following empirical chapters, explaining how Japanese economists built their analytical frameworks on the inspiration provided by these three economic giants, two accounts illustrate their importance. First, in 1983, Japanese economists solemnly celebrated the centennial of either the birth or the death of these three great thinkers, who had influenced them so strongly. Karl Marx had died on March 14, 1883; Joseph A. Schumpeter and John M. Keynes were born, respectively, on February 8 and June 5. Two influential economic magazines in Japan, *Tōyō Keizai* (*Oriental Economy*) and *Ekonomisuto* (*The Economist*), each issued a special edition declaring their deep respect for these great teachers. The profound effects of these thinkers on Japanese economists were quite different, according to Tsuru Shigeto. "Keynes was an intellectual aristocrat who was closely associated with power and wealth, Schumpeter was an erudite person with a lonely soul, admiring his own purity, and Marx was a great thinker who pushed history forward and possessed an amazing vision of predicting the long-term trend of economic development" (Tsuru 1983a:1). *Jissen-ha* economists learned from Marx the importance of empirical data for economic analysis; from Schumpeter, the limits of economic theories; and from Keynes, how economics could have a clear nationality (Tsuru 1983b:117–19).

Second, the impact of Marx, Schumpeter, and Keynes on *Jissen-ha* economics is highly visible in its policy orientation. In 1967, when the economic miracle had largely materialized, the *Japan Economic Press* (*Toyo keizai shinposha*) conducted a series of interviews with eight prominent Japanese economists on their general views of the Japanese economy: Arisawa Hiromi, Nakayama Ichirō, Tōbata Seiichi, Tsuru Shigeto, Shimomura Osamu, Ōuchi Hyoe, Takahashi Kamekichi, and Horie Shigeo. (Most of these men are discussed in this study.) Afterward, one of the interviewers, Koizumi Akira, tried to classify their positions into three categories: the market economy, represented by Friedrich A. Hayek; the mixed economy, represented by John M. Keynes; and the planned economy, represented by Karl Marx. He found that these eight economists' theoretical orientations were similar to those of either Keynes or Marx, and that none favored Hayek, though he had become popular with the younger generation at that time. Instead of the static Hayek, this generation of Japanese economists preferred the dynamic Schumpeter. Another interviewer, Miyazaki Yoshikazu, pointed out that the perspectives of these Japanese economists were either short-term Keynesian plus long-term Schumpeterian or short-term Keynesian plus long-term Marxian (Koizumi and Miyazaki 1967b:313–18). Of course, when Marx's, Schumpeter's, and Keynes's ideas were incorporated into *Jissen-ha* economics, they were no longer integral or comprehensive economic theories with fullfledged presentations of variables and generalizations; they became a hodgepodge, combining divergent views on various issues with adjustments to local conditions.

What particular elements of Marx's, Schumpeter's, and Keynes's theories inspired the policy agendas of Japanese developmentalism in different periods?

Marxism has had a profound effect on Japanese economics. Tamanoi Yoshirō observes that "Marxism was the only foreign theory that was widely institutionalized in Japanese academia before World War II . . . it exerted a great effect on the Japanese intelligentsia not only in the prewar period but also today. In this sense, one cannot talk about modern Japan without Marxism" (Arisawa and Tamanoi 1973:62). Most *Jissen-ha* economists shared the Marxian belief in economic planning. At the same time, however, they differed from orthodox Marxism in certain important ways. In contrast to the cosmopolitanism asserted by classical Marxism, for example, Arisawa Hiromi's version had a strong nationalist orientation; it emphasized ways to strengthen Japan in the competition among nation-states, especially between Western and non-Western countries. Accordingly, this version focused on production force based on technology and often acknowledged the role of big firms in innovation, rather than emphasizing the relations of production and treating big firms as agents of monopoly capital. Arisawa's version of Marxism, moreover, prescribed the avoidance of class conflict and advocated cooperation between management and labor, especially when the nation was in crisis.

Schumpeter's reputation in Japan is higher than that in any other countries. His idea of innovation, in the Japanese context, was no longer an academic concept for making sense of the dynamics of economic growth, but instead was perceived as a practical strategy to "upgrade the industrial structure of the Japanese economy" so as to enable the nation to gain a strategic position in international competition. Gotō Yōnosuke once explained the sense in which he introduced Schumpeter's idea of *innovation* in the 1956 White Paper on the Economy. He said that "according to Schumpeter's definition, innovation refers to new technology, new products, new business organizations, and the creation of new markets. In this white paper on the economy, the meaning of innovation is further broadened. It suggests the modernization of Japan's economic structure" (Gotō 1956:14).

Keynesian economics is applied in Japan not as a macro economic policy to adjust market fluctuations, or to sustain economic growth and full employment in general, as in many Western industrialized countries, but as part of an industrial policy to induce private firms to innovate in order to meet the international challenge of liberalizing trade and capital investment. Shimomura Osamu (1967:168) once made a clear distinction between the welfare state and Japanese developmentalism in regard to the implications of Keynesian economics. He argued that the application of Keynesian economics

> does not have to be limited to the economic situation when effective demand is needed. In that way, the issue of development is confused with the issue of full employment. The nature of development lies in innovation. Development is nurtured by promoting productivity, upgrading industrial structure, and enlightening human creativity. In short, it aims at paving a way for new and still higher productivity.

Fred Block (1994) points out that advocating long-term state intervention to sustain economic development is also a theme in Keynesian economics, but it is usually neglected because it sounds too radical in Anglo-Saxon economies. In the Japanese economy, however, which has a long tradition of state intervention, this theme is well received.

Another tradition of economic thinking

The Japanese experience in economic development has demonstrated an alternative path of industrialization to the Anglo-Saxon experience; this development has been regarded as a great economic challenge to Western countries. A more profound challenge from Japan, however, is intellectual because Japanese developmentalism represents a different tradition in the history of economic thinking. This tradition, which can be traced back at least to the German historical school, competes with that represented by neoclassical economics (Pyle 1974).

Murakami (1992 vol. 2:143) pointed out that neoclassical economics regards capitalism as its research subject but that the concept itself is ahistorical. In contrast, Japanese developmentalism treats industrialization as its subject, and this concept is historical. Neoclassical economics focuses on a particular aspect of virtually all human behavior, and investigates facts and discovers truths about them. In contrast, Japanese developmentalism emphasizes the concrete processes of production, distribution, exchange, and consumption of goods and services in Japanese industrialization. Japanese developmentalism rejects neoclassical economists' claim that economic laws are universal and insists on the relativity of economic theories. This view is consistent with Veblen's proposition that economics is an evolutionary science because the conditions of economic life are subject to variation. Most *Jissen-ha* economists belonged to either *Marukei* or *kinkei* in some way by academic definition, but in regard to policy issues they overcame the ideological restrictions of a single economic doctrine and borrowed selectively whatever proved useful.

Methodologically, neoclassical economics derives economic laws through logical and mathematical deduction, disregarding the ethnographic facts about human behavior in any given society and the cross-cultural data about any economic system (Schneider 1974:23). Once these logical principles are derived by introspection, they become the axioms from which the "data" and the "facts" about other societies are to be "generated" or deduced. Produced in this way, models in neoclassical economics are inevitably derivative and universal (Gudeman 1986:32). In contrast, the major theoretical propositions of *Jissen-ha* economics were derived through induction. They were based on empirical studies of economic reality and were concerned with the timely issues confronted by the Japanese economy.

Neoclassical economics is based on methodological individualism and explains macro economic phenomena as an aggregation of individual behaviors. In this sense, according to Sawa Takamitsu ([1982] 1989:17), neoclassical economics is influenced by the *physics imperialism* that emerged in the nineteenth century; methodological individualism resembles the method of atomization in physics. Japanese developmentalism, in contrast, treats economic phenomena institutionally, emphasizing how the nation-state increases its wealth through promoting the power of production by employing a state industrial policy, business networks, and Japanese management.

Finally, neoclassical economics claims to be value free. There is a greater tendency among economists to be more neutral than others about the relative value of particular industries. In contrast, Japanese developmentalism regards the economy as a social system that has ethics. For this reason, the description by John Neville Keynes (the father of John M. Keynes) of the characteristics of the German historical school is also a precise summary of the standing propositions of developmentalism in Japan:

> The school explicitly calls itself ethical; it regards political economy as having a high ethical task, and as concerned with the most important problems of human life. The science is not merely to classify the motives that prompt economic activity; it must also weigh and compare their moral merit. It must determine a standard of the right production and distribution of welfare, such that the demands of justice and morality may be satisfied. It must set forth an ideal of economic development, having in view the intellectual and moral, as well as the merely material, life; and it must discuss the ways and means – such as the strengthening of right motives, and the spread of sound customs and habits in industrial life, as well as the direct intervention of the state – by which that ideal is to be sought after. (Keynes [1917] 1984:80)

The preceding analysis illustrates both the dynamic and the static characteristics of the modern Japanese economic ideology, which has inspired Japanese industrial policy. In the empirical chapters that follow, I demonstrate how the major propositions of Japanese developmentalism evolved over time and show what factors in the historical environment can explain these changes.

3. The managed economy

The managed economy was the leading paradigm in Japanese industrial policy during what Tsurumi Shunsuke calls the "fifteen-year war." This period began with the Manchuria Incident on September 18, 1931, in which the Japanese army occupied northeast China, and ended with Japan's surrender to the Allies on August 15, 1945. The period 1931–45 was one in which "history was geared to social change; the fate of nations was linked to their role in an institutional transformation" (Polanyi [1944] 1957:28). Responding to the Great Depression, fascism, socialism, and the New Deal emerged as three "live forces" in writing the most important page of human history in this century. During this period, the Japanese economy experienced some profound changes that strongly influenced its postwar development.

Writing about the significance of the Japanese experience from this period to its postwar history, Itō Takashi (1976:16–20) pointed out that many distinctive phenomena in postwar Japan cannot be understood properly without reference to the Japanese experience over these 15 years. Nakamura Takafusa (1974a:164) wrote that "the system established to control material and money directly during the war has almost disappeared. Many of its variants, however, have remained as legacies of the war and constitute the foundation of the economic institutions even today." One of the most important parts of this foundation, states Chalmers Johnson (1982), was the industrial policy practiced by the Japanese state. According to Ryūtarō Komiya (1986:23), the Japanese economists who lived through that experience "were influenced both consciously and unconsciously by the socialist planned economy and by their wartime experience of economic controls. They believed that the government must exercise strong leadership, formulate plans, and guide and regulate the activities of the private sector across the whole gamut of industrial activity."

Recent studies published in Japan stress the significance of the 1931–45 period to the development of the contemporary Japanese economic

67

system to an unprecedented level. Okazaki Tetsuji and Okuno Masahiro (1993b:ii–iii) write, with some exaggeration, that "the Japanese economy before the 1930s was basically an Anglo-Saxon type of classical market economy. . . . This classical economic system was transformed to what we know now the 'Japanese type' of economic system. To be specific, the contemporary Japanese economic system originated from the 'total war system' which was artificially created for the purpose of war mobilization." Noguchi Yukio (1995) argues that it was during the war that the Japanese economy became "alien." Today's Japanese economy still operates by the war system. The continuities of the wartime legacies are reflected not only in institutions, but also in economic principles. The emphasis on production and the rejection of competition have been two guiding principles in this system.

What were the dynamics behind the departure of Japanese capitalism from its pre-1930 practice? Given the simultaneousness of the great transformation of capitalism in world history, should we treat the Japanese experience as similar to the Anglo-Saxon experiences or perceive it as a distinctive pattern of its own? In this chapter, I show that although the major industrialized countries all suffered in the Great Depression, the Japanese response to the situation resembled the fascist pattern in several important ways.

As a leading concept used by Japanese scholars in studies of the Japan of the 1930s, the relationship between fascism and modernity has been a key point at issue. In the 1950s, fascism was regarded as the major reason for the war, and studies of fascism concentrated on its evolution and structure. When Keynesian economics became influential in the 1960s, a stream of studies began to focus on how modern economic policy originated in Japan during the 1930s. The continuity argument of the 1960s stressed the link between the prewar and postwar periods. In the 1970s, Japanese academic attention was extended to the society of the 1930s. Fascism and modern capitalism (*gendai shihon shugiron*) have been two competing perspectives (Hara 1982:3–4). Before the 1990s, fascism basically was perceived as irrational in contrast to modernity. In the 1990s, Yamanouchi Yasushi and his associates have tried to incorporate these two competing perspectives into a coherent theory by asserting that total war played a very important role in modernizing societies in both fascism and the New Deal (Hooks and Jussaume 1995; Prinz 1995; Yamanouchi 1995a). Yamanouchi made two distinctions between different facets of fascism. First, fascism involved racial discrimination externally against other ethnic groups. Internally, however, it intended to eliminate the gap among different social classes (here it should be noted that fascism also depended on coercion concerning domestic affairs). Second, the purpose of fascism – to dominate the world by military power – was certainly irrational. Nevertheless, to achieve this irrational goal, fascist programs adopted many rational means. In order to mobilize their own countrymen to carry out the mission of conquering the world, fascist regimes tried to eliminate social conflicts and social exclusions through compulsory equalization (*Gleichschaltung*) and rationalized society (Yamanouchi 1995a:11–12).

In the English literature, fascism has been rejected as a meaningful concept with which to interpret the nature of Japanese politics in 1931–45. It was argued that "fascists may have been part of the total political scene, but only as a minor side current." (Duus and Okimoto 1979:67). Compared to the German and Italian cases, Japanese fascism had no mass movement or the cult of the supreme leader, but a focus on agrarianism, a central role for military officers (Maruyama 1967). As Andrew Gordon (1991:334) points out, however, the rejection of this concept in the analysis of Japanese history of 1931–45 reflects "an implicit Eurocentrism and an explicit nominalism." Rather than deriving a standard criterion from the German or Italian case, Gordon (1991:335) suggests, we should emphasize the "common ideas that justified the new regimes, and the common programs they adopted." Fascism, as a "common historical process unfolding in different nations over the same broad timespan," may provide many insights in understanding the contemporary diversity of capitalism. As Simon Reich (1990) demonstrates, countries that experienced fascist regimes had much in common, not only at that time but also in their postwar economic policies. Denying the impact of fascism by stressing the survival of limited pluralism involves overlooking the profound institutional and ideological changes that were strongly influenced by fascism. Rather than adopting a "rigid periodization of history" or an "arbitrary assumption about the normal mode of development" (Duus and Okimoto 1979:65) (either of them would result in a holistic argument), I treat fascism as one important variable that influenced the transformation of Japanese capitalism in 1931–45 in certain ways.

In this chapter, I first consider how the governance of the Japanese economy departed from the pre-1930 practice in 1931–45. I do not mean that the change in Japanese capitalism in this period had nothing to do with the pre-1930 period, but I stress the magnitude of the change itself. The state emerged as a major actor in the economic arena in the aftermath of the Great Depression and in the increasing international tension between Japan and other countries after the Manchuria Incident in 1931. It implemented a series of policy innovations in an effort to strengthen the national power of production. The state not only greatly strengthened its planning capacity, but also established tight control over resource allocation. Influenced by the state's industrial policy, business organizations also changed profoundly in 1931–45. Starting the program of managed economy in a capitalist environment, the state depended heavily on nonstate institutions to control the economy. Cartels, control associations, the main bank system, the practice of subcontracting, and the industrial patriotic associations became common institutions restraining the market forces. The great transformation of institutions and ideologies indicates the rise of developmentalism in Japanese industrial policy.

How did fascist ideology influence this transformation? I portray the impact of fascism on Japanese industrial policy in a broad historical context. First, the Japanese perception of the inevitable military conflict with Western countries induced a strategic view of the economy. The Japanese believed that after the Great Depression, the trend toward the bloc economy was replacing free trade in the international economy. As a result, the conflicts of interests among nation-states were intensified. During this process, Japan had suffered from racial discrimination by the Western powers. Sooner or later, Japan would be involved in a total war with Western countries in order to redefine the international order. To prepare for this total war, Japan had to organize the entire economy around national defense.

Second, in response to the challenging international environment, two nationalist movements emerged, which shifted the unit of analysis in Japanese economic ideology from the individual and the social class to the nation-state. The *tenkō* (conversion) movement by former communists rejected the Marxist assertions of cosmopolitanism and class struggle; the *kokka kakushin* (state reform) movement launched a sweeping attack on individualism, as reflected in the laissez-faire doctrine, in order to get rid of the evils of capitalism. In place of individual and class interests, the public interest became the chief concern, and the nation-state was perceived as the only proper level at which to analyze the situation and to prescribe economic strategy.

Third, through brain trusts – the special channels that linked academia with high-level politics – the diffusion of foreign economic ideas strongly influenced state policy making in 1931–45. The German theory of *der totale krieg* (total war) and the practice of national socialism, the Marxian theory of production force and the Soviet practice of the planned economy, and the American New Deal were studied seriously and provided the theoretical foundation for the managed economy. Economic hardship during the Great Depression mad₋ the Japanese believe that the laissez-faire doctrine was obsolete. Because individual economic actors would behave according to the profit principle, the market could not effectively allocate resources for war mobilization. The state had to assume leadership to achieve this goal.

Finally, the institutions that evolved in the managed economy, as a product of the politics of industrial policy, were constrained by the structure of the state and by state–business relations. The effort to strengthen the state's capacity for integrating policy encountered strong resistance by bureaucratic sectionalism in the state, which was rooted deeply in the Meiji Constitution. The state, despite its attempts, could not centralize the power of planning and implementing the managed economy in a single bureaucratic agency until 1943. Meanwhile, even though the state had gained great power of control over the economy, the private sector, supported by the anticommunist orientation of the fascist ideology, could still block some radical policy initiatives by the state, such as the efforts to control profits, to separate management from ownership, and to bestow official status on managers. By the end of World War II, however, the power of the Japanese state in economic intervention was far greater than at the beginning of the 1930s.

The emergency era

Crisis is the father of policy innovation. The paradigm of the managed economy in Japanese industrial policy emerged in the chaos between the late 1920s and the end of World War II. According to Andō Yoshio (1987:403), the managed economy had two separate but related origins: the policy measures for counteracting the Great Depression and the general mobilization for war. The Japanese called this the *hijoji* (emergency era). As Arisawa Hiromi (1976:19) described it:

> In political history, the first ten years of the Showa era (1926–1935) were a period full of terrorism and coups, in which Japan stepped quickly towards war and fascism, beginning with the fire in Man-

churia (northeast China). In economic history, it was a period in which Japan experienced a rapid transition from "financial panic" and the "Showa crisis" to hyperinflation and militarization of the national economy against the background of the 'May 15th Incident' and the "Manchuria Incident."

The emergency era came to Japan two years earlier than did the Great Depression to other countries. Beginning in mid-March 1927, Japanese banks suffered a storm of withdrawals from savings accounts, resulting in the failure of 31 banks in two months. In 1928 the government enacted the Bank Law, aimed at rationalizing the Japanese banking system by eliminating small banks. As a result of this measure, Mitsubishi, Mitsui, Sumitomo, Yasuda, and Daiichi became the "big five" financial actors. To tighten finance and reduce the national debt, Inoue Junnosuke, the finance minister in the Tanaka cabinet, also lifted the ban on gold exports. By doing so, however, he opened the Japanese economy to the international market at an inappropriate time. When the Great Depression occurred in the West, its influence, together with Inoue's deflationary policy, drove Japan into the Showa crisis. Between 1929 and 1931 Japan's GNP declined 18%; exports, 47%; household consumption, 17%; and investment in plants and equipment, 31%. The rate of capital gains in manufacturing fell from 5% in 1929 to 1% in 1931. The stock market also crashed. If we set the January 1921 market average at 100, the average stock price in 1930 was only 44.6. In urban industrial areas, cartels and trusts were created to deal with the failure of the market, which had caused the unemployment of an estimated 2 to 3 million persons (Arisawa 1976:53–4). (At that time, no reliable statistics were kept in Japan.)

The economic hard times also aggravated labor disputes. In 1930, 195,805 Japanese workers were involved in 2,289 disputes and 81,329 took part in 906 strikes. In rural areas, the net production of agriculture, forestry, and fishing in 1931 was equal to only 57% of production in 1929. Many families felt compelled to sell their daughters to serve as prostitutes. In one hard-pressed village, one-fourth of the young girls were sold; the village office was even made into a market for transactions in prostitution.

How did the country respond to this unprecedented crisis? Responding to the isolation imposed by the international environment, Japan engaged in an arms race with the United States between 1918 and 1921 in an effort to prepare for military confrontation in Asia. Then, at the Washington Conference, Japan changed its policy to one of cooperation with the Western countries by making a number of commitments: first, to respect the sovereignty, independence, territorial and administrative integrity of China; second, to provide China with the fullest and freest opportunity to develop and maintain itself as an effective and stable government; third, to use its influence to promote equal opportunity in commerce and industry for all nations throughout the territory of China; and fourth, to refrain from taking advantage of conditions in China in order to seek special rights or privileges that would abridge the rights of subjects or citizens of friendly states, and from countenancing actions inimical to the security of such states (Crowley 1966:28–9). Nevertheless, after a short period of peace resulting from the naval status quo established at the Washington Conference, the Japanese military came to believe that restricted military force would not enable Japan to protect its interests in Manchuria and China. At that time, the nationalist movement in China and the presence of the Soviet army in the Far East were perceived as real threats to Japanese interests. In 1927 the Tanaka Giichi cabinet adopted an aggressive policy toward the mainland, explicitly claiming Manchuria and Mongolia as Japan's lifeline. This cabinet asserted that "if disturbances should spread to Manchuria and Mongolia and menace Japan's special position and interests in these regions, the Imperial government must be prepared to combat this menace, regardless of where the danger may originate" (Crowley 1966:32).

On September 18, 1931, the Japanese army provoked the Manchuria Incident, which was aimed at solving Japan's economic problems by expanding Japanese military power in mainland Asia. Although this incident was organized by a small group of radical military officers, the consequences for the nation were far-reaching. The incident drove Japan into military confrontations, not only with China, which it invaded, but also with Western powers that had vested interests in East Asia. Japan was branded as an aggressor and was ostracized by the world. Because Japan strongly opposed any intervention by the League of Nations, the country became more and more isolated from the international community. In 1933, when the League of Nations refused to recognize the Manchurian government and ruled, after an investigation, against Japan, Japan withdrew from the organization. Finally, Japan committed a great military error by waging two wars: the war with China, beginning in 1937, and the war with the United States, starting in 1941.

These military conflicts had some serious economic consequences.

First, the rapid increase in military expenditures created huge government debts. The military expenditures of the Japanese government in 1931, the year of the Manchuria Incident, totaled 1,477 billion yen; in 1932, 1,950 billion; in 1933, 2,255 billion; in 1934, 2,163 billion; in 1935, 2,206 billion; in 1936, 2,282 billion; and in 1937, 3,452 billion yen (Rengō Jōhōsha 1938:17). Second, the huge budget for military expenditures inevitably weakened Japan's ability to make international payments. The trade deficit in 1932 was 67 million yen; in 1933, 85 million; in 1934, 142 million; in 1935, 15 million; in 1936, 131 million; and in 1937 the deficit climbed to 636 million yen (Rengō Jōhōsha 1938:203). Because of these pressures, the problems of how to allocate limited resources at the macro level and how to promote production in order to survive the wars became the most critical policy issues for the Japanese state.

The program of the managed economy

As the Great Depression undermined the belief in laissez-faire, state intervention in the economy was strengthened in all major industrialized countries. These trends together constituted what Karl Polanyi (1957) called the *great transformation* of the modern economy, which resulted not only in German nationalist socialism and the Japanese managed economy, but also in the New Deal in the United States and the practice of planned economy in the Soviet Union. The practice of managed economy in Japan represented a major departure from liberal capitalism in which a distinctive economic system emerged. Through industrial reorganization, the state and nonmarket institutions became the major means of organizing economic life. They largely replaced the functions of markets: not only financial and labor markets, but also the markets for producer and consumer goods.

The evolution of the managed economy had three stages. The first stage occurred between 1931 and 1937, starting with the enactment of the Important Industry Law. At this stage, "the state tried hard to avoid exercising its power in the managed economy. As an alternative, it tried to realize its will through independent management by industries, depending upon the initiative of entrepreneurs in economic control and pursuing the goal of managed economy through protection and assistance to the private sector" (Arisawa 1937a:1) After the Japanese army started its full-scale invasion in China in 1937, the state assumed direct control over the economy by enacting the National General Mobilization Law in 1938. "In this new stage," argued Arisawa (1937a:1–2), "the goal of managed economy has become different. It is no longer possible to realize this goal by simply depending upon entrepreneurs' initiative. The state has to exercise its power and directly assume its leadership in economic activities. In a semi-war situation, an economy led by the state has to be coercive." After the Pacific war broke out, state control over the economy was further strengthened.

Can we categorize the pre-1930 Japanese economy as liberal capitalism, as Noguchi (1995) and Okazaki and Okuno (1993) suggest? The answer is no. The Japanese economy in pre-1930 had both a high weight of agriculture that was dominated by a landlord system, which was in many ways feudal or semi-feudal, and a hierarchical industrial sector that was dominated by *zaibatsu* whose membership was primarily based on the family ties and was exclusive to outsiders (Nakamura 1995a; 1995b). Besides, as a latecomer in industrialization, Japan had been strongly influenced by Germany in state building, economic ideology, social policy, and the perceptions of technology and national security since the Meiji period (Johnson 1982; Pyle 1974, 1989; Samuels 1994). The Japanese adopted the German model as an alternative to Anglo-Saxon liberal capitalism in order not only to build a "rich nation" and a "strong army," but also to maintain the conservative control of industrial society. In many ways, the rise of developmentalism in 1931–45 needs to be understood as an extension of the pre-1930 period.

Then, how should we interpret the drastic changes that took place in 1931–45 in the Japanese economy in relation to pre-1930? I argue that the institutional recomposition in 1931–45 can be regarded as a great leap. Although the leap was in the previous direction, its magnitude was so great that it looked as if the ending point was fundamentally different from the starting point. It was the special historical environment in 1931–45, the unprecedented crises, wars, and the rise of fascism, that triggered the great transformation. To analyze the process of industrialization which led Japan to fascism is beyond the scope of this study. What I want to emphasize here is not whether every element of the contemporary Japanese economic system originated in 1931–45 but what kind of major changes took place in this period. Without distinguishing 1931–45 from pre-1930, it does not make much sense to discuss the continuities between 1931–45 and the postwar period because the governance structures of the postwar Japanese economy can be hardly compared with that in pre-1930.

The governance of the Japanese economy underwent a great transformation in 1931–45. The rise of the state was the most important change in the managed economy, which greatly resembled the German experience (Johnson 1982; Reich 1990). Although state intervention had a long tradition in Japanese industrialization, the systematic practice of industrial policy did not begin until the second half of the 1920s (Johnson 1982). During 1931–45, bureaucrats acquired great power in policy making in relation to politicians and business leaders. In the 1930s, corrupt politicians and selfish capitalists were regarded in Japan as the major evils of capitalism. The power of the political parties declined rapidly. By 1941, all parties were forced to dissolve (Berger 1977). In contrast, the *kakushin kanryō* (reform bureaucrats) – the major designers and practitioners of industrial policy – emerged as a new political force. Because industrial policy in the 1930s was related closely to the war mobilization, bureaucrats were strongly supported by the military. The National General Mobilization Law enacted after the China war broke out in 1937 bestowed on the state bureaucracy an incomparable command of power. This law was characterized by its highly abstract general principles. It bestowed on the state bureaucracy the authority to make detailed policies for conducting the managed economy by executive order, without approval from the Diet. This was a direct application of the "ultimate power in emergency" (*hijō daiken*) defined by the Meiji Constitution of 1889. According to the Meiji Constitution, the sovereignty of Japan belonged to the emperor. In case of war and other military emergencies, the emperor had the power to issue orders to the Japanese people, not through the government but directly through the military. None of the rights held by Japanese citizens, as defined by Article 31 of the Meiji Constitution, could prevent implementation of the emperor's power in time of war and national emergency. Moreover, as Andō Yoshio (1987:75–6) pointed out, "Given the administrative and technical aspects of implementing the program of the managed economy, the actual power held by bureaucrats was virtually beyond the restrictions set by laws."

Strategic planning was a major task of the economic general staff. The Japanese state tried hard, though not completely successfully, to strengthen its capacity to centralize the power of policy making and policy implementation. In 1935, the Cabinet Survey Bureau (CSB) (*nai-*

kaku chōsakyoku) was established under the leadership of the Okada Keisuke cabinet. In early 1937 the CSB was replaced by the Cabinet Planning Agency (CPA) (*naikaku kikakuchō*). As the Japanese army extended its invasion of China in 1937, the Konoe cabinet established the Cabinet Planning Board (*naikaku kikakuin*) by merging the CPA with the Cabinet Resource Bureau. These bureaucracies, called *kokusaku kikan* (national policy agency), were in charge of formulating long-term policies for the state. They were under the direct control of the prime minister. Bureaucrats in these agencies designed policy from the standpoint of the state as a whole, rather than at the level of individual ministries. Because of strong resistance from competing bureaucracies such as the Ministry of Finance, however, the function of these agencies was limited to making rather than executing policy. In 1943, when the failure of the Pacific war seemed inevitable, the Japanese state finally centralized the functions of policy making and execution in a single bureaucratic agency, the Ministry of Munitions. Even in this ministry, however, a deep division between the army and the navy remained. Nevertheless, by the end of World War II, the state's capacity for policy making and integration had improved considerably.

In contrast to state intervention in liberal capitalism, which basically took the form of macro economic policy, state intervention in fascist programs went down to the micro level (Reich 1990). National general mobilization meant the "control and use of human and material resources in order to mobilize the national forces most effectively for the purpose of national security in war (including any incident which is equivalent to war)" (Yomiuri Shinbunsha 1971:211). The practice of making long-term strategic plans for promoting production was first sponsored by the Japanese army through the Japan–Manchuria Research Association of Finance and the Economy (*Nichiman zaisei keizai kenkyūkai*) under the leadership of Ishiwara Kanji. Then it became the joint responsibility of the Ministry of Commerce and Industry. The long-term planners urged Japan to develop heavy-chemical industries, to promote exports in order to increase Japan's import capacity, and to adopt an easy money policy in order to promote production as quickly as possible, given the imminent crisis in Japan's foreign relations. After the China war broke out, the Cabinet Planning Board started making annual plans for general mobilization. Because Japan had few natural resources and because the Japanese economy depended heavily on trade, the main aim of these plans was to guarantee the satisfaction of the huge demands for munitions during the China war and the Pacific war within the ultimate constraints of Japan's capacity to make international payments. In these plans, the quotas set by the state for each industry depended on the amount of imports permitted. By making and implementing these plans, the state completely controlled resource allocation among sectors and industries. The state always set an order of priority according to the value of each industry or sector to war mobilization. Military demands always had the highest priority, and civilian needs in daily life were minimized (Tanaka 1975:21). This practice became one of the most basic policy instruments adopted by the Japanese state in the postwar period.

State intervention in strategic industries during this period also took the form of nationalization of management, such as in the electrical industry. As Okumura Kiwao ([1966] 1972) recalls, the electric industry suffered greatly during the Great Depression because the oversupply of electrical power by five monopolies created chaos. As national security became a major issue, the state nationalized the management of the electric industry in 1938, though the ownership remained private. After the Pacific war broke out, the distribution of electrical power was also subject to state control. During the war, the state also created many public corporations (*kōdan*) in the industries that were closely related to civilian daily life, such as transportation, food production, agricultural development, and housing. These corporations were owned by state capital and were managed directly by the government. They were established to maintain social stability during the war (Arisawa 1976:203).

To achieve its strategic goal, the state made a great effort to constrain market forces. This was achieved through both state regulations and nonstate institutions.

The state began to control the business activities of private companies through intensive regulation of the managed economy. According to Nakamura Takafusa (1974a:55–7), these regulations covered all important dimensions of the economy. With regard to human resources, the state was given the power not only to draft personnel by demanding cooperation from civilian individuals and corporations, but also to issue orders to employers regarding conditions of employment, layoffs, wages, and dispute resolution. The state also controlled the production, repair, distribution, and exchange of production materials. It had the power to set limits or prohibitions on imports and exports, and to decide on levies, tax reductions, and tax exemptions. With regard to business operations, the state could issue orders to limit or forbid establishing new firms, increasing capital, conducting mergers, changing the nature of a business, and issuing stocks and dividends. In addition, it could control capital investment by financial institutions. With regard to business organization, the state could issue orders to reach an agreement on the conditions for economic control by the private sector and to organize associations for carrying out the managed economy. Finally, the state had the power to control prices in the market – not only the prices of consumer goods themselves, but also those for shipping, insuring, leasing, and processing the goods.

The practice of managed economy by the Japanese state was not completely successful due to the strong resistance from business circles. Even within the state bureaucracies, the efforts to centralize policy making and implementation failed to overcome strong sectionalism completely. Nevertheless, by the end of World War II, the Japanese state had established much stronger control over the economy in comparison with 1930.

Nonmarket institutions also constituted an important part of the managed economy. In the early 1930s, according to Yoshino Shinji (1966), cartels were regarded by the Ministry of Commerce and Industry (MCI) as the only way to moderate the damaging effects of the Great Depression on the Japanese economy. According to the Important Industries Law (*jūyō sangyō tōseihō*) enacted in 1931, when more than half of the firms in one industry joined a cartel, the state had the authority to force the rest of the firms to follow the agreements regarding production, sale, and prices set by the cartel. Meanwhile, the MCI made a great effort to standardize the production process and products in the rationalization movement in order to strengthen the efficiency of medium-sized and small firms. When the China war broke out, munitions-related demands increased rapidly; this resulted in a crisis in Japan's international payments, which, in turn, accelerated inflation. From then on, according to Miyajima Hideaki (1987:103), the state not only organized those industries that did not have cartels, it also intervened directly and comprehensively in the production and pricing policies of private companies that had previously made independent decisions. On the eve of the Pacific war, the Japanese state promulgated the Important Industries Association Ordinance, which resulted in the establishment of more than 20 control associations. The private sector won the battle with the bureaucrats to determine who would operate the control associations. These associations were entrusted by the state with administrative power but were operated by the private sector. They had the authority to decide not only the amount, varieties, and methods of production, but also terms, prices, partners, and timing of transactions. They also had the power to determine profits, dividends, and bonuses (Nakamura 1974a:97–101, 128–33). On the surface, these associations were under the control of the private sector. In reality, however, they were controlled by the state, especially because many staff members in the control associations came from state bureaucracies (Andō 1987:416–17). This was very similar to the German experience.

The main bank system also developed in the managed economy, which not only changed the source of corporate financing, but also formed a foundation for business groups to organize themselves around the major commercial banks. After 1937, the major source of capital for private companies shifted quickly from direct financing through stock sales to indirect financing through bank loans. By 1944, the percentage of stocks in total capital supply declined to 6.1% from 35.5% in 1937, whereas that of bank loan increased from 31.9% in 1937 to 90.9% (Teranishi 1993a:79). Beginning in early 1944, the state assigned each munitions company one bank as its chief capital provider. This structure was the origin of the postwar type of *keiretsu*. Supported by indirect financing, managers obtained greater autonomy. The time span for which interest or efficiency was estimated in Japanese business operations was extended. Meanwhile, the leading ideology of the managed economy rejected the profit principle in business operation and asserted the importance of the public interest. When the function of the market in resource allocation was largely replaced by bureaucratic control in the mobilization for war, the issue of efficiency at the micro level became less important to companies that held monopoly positions. In the end, the managed economy became very inefficient, and companies often emphasized production regardless of the cost involved.

Subcontracting was another important development of Japanese business organization under the managed economy. This was an important means of organizing various elements of the economy in the collective effort to strengthen the national power of production. In 1940, 80% of Japanese firms employed five or fewer persons and contributed only 7.4% of the total industrial production; 97% of the firms employed fewer than 30 persons and contributed 27.1% of the total production (Ueda Hirofumi 1987:200). To allocate limited resources more effectively and to promote the national power of production, the Japanese state adopted a *tenhaigyō* (transfer or close business operation) policy to force the inefficient medium-sized and small firms out of business and to organize the munitions-related firms, especially in the machine-tool and electronics industries, to join with the big manufacturers. This trend was further stimulated by the outbreak of the Pacific war, in which the production power of big companies fell far behind military demands. According to government documents, "As the current war develops, strategic industries need to be more organized. Business grouping must be promoted in order to maximize production power" (Ueda 1987:210).

Labor relations were stabilized under coercive state intervention. Orthodox Marxist scholars in Japan usually regard the managed economy as an alliance between the state and monopoly capital. According to Chalmers Johnson (1982) and Andō Yoshio (1987), however, the Japanese state often acted as a buffer between the conflicting interests of capital and the working class in order to maximize national resources in support of the war. Ōkōchi Kazuo (1970:97) shows that industrial patriotic associations asserted the autonomy and creativity of employees in the workplace, and regarded employees as human resources and the secret of success. Driven by the goal of strengthening the national power of production, these associations became a system of locating, mobilizing, maintaining, and training workers in the managed economy. This legacy exerted a strong influence on the institutionalization of Japanese management in the postwar period. State control over labor relations from 1931 to 1945 reveals an important facet of Japanese nationalism: To mobilize workers for the national program, the state had to provide a certain degree of economic equality in distribution. Workers would support the goal of strengthening the national power of production only when they believed that their interests were reflected in the state program. Otherwise, even under coercion, workers might not cooperate with the state.

The National General Mobilization Law granted the state the power to select munitions companies (*gunju kaisha*) from the private sector. In munitions companies, the major manager received official status as the responsible head of production (*seisan sekininsha*), but without pay, and all employees became responsible workers for production (*seisan dantōsha*). Everybody in munitions companies had to obey the orders of the responsible head of production; whoever violated an order was subject to a legal penalty. Before the war ended, the state had designated more than 600 firms as munitions companies. In this process, according to Nakamura Takafusa (1974a:133), "the institution of private enterprises was changed to a production system that had a command system. It was composed of 'the responsible head' and 'the responsible workers,' and was under the control of the state. It looked like a military institution with a ranking system which was divided into the army commander, the divisional commander, the brigade commander, and the regimental commander." These munitions companies always had a major advantage in obtaining resources in the annual general mobilization plans. During the Pacific war, the Japanese state identified iron and steel, coal, light metal, shipbuilding, and aircraft as the five major strategic industries. The administrative power of these industries was taken away from individual ministries and given directly to the prime minister (Arisawa 1976:204–6).

In the 1930s, two factors distinguished the Japanese managed economy from American liberalism and Soviet socialism. First, the goal of industrial policy differentiated Japan from the United States but made it similar to the Soviet Union. Even though the Soviet Union was dominated by the dichotomy between socialism and imperialism in its worldview, whereas Japan was overwhelmed by the perception of racial and ethnic discrimination on the part of other great powers, they all believed that the international conflicts would eventually result in direct military confrontation among nation-states, and that industrial policy must be implemented to support and prepare for war by strengthening the national power of production. In the United States, in contrast, the goal of economic policy was limited to the issues of unemployment, monopoly, and regulation, though the New Dealers believed that "a solution of the nation's greatest problems required the federal government to step into the marketplace to protect the interests of the public" (Brinkley 1989:89). Second, the means of achieving the goal distinguished the Japanese managed economy from the Soviet planned economy. In the Soviet Union, the state nationalized all industries and made coercive plans for individual firms. In Japan, in contrast, the operation of the managed economy still depended on private ownership, even though state intervention had been strengthened enormously. These two competing alternatives mattered greatly, not only in military confrontation during the war, but also in economic competition in peacetime. Among other important reasons, the rapid transition of the Soviet economy to heavy-chemical industries and more effective government planning contributed significantly to the victory of the Soviet Union in World War II. In contrast, the economic system chosen by Germany and Japan failed to support them effectively in the military confrontation. Conversely, the German and Japanese economic system, after certain adaptations, demonstrated great strength in peacetime, whereas the socialist system gradually lost its dynamic in economic development.

The trend toward a bloc economy

What was the dynamic behind this great transformation of the Japanese economic system in 1931–45? I argue that fascist ideology played a very important role in prescribing the strategy of change. The strategic view of the economy, which distinguished the fascist program from the New Deal, was directly derived from the Japanese perception of the world system at the time. In the Japanese worldview of the 1930s, the international economy after World War I had fallen into disorder. The Japanese believed that the intensive competition among the great powers for resources and markets in colonial areas would inevitably lead internationally to bloc economies.

It was argued that the international market worked relatively well before World War I, as nations produced goods according to the principle of comparative advantage. This international division of labor, however, was destroyed by the war. As Yoshino Shinji, who served as deputy minister and minister of commerce and industry in the 1930s, pointed out (1930:1):

> As all major industrialized countries were involved in the war, the balance of materials between supply and demand in the global market was ravaged. International commercial transactions became seriously restricted. As a result, the whole world suffered from the shortage of materials. In those countries which were directly involved in the war, the munitions demands for all kinds of materials were increasing day by day. Under such circumstances, the theory of economic self-sufficiency, which asserted that a nation should produce all necessary materials domestically, became very fashionable everywhere.

Unlike World War II, after which the Bretton Woods system established an order for the international economy, World War I resulted in chaos because most industrialized countries adopted a protectionist policy to safeguard their own industries. According to a study by the Shōwa Research Association (SRA), a private brain trust of the Konoe Fumimaro cabinet, it was Great Britain that first established the mutually favorable trading system. Subsequently, all major industrial countries tried to obtain privileges from certain geographical areas. This practice not only made entry into markets more difficult for other industrialized countries, it also intensified the competition for markets among later-developing countries (Shōwa Kenkyūkai 1939:18–19). The Japanese held that the international peace might be threatened when a nation monopolized the production of certain goods (Yoshino 1930:16–17, 78).

According to the *lifeline* (*seimeisen*) theory, whose Japanese origin could be traced back to the Meiji period, a suzerain country's economy could not survive without a huge geographic region outside its own territory to supply resources, labor, and markets in the form of colonies. This theory asserted:

> Every country should obtain all its needs within its own territory or areas under its control, and seek its own markets in the same areas as much as possible. It is a trend to restrict trade with areas that are outside a nation's influence and to avoid the use of gold or the currency of a third nation in the settlement of foreign accounts . . . foreign trade in the future will be simply a means of maintaining and developing a nation's own economic sphere, a bare function of national policy. (Sugimori 1940:967–8)

How should Japan act in this new era of bloc economies? Ayusawa Iwao (1940:801–2), the deputy director of the Foreign Relations Bureau of the Japan Economic Federation, believed that the European style of economic nationalism, which protected one country's domestic market from foreign products, was "uneconomical," "unsafe," and "inefficient." This kind of economic nationalism, stated Iwao, was a direct explanation for the "inhumanity of the war in Europe." He argued that regionalism was a better alternative as "a system of ensuring security, order and peace, not for the whole world at once, as the League attempted to do and failed, but within three or four separate regions of the earth such as America, Asia, Western and Eastern, etc." Matsui Haruo (1938:251), the director of the Cabinet Resources Bureau, said, "We by no means reject the international nature of our economy. Nor do we deny the inevitability that any economy will develop into the global economy. We must admit, however, at least to some extent, that many countries' economies in the trend toward bloc economies have emphasized the principle of economic self-sufficiency and have exercised a planned economy."

To be specific, the Japanese advocated a regional economic bloc under Japanese leadership. Because Japan had few natural resources, it was argued, its economy could not operate independently. Therefore it was very important for Japan to establish an economic bloc that placed Manchuria, China, Korea, and Taiwan under its control because the resources in East Asia were regarded as critical to the Japanese economy. These included Korea's coal, iron, aluminum, magnesium, cotton, and wool; Manchuria's iron, coal, aluminum, gold, industrial salt, and agricultural forestry and products; and northern China's coal, cotton, salt, wool, and meat. After the China war broke out, Matsui (1938:254) stated that Japan's expectation regarding Manchuria and Mongolia was to develop them into a supply base for industrial materials and fuel, and meanwhile to cultivate them as a market for Japanese products. In the future, he suggested, Japan must attempt to absorb these areas into an integrated economic bloc, which would further strengthen the Japanese economy by allocating resources effectively throughout the bloc. To realize this goal, Matsui (1938:250, 258) further suggested, Japan should establish a division of labor in the region by using economic planning, and should extend the practice of the managed economy to the entire region in order to mobilize capital, labor, technology, and management there more effectively. As a concrete measure for creating regional economic integration, Japan should sign commercial treaties with Manchuria and China to make tariffs, business organizations, and financial and monetary systems compatible.

In the end, the effort to build an economic bloc under Japanese control resulted in the proposal for the Great East Asia Co-Prosperity Sphere under the leadership of the Konoe Fumimaro cabinet in 1941. The ideological core of this proposal was Asianism. In the words of the president of Seiyūkai, Kuhara Fusanosuke, "It is essential to make Asia a region for the Asiatics by ousting the aggressive Western influences and by establishing a regional life for Asiatics in East Asia" (Okada Tadahiko 1940:970). In his study of the SRA, the designer of this proposal, Baba Shūichi, points out that although this regional order was perceived as a rational alternative for Japan and Asia in the existing international disorder, which established "a defensive and developmental regionalism," the Japanese military viewed Japan as the head of Asia and regarded the building of the Great East Asia Co-Prosperity Sphere as a mission of the Japanese empire (1969). To practice this theory in the 1930s, according to Ōtake Hideo, both Japan and Germany chose to depend on military power and coercive pillage. They dared to risk involving themselves directly in military confrontation with the older great powers (Ōtake 1992:49).

A great power as victim of racial discrimination

In his analysis on Japanese developmentalism, Murakami Yasusuke (1992) points out that nationalism has been an important part of modern politics despite the denial by the progressive view of history. In Japanese developmentalism, as I discussed in Chapter 2, nationalism was an indispensable component. What role did nationalism play in the managed economy? What was the implication of nationalism in that special historical environment?

In 1931–45, the implication of Japanese nationalism for industrial policy was reflected in the perception that Japan had been racially discriminated against in the competition for spheres of influence in China by the Western great powers. In order to fight for justice, Japan had to prepare for the final military confrontation by developing heavy-chemical industries.

Since the Meiji Restoration, the Japanese had taken the slogan "rich nation, strong army" as their national policy, believing that Japan's position in the world system would be determined by its military strength. Accordingly, Japanese involvement in the international economy was accompanied by a series of military expansions. Japan gained Taiwan as its first colony in 1895, after it won the Sino-Japanese War, and colonized Korea in 1910. In 1905 Japan defeated Russia, one of the biggest Western powers in East Asia, and gained many special privileges in Manchuria and northern China. Taking advantage of the opportunity during World War I, Japan further increased its presence in China as one of the Big Four, along with the United States, Britain, and Russia. After the Japanese Army provoked the Manchuria Incident in 1931, the conflicts of interest between Japan and Western countries accelerated.

During World War I, U.S. President Woodrow Wilson first proposed the principle of *self-determination* for the late-developing areas. This principle was then asserted by the League of Nations to reduce international tensions. The Japanese, however, did not believe that the Western countries would truly adhere to this principle. Masaharu Anesaki (1921:144–5), a professor at the Imperial University of Tokyo, stated:

> The general distrust of the Western nations with regard to their practice of international morality is a great obstacle for the Japanese. . . . Some Japanese ask: Can British rule in India be called just? Has not the American occupation of the Philippines a strong military aspect? Has not the Far East for some time been the prey of international competition? Has not Japan often been frustrated in her legitimate claims? These impressions, either well founded or suspiciously construed or instilled by dubious agents, are pretty widely current among the people. Thus a pointed question is often asked: How could the British or the Americans have become so suddenly converted in their moral sense that they really stand for peace and justice, for the liberty of smaller nations and against German aggression?

After young officers in the Japanese Army provoked the Manchuria Incident, Japanese public opinion enthusiastically supported the actions of the Japanese military. According to Japanese logic, the military had done nothing wrong because Manchuria was the lifeline of the Japanese economy and the "common object of the Big Four was the acquisition of a privileged position in China" (Crowley 1966:3–4). When the Japanese invasion caused a strong international protest, the whole issue was interpreted as a fight against racial discrimination by whites (Ogata 1969). The Japanese believed that Japan had every reason to claim equal status with the Western countries as one of the great powers: It had won the war with China, formerly the only power in East Asia; it had defeated Russia, "one of the strongest white nations, with a most powerful army"; it had begun to export industrial products to other countries, transporting them on its own ships; it had made a great effort to modernize its domestic institutions and to imitate the Western countries; and it had already become one of the Big Five. The prominent Japanese politician Shigenobu Ōkuma (1921:169–70) argued that "some whites regard the development of Japan as an unjustifiable encroachment upon their own rights. They either instigate racism against Japan as nonwhite or plan to organize a league of white nations to perpetuate white supremacy in the world." To the Japanese, the assertion of the self-determination principle in Chinese affairs was simply a Western strategy to contain Japan's interests in China. Tokichi Tanaka (1933:376–7) asserted that "The United States and other Western powers can afford a laissez-faire policy in China because their interests there are relatively inconsiderable and are not essential factors in their own existence. Japan cannot share that fortunate detachment from the fate of a nation of 400 million people at her door."

Although the Japanese stressed the issue of racial equality in their dialogue with the West, they applied a double standard on this issue by asserting that racial equality in international affairs applied to the relationship between Japan and the Western countries, but not to that between Japan and its Asian neighbors. Japan considered itself one of the great powers, whereas other Asian countries were the periphery. Sabutarō Tachi (1934:574, 581–2), who had been a professor at the Imperial University of Tokyo and had served as legal adviser to the Japanese delegation at both the peace conference after World War I and the Washington Conference, asserted in a lengthy article:

> Originally the purport of the Open Door policy was to secure equality of treatment among nationals other than Chinese in commercial matters within the Chinese districts forming part of the spheres of influence or interest of some major Powers. . . . As China is not to be considered as a direct party in the relations concerning the Open Door principle, it would be out of the question for China herself to raise the question of the validity of rights or privileges stipulated in previous arrangements between herself and some powers, on the strength of stipulations concerning that principle, unless express provisions to that effect were especially added to the stipulations in question.

Following the same logic, Ayusawa Iwao (1940:800) regarded the establishment of the League of Nations as an "unfortunate misapplication of 'democracy'" because it placed "all States, regardless of their political or economic importance, indiscriminately on an equal vote to big powers with a population of more than 100 million as well as to tiny political units, with only a few million inhabitants." These statements lay bare the sophistry of the belief that what Japan intended to do was to liberate Asia from Western imperialism.

The perception of being racially discriminated against contributed directly to Japan's national war mobilization. According to the leading Japanese politician Konoe Fumimaro (Yomiuri Shinbunsha 1971, vol.

16:10–11), who twice became prime minister in the 1931–45 period, the great powers were divided into the haves and the have-nots. This unfair distribution of power and wealth was the ultimate source of international conflicts: "As long as the international injustice exists, there will be no genuine peace." The struggle for resources and markets among the great powers in East Asia would inevitably result in war between Japan and the Western countries – either the Soviet Union, Great Britain, or the United States. To fight for their interests in East Asia, the Japanese had to prepare for a total war in the near future. This is why the Japanese response to the Great Depression, in comparison with the New Deal of the United States, had a strong strategic orientation from early on. In this sense, the cognitive gap between the outdated Monroe Doctrine and the self-determination principle, as well as the perception of racial discrimination by Western countries, constituted one of the most important dimensions of Japanese thinking that gave rise to the military version of developmentalism in 1931–45.

Tenkō (conversion)

To mobilize the whole country for war, fascist ideology, which asserted the national interest, had to defeat two major rival views that predominated in the Japanese economic ideology before 1930: Marxism, which asserted the interest of the working class, and laissez faire, which advocated the interest of individual shareholders. Two nationalist movements arose in response to Japan's domestic and international crises that sustained the transition of the unit of analysis in Japanese economic ideology from the individual and the social class to the nation-state. In the *tenkō* (conversion) movement, former communists renounced their ideological commitment to the Marxian doctrine of class struggle and cosmopolitanism and converted to the indigenous political values of the emperor system. In the state reform movement (*kokka kakushin undō*), right-wing radicals launched a powerful attack on the laissez-faire doctrine, which regarded the interest of individual capitalists as the highest priority. They urged the Japanese state to play a dominant role in the economy in order to get rid of the evils of capitalism. Yamaguchi Yasushi (1979:140–52), a prominent Japanese scholar of fascism, points out that the rise of fascism in the 1930s was the result of a merging of two major themes in European political thought of the late nineteenth century: nationalism and socialism. In Japan, I argue, the *tenkō* movement indicated a shift of socialism toward nationalism because the class struggle and cosmopolitanism were no longer regarded as major concerns. The *kokka kakushin* movement demonstrated the rapid transition of Japanese nationalism toward socialism as the claims of individual interests were replaced by the claims of public interest. These two movements, by giving the ideology of the managed economy both an anticapitalist and an anticommunist orientation, have had a profound impact on the evolution of Japanese developmentalism.

The *tenkō* movement was a strong reaction to the influence of communism in Japan. Marxism became influential in Japanese economics after World War I. Its assertion of class struggle became a powerful framework for analyzing the reality of the Japanese economy. According to this conflict perspective, Japanese capitalism was characterized by exploitation of the surplus value created by the working class; this exploitation eventually would lead the nation to revolution. *Tenkō* began in 1933, when Japan was filled with feverish nationalist sentiment after the Japanese army provoked the Manchuria Incident in northeast China. Facing strong criticism from the international community, the Japanese public showed strong support for the actions of the military. Under such circumstances, two imprisoned leaders of the Japanese Communist Party, Sano Manabu and Nabeyama Sadachika, made a public statement on 8 June 1933 renouncing their Marxist ideology. Their action shocked the whole country and was copied by their comrades. Within one month, 30% (415 of 1,370) of the unsentenced political prisoners and 34% (133 of 393) of the sentenced political prisoners who were involved in the Japanese communist movement repented. By the end of the third year, only 26% (114 of 438) retained their original political beliefs (Tsurumi 1982:10–11). From then on, whenever Japan's engagement in military adventures reached a new level, there was a wave of *tenkō*.

In addition to the conversions following the Manchurian Incident in 1931, two other peaks of *tenkō* occurred: one in 1937, after Japan started its full-scale invasion of China, and the other in 1941, when Japan started the Pacific war. In the beginning, *tenkō* took place among the believers in political Marxism, which directly advocated political action against the capitalist system. It was later extended to the believers in intellectual Marxism, including democratic socialism, who regarded Marxism as an academic perspective. Eventually *tenkō* swept away "all modern ideologies which came from the West, including bourgeois liberalism" (Maruyama 1982:119).

Tenkō transformed the unit of analysis from class to the nation-state in former communists' thinking. According to a police report, 31.9% of political prisoners claimed that "the consciousness of being a member of the Japanese nation" was their major motive for renouncing their Marxist beliefs (Tsurumi 1982:12). After Nabeyama announced his *tenkō*, he told the mass media that when he learned that Japan had left the League of Nations, he believed the country would be involved in a major tragedy in the near future. When he recognized that Japan was risking great danger, he felt that his heart had returned to his own nation from the working class, to which he belonged. He believed that Marxist doctrine was wrong in assuming that the failure of an imperialist country in war would result in the victory of proletarians in that country. "Once in war," Nabeyama argued, "the bullet from the enemy will kill whomever it hits without distinguishing between capitalists and workers, no matter who is the enemy, either the Soviet Union or China" (Iriye, Furutani, Yamazaki, and Takagi, 1984:539). The same change is evident in the famous liberal Koizumi Shinzō, who held strong cosmopolitan beliefs in both the prewar and postwar periods. As his wartime diary shows, Koizumi "lost sight of the people outside Japan" and concerned himself only with his own nation (Tsurumi 1982:17–18). At that time, the Marxist doctrine of class struggle was perceived by many Japanese communists as a threat to the national identity in a late-developing country such as Japan. Because imperialism tended to divide nation-states according to their status in the world system, just as capitalism divided people by classes in a single country, Japanese communists felt that the cosmopolitanism contained in orthodox Marxism could not answer the Japanese question of national independence, and that Marx's analysis of class struggle was now perfectly applicable at the international level rather than the national level. A "national or state socialism, premised on organic ethnic unity which does not allow class struggle" (Hoston 1983:106) fit the Japanese situation much better. The *tenkō* movement represented an effort by Japanese Marxists to adapt the European ideology of Marxism to their native context, seeking a "predominant means" to reconcile Marxism with nationalism in a difficult international environment (Hoston 1983). The nationalist logic of *tenkō* provides us with a clue to understanding not only why Marxists have participated so often in state policy making, together with state bureaucrats, business leaders, and even the military, but also why the Japanese were able to transcend class-based domestic conflicts to achieve nationalism when the nation was under external pressure.

The *tenkō* movement had a profound effect on the Japanese labor movement. After the China war broke out, the left-wing labor unions rapidly became conservative. The right-wing National Federation of Labor Unions (*zennihon rōdō sōdōmei*) even issued a "Public Statement Regarding Stopping Strikes." In this document, it was announced,

> Japanese people now are sacrificing their lives for the nation with loyalty, and the working class and the nation's industrialists are also cooperating with each other based on their proper consciousness in a national effort to overcome the difficulties. We believe that our task is to protect the rear base of the nation as soldiers who fight at industrial front in this time of emergency. . . . Based on the above belief and perceiving the uncertain future, we declare the following principles for the labor movement: first, we search for a peaceful and moral solution for the conflict during this period, and expect the complete suspension of industry-wide strikes; second, we suggest that a council of industrial cooperation be established immediately, which includes both government officials and civilians, in order to promote productivity that stands behind the gun and assures peace in industry; third, we urge the legal recognition of workers' right to organize and the immediate realization of state control over industry and labor as a national policy for the present as well as the future. When the generals and soldiers of the Imperial Army are sacrificing their lives for the nation without distinction between rich and poor, we hope wholeheartedly that in domestic industries there is not one worker who goes slowly at work and not one capitalist who still pursues individual interest. (Ōkōchi 1971:82–3)

According to Shunsuke Tsurumi (1982), *tenkō* was rooted deeply in the Japanese psychology of insularity, which resulted from the national isolation policy of the Tokugawa *bakufu*. This characteristic had been "a latent feature of the Japanese experience" and "an unexpressed postulate of Japanese thinking." This insular psychology had once been overcome by enthusiasm for pursuing modernity in a cosmopolitan environment, as the Japanese believed that Japan had already become one of the great powers in the world. In such an era, the assertions of individual and class interest prevailed in economic discussions. Once the nation became involved in international conflict, however, the insular psychology revived. It called for unconditional support of one's own country because "whether it is right or wrong, it is my country." Driven by this psychology, any unit of analysis other than the nation-state lost legitimacy in political discourse. Japanese communists had formerly believed that class struggle and cosmopolitanism were the only way to a socialist society. When these concepts failed to explain the reality of the international political economy, however, they no longer seemed rational to Japanese communists. As a result, these communists shifted their reference system from a materialistic framework to a moral and ethical one in which the family, the community, and the nation had the highest priority (Johnson 1990 [1964]).

The state reform movement

The state reform movement of the 1930s reflected the transition of Japanese nationalism to socialism, which undermined the legitimacy of methodological individualism in Japanese economic thinking, cleared the way for the claim of national interest and provided ideological legitimacy to constrain market forces. The major target of criticism of this movement was laissez-faire capitalism. It was argued that "the social system of Japan is not perfect. The sway of capitalism allows only a small and privileged class to spend for comfort and pleasure; the masses are plunged into misery; they struggle against heavy odds" (Fujisawa 1932:443). Concerned with the issue of economic inequality between social groups, the activists of the state reform movement were particularly angry at business leaders and politicians. They believed that "the political parties, the *zaibatsu*, and a small privileged group attached to the ruling class are all sunk in corruption. They conspire in parties to pursue their egoistic interests and desires, to the neglect of national defense and to the confusion of government" (Marshall 1967:104).

The state reform movement had two major groups of supporters: the right-wing radicals, consisting of young military officers who often acted as a destructive force to undermine the old system, and the reform bureaucrats (*kakushin kanryō*), who often served as a constructive force in building new institutions for the managed economy (Hata 1983:112–13). The strength of the young military officers in 1930s' politics was generated by the strong resistance of the rural areas to rapid industrialization, which intensified the social conflicts between different sectors of the economy. Rural areas traditionally had been the major sources of recruitment for the Japanese military, and they suffered great economic hardship in the Great Depression. Consequently, some young military officers were extremely critical of laissez-faire capitalism. This opposition, by many accounts, resulted in a series of terrorist assassinations in 1932. The major targets were political and business leaders. In February, Inoue Junnosuke, the former minister of finance and the head of the Democratic Political Party, was assassinated, as was Dan Takuma, the leader of the Mitsui *zaibatsu,* in March. In May a group of young military officers broke into Prime Minister Inokai Tsuyoshi's home and shot him to death. This event marked the end of an era in which the party that had won the election would be able to organize the cabinet by itself. These assassinations by right-wing radicals shook the political foundation of laissez-faire capitalism, creating an opportunity for the reform bureaucrats to emerge in the political arena.

The reform bureaucrats were the major agents of the managed economy. Although their opinions and behavior differed, they had some characteristics in common. Most had an intimate knowledge of Germany, many had experience in operating a planned economy in Manchuria, all were influenced by Marxism in their early years, and in the 1930s they all had a strong nationalist orientation (Hata 1983:124). In addition, these reform bureaucrats had a strong technocratic orientation. They not only had mastered the planning skills but also had the ability to turn their ideas into concrete policy proposals. In politics, they were often able to manipulate policy making because the older politicians in the political parties could not keep up with the latest developments or understand the demands of the younger generation (Kawahara 1979:10). The current crises created an opportunity for these bureaucrats. They were able to persuade other political elites and the general public that Japan had entered a period of national crisis in both international and domestic affairs, and that the situation required an application of their expertise, which the parties could not provide (Berger 1977:32).

The relationship between Marxism and the ideology of the state reform movement was very delicate. The left wing of the latter shared Marxists' criticisms of Japanese reality. As Masagi Chifuyu, a bureaucrat at the Cabinet Survey Bureau (CSB), reported to the court after he was charged with having a communist orientation and arrested in 1941, the CSB bureaucrats as a group were critical of the evil of laissez-faire capitalism. They had strongly asserted the need for a managed economy and their support for strongman politics. Although the CSB did not approve of Marxist theory officially, its bureaucrats were quite sympathetic to its criticism of capitalism. In order to develop a theory of managed economy, the CBS bureaucrats tried to incorporate the practices of the Soviet planned economy and of the Nazi economy (Ōtake 1981:103).

The right wing of the state reform movement, however, rejected the Marxist solution to class struggle. It was argued that Marxism perceived society as a mechanical structure founded on selfishness, which was no different from the laissez-faire doctrine. "If we seriously intend to overthrow capitalism because of its ethical deficiencies," contended Fujisawa (1932:447), "we shall thereby strangle Marxism, which is being nurtured by the pressure of capitalist influences on our lives." As an alternative to the Marxist solution of class struggle, the right wing of the state reform movement asserted that Japan should adopt

> the practicable oriental idealism that accepts society as a cooperative organization founded on morality and the family system [because] the Japanese Empire is a huge family, and the people are tied by close blood relationships into a tight spiritual unity. It is thus quite different from states in Europe and America that have been organized to meet the rational needs of the people. . . . Instead of the principles of freedom and equality for individuals held essential in occidental states, the Japanese rely on parental love and deep affection among brothers and sisters. These feelings are more deeply rooted and permanent than the rational claims for freedom and equality. Though dormant in the bosoms of the people in ordinary times, they manifest themselves unmistakably in times of national emergency. (Fujisawa 1932:448–9)

The left wing and the right wing of the state reform movement had one view in common: They advocated the leadership of the state in the operation of the national economy. As "an agent of reform," argued Ryū Shintarō, "the state is the only force capable of challenging the capitalist system," and "stricter state controls could modify Japanese capitalism on behalf of the national welfare" (Fletcher 1982). The right wing, represented by Kita Ikki, pushed this idea one step further by directly advocating national socialism. Kita held that the state should limit private wealth, and that the major industries should be owned and managed by the government (Fletcher 1982:51). Despite the influences of democracy, socialism, and liberalism in their early lives, emotional nationalism turned many Japanese toward the state in a struggle to "break the deadlock of the current situation."

In the ideology of the state reform movement, the choice between liberal capitalism and the Japanese managed economy was rendered as a cultural choice between Western values and Japan's indigenous values. The entire history of pursuing capitalism, which started with the Meiji Restoration, was under critical reexamination. It was argued that "because of indiscriminate introduction of occidental capitalism since the beginning of the Meiji Era, selfish principles, disregarding the solidarity of the family, have crept unawares into our national thought" (Fujisawa 1932:449). Influenced by Western utilitarianism, "leaders in politics and business also encouraged the spread of the new social motives and standards of value. . . . As they developed, business and industry themselves helped to diffuse material ideals, and our civilization took on many aspects of capitalism" (Fujisawa 1932:444). The real danger, it was argued, lay in the fact that capitalism was mercenary in spirit, and at that time it completely dominated Japan. The only solution to this problem, he argued, was to abolish this framework completely. In the Japanese perception of capitalism, there was little room for Western liberal ideas. Therefore, when market forces needed to be constrained, the Japanese had to turn to their indigenous values as an alternative. For this reason, Japan's indigenous values were often in conflict with the process of industrialization, as indicated by sporadic and periodic revivals and declines in their popularity.

From "economic man" to "functional man"

The transition toward the managed economy was not only interpreted as a cultural choice. It was also perceived as a competing version of modernity to liberal capitalism. Itō Takashi once pointed out that "scholars usually put too much emphasis on 'the sem-feudal nature' and the 'irrationality' of Japanese fascism without acknowledging the discussion and policies of industrial rationalization conducted by the 'reform forces.'" Avraham Barkai (1990:103–4) also observes that in the 1930s some Nazis were sufficiently well read to look for a theoretical foundation for the German economy, and that Adam Müller and Friedrich List attracted a great deal of attention from the Nazis and their collaborators. The Nazi economic principles were regarded as the realization of "the traditional idea of a German state economy," and "the economic ideal of National Socialism" was perceived as reviving the "best characteristics of German economic theory."

The German historical school's assertion for social policy had been perceived in Japan, since the Meiji era, as an alternative to liberal capitalism to prevent growing class consciousness and social unrest in industrialization. Kanai Noburu, the founder of the Social Policy Association, had recognized the relationship between nationalism and the issue of economic equality and regarded the "prevention of the social problem as a prerequisite to success in foreign affairs" (Pyle 1974:144). Influenced by this perspective, the Japanese state enacted the Factory Law in 1911 and began to sponsor the rural improvement movement at the turn of the century (Pyle 1989). As a result of the Taishō democracy, however, social policy in the 1920s became more liberal. Some bureaucrats and politicians intended to establish an industrial order by legislations protecting labor's right to organize unions, and the labor disputes developed rapidly in the 1920s (Garon 1987).

In 1931–45, social policy once again turned conversative. This conversatism, however, was perceived as quite modern. After being reinterpreted in relation to war mobilization, social policy was believed as the key solution to the dilemma between nationalism and the issue of economic equality among different social classes. Ōkōchi Kazuo, professor of economics at the Imperial University of Tokyo and a leading figure in the SRA, argued that without a proper social policy, aggregated capital would not be able to "sustain the order of reproduction." Such a social policy was "a capitalist effort to eliminate the contradictions contained in the capitalist system." Because individual capitalists always acted in their own interests and did not support the adoption of social policy, the state must take action on behalf of aggregated capital (1941). Ōkōchi further argued that economic ethics for social policy were not introduced by external forces but was demanded by the economy itself ([1942] 1969a:99, 414–15).

Ōkōchi closely linked social policy with war mobilization. Rejecting Adam Smith's concept of "economic man," he proposed a new concept, "functional man," to describe the role of individuals in the managed economy. Ōkōchi argued that production in the managed economy was not sustained by individuals' pursuit of profits but by their support for national interest. Individuals should have a clear consciousness of their social function as integral parts of the body of the managed economy that reflected the will of the state. Adam

Smith assumed that economic man was motivated by profits. The market was unconsciously guided by the "invisible hand." In contrast, the "responsible ethics" based on the social consciousness of functional man was directly connected with government planning for promoting the national power of productivity (Ōkōchi [1942] 1969a:421, 424). In Ōkōchi's argument, social policy was bestowed with new significance. It aimed no longer only at preventing the extremes of social disruption that industrialization gave rise to, but also at uniting the Japanese people in national emergency and mobilizing the working class into war. This greatly enhanced the legitimacy and persuasiveness of Ōkōchi's theory in the debate on the state labor policy during the war, which was characterized by compulsory equalization.

Ōkōchi's theory caused great controversy in the postwar era. Some argued that according to Marxian historical materialism, social revolution would occur only when the relations of production became the shackles of production. Therefore it was progressive to promote production force in heavy-chemical industries and even in military industries during the crisis of capitalism and in wartime. "Because of repression, Marxist economics in this period shifted its focus to the 'theory of production forces.' It focused neither on class and exploitation, nor on the anti-war movement. Instead it utilized the war as a 'precondition,' and concentrated on promoting production in an effort to approach production relations" (Uchida 1948:39). Others, however, strongly questioned the role played by this theory. They argued that although this theory criticized the state policy and advocated better conditions for the working class during the war, it did not criticize the war itself. Rather, it showed the "same determination as the soldiers on the battlefield and had the professed intention of building a more rational state institution in order to carry out the war" (Takabatake 1960:206). In a recent analysis of the relationship between war mobilization and modernity, Yamanouchi Yasushi (1995a:35–8) points out that the war mobilization system played an important role in "historically constituting the daily life of modern society." Ōkōchi regarded the social distribution and sustenance of labor as indispensable to production activities and bestowed public meaning on the family life of workers. As a result, family life could no longer be regarded as a private sphere, separate from the state and civil society. In this sense, social equality, a major tenet of postwar democracy, had been largely defined by the socialization of the system during the war, and the term *welfare state* can be considered a synonym for *warfare state*.

Ideas of the managed economy

Economic ideas played an extremely important role in formulating the state policy in the managed economy. When the laissez-faire doctrine was discredited by the Great Depression, the Japanese searched for new solutions from various sources, especially Western countries. These elements from various sources together constituted a coherent logic for the managed economy.

The German theory of total war was the theoretical foundation for the ideology of the managed economy. It bestowed strategic significance on the economy. It argued that the recent world war had witnessed the mass production of advanced weapons, such as aircraft, tanks, and submarine, which were based on the progress of technology and the development of advanced industrial organization. The rapid development of communications and transportation represented by the railway, the automobile, and the telegram had made the building and employment of big military forces possible. As a result, war could take place on a world scale and could become an unprecedented mega-war. Under such circumstances, it was obvious that the organization of the army and navy, their equipment and their strategies would depend upon the level of production and the transformation of the country. In this sense, the impact of world war on economic development was not limited to the technical part of the war, but also included its social and political dimensions (Mori 1933:3–4). World War I involved 66.3% of the land, 88.1% of the population, 85.6% of the trade, 83.4% of the ships, and 84.4% of the railways on earth. "In a world war, the magnitude of the war is great, the cost of the war is surprisingly high, and tremendous munitions are needed to support the war. Therefore it is essential to conduct the general mobilization of all industries" (Arisawa 1934:54).

To prepare for a total war, heavy-chemical industries were perceived as critical, as they were directly related to the production of weapons. Given the inevitability of military conflict with other great powers, Yoshino Shinji (1930:141–2) argued that even in peacetime, Japan had to strengthen its military capacity by developing a defense-oriented economy based on heavy-chemical industries. Arisawa Hiromi

(1949c:72) pointed out that "without heavy-mechanical, automobile, tractor and modern chemical industries, without the advanced technology of metal production and training in precision manufacturing, a country's economy simply will not have the foundation to produce advanced weapons . . . the organization of Japan's munitions production system cannot be accomplished without rapidly upgrading industrial structure."

To sustain a total war, allocating national resources for strategic purposes was the major concern of the managed economy. The Japanese army had started making war mobilization plans in the mid-1910s. Until World War I, the Japanese military had fought for its interests only in the governmental budget and seldom had spoken on economic policy. This attitude, however, changed dramatically during World War I. In 1915, enlightened by the German experience, the chief of the Military Geographical Division, Koiso Kuniaki, who later became the prime minister, wrote a famous book titled *The Defence Sources of Imperial Japan*. In this book, Koiso and his staff estimated the total amount of food, clothing, and other materials needed for both civilians and military personnel. They also estimated the impact of war on domestic production, and suggested various methods of promoting production and guaranteeing resources (Katō 1979). Matsui Haruo, director of the Cabinet Resource Bureau in the 1930s, was influenced strongly by Konozuka Kiheiji, his teacher in the Law Faculty at the Imperial University at Tokyo. Konozuka argued that to prosper, Japan must cultivate and sustain the development of national resources. The general mobilization of national resources did not have to be limited to war; it could also be used for economic development (Yomiuri Shinbunsha 1971, vol. 16:152). "Industries that are strategic to national defense" must be supported by the state through a discriminatory policy in resource allocation.

To achieve these goals, it was argued, market forces must be restrained. This principle was initially derived from the criticism of liberal capitalism. Matsui Haruo (1934) asserted that European economic thinking in the nineteenth century began with contempt for the state but ended with respect for the state. By the end of the century, the doctrine that "the best government governs least" had been replaced by Friedrich List's national economy, Karl Marx's class struggle, and Karl Rodbertus's and Ferdinand Lassalle's national socialism. Addressing economic issue from the viewpoint of the national economy was also the basic assumption in Japanese industrial policy. Senior bureaucrat Yoshino Shinji (1930:102–3) argued that from the perspective of the national economy, Japan had to rationalize its industrial structure and eliminate excessive competition among many medium-sized and small firms in a single industry by creating cartels. In this regard, fair competition was not an issue because some individual companies' interests had to be sacrificed for the national economy. Suetaka Shin (1936:25–6) wrote that the laissez-faire doctrine held that the balance of interest conflicts among social classes could be achieved by the invisible hand. In reality, however, such conflicts could not be easily balanced when the laissez-faire principle was at work. The maximization of productivity by the invisible hand was achieved at a great social cost. These conflicts had to be tempered by state control. This was particularly important in an era of confrontation between nation-states when munitions production needed to be ensured.

Replacing profit with public interest was another major assertion when the managed economy aimed at revising liberal capitalism according to the total war theory. To support the war, it was argued, the state must control the profits of firms, separate ownership from management, and give official status to managers (Arisawa 1937c; Ryū 1939). The "separation between social function and capital ownership" was regarded a trend that would eventually result in *state capitalism* – "the stronger the economic control, the closer to state capitalism" Arisawa (1937b:212). Public interest (*kōeki*) became the highest priority in the ideology of the managed economy. According to the blueprint for Konoe's economic "new order," designed by the SRA in 1941, public interest was not a moral claim from outside the economy but an "internal" prerequisite to the operation of the managed economy. If every economic actor took public interest as the highest priority, this document argued, all kinds of economic activities would promote production, and the enhanced production would benefit the entire society.

In the ideology of the managed economy, concern for the public interest was directly connected with concern for production. According to the principle of the public interest, the profits of private firms should be constrained; the principle of business operation should be shifted from the profits of the firm to the firm's function and utility for the national economy. Because the goal in the ideology of the managed economy was to promote the national power of production, it was argued that the public interest would not take part of the profits away

from firms, but would demand that firms spend their profits on reproduction. In other words, the firm's profits had to be limited to a certain
level, and the surplus had to be used directly for reproduction (Sakai
1979:367–8). In the ideology of the managed economy, the property
right of a private company was defined as a "limited right of disposal
which is also accompanied with responsibility." This meant that
"different from capitalism, companies no longer regard the profit of
private shareholders as their goals. Instead, they take serving the welfare of all citizens in the country as the ultimate goal." This concept of
property rights differed significantly from the "absolute right of
disposal" in liberal capitalism that admitted the "dictatorship of
capitalists" (Kojima 1938:81).

To plan for a total war, the leadership of the state was perceived as
the most important means of reorganizing industries in the managed
economy. *Economic general staff (keizai sanbō honbu)* was the
straightforward phrase used by the Japanese to describe the role of the
state in the managed economy. It was argued that to sustain the war, it
was necessary to mobilize all the "forces behind the gun," which included not only natural resources and human capital, but also the
organizational skill that would enable the nation to coordinate all
elements in the national economy more smoothly for military purposes. Matsui Haruo (1938:35) asserted that "since modern war is by
no means a war only by military forces but by national forces as a
whole, the state is becoming increasingly important. It has to plan and
organize the comprehensive employment of national resources even in
peacetime." Wada Hiroo, another important reform bureaucrat (see
Ōtake 1981:132), argued that "the character of the modern state lies in
its strong intervention in the national economy. . . . The problems can
never be solved as long as we conduct out the managed economy based
on independent management by capitalists. We can expect the problems to be solved only when the state begins to take responsibility for
conducting a genuine, comprehensive, coherent, and active managed
economy." Arisawa Hiromi (1934:117) commented, "Just like an
army which developed quickly from a handful of warriors to millions
of well-trained soldiers, the development of industry also demands
organization in order to formulate plans and issue orders. The power
to supervise the planning and implementation of industrial mobilization should be bestowed on such experts, who know business and
production well and can act as commanders in the battlefield." To

survive a total war, Arisawa Hiromi contended, the state has "to employ every economic instrument, mobilize all available materials in order to fight until the last minute."

In the ideology of the managed economy, however, there were some competing arguments about the role of the state. Suetaka Shin (1936:26–7) argued that "we need to remember firmly that the managed economy is neither socialism nor communism. It does not reject capitalist institutions completely, but admits them and eliminates their problems in order to make them work." Kojima Seiichi (1938:2, 80) pointed out that German industrial control was based on the leadership principle. It was different from both liberal capitalism and socialism. On the one hand, it rejected the laissez-faire principle, which emphasized the profit of private individuals and asserted the priority of the public interest. On the other hand, it did not eliminate private property and individual interest, as in socialism, but respected private ownership. Criticizing the Nazis' control over the economy as too bureaucratic is simply a big misunderstanding of the different natures of Nazi Germany and communist Russia. In the long-term plans for promoting the national production power drafted by Miyazaki Masayoshi, various types of governance structures were suggested to control different industries. According to this plan the electricity, aircraft, and weapons industries should be nationalized, taking the Soviet model; the oil, coal, iron-steel, automobile, and chemical industries should take the German and Italian models, establishing an industrywide agreement; other industries might also have this kind of agreement plus the administrative guidance of the state. In order to best mobilize the existing institutions for this effort, it was argued, the Japanese state should depend on the independent self-control of the private sector and meanwhile strengthen the state's control to make it work for the national goal (Kobayashi 1995).

Brain trusts in Japanese politics in the 1930s

The impact of foreign economic ideas on the formation of the paradigm of the managed economy in state industrial policy was sustained by strong links between academia and the state. Because the managed economy was an unprecedented effort by the state to intervene in the economy, its planning was far beyond the state's capacity. In addition, as mentioned earlier, the deeply rooted sectionalism in state bureaucracies was a serious barrier to comprehensive policy integration (the effects of bureaucratic sectionalism are discussed later in this chapter). Responding to the urgent need for policy integration, brain trusts emerged to help politicians develop new ideas and policy proposals. Through these special links between academic and political elites, the ideas of a small number of economists acquired political currency, enabling an academic agenda to permeate policy making. The activities of these brain trust members were regarded in Japan as the origin of *brain politics,* which often resurfaced and played an important role at turning points in postwar Japanese history (Kaminishi 1985).

Among several agencies that performed the function of linking ideas and politics, a number of brain trusts created by Ishiwara Kanji and Miyazaki Masayoshi played a very important role in designing the first grand strategy for the Japanese state before the China war broke out. Ishiwara was the most famous strategist in the imperial army. He believed that Japan would eventually have a major military confrontation with the United States. In order to prepare for this final confrontation, Japan must promote its national production power comprehensively. To do so, Japan must control China in order to obtain necessary resources. Based on this belief, Ishiwara directly planned the Manchuria Incident in 1931 while serving as a staff officer of the Kwantung army. Miyazaki Masayoshi was the head of the Soviet Division in the research department at the Manchuria Railway when the Manchuria Incident occurred. He visited the Kwantung army after the incident and discussed his plan of establishing a research institute in charge of planning how to operate the Manchurian economy according to Japan's national strategy. As a result, the Investigation Committee of the Manchuria Railway (*Mantsu keizai chōsakai*) came into being and Miyazaki became the director of its First Department. In 1933, Ishiwara became director of the Division of Military Action at the General Staff, in charge of planning the long-term strategy in relation to the economy. He immediately authorized Miyazaki Masayoshi to establish the Japan–Manchuria Financial Economic Research Institute (Nichiman zaisei keizai kenkyūkai) to plan Japan's grand strategy for the coming confrontation with the United States. Assisted by a number of economists from the Imperial University of Tokyo, including the chair of the Faculty of Economics, Hijikata Seibi, Tōbata Seiichi, and Koga Hidemasa, this institute sponsored about 27 research projects on increasing state intervention and government planning in other industrialized countries (Kobayashi 1995; Peattie 1975).

In 1936, driven by the increasing tension between Japan and the Western countries, Miyazaki and his associates designed a grand strategy for Japan, which included two separate but related plans: One was for Manchuria and the other was for Japan. The plan for Manchuria began to be carried out in 1937. To achieve this goal, the Japanese state sent many elite bureaucrats to Manchuria, headed by Kishi Nobusuke. Ishiwara and Miyazaki's dream of preparing for the major confrontation with the United States by promoting Japan's national power of production in 10 years of peace was ruined by the outbreak of the China war. Nevertheless, the experiment of running a managed economy in Manchuria, as Chalmers Johnson and others have demonstrated, trained a group of bureaucrats who came back to Japan to carry out a domestic version of the managed economy (Johnson 1982; Kobayashi 1984, 1995; Nakamura Takafusa 1974a, [1978] 1993). When the China war started, the plan for Japan was forced to shift its focus from promoting and accumulating the national power of production to mobilizing national resources to support the war. Nevertheless, the institutional reforms instituted for the former plan were employed to serve the latter.

The Cabinet Planning Board (CPB) was the major player in designing the managed economy after 1937. It was a successor of two former brain trusts in the Japanese state: the Cabinet Survey Bureau (CSB) and the Cabinet Planning Agency (CPA). Many bureaucrats in the Cabinet Survey Bureau (CSB), the CPA, and the CPB, which were created to develop *kokusaku* (national policy), also held membership in private brain trusts, such as the SRA and the National Policy Research Association (NPRA), both formed in 1933, where intellectuals, journalists, politicians, bureaucrats, business leaders, and military officials gathered to discuss the emergent policy issues. Because the bureaucrats at the CPB were in charge of planning the state program of managed economy, what they learned in these brain trusts was reflected immediately in policy. Furthermore, the bureaucrats in the brain trusts crossed the boundaries of individual bureaucratic agencies within the Japanese government, and thus helped to nurture a collective view of the situation and of policy measures. In this sense, the brain trusts were the intellectual leaders in forming the paradigm of the managed economy.

The SRA played the major role in designing the Konoe new order on the eve of the Pacific war. This association was established by Gotō Ryūnosuke as a private brain trust for Prince Konoe Fumimaro. During his one-year trip to Europe and the United States between June 1932 and May 1933, Gotō heard a speech delivered by Hitler to a mass gathering in Berlin, saw Stalin at the ceremony for the annual celebration of the Bolshevik Revolution in Moscow, and watched Roosevelt's campaign for his New Deal policy in the United States (Sakai 1979:11). These experiences convinced him that it was also urgent for Japan to conduct sweeping reforms. After Gotō returned to Japan, he visited Konoe, with whom he had spent his college years at the Imperial University in Kyoto. Konoe and Gotō shared the view that the current pattern of decentralized policy making in the Japanese state could no longer respond to the emergent needs of the time. They agreed to establish a brain trust to conduct research on national policies because they believed that the state policy needed a theoretical foundation (Showa Dōjinkai 1968:7).

The membership of the SRA indicated its theoretical orientation. This membership passed through several stages. According to Baba Shūichi's (1969:117–24) analysis, the SRA started as a group of liberal intellectuals (13 of the 15 had graduated from the Imperial University of Tokyo, 7 of the 15 were professors, and none were bureaucrats). By March 1935, however, the membership of the SRA had changed considerably. Among the 15 members of the Standing Committee, only 5 of the original members remained. The 10 new members included 4 famous reform bureaucrats and 3 Marxists. More important, in contrast to the original group, 10 members of this group had experienced in their college years the "disturbing era in Japan's political and academic history in which the Taishō democracy shifted to Marxist movements" (Baba 1969:121). This experience was important in understanding the theoretical orientation of the SRA. By November 1936 the SRA's core membership was dominated by reform bureaucrats, comprising about 15 of the 34 members. Other members included intellectuals, most of whom were professors at the Imperial University of Tokyo; journalists from *Tōyō Keizai Shinpōsha* (*The Oriental Economic Press*), one of the most influential economic magazines in Japan; and some politically oriented business leaders. The impact of the SRA was also reflected in the fact that many of its academic members also served as advisors or trusted investigators in some important bureaucracies, such as the Cabinet Survey Bureau. Several important figures who influenced Japan's postwar industrial policy, including Arisawa Hiromi, Nakayama Ichirō, Tōbata Seiichi, and Ōkita Saburō, were involved in the SRA's activities.

In the late 1930s, the SRA made a systematic policy proposal for building an economic order. This proposal asserted that the state should control the profits of private companies, separate capital from management, and give managers official status. It also called for a transformation from a "profit orientation" to a "production orientation." Arisawa Hiromi played an important role in making this proposal. Arisawa was not a formal member of the SRA at the time, but was secretly entrusted by the SRA with doing research after he was released from jail after being arrested with a group of Marxists for involvement in communist-related activities. After Arisawa wrote the first draft of the proposal, Ryū Shintarō, an economic commentator in charge of the Economic Section at the SRA, finalized the proposal by adding the suggestions given by the SRA members at several internal discussions. The SRA's proposal was echoed by bureaucrats at the Cabinet Planning Board, who put forward the "Outline of the New Economic Order" in September 1940, expressing an identical policy orientation (Gao 1994; Sakai 1979).

Intellectual sources of the managed economy

The German impact was the most important intellectual sources in the ideology of the Japanese managed economy. The German experience was regarded as the most important reference system in the discussion of the managed economy in the 1930s. According to Mark R. Peattie (1975), during Ishiwara's three-year stay in Germany in the early 1920s, he held weekly discussions with former officers on the German General Staff, doing intensive research on European military history. Ishiwara's early distinction between short-term and long-term war was reconfirmed not only by numerous historical case studies, but also by Hans Delbruck's strategic theory, which distinguished between the strategy of annihilation and the strategy of exhaustion. The Japanese version of the total war theory was largely based on Ishiwara's distinction between decisive war, which aimed at destroying the enemy by general attacks on the battlefield, and continuous war, in which final victory would be decided not only by the military factor, but also by political, economic, and social factors. The Japanese version of the economic general staff was also based on the German model. In his book *On the Economic General Staff,* published in 1934, Matsui Haruo compared the agencies in charge of war mobilization in Germany, France, Italy, the Soviet Union, Britain, and the United States. He believed that the German experience was most suitable to Japan because the state's control over the economy enabled Germany to mobilize its national resources successfully during World War I. Matsui later became the chief economist at the Cabinet Survey Bureau and then the director of the Cabinet Resource Bureau.

Fascist ideology was weighted high in the ideology of managed economy. It was not, however, the only intellectual root. The Japanese incorporated elements from various sources for the same purpose. A modified Marxist perspective, which excluded the assertion of class struggle and cosmopolitanism while emphasizing planning, was significant to the evolution of Japanese developmentalism in two ways: One was support for the adoption of social policy as a precondition for mobilizing the working class into the nationalist program of state policy; the other was the effort to adjust or reform the irrational elements of economic institutions in the national crisis. Both of these issues resurfaced repeatedly in the postwar period. A distinction has been made between political and intellectual Marxism. Political Marxism advocated direct action against the capitalist system. In contrast, intellectual Marxism simply served as an analytical framework in academic discussions. Although the *tenkō* movement led to the demise of political Marxism, with its support for class struggle and cosmopolitanism, intellectual Marxism remained influential among reform bureaucrats. Not only were they convinced by Stalin's analysis of the "general crisis of capitalism," they also believed that the success of the first five-year plan in the Soviet Union showed promising prospects for socialism. In their search for a theoretical foundation for the policy regarding the managed economy, these bureaucrats studied Marxism seriously. Wada Hiroo, for example, a high-ranking bureaucrat in the CSB and later in the CPA, was familiar with Marx's *Das Capital,* Bukharin's *Imperialism and the World Economy,* Kautsky's *The Problems of Agriculture,* and Lenin's *The Development of Capitalism in Russia* (Ōtake 1981:69–70). Bureaucrats at the CPB even organized a group to study *Das Capital.* In 1941 this group was arrested on the charge of having a communist orientation.

In addition to Marxism, the Soviet experience of operating a planned economy drew the special attention of the planners for the Japanese state. Miyazaki Masayoshi, who drafted the two most important plans for promoting production power for both Manchuria and Japan, was an expert on Russia. He had personally witnessed the Russian Revolution as a foreign student at Petersburg University. After he graduated in 1917, Miyazaki joined the Manchuria Railway and became the head of the Soviet Division in the research department. He spent four months in the Soviet Union in 1923, collecting materials on the Soviet economy and doing intensive research on the new economic policy adopted by the Soviets at the time. According to Kobayashi Hideo (1995:53), Japan's Russian specialists who had followed the situation after the revolution numbered no more than 10, and Miyazaki was a major figure. Under Miyazaki's leadership, by 1925 the Manchuria Railway had collected more than 30,000 books and other publications on the Soviet economy. It became a leading center for Soviet studies in Asia. Miyazaki hired many Japanese and Russians to study these materials and translate them into Japanese. By 1931, they had translated and published 83 volumes of books on the Soviet economy in Japan. Miyazaki was deeply impressed by the first five-year plan of the Soviet government. According to this plan, in 1928–33, the Soviet Union's national income would increase 5.4 times and industrial production 2.1 times. Besides, this plan emphasized heavy industries. If it succeeded, the Soviet Union would be transformed from an agricultural country into an industrialized country (Kobayashi 1995:63–4). Later, Miyazaki estimated that the Soviet Union had achieved in 10 years what Germany, France, the United States, and Britain took 58 years, on average, to accomplish, and he identified various elements of the Soviet Union's economic policy that he used later for planning the managed economy in Manchuria and Japan (Kobayashi 1995:95–6). The study of the Soviet Union was also conducted in the state bureaucracy. The CSB set up a Soviet Section to study the Soviet economy, with 20 staff members headed by an army major. Japanese bureaucrats studied the Soviet economy for two reasons. First, the Soviet Union was perceived as a major military rival that was contiguous to Manchuria. The Japanese army was under strong pressure because the Soviets had rapidly increased their economic and military power through long-term government planning. Second, when the Japanese state began its own general mobilization of national resources and promotion of production, the balance between different economic sectors and industries at the macro level became problematic. Thus the Japanese bureaucrats believed that the Soviet experience of operating a planned economy was an important point of reference (Yomiuri Shinbunsha 1972, vol. 17:49–50).

The New Deal policy in the United States also attracted attention.

The Tennessee Valley Authority, which was heralded as a well-known achievement of the New Deal, became the model for Japan's nationalization of management in the electrical industry in 1938. The chief concern of Japanese bureaucrats at that time was the form of organization that was needed to carry out a major program such as the New Deal. To study the New Deal policy, the CPA and later the CPB imported all of the major business magazines published in North America and collected many volumes of the *United States Government Manual*. When the policy proposal for nationalizing the electrical industry was made, Okomura, the major designer of this policy, was sent on an 18-month tour to study how the Western countries administered their electrical industries. The Tennessee Valley Authority, together with the British grid system, which played an important role in mobilizing national electrical power during World War I, became the models for the Japanese (Okumura 1966).

Conflicts about the establishment of the national policy agency

Although state intervention was the predominant issue in Japanese economic ideology during the 1930s, the efforts to strengthen this capacity further encountered two types of institutional resistance: strong sectionalism within state bureaucracies, which weakened the state's capacity for policy making and policy integration, and strong resistance to state intervention from the private sector.

The state's effort to centralize the power of policy making provoked a series of political struggles focused on the issue of the "national policy agency." In the 1930s, the power of the cabinet, especially of the prime minister, in making and integrating policy was one of the key issues, and bureaucratic sectionalism was perceived as the major obstacle to the state capacity. According to Rōyama Masamichi, the intellectual leader of the SRA and an influential scholar in the 1930s, the root of bureaucratic sectionalism was the cabinet system established in the Meiji period, which aimed at balancing power internally among various oligarchies. Rōyama pointed out, in his examination of the Meiji Constitution, that

> [m]any writings on the political history of the Meiji period emphasize the political function of the cabinet as a place where the power of *han* cliques united and as their means of fighting with political parties in

the Diet. Little research has been conducted, however, on the function of the cabinet as a central administrative agency. The cabinet should act both as an agency to make and carry out policies regarding national affairs and as an integrative agency that possesses the function of administrating individual ministries. ([1936] 1965:127)

According to Rōyama's analysis, sectionalism was a product of contradictions in the functional arrangement of the Imperial Constitution of 1889. On the one hand, this constitution gave the prime minister the power to control ministries. On the other hand, however, it acknowledged the right of individual ministers to assist the emperor directly. In the Meiji Constitution, supreme authority was vested in the emperor, and all state organs – the state ministries, the military, the Privy Council, the Imperial Household Ministry, and the Diet – were responsible to him. This arrangement strengthened the individual ministries by giving them the right to act in their own interest in the name of "serving the nation." Thus Rōyama ([1936] 1965:131–2) argued that sectionalism within the state bureaucracy was institutionally authorized by the Imperial Constitution of 1889. A key point at issue, he believed, was that the Meiji Constitution failed to provide the prime minister with a bureaucratic agency under his direct control, though ostensibly it bestowed great power on him. As a result, the prime minister could act only as the "speaker of the cabinet," while sectionalism gradually gained strength in the decentralized and independent administrations of individual ministries. In this sense, the Meiji Constitution of 1889 failed to centralize political power within the state bureaucracy, though the building of the state after the Meiji Restoration established effective control over the society.

The state bureaucracy defined by the Meiji Constitution was characterized by the coexistence of *vertical centralization* and *horizontal decentralization*. At that time, the ministers' equal access to the emperor enabled them to develop their personal networks in a linear fashion. The state bureaucracy grew like a tree, with the emperor at the top. At the same time, however, it was difficult for the state to achieve policy integration at the horizontal level because each ministry, bureau, or division often exercised veto power over decisions made by its counterparts. Although the ministers were expected to act as members of the cabinet, cooperating with each other in policy integration, in reality each one always acted as "the head of an individual ministry," standing for the interests of his own domain (Ide 1982:252–3). Gordon M.

Berger (1977:233) comments that "although Japan moved with relative smoothness from a semicentralized administrative system of *bakufu* and *han* in the Edo period to a centralized nation-state after 1868, the process of political integration was not considered complete by Japanese leaders even in 1940." Andō Yoshio (1987:77) made a similar point, saying that state building after the Meiji Restoration did not complete the centralization of power institutionally and failed to abolish sectionalism, which was characterized by the multiple political centers and independent administrations of state bureaucracies.

Although the establishment of an economic general staff was regarded as indispensable for conducting the managed economy in the 1930s, implementation of this idea encountered strong institutional barriers. First, making national policy required crossing the administrative boundaries of individual ministries, as well as integration and cooperation among several bureaucracies. This goal conflicted with the deeply rooted tradition of *nawabari arasoi* (dispute over jurisdiction). In an effort to protect and promote its interests, each state bureaucracy fought hard to turn its ministerial policy into national policy. Even some reform bureaucrats still upheld the positions of their home agencies in discussions of national policy. Second, no integrative agency existed in the state bureaucracies at that time; many reform bureaucrats regarded the establishment of a new agency as the most efficient way to increase the state's power in policy making. Nevertheless, any move to set up a new agency faced strong resistance because it threatened to reduce the power of existing bureaucracies. Bureaucrats at the CSB intended to take over the budgeting power of the Ministry of Finance, arguing that because they were the ones who made national policy for the prime minister, they should have the power to decide how to spend the money. In this political struggle, however, they were defeated decisively by the Ministry of Finance. Also, before the CPB was established in 1937, the army proposed to set up a more powerful agency as a genuine economic staff with the intention of controlling it. This move, however, was blocked by the navy and other bureaucracies because the new agency's planning power would have conflicted with the administrative power of individual ministries, and especially with the budgeting power of the Ministry of Finance (Ide 1982:118). Eventually the CPB was defined as an office of general affairs for national mobilization; it failed to obtain a status superior to that of individual ministries.

Another dimension of the efforts to counter the impact of sectionalism in the 1930s was a reduction in the number of cabinet ministers involved in final important decisions and a change in their role in the administration. In its proposal for Konoe's new order, the SRA suggested that ministers should separate their role as administrators of individual state bureaucracies from their role as cabinet members in charge of policy integration. Their administrative role should be reduced, and their role in policy integration should be strengthened. Meanwhile, the number of ministers should be reduced to six to make policy integration at the cabinet level more efficient. The SRA also suggested that the prime minister should directly control the Cabinet Bureau of General Affairs and the CBP. The former would be in charge of integrating individual ministries, which would have the power of selecting personnel and promoting bureaucrats for administrative positions at different levels in those ministries; the latter would be responsible for making comprehensive plans for the national economy. For greater efficiency, the CPB should assume the power over government budgeting held by the Bureau of the Budget at the Ministry of Finance in order to plan the budget from the viewpoint of the government as a whole, not from the viewpoint of individual ministries. It should also absorb the Cabinet Bureau of Legal Affairs in order to legitimize state policy more quickly (Sakai 1979:121–6). During the war, the Japanese state established the "five-minister meeting" (*gosō kaigi*) system, in which major decisions were made by the prime minister, the minister of foreign affairs, the minister of the army, the minister of the navy, and the minister of finance.

By the end of World War II, the state capacity in policy making and policy integration was strengthened considerably in comparison with the pre-1930s era. Nevertheless, the issue of who is in charge still remains significant in Japanese politics. Karel van Wolferen (1989:5), among others, argues that statecraft in Japan still entails a balance between semiautonomous groups that share power; furthermore, "no one is ultimately in charge." Even in the 1990s, many Japanese politicians still believe that strengthening the prime minister's power is an urgent issue.

Contests over the "economic new order"

The constraints on the managed economy also came from strong resistance by the private sector. The politics of industrial policy exerted a great impact on the institutions that were created to carry out the managed economy. Two cases – the struggle on the issue of corporate control and the evolution of the main bank system – indicate that the rise of the state in the managed economy did not develop a one-way direction, but was shaped by the joint forces of various economic actors who were involved in politics. The private sector failed to resist the general direction of the managed economy because the ongoing war with China and the growing tension with the Western countries provided bureaucrats and the military with strong legitimacy for the managed economy. Nevertheless, the private sector was able to block some radical policy proposals made by state bureaucrats. In contrast, the state bureaucracy succeeded in enacting the National General Mobilization Law in 1938 and obtained unprecedented power in controlling the economy. However, it failed to exercise this control solely by itself and had to depend on nonstate institutions to realize its policy goals. This was why the Japanese managed economy was characterized by both an anticapitalist and an anticommunist orientation.

After Japan started its full invasion of China, the military pressured the government to pass a national mobilization law. The proposal for the National General Mobilization Law drafted by the CPB encountered strong resistance from the political parties when it was presented to the Diet in January 1938. The major criticism was that this law, by entrusting the state bureaucracy with complete authority to decide how to conduct the managed economy, would take legislative power away from the Diet, leaving it to exist in name only. Both the *minseitō* and the *seiyūkai* charged that the proposal contradicted the constitution, gave the bureaucrats too much power, and did not distinguish clearly between wartime and peacetime in determining when this law would be applied. They held that the scope of state control over the economy should be defined by law. The state bureaucracy replied that no one could predict what would happen in a war; therefore it was impossible to define everything clearly. During the hearing process at the Diet, however, a series of events forced the political parties to change their position on these issues. First, the headquarters of both the *minseitō* and the *seiyūkai* were occupied by right-wing activists. Second, the head of the *shadaitō*, which supported the proposal for this law, was attacked by a group of radicals, who accused him of showing sympathy to this socialistic proposal. Third, a military officer at the hearing shouted at a Diet member who asked him a question. Eventually the bill was passed without any major revisions (Yomiuri Shinbunsha 1971, vol. 16:150–276).

Nevertheless, in 1941 the private sector succeeded in blocking radical policy proposals made by the SRA and the CPB for the economic new order. At that time, Germany had won a series of military victories (the invasion of Norway in April and the conquest of France in June), and the Japanese military intended to take this opportunity to occupy Southeast Asia. The military officers and reform bureaucrats held that Germany's victories had resulted directly from its political institutions. They believed that Germany was strong because of its totalitarianism and its planned economy, and that Britain and France had encountered trouble because of their utilitarianism, capitalism, and democracy. Liberalism would not help Japan win the war and the international competition; it had to be replaced by totalitarianism.

The policy proposals prepared by the SRA and the CPB for Konoe's new order asserted that direct state control over the profits of firms, the separation of management from ownership, and official status for managers would ensure the effectiveness of the managed economy. According to these documents, the old pattern of economic control was from "outside" and "above": That is, the system controlled the distribution of resources at the macro level but did not control production at the micro level. As a result, private firms would either cease production when there were not enough potential profits or would skimp on labor and materials in order to reduce costs and make more profits. This kind of control also created many black markets for production materials and foreign exchange. Exercised in this way, economic control had lost its significance. As long as firms were driven by the profit principle, the managed economy could not work smoothly. Therefore the business philosophy had to be changed from the profit principle to the production principle, and laissez-faire capitalism had to be revised. To achieve these goals, these proposals asserted further, the state should regard production rather than profits for shareholders as its leading priority in industrial policy. When necessary, the state should nationalize manufacturing industries or establish a mixed economy. In such a system, managers of enterprises would function as public servants. Their only responsibility to shareholders would be to guarantee certain amounts of profits, as determined by the state. They should commit themselves primarily to the state; their performance should be evaluated largely on the basis of their contribution to production (Sakai 1979).

Although these policy proposals by the SRA and the CPB were well received by intellectuals and reform bureaucrats, they were seriously criticized and opposed by a united front consisting of business leaders and the "spiritual right wing" (*seishin uha*). Seven national business associations made public statements attacking the SRA's proposal from two perspectives. First, they stated, the most urgent task for the Japanese economy was to promote production. Therefore the state should not initiate any radical change that would shake the foundations of present economic institutions and thus might decrease production. The pursuit of profits was not necessarily inconsistent with national interests, and it should not be criticized. Rather, the state should encourage businesses to pursue profits in order to stimulate production. Second, the Japanese economic institutions were not based on the laissez-faire principle but on the "Japanese spirit," which emphasized the harmony of the Japanese people. The state policy regarding the managed economy should also follow this spirit. Direct state control over the profits of private firms would not promote production because it would deviate from the Japanese way of doing business. Ownership and management should not be separated, and managers in private firms should not be appointed by the state. Even when state control was necessary and inevitable, it should be exercised by businesspeople themselves. With allies in the Ministry of Home Affairs, the business leaders succeeded in blocking this move. A group of reform bureaucrats in the CPB, including Wada Hiroo and Inaba Hidezō, who were involved in planning for the new order, were charged with engaging in *aka* (communist) activities and arrested. To escape from a possible purge, Ryū Shintarō, who was in charge of making the proposal at the SRA, left for Europe. Eventually, the Japanese state adopted a moderate policy for the new order (Gao 1994). The statement "to separate capital from management and to shift priority from profit to production" in the SRA's proposal and the CPB's plan was revised to read: "The enterprise is an organic entity of capital, management, and labor. As a component of the national economy, its activity should follow the comprehensive plan of the state and at the same time should be based on the creativity and responsibility of managers and automatic management."

The evolution of the main bank system was another example of how the pattern of state intervention in the managed economy was shaped by joint forces. To support the China war financially, the Japanese state started to control the supply of capital through a series of executive orders. It enacted the Law Concerning Temporary Adjustment of Capital in September 1937, the Ordinance Regarding Company Dividend and Finance in 1939, and the Ordinance Regarding the Capital of Banks in 1940. Any company whose total amount of capital was more than 200,000 yen was subject to the regulation of the Ordinance Regarding Company Dividend and Finance. This ordinance used the dividend rate between December 1937 and November 1938 as the standard rate. Any company that wanted to pay a higher dividend had to apply for approval from the government. Between April 1939 and October 1940, only 50 approvals were granted among 130 applications for increasing the dividend rate. This resulted in a sharp price decline in the stock market in 1940–1 (Okazaki 1993:110–11). To finance munitions industries during wartime meant not only huge profits but also high risks. To reduce the risks, the banking industry in 1937–41 created 130 *loan syndications,* collective investments from multiple financial institutions in a single project on their own initiative. The state changed these loan syndications to the Cooperative Investment Group, which was composed of the 10 biggest commercial banks, the Industrial Bank, and the 5 biggest trust funds in August 1941, and then to the National Finance Control Association in May 1942. The syndication loans in 1937–41 constituted only 14% of the total finance provided by those banks that practiced these joint syndications. In contrast, after the National Finance Control Association was created, it controlled most of the capital supply. When the Munitions Industry Law was enacted in October 1943, the state instituted direct control over corporate financing. According to this law, the operation of munitions companies, which numbered 600, did not need approval from shareholders if they received an order from the state bureaucracy, and they could even refuse to make the information on management available to shareholders. By doing so, banks lost their function of monitoring companies, and managers' autonomy increased rapidly (Okazaki 1993; Teranishi 1993a, 1993b).

Conclusion

In this chapter, I have described the great transformation of Japanese capitalism in 1931–45. In this period, most of the characteristics of the contemporary Japanese economic system appeared. The state emerged as the economic general staff, and its capacity in economic intervention was strengthened enormously. Meanwhile, various nonmarket governance structures developed to restrain market forces, and the embryonic form of contemporary Japanese management, characterized by permanent employment, the seniority-based wage, and the company-based union, also developed. Many elements of these institutions had existed before the managed economy was created. Nevertheless, they were institutionally recomposed into a coherent economic system in 1931–45. Although all major industrialized countries were confronting both the Great Depression and World War II, Japan, along with Germany and Italy, demonstrated a pattern considerably different from the responses of both liberal capitalism and socialism.

Behind this great transformation, a set of economic ideas and ideologies was at work. Foreseeing a total war among nation-states, the ideology of the managed economy viewed the economy strategically. In order to sustain the military adventure, this ideology gave production top priority in industrial policy. To achieve these goals, it demonstrated a strong anticapitalist orientation marked by constraint on market competition and rejection of the profit principle. In the meantime, due to strong resistance from business circles and ideological constraints, this ideology also had a strong anticommunist orientation. The ideology of the managed economy, incorporating ideas from various sources, not only became the framework for the industrial policy practiced by the Japanese state in 1931–45, but also laid out the general principle for Japanese developmentalism in the long run.

In the dynamics of this transformation, the impact of nationalism deserves special attention. Given the perception that the Great Depression would inevitably lead to military conflicts among nation-states and that Japan must prepare for a total war, the nation-state became the unit of analysis in economic analysis. When the country was under strong international pressure, communists abandoned their Marxist beliefs in class struggle and cosmopolitanism and stood on the same side as management and the state for the first time in modern Japanese history. In the meantime, the claims for individual interests and shareholders' profits were strongly rejected. Both the *tenkō* and the state reform movements prevented the possibility that the Japanese economy would move toward either a more socialistic economy or a more liberal capitalism and pushed Japan in a third direction. Under the influence of nationalism, the ideological distinction between conservatives and progressives became more ambiguous. To formulate the strategy for the managed economy, Marxist ideology coexisted with fascist and liberal ideologies. The military could even hire Arisawa Hiromi, who was suspected of engaging in communist activities, in its preparations for war (Gao 1994; Sakai 1979). The situation of several persons who were regarded as progressive in the postwar period, such as Arisawa Hiromi, Wada Hiroo, and Ryū Shintarō, was complicated. On the one hand, they could be arrested for, or accused of, communist-related activity. On the other hand, the policy proposals they drafted for the Konoe cabinet were regarded as more radical even than those of the military. Therefore, it would be simplistic to label these complicated figures according to only one aspect of their activities.

The development of the managed economy, moreover, was shaped by joint forces in the politics of industrial policy. The political and ideological restraints had a great impact on the development of the wartime economic system. The state failed to establish complete, direct bureaucratic control because the attitudes of the military, business, and the bureaucrats toward the managed economy were complicated. The military supported control by the state bureaucracy and the efforts to militarize the national economy. Nevertheless, military leaders also recognized that their goals could not be achieved without support from business. Therefore they had to admit the principle of capitalism. Although the bureaucrats flew the banner of public interest and asserted the necessity of a planned economy, they dared not reject capitalism completely because business leaders could use the element of anticommunism in the ideology of fascism to mount a counteroffensive. In contrast, the private sector had no excuse for opposing the managed economy because support of the war was perceived as the highest priority of the nation at that time; thus they failed in their political struggle with the state bureaucracy concerning the National General Mobilization Law in 1938. To secure their interest in the managed economy, however, the private sector insisted that the managed economy should be operated according to the principle of capitalism (Asanuma in Kawahara 1979:38). They mounted a successful counterattack by labeling the radical bureaucrats as communists.

The practice of the managed economy resulted in the birth of a distinctive economic system that in many ways departed significantly from orthodox liberal capitalism. As Ōkōchi Kazuo (1949:189–90) pointed out long ago, the wartime economy did more than destroy the normal life of civilians and wasted huge amount of material and human lives. It also stimulated munitions production and changed the structure of the economy. More important, it had a great impact on the economic order of capitalism and artificially shortened the process of development of capitalist institutions in the form of top-down. Therefore, it had important implications for the future by serving as the medium of continuity between the prewar and postwar economies, which were very different in nature. Although this economic system was created to carry out the war, it had great historical impact on economic institutions. Even after the war ended, this impact would not disappear.

4. Priority production

Japanese industrial policy in 1946–9 was still dominated by the paradigm of the managed economy. Although many elements of the wartime economic system were greatly challenged by the democratic reforms of the occupation authority, the practice of *priority production* (*keisha seisan hōshiki*), which referred to concentrating human, financial, and material resources in the coal, iron and steel, and fertilizer industries in order to provide basic materials for postwar economic reconstruction in all industries, contributed greatly to transforming the wartime legacies into the postwar economy.

Japan's defeat in World War II opened a new chapter in its history. Like Germany, Japan experienced a storm of democratic reforms by the Occupation Authority. What was the impact of these reforms on postwar Japan? For a long time, 1945 was considered by many people the "birthday for a new Japan" (Noguchi 1995), a "Year Zero, when everything could be remade and redone" (Fallows 1994:120). In academic discussions, the discontinuity argument presented by Yamada Moritarō prevailed. It held that the postwar democratic reforms changed Japanese capitalism fundamentally because the production cycle of the Japanese economy was no longer sustained by militarism and colonies, the land reform eliminated the landlord class, and the majority of economic output shifted from textile industry to heavy-chemical industry (Ōishi 1974). This view was influential not only in Japan, but also in Germany. As Simon Reich (1990:4) points out, the astonishing achievement of Germany in postwar economic growth has been interpreted as being "like a phoenix [rising] from the ashes," which had nothing to do with the German experience in the dark valley.

This view of history began to be challenged in Japan in the 1960s. Ōuchi Tsutomu contended that the changes in the Japanese economy since 1931 were driven by the development of what he called *state-monopoly capitalism*, which constituted the foundation and the original pattern of postwar Japanese capitalism. Many postwar reforms,

121

such as the land reform and the *zaibatsu* dissolution, reflected the state policies and the trends that had already begun before the China war that started in 1937. The changes driven by state-monopoly capitalism before 1945 were immature due to various political barriers. The postwar democratic reforms eliminated these barriers and created a favorable environment for the development of state-monopoly capitalism (Ōishi 1974). Since the 1970s, the continuity argument has shifted its focus from the continuity between the prewar and postwar periods to the continuity between the wartime (1937–45) and postwar periods. Nakamura Takafusa ([1978] 1993) points out that "the prewar period and the postwar period can not be connected by jumping the war period. Many social and economic institutions, technologies, life styles, and customs were created during the war and were inherited in the postwar period. Even if they were not created with a long-term perspective at the time, in the end they defined the postwar patterns of companies, industrial organizations, and life styles."

In the 1990s, the debate between these two competing views is more heated than ever.

Yamanouchi Yasushi (1995a) points out that modern Japanese history during the fascist period was perceived as abnormal because the trend toward democracy during the Taishō period was interrupted and a coercive regime based on an irrational ultrastate ideology led the nation to the war that drifted off the course of modernization. In reality, however, the total war program changed the social structure greatly, in many ways modernizing Japanese society. Noguchi Yukio (1995), along with the research group headed by Okazaki Tetsuji and Okuno Masahiro (1993b), examined a number of key institutions in the Japanese economic system, including state bureaucracy, the main bank system, and Japanese management. They found that the major components of these institutions can be traced back to the 1930s. The end of World War II has often been used as the cutoff point in the examination of either continuities or discontinuities. Hara Akira (1995a), however, points out that 1937–50 should be regarded as a coherent period because the managed economy did not end with the war but continued until the implementation of the Dodge Plan at the end of the 1940s.

To those who believe in the discontinuity argument, this continuity argument has neglected some fundamental changes that occurred during the occupation period. Hara Akira (1995a) argues that the postwar democratic reforms, especially the land reform and the *zaibatsu* dissolution, greatly changed the structure of the Japanese economy. In addition, the new constitution significantly changed the nature of government finance. By minimizing public expenditure on national defense, the economy no longer had a military nature. Nakamura Masanori (1995b:64) points out that Noguchi's 1940 system argument downplayed the impact of the changes in Japan's political, economic, and social structures brought by the postwar reforms and the strong growth of the Japanese economy. Even though similarities between the wartime and postwar periods can be observed, their implications for the economy, which are determined by the structure they are based on, are completely different.

Where does this big cognitive gap come from? Ōishi Kaiichirō provided a convincing answer. He pointed out that the key issue in the old debate between these two competing arguments was the conceptualization by which the continuities and discontinuities were measured. Yamada Moritarō's discontinuity argument emphasized economic structures. In contrast, Ōuchi Tsutomu's continuity argument focused on the economic system (Ōishi 1974:86). The impact of this difference in methodology on later research is huge. In the ongoing debate concerning the origin of the contemporary Japanese economic system, the two sides still differ in conceptualization. Today's continuity arguments inherit Ōuchi Tsutomu's tradition, perceiving the institutional evolution of modern Japanese capitalism as a continuous and coherent process. In contrast, the discontinuity arguments follow Yamada Moritarō's conceptualization, emphasizing the structural changes in postwar Japanese economy. Because these two competing arguments differ significantly in their measurements and emphasize different facets of the economy, neither of them should be regarded as a holistic argument about the entire economy. As I focus on the institutional evolution of the Japanese economic system in this book, the continuities of the wartime legacies are certainly more important than the discontinuities. At the same time, however, it is also meaningful to examine how liberal capitalism has influenced the survival of the wartime legacies.

In this chapter, I first show the complicated situation in 1946–9. On the one hand, many components of the wartime system were strongly challenged by the democratic reforms: The military forces were completely eliminated; the secret police was abolished; parliamentary democratic political practice was installed; the landlord class disappeared in the land reform; the *zaibatsu* were dissolved; the labor unions received the right to strike; the national educational system was reformed; and Japanese women were given the right to vote. Many of these reforms have been irreversible, and they created a new environment for the Japanese state to practice its industrial policy. Although the developmental orientation survived, it had to operate according to different rules.

On the other hand, the control of state bureaucracy over the economy was even further strengthened, and both the ideology and personnel of the managed economy were largely inherited to combat the economic crisis. Because the major purpose of this study is to examine the evolution of Japanese developmentalism, this chapter focuses on why many key institutions of the wartime economic system remained when the country underwent drastic democratization in 1946–9.

First, the strategic view of the economy survived. Demilitarization certainly changed Japan's national purpose, and the focus of state industrial policy was no longer to sustain the total war. Due to the economic hardship resulting from hyperinflation and a severe shortage of materials, however, national survival was still an urgent issue, and production continued to be the top priority in state industrial policy. The state, backed up by the General Headquarters (GHQ), had to centralize further its policy making and policy integration, establishing the powerful Economic Stabilization Board (ESB) (Keizai antei honbu), and continued to practice a discriminatory policy in resource allocation: It not only channeled the major resources to strategic industries according to its policy agenda, but also controlled the distribution of materials of daily living to consumers (Gao 1994).

Second, the influence of nationalism declined significantly at the grass-roots level after Japan's defeat in World War II, and the state's assertion of national interest in the priority production program encountered strong criticism based on individualism and class consciousness, which revived rapidly during the democratic reforms. Nevertheless, an isolated self-perception and distrust of the occupation policy remained influential in policy-making circles. Japanese policy makers believed that they could depend neither on foreign aid nor on the market for economic reconstruction; the state must take the lead in promoting production to survive the economic crisis and start the postwar reconstruction.

Third, economists who were strongly oriented toward state intervention from different perspectives were either very close to the leading politicians or occupied important offices themselves in this period. Arisawa Hiromi, the designer of the priority production program, who represented the legacy of the managed economy, became the chief advisor to Prime Minister Yoshida Shigeru; Ishibashi Tanzan, a devoted Keynesian, became the minister of finance and then the director of the ESB. He contributed greatly to the adoption of an easy money policy in priority production. Tsuru Shigeto, a Harvard-trained economist who was in charge of integrating macro economic policy at the ESB, championed the New Deal type of economic policy and created the distribution system for the priority production program. In addition, a group of former bureaucrats, represented by Wada Hiroo and Inaba Hidezō, also gained great power in state bureaucracy (Gao 1994).

Fourth, as a side effect, the democratic reforms eliminated barriers that had prevented the further evolution of Japanese developmentalism in 1931–45. Two examples were the state bureaucracy and corporate governance. The political reforms of the occupation authority either eliminated or significantly weakened the major political elements that could challenge the power of bureaucrats in policy making. In the meantime, the occupation of Japan was indirect (in contrast to the direct occupation of Germany); the GHQ exercised its authority through the Japanese government. These factors enabled the state bureaucracy to gain unprecedented power in economic intervention (Gao 1994). The *zaibatsu* dissolution forced *zaibatsu* families to sell their stocks and drove them out of the companies. This indeed democratized the Japanese economy in an important way. A new generation of managers who came to power as a result of *zaibatsu* dissolution, however, paid little attention to profits because indirect financing from the main bank system provided them with great autonomy. This sustained the further development of the anticapitalist orientation, marked by the rejection of the profit principle in management that had started in 1931–45 (Okazaki 1993).

Finally, the continuities of the wartime economic system, from today's perspective of comparative capitalism, can also be attributed to the nature of the occupation policy adopted by the GHQ. First, the major purpose of GHQ's reforms was to demilitarize Japan rather than to convert the Japanese economy to liberal capitalism. Thus, the institutions that were perceived as contributing directly to the rise of fascism, such as the landlord system and the *zaibatsu,* received great attention. Other institutions, such as the state bureaucracy, trade associations, and the main bank system, remained untouched (Hara and Miwa 1992:362–4; Noguchi 1995:77–8). In this sense, as Yamamoto Michiru points out, "even without the Cold War, the occupation policy would be sooner or later changed anyway" (cited in Noguchi 1995:78). Second, some GHQ officials were greatly influenced by the New Deal policy. They showed a strong orientation toward state intervention in their policy regarding Japan; this orientation powerfully supported those Japanese policy makers who represented the legacy of the managed economy. Third, due to the Cold War, the U.S. government changed its policy toward Japan from punishment to support. As a result, many reforms, especially the *zaibatsu* dissolution and the prevention of overcentralization of corporate power, did not end as planned.

Democratic reforms and the economic crisis

The state industrial policy in 1946–9 encountered an environment shaped by two contradicting factors. On the one hand, Japan underwent a series of democratic reforms instituted by the Occupation Authority in 1946–9. These reforms changed the structure of the Japanese economy considerably and created a number of discontinuities with the wartime system. On the other hand, the Japanese economy suffered from a great economic crisis caused by hyperinflation and a severe shortage of materials.

The democratic reforms had a great impact on the Japanese economy.

First, demilitarization and the adoption of the new constitution changed the Japanese national purpose. Since the Meiji Restoration, "rich nation, strong army" had been Japan's national purpose. During the 15-year war, the economy had been given strategic significance and state industrial policy had been a very important part of the war mobilization effort. Since 1938, the state had replied on the emperor's "ultimate power in emergency" to control the economy. Under the new constitution, the emperor was no longer the ultimate source of sovereignty but merely a symbol of the nation. In Article 9, Japan also gave up its right to have military forces and to wage war with other countries. The new constitution also strengthened the power of the Diet while restraining the power of bureaucrats in determining government finance. The new finance law also constrained the government budget for military purposes (Hara 1995a:93). These changes, together with Japan's defeat in World War II, not only changed the goal of state industrial policy, but also caused the rapid decline of Japanese nationalism at the grass-roots level.

Second, the dissolution of the *zaibatsu* changed the nature of Japanese business groups. In this reform, all stock-holding companies were forced to sell their stocks: Not only the 4 major *zaibatsu* – Mitsubishi, Mitsui, Sumitomo, and Yasuda – but also the 11 "new" *zaibatsu* such as Asano, Nakajima, and Furukawa. In addition, the practice of inter-firm exchange of senior managers was prohibited, and 56 *zaibatsu* family members were forced to sell their stock and were prohibited from taking any managerial position in their companies. Also, many business leaders were purged because of their involvement in the war and their relationship with the military. The dissolution of the *zaibatsu* eventually proved to be incomplete because only 18 firms were identified as having excessive economic power and were subject to decentralization after the U.S. government changed its policy toward Japan. Even so, the dissolution of the *zaibatsu* has had some long-term impact on the Japanese economy. For example, after the dissolution, holding companies were outlawed. The relationship among *keiretsu* members are much looser in comparison with those of the *zaibatsu*.

Third, influenced by the New Deal, the Occupation Authority demonstrated a prolabor policy in the early stage of occupation. It held that labor unions would be an effective counterforce to the *zaibatsu* and would prevent the revival of Japanese militarism. From the beginning, the GHQ ordered the Japanese government to lift the ban on labor movements, to acknowledge the rights of labor unions, and to revive the labor protection law and the labor conflict arbitration law. With the support of the GHQ, the Japan Federation of Labor Unions, which supported the Socialist Party, was established on 1 August 1946, with a membership of 850,000 workers and 1,699 labor unions. The Japanese Association of Industrywide Labor Unions, which claimed to be politically neutral, was established later in that month, with a membership of 1,630,000 workers and 34 industrywide labor unions. The adoption of three labor laws – the Work Standard Law, the Labor Union Law, and the Labor Relations Arbitration Law – laid the foundation for postwar democracy. Even though the GHQ changed its policy toward Japanese labor unions as the Cold War began in Asia, the rising labor movements, which were stimulated by the GHQ's initial policy, changed the balance of power between labor unions and management in the political struggle (Masamura 1985).

Fourth, land reform eliminated the landlord class. Tenant farmers, who had suffered from high farm rents, became landed farmers. This greatly stimulated their enthusiasm for production and investment. The increasing productivity resulted in the migration of the agricultural population to urban areas, which became an important foundation for high growth.

Although these drastic changes created many discontinuities, the economic crisis still demanded strong intervention by the state. According to an American observer:

> in the three years under the occupation two basic but divergent trends have been paramount. A hare-and-tortoise race has been in progress between a mounting inflation on the one hand and a slow revival of industrial activity on the other hand. The two are, of course, in effect tied together. Inflation has retarded industrial recovery while the dearth of output in the face of mounting monetary claims to goods has only accentuated the price spiral. (Cohen 1949:447)

The shortage of both production and the materials of daily life had several causes. First, much of Japan's wealth was destroyed in World War II. Japan had spent all of its energy and staked all of its wealth on a 15-year total war. After Japan surrendered to the Allies on 15 August 1945, awakening from the nightmare, the Japanese found that this war had cost their country one-fourth of its national wealth, including buildings, harbors, canals, machine tools, products, railways, ships, vehicles, electricity, gas, and sewer facilities, telephones, and other communication facilities. Nine million people lost their homes (Arisawa 1976:241). Second, the defeat in World War II resulted in a great contraction of Japanese access to the international market. Japan lost all of its colonies; apart from areas occupied later, these had constituted 44% of its prewar territory. The Japanese could no longer obtain cheap materials, cheap labor, and captive markets from these countries; thus the coal supplies for operating the economy were reduced considerably. Japan was also prohibited from engaging in international trade until 1948. Third, Japan could no longer obtain supplies of materials from outside the country. Meanwhile, domestic demand increased rapidly because of the repatriation of millions of military and civilian Japanese from overseas. Finally, as a result of the defeat, Japan experienced a crisis of underproduction because manufacturing equipment was either destroyed or overused. If the 1934–6 level is taken to be 100%, the production of rice in 1945 was 66.5%; wheat, 76.0%; cotton yarn, 4.2%; cotton textiles, 1.4%; raw silk, 12.8%; coal, 58.0%; iron, 35.6%; and marine products, 44.5% (*Tsūsanshō* 1954:35). If the 1937 level is taken as 100%, the production level of the national economy in 1945 was 37%. In 1946 it was only 20%, rising to 25% and 33% in 1947 and 1948, respectively (Economic Planning Agency 1990a:10). In addition, Japan had one of the worst harvests in its history in 1945, and the shortage of food became a major crisis.

Hyperinflation aggravated the economic situation for another reason. When Japan wantonly engaged in military adventures in the 1930s and early 1940s, the Japanese state spent most of the government budget on munitions. In 1930, military expenditures accounted for 32.3% of the budget. In 1937, when Japan increased its aggression in China, this proportion jumped to 69.0%. At the end of World War II, it increased further to 85.5%. To support the 15-year total war, the Japanese state incurred a huge amount of public debt. At around the time of the Manchuria Incident, 1.1 billion yen in bonds were issued. Between 1937, when the China war started, and the end of World War II, the Japanese state issued 98 billion yen in bonds; from 1931 to 1945, it issued 99.1 billion yen. In 1930 the Japanese state had only 6.1 billion yen in public debt, but by the end of 1945 the accumulated public debt had risen to 143.9 billion yen (Arisawa 1976: 242–3). This huge public debt, combined with underproduction, became the fuse for hyperinflation in the early postwar era. If the 1937 level is taken as 100, Japan's wholesale price index for major industries in 1945 was 442. This index was 1,210 in 1946, 3,860 in 1947, and 10,508 in 1948 (Economic Planning Agency 1990a:10).

The priority production program

What happened to the governance of the Japanese economy in the storm of democratic reforms that was presumably a frontal challenge from liberal capitalism to Japan's wartime buildup?

In fact, the practice of the managed economy did not continue without interruption. Immediately after Japan's surrender, the bureaucrats lost their confidence in practicing the managed economy. As a result, the state ended its controls over 19 production materials and food three times: on 20 August, 9 October, and 15 November 1945. In the meantime, the Occupation Authority focused on political reforms and did not intervene in the operation of the economy. When these controls ended, inflation was aggravated quickly. Jerome Cohen pointed out that "the early reluctance of SCAP [Supreme Commander for Allied Powers] to intervene in this area, and the incompetence of successive Japanese cabinets, produced an administrative fumbling which, if anything, accentuated the dislocations and impaired recovery efforts provided in other fields by factors such as food and raw material imports" (Cohen 1949:447). As the economic situation grew worse, the Japanese state, under strong pressure from the GHQ, established the ESB in May 1946 to carry out the priority production program. This program transformed the wartime legacies of state intervention into the postwar economy. Ideologically, the theory of priority production had clear continuity with the wartime managed economy: It regarded national survival as the major goal in state industrial policy and the promotion of production as the top priority.

The state strengthened its capacity for economic intervention in 1946–9 to an unprecedented degree. As Hata Ikuhiko pointed out, "never has the Japanese bureaucracy exercised greater authority than it did during the occupation" (cited in Johnson 1982:176). The dominance of state bureaucrats in policy making not only remained but was even further strengthened. In 1931–45, the bureaucrats' policy-making power had been constrained by military and business leaders. In 1946–9, in contrast, these competitors were no longer a threat to the bureaucrats' power. The military disappeared forever; many business leaders were purged; and the dissolution of the *zaibatsu* significantly weakened the power of business as a whole in politics. Meanwhile, the major politicians, such as Prime Ministers Yoshida Shigeru and Katayama Tetsu, had been outsiders in politics during the war, and they lacked the expertise to operate a managed economy. The only element that could constrain the bureaucrats' power in 1946–9 was the occupation authority. Because of the indirect occupation, however, the GHQ had to depend on Japanese bureaucrats for all kinds of daily operations. This greatly strengthened bureaucratic power because the policies adopted by the Japanese state were perceived as orders from the GHQ. Although the state bureaucracy was deeply involved in the war, it survived the postwar democratic reforms.

Strategic planning remained the leading principle in state industrial policy. In 1931–45, there was no ultimate authority that could give orders to individual ministries, and the decentralized administrative agencies often failed to reach agreement on policy issues. Backed up by the GHQ, however, the Japanese state was able to centralize the power of policy making and implementation effectively. The ESB, which was established in July 1946, largely realized the dream of the *economic general staff*. With a "superior status over individual ministries," this bureaucracy gained great power in policy integration, and its director had the authority to "direct" and "order" other ministers (Keizai Kikakuchō 1964:11–12). Under pressure from the GHQ, the Japanese state in April 1947 transferred all planning functions pertaining to economic administration from other ministries to the ESB. The ESB became the only agency in the Japanese state bureaucracy in charge of government planning and policy integration; its powers included balancing the supply and demand of materials, trade, and labor, and regulating prices, finance, transportation, and construction. All ministries had to implement the policies designed by the ESB. In April 1947 the ESB was enlarged from 5 departments to 10 bureaus plus 2 departments, 48 divisions, and a minister's secretariat; its personnel numbered more than 3,000 (Keizai Kikakuchō 1964:47–8; also see Johnson 1982). Individual ministries competed with each other in sending their best staff members to this agency in order to protect their own interests. In this sense, the ESB was the most powerful state policy-making bureaucracy in Japanese history. Its capacity in policy making and integration was much stronger than that of the CPB and the Ministry of Munitions in World War II.

To reduce the shortage of materials, the state regarded the promotion of production in the coal, iron and steel, and fertilizer industries as the top priority. To promote production in these industries, the Japanese state relied on two instruments. One was the plan concerning the demand and supply of resources, which was exactly the same as the annual plan of material mobilization during World War II. The other was tight control over resource allocation based on the Law Concerning Temporary Adjustment of Resources between Supply and Demand (*Rinji busshitsu jukyū shōseihō*), which replaced the National General Mobilization Law in October 1946. This law granted the state the power to assign important production materials, to set quotas for distribution of these materials, and to limit or prevent their use. The combination of these two instruments was no different from the mechanism of the managed economy in World War II (Okazaki 1995b:276). To support the priority production program financially, huge government loans were given to key industries through the Reconstruction Finance Bank (RFB). In addition, the Standard of Loan Issuing by Financial Institutions adopted by the state defined the priority of financing among different industries for private financial institutions. The wartime practices of loan syndication and cooperative investment continued, and the Bank of Japan replaced the wartime financial control association in integrating financing of key industries (Okazaki 1995b:276–7).

Although the wartime establishment was the major target in the postwar democratic reforms, the anticapitalist orientation – marked by constraint of market competition and rejection of the profit motive – was still highly visible in the Japanese economy during 1946–9.

Constraining market competition was a major policy agenda in the priority production program. Without strong constraints on competition, it was argued, the speculative behavior in the black markets would worsen inflation, and production might deteriorate further because of the severe shortage of materials. This would not only cause social instability, but also destroy the entire economy. In 1931–45, the state depended on the control associations in each industry for resource allocation. In late 1945, the state intended to continue relying on these associations to manage the economy. Because this proposal violated the antimonopoly principle asserted by the GHQ, it was disallowed. Instead, the control associations were transformed into different trade associations. These trade associations still helped the state in "setting production quotas, coordinating material demand and supply, mediating between consumers and producers, making statistics, and investigating the industry" (Okazaki 1995b:276). At the same time, the state established 15 public corporations (kōdan), which were in charge of the distribution of materials through a strict stamp system.

State control affected not only production materials, but also extended to items for daily living, such as food, household fuel, cloth, and soap. In these areas, the function of the market in resource allocation was largely replaced by bureaucratic control (Arisawa 1976:281; Keizai Kikakuchō 1964:57). In this system, the ESB sent the distribution plan to individual ministries after it had estimated the supply and determined the quotas for distribution. On the basis of the ESB's plan, individual ministries then decided the quota for each consumer-goods industry in each county. The ministries of the central government or the local governments then decided the quota for each registered wholesaler or retailer. Trading the materials that were subject to state control without government authorization was forbidden. Producers and distributors were required to sell the materials to those who were designated in the document. Retailers could buy these materials from the wholesalers within the quota set by the state only after they presented the stamps they had collected from consumers. Wholesalers also had to follow this rule in their transactions with producers (Keizai Kikakuchō 1964:19–26). To enforce the state's control over resource allocation, the ESB assigned 349 professional inspectors, whose major duty was to investigate and disclose economic crimes such as hoarding materials. At that time, the ESB was so powerful that there was a well-known saying: "Even crying babies become silent when they hear the name of the ESB" (Arisawa 1976:281).

The profit principle was still rejected in 1946–9, but now in relation to democracy. The tendency to shift company power from shareholders to employees was further stimulated by both the GHQ's policy and the state industrial policy. The development of labor unions greatly strengthened the power of employees in the company. The *zaibatsu* dissolution destroyed the monitoring function of the holding companies. For the purpose of redistributing wealth, capitalists had to pay a heavy property tax, which was about 1% of Japan's GNP in 1946. Twenty-nine percent of this property tax was paid in stock, further weakening the power of shareholders. At the same time, to promote economic democratization, the Ministry of Commerce and Industry adopted a policy of restraining the power of shareholders by encouraging employees to hold the shares of their companies and by financing companies through banks rather than through financial markets. Influenced by this policy, the shareholders' right was restrained not only in intervening in the management of the company, but also in receiving dividends (Okazaki 1993:120–7). The new generation of company managers after the *zaibatsu* dissolution regarded employee sovereignty and the separation of ownership and management as the foundation of democracy. The leading members in the newly established Japan Committee of Economic Development (Nihon Keizai Dōyūkai) even regarded Ryū Shitarō's *Nihon keizai no saihensei*, the ideological manifesto of the Konoe government's economic new order during the war, as the latest knowledge concerning management and used it as the textbook for group discussions (Sakurada and Shikanai 1983:183–7).

Supported by the GHQ's labor policy, the organization rate of labor jumped from 3% in the prewar period to about 50% in 1947. The Council of Management Consultation (Keiei kyōgikai or CMC), established in many companies, also functioned to restrain the profit principle. In the iron-steel industry, for example, 78% of the companies established the CMC. The purposes for consultation ranged from production, efficiency, and working conditions to benefits, organizational design, and management (Nishinarita 1994). In contrast to the wartime period, in which rejection of the profit principle by Japanese management was sustained by state control through coercion, the continuity of this policy after the war was sustained by the new dynamics of democratization. In this sense, the experience of restraining company profits in 1946–9 transformed a wartime legacy into a peacetime practice. Although profit and efficiency became the top issues as management regained power after implementation of the Dodge Plan, as the next chapter indicates, they were soon traded off for the need to incorporate labor into the effort of promoting productivity in the late 1950s.

The state's capacity for economic intervention was strengthened enormously in 1946–9. In 1931–45, businesses were able to block the radical proposal of reform bureaucrats to control the profits of private firms and to bestow official status on managers. Meanwhile, sectionalism in the state bureaucracies considerably undermined efforts at policy integration. In 1946–9, however, both of these barriers were broken by pressure from the GHQ. Throughout that period, the managed economy dominated Japan's industrial policy, though various efforts were made to move in new directions.

The indirect occupation was an important factor in the inertia of the managed economy. A brief comparison between Japan and Germany, which was occupied directly, illustrates a crucial difference. In both countries, wartime practice continued to function for some time after the war because of the economic crisis. Continuity in Germany was accomplished primarily by the occupation authorities, who were in charge of the daily operations of the occupation; in Japan, operations were overseen primarily by the Japanese government because the occupation was indirect. Consequently, when a change in state policy was required by a change in the situation, the German economists who gathered at the Independent Advisory Council of Academic Economists to the Bizonal Economic Administration advocated a radical decentralization of the economy. Ordoliberalism, represented by Alfred Muller-Armack and Walter Eucken, emphasized individual freedom. This policy prevailed and became the major dynamic in the German transition from a wartime to a peacetime economy (Giersch, Paque, and Schmieding 1992:26–44). In contrast, because the Japanese government assumed the operation of the economy by inheriting the managed economy, change could hardly be generated from within the government. In this sense, the implementation of the priority production program in 1946–9 played an important role in institutionalizing the continuities of Japanese capitalism (Gao 1994).

Because Japan experienced a series of drastic reforms under the occupation, the environment for the priority production program was quite different from that for the managed economy in 1931–45. Nevertheless, adoption of the priority production program by the Japanese state in 1946–9 was important in transforming the managed economy of 1931–45 into the institutions of the Japanese economy in the postwar period. It provided legitimacy to the policy instruments and economic institutions that were developed to strengthen the intervention of the Japanese state during the 15-year war, and enabled them, as did the state bureaucracy, to survive the drastic reforms during the occupation period. At that time, as this chapter shows, many efforts were made to change the course of history. Many Japanese believed that they had a variety of choices concerning economic institutions in a democratic new Japan. Nevertheless, the legacy of the managed economy prevailed in this period for complicated reasons relating to international and domestic political economy. For a long time, it was widely believed, both in Japan and in the West, that it was rational to continue the managed economy under the given circumstances. In the 1990s, however, observers have begun to sense how strong the institutional inertia of the managed economy can be: The wartime practices are now perceived as the origin of many major problems confronting the Japanese economy today.

The prominence of economists in policy making

The 1946–9 period was a golden era for economists participating in state policy making. The ties between the state and the economists that quickly developed in 1931–45 were further strengthened. Not only did several economists deeply involved in policy making in the managed economy become important advisors to the leading politicians, a number of others even took important posts in bureaucracies to apply their own ideas directly in making state policy. A group of economists gathered at the Special Survey Committee at the Ministry of Foreign Affairs (SSCMFA), which was organized by Ōkita Saburō, a young bureaucrat at that ministry, provided the Japanese state with the first blueprint for postwar reconstruction in 1946. The SSCMFA started its research on 16 August 1945, the day after Japan's surrender to the Allies. The membership of this committee included many economists who became prominent in postwar Japan. These economists can be divided into three groups. The first group included some important spokesmen for Marxism, including Ōuchi Hyōe, Arisawa Hiromi, Uno Kōzō, and Yamada Moritarō. The second group consisted of the *Kinkei* (modern economists), including Nakayama Ichiro, Tōbata Seiichi, and Tsuru Shigeto. The third group was the first generation of government economists, including Inaba Hidezō, Ōkita Saburō, and Goto Yōnosuke. The men in the third group were very active in politics and later became important liaisons between academia and the state. Many members of the SSCMFA had been involved in the activities of the SRA before it was dissolved in 1941. Arisawa Hiromi, for example, secretly drafted the policy proposal for Konoe's economic new order. Nakayama Ichiro and Tōbata Seiichi were members of the SRA.

According to the first blueprint for Japan's postwar economic reconstruction made by this group, the postwar international economy would be divided into two blocs, which were controlled by the United States and the Soviet Union. Japan would be in a sensitive position between these blocs, and both sides would have a great impact on the Japanese political economy. The operation of the economy could not depend solely on a laissez-faire policy. After the Japanese economy was democratized, it would be necessary to nationalize monetary institutions as well as some basic industries, to make economic plans, and to exercise strong state control. To strengthen the Japanese state's capacity in economic planning, these economists suggested that the Soviet Union's five-year plan, the American New Deal, and Britain's postwar recovery plan serve as models. The future of the Japanese economy, this group argued, would depend on whether the U.S. economy integrated the East Asian economy as a whole, while allowing cooperation based on a division of labor within this region, or whether it would integrate the Chinese economy alone, because China had replaced Japan as the major Asian country after World War II. The committee also believed that industrialization in China, India, and other Asian countries would not only reduce Japanese exports of light industrial products to these countries, but would also increase their competitiveness in the international markets and make importation of industrial raw materials from these countries more difficult. Under such circumstances, this group argued that Japan should participate in the division of labor in the international economy by focusing on heavy-chemical industries. To promote trade, Japan would have to upgrade its technology. Only when Japan had established its technological superiority could it export industrial products to other Asian countries. In this first plan for Japan's postwar reconstruction, Japanese economists had already identified the future strategy for economic development. They held that because Japan lacked resources and had abundant cheap labor, it should focus on labor-intensive but material-saving and quality-improving technology (Gaimushō [1946] 1990:149–51).

Arisawa Hiromi, Nakayama Ichirō, and Tōbata Seiichi soon became major advisors to the prime minister, Yoshida Shigeru. The personal ties between these economists and Yoshida were established by Yoshida's father-in-law, Makino Nobuaki. Makino was the second son of Ōkubo Toshimichi, one of the major leaders in the Meiji Restoration. Makino himself was also an important politician who had previously served as minister of education, minister of agriculture and commerce, minister of foreign affairs, minister of home affairs, and minister of imperial affairs. Beginning in the 1930s, Makino often played *go* with Wada Hiroo, Tōbata Seiichi, Nakayama Ichirō, and Arisawa Hiromi. These activities continued in the postwar period; Makino regarded these men as the backbone of Japan in the future. After Yoshida became minister of foreign affairs in the Shidehara cabinet in early 1946, Makino urged him to obtain advice from these economists on how to proceed with economic reconstruction. When Yoshida talked with the economists, he was deeply impressed (Takemi 1968:106–9). Consequently, when he became prime minister in March 1946, he tried to persuade Tōbata Seiichi, a professor of agricultural economics at the University of Tokyo, to be his minister of agriculture;

Ōuchi Hyōe, a professor of economics at the University of Tokyo, and then Nakayama Ichirō, a professor of economics at Hitotsubashi University, to be his minister of finance; and Arisawa Hiromi, a professor of economics at the University of Tokyo, to be the director of the ESB. Although Arisawa, Nakayama, and Tōbata did not accept Yoshida's offers, they became his major economic advisors. Yoshida met them regularly at lunch meetings to discuss economic issues. It was at these meetings that the idea of priority production came into being.

To carry out the priority production program, Arisawa Hiromi chaired the Coal Committee, a private brain trust to Yoshida. Its membership consisted of Inaba Hidezō, Tsuru Shigeto, Okita Saburō, and Gotō Yonosuke from the ESB; Yoshino Toshihiko from the Bank of Japan; Oshima Kanichi from the Ministry of Finance; and Sato Naokuni from the Ministry of Commerce and Industry. The detailed program for priority production was developed by this committee. Later, when the ESB drafted the Five Year Plan for Economic Recovery, Arisawa served as the director of the special committee in charge of the macro framework for the plan. Influenced by his logic concerning priority production, this plan asserted that the future of Japan's economy should be based on the heavy chemical industries; this implied that Japan would go beyond any restrictions set by the GHQ. Meanwhile, the plan stated that the government would wait another two years before it adopted any strict policies to stabilize inflation (Hara 1990:14).

Taking government posts was another effective channel for diffusing economic ideas to state policy making. Ishibashi Tanzan, an economics commentator, and Tsuru Shigeto, an academic economist who taught at Harvard before the Pacific war broke out, directly took government office. Ishibashi became the minister of finance in the first Yoshida cabinet and then the director of the ESB. These positions enabled him to carry out a Keynesian financial policy for the priority production program. Tsuru was the chairman of the Comprehensive Policy Integration Committee in the Wada ESB, which was in charge of the macro integration of the state's economic policy.

Japanese economists had a strong impact on state policy making in 1946–9 for several reasons. First, after Japan's defeat in World War II, the whole country fell into what was called *postwar lethargy* (*sengo kyodatsu*), a spiritual shock that was aggravated by economic crisis and political instability. Suffering from ruin and famine in the struggle for survival, many Japanese fell into a "stupor"; they had no idea of where to start again after they lost the sense of mission, which had been sustained by nationalism that had been closely associated with military expansion since the Meiji era (Maruyama 1951:176). The bureaucrats were not sure, after operating the managed economy for a long time, whether they could continue this practice when Japan was experiencing radical democratization. The business leaders were either overwhelmed by worry about their future during the dissolution of the *zaibatsu* or were driven by the need to rebuild the factories that had been ruined by the war, so they had no time or energy to think about the long-term plan (Arisawa and Ōkita 1966:281). Under such circumstances, the economists' ideas about postwar reconstruction were highly appreciated. Second, the severity of the unprecedented economic crisis in 1946–9 was far beyond the coping capacity of the bureaucrats. The Japanese state was well known for its effectiveness in routine work but was vulnerable in an emergency. For this reason, the leading politicians could no longer depend on bureaucrats but were eager to search for new ideas from outside the state bureaucracy. Third, the postwar democratic reforms strengthened the willingness of Japanese intellectuals to be involved in politics. As the state control of thought disappeared, the intellectuals' impact on policy debates increased greatly. And finally, the personal ties that had developed before and during the war among economists, bureaucrats, and politicians provided a natural foundation for the link between academia and the Japanese state.

A lonely nation in the world

In what kind of intellectual environment was the ideology of the managed economy inherited? Why could it continue, given that the democratic reforms had shaken the country profoundly? Part of the reason was that nationalism still remained quite strong in policy-making circles, though it was no longer popular at the grass-roots level. Nationalism was no longer associated with military expansion, but was concerned with how to protect Japan's national interest during the occupation. A combination of elements, including concern about war reparations, the perception of the new challenge to Japan from developing economies in Asia, and the distrust of the GHQ's policy regarding Japan's postwar construction, kept the concern for national interest alive. The nationalist orientation in the early postwar period was reflected in three propositions: first, to proceed independently with postwar reconstruction; second, to give production top priority in state industrial policy; and third, to emphasize the development of heavy-chemical industries.

Arisawa once recalled that 1946–9 was the only period in which Japan was full of the "spirit of independence" and "patriotism" (Arisawa and Ōkita 1966:279). What were the dynamics behind the patriotism shared by policy makers? An analysis of their statements reveals two factors. First was the desire to protect the Japanese economy from the turbulence of the international market. Tsuru asserted that "the so-called independence, as often mentioned, means to eliminate the American aid that we are receiving now (which constituted 5 to 10 percent of Japan's national income) as soon as possible, and to gain a balance in international payments. The establishment of economic independence means that the Japanese economy will not be shaken recklessly by the turbulence of foreign economies" (cited in Miyazaki 1985:28).

Second was the anger and indignation about (in Arisawa's word, *uppun*) or distrust of the occupation policy. As Arisawa stated:

> the proposals for economic reconstruction were rejected by the Occupation Authority, the production equipment was taken away for war reparations, and the factories could not be run effectively due to the order to decentralize the excessive economic power. If these continued, we would not be able to do anything in the future. . . . Once I felt that we had been driven to a situation where there was no way out but to improve our life by ourselves, I strove with a strong will to win (Arisawa and Ōkita 1966:279)

This was why Arisawa asserted the need for strong intervention by the state. Ishibashi Tanzan shared this patriotism. From the beginning of his tenure as the minister of finance, Ishibashi was involved in conflicts with the GHQ. He strongly insisted that war compensation be provided to Japanese companies and regarded the GHQ's opposition to this proposal as unsympathetic to Japanese postwar reconstruction. Masuda Hiroshi (1988:104–5), in his study of Ishibashi Tanzan, points out that "In his heart, Ishibashi distrusted the Occupation Authority because if it failed [in Japan], it could simply go home."

The idea of priority production

The idea of priority production first emerged in July 1946 in the discussion of how to choose the limited imports allowed by the GHQ to survive the economic crisis and sustain the postwar reconstruction.

During World War II the Japanese state, under the General Mobilization Law, ordered many companies to produce munitions. As a result, these companies owed huge amounts of debt. Without compensation from the government, these companies and the banks that provided them with loans would confront a major financial problem. The Japanese government, represented by Minister of Finance Ishibashi Tanzan, intended to pay war compensation to these companies, which was estimated to be as high as 95 billion yen. This proposal, however, reflected a dilemma. On the one hand, without financial compensation from the state, many private companies might become bankrupt; consequently, the unemployment rate would rise. On the other hand, war compensation might exacerbate the severe inflation. The proposal was eventually rejected by the GHQ in July 1946 after a series of negotiations (Masuda 1988:61–74). Under such circumstances, Prime Minister Yoshida Shigeru asked General Douglas MacArthur to provide help in order to survive the economic hardship that would follow. MacArthur agreed to provide a limited amount of goods and asked Yoshida to prepare a short list. Therefore the Japanese government had to determine which goods were most important.

In this context, Arisawa Hiromi came up with the idea of priority production. When Yoshida asked his economic advisors to identify the most important materials for the Japanese economy, Arisawa and his colleagues in Yoshida's brain trust listed iron and steel, crude petroleum, rubber, smokeless coal, and trailers. The rationale behind this selection was that the imported crude petroleum would be used in iron and steel production. Iron and steel then could be used to improve the production of coal. Because coal was the only source of energy available domestically at that time, coal production would be critically important to production in other industries. Arisawa (1948c:69) asserted that

> we should concentrate our priority in economic policy on the production of coal, the only manipulable basic resource we have, and organize the economy around coal for a while . . . for a coal-oriented economy. Needless to say, this is unstable and cannot be sustained,

nor will it be necessary . . . for long. Since it is impossible to stimulate production across the board simultaneously due to insurmountable difficulties and barriers, we have to choose a priority in our economic plan in order to increase production quickly in basic industries, aiming at a turning point in the promotion of productivity.

In Arisawa's vision, the priority production program was not an ad hoc response to the economic crisis, but a grand strategy for postwar reconstruction. This strategy had three policy objectives. First, it aimed at promoting production in order to overcome the absolute shortage of materials. Second, after production had reached a certain level, the state should tighten the money supply in order to eliminate hyperinflation. Third, the state should tighten the money supply only after production had returned to 60% of the prewar level so that the Japanese economy would have a solid foundation for surviving the following stabilization panic (see the following discussion). Stabilization and reconstruction were two important but competing agendas for policy makers. To stabilize the economy, inflation had to be eliminated. To do this, the state had to tighten the money supply. If the money supply was tightened, however, production would decrease and the reconstruction process would be slowed down because reconstruction demanded capital. The supply of capital, however, would increase the amount of currency in circulation, which would aggravate inflation. Arisawa was aware of this dilemma but gave reconstruction more importance than stabilization. This reflected a strong developmental orientation. Drawing on the German experience of economic stabilization after World War I, Arisawa argued that the state should not adopt a tight money policy too early to eliminate inflation because it might cause what he called *stabilization panic* (*antei kyōkō*). As with the German experience, industrial production might decline as much as 50% when the state tightened the money supply. Thus, to avoid this panic, the state should not tighten the money supply until production had returned to at least 60% of the prewar level (Arisawa and Ōkita 1966). According to Arisawa's (1948b) rationale, the only effective way to eliminate inflation was to solve the problems of the absolute shortage of materials by promoting production. Greater production could solve the problems of inflation and the shortage of materials simultaneously.

After a series of discussions with Inaba Hidezō, Yamamoto Takayuki, and other bureaucrats in the Ministry of Commerce and Industry, Arisawa developed his ideas of priority production into a policy proposal. Prime Minister Yoshida then established the Coal Committee, which was headed by Arisawa. In July 1946, Arisawa Hiromi, Inaba Hidezō, and Ōkita Saburō started their research on the priority production plan. They set the goal of increasing monthly coal production to 2.5 million tons, or 30 million tons annually, and designed a nationwide program to achieve this goal.

Arisawa's logic for priority production was based on the Marxist theory of reproduction in a war economy. According to that theory, a war economy was characterized by constantly decreasing reproduction. The theory consisted of a series of formulas: $c + v + m$; $c + v(m - x)$; $c + v$; $c + (v - x)$; $(c - y) + (v - nx)$ (c = constant capital, v = variable capital, m = surplus value production, x = the amount of military consumption in variable capital, and y = the amount of military consumption in constant capital). In the war economy, the production of munitions was regarded as the top priority. Although it cost a huge amount of resources, it was pure consumption that had nothing to do with the process of reproduction. Therefore it took resources not only from the production of civilian goods but also from the production of industrial materials, and thus weakened reproduction itself. Although Japan's resources were allocated quickly away from munitions production after the war ended, Arisawa argued, they were not channeled into the production of industrial materials but into the production of consumer goods. The latter were much more profitable than the former because of the severe shortage of products for daily living. As the limited domestic resources were directed away from the production of industrial materials, reproduction would become problematic, and the Japanese economy would risk collapse after running out of stock. Only under priority production could the increased coal supply be used to reconstruct the entire economy. Because coal was the only source of energy available in Japan, it was the most important for production in all other industries (Nakamura and Miyazaki 1990:160; Shimazaki 1971:309–11).

Arisawa's idea of priority production was heavily influenced by the ideology of the managed economy in 1931–45, for which Arisawa himself was one of the most important theorists.

First, Arisawa still viewed the economy strategically and asserted the need for strong intervention by the state. In his perception, the key industries, such as coal, iron and steel, and fertilizer, were indispensable for the postwar reconstruction. Arisawa (1948d:79) argued that "in the case of an underproduction panic, the materials are in a comprehensive shortage. Even if we want to produce material, we don't have materials with which we can produce materials. Coal is in shortage. In order to increase coal production, iron and steel are needed. To increase iron and steel production, however, coal is needed. A circle exists here. If we follow the circle, we will not be able to find a way out. The clue for a solution is to break the circle." After the strategic industries were identified, the state must make a great effort, through its industrial policy, to sustain the development of these industries, "give bold and special treatment to miners by providing food, housing, medicine, and health care," and "forbid the unnecessary use of timber, iron and steel products and rubber" (Sekitan Shōiinkai [1946] 1990b:160).

Second, Arisawa still regarded production as the top priority in state industrial policy. This prevailed over other policy objectives such as equality or stability. The priority production program benefited big companies greatly while putting consumers and medium-sized and small companies at a disadvantage. It also created instability, as it stimulated inflation. Arisawa's major concern, however, was the survival of the entire economy, not equality among particular social groups. He believed that the causes of the economic crisis were the absolute shortage of food and underproduction in the mining industry, and was convinced that Japan must promote production by all means. As Albert Hirschman (1958) once pointed out, emphasizing economic growth over economic stability is a common characteristic of development-oriented economies.

Third, to achieve the policy objective, Arisawa asserted the need for strong control over the market. Without tight state control of resource allocation, argued Arisawa, the market forces would channel all stocks of limited domestic resources into the production of consumer goods because (as stated earlier) they were very profitable. Little would be left for production of industrial materials. The major purpose of state control was to ensure the survival of the national economy by concentrating domestic resources in the key industries. To constrain the market, the state would institute whatever organizational or institutional reforms were needed in the governance structure of the economy. Within the state bureaucracy, "bureaucratic confusion and inefficiency should be prevented"; the state should "establish a cooperative system for coal production, integrating all relevant bureaucracies," and "should establish the Coal Committee within the Economic Stabilization Board or put it under the direct control of the Prime Minister in order to integrate bureaucracies." If the private coal mines failed to achieve the production goals set by the state, "the government should change their managers or even buy up ownership by coercion" (Sekitan Shōiinkai [1946] 1990a:87). Arisawa held that ownership of the coal industry would not have to follow the principles of capitalism. If the current system of private enterprise restricted production, it could be changed to public management (Sekitan Shōiinkai [1946] 1990b:161).

Fourth, class struggle and social revolution should be avoided in this economy. At that time, the Russian and German traditions of democratic socialism were very influential in Japan. The concept of *sozialisierung* (socialization) became very popular in Japan's political discourse, reflecting the loss of the strength of capital and the people's distrust of the state. Progressive forces advocated the participation of the working class in management; some radicals even supported the nationalization of basic industries. Arisawa also argued that the participation of the working class in management was progressive because it would help to eliminate the feudal relationship in private firms, although that participation was far from the liberation of the working class (Arisawa 1948a, 1948b, 1948c, 1948d, 1948e, 1948f). According to Marxist criticism, Arisawa's vision did not address the issue of class, but "was simply theoretical thinking about the policy of state monopoly capitalism," which had to be questioned because of its "responsibility to history" (Shimazaki 1971:314).

The GHQ and the ESB

The ESB was established in July 1946 to take charge of the priority production program. This was the first effort of the Japanese state, backed up by the GHQ, to centralize its power in policy making and integration. Early that year, the GHQ ordered the Japanese state to tighten its control over the market in order to fight hyperinflation, and then to establish the ESB and give it great authority. As mentioned at the beginning of this chapter, Japanese bureaucrats lost their confidence to continue operating the managed economy immediately after the war ended, and they intended to reintroduce the function of the market by withdrawing state control. On these occasions, between August and November, the Japanese state ended its control over many food and production materials (Arisawa and Ōkita 1966; Keizai Kikakūchō 1964:9). On 26 December 1945, the GHQ sent a memorandum to the Japanese government rejecting the Japanese proposal to end controls over the price and distribution of daily-life products and stressing the necessity of tight state control over resource allocation (Keizai Kikakuchō 1964:9–10). In January 1946, under pressure from the GHQ, the Japanese state decided to take emergency measures to deal with the economic crisis. On 1 March 1946, after more than 10 meetings among economic ministers, the state decided to establish the ESB as the agency for policy integration among individual ministries. At the same time, the GHQ made a similar proposal.

On May 17, the GHQ issued a number of direct guidelines to the Japanese government regarding the function of the ESB. Among the most important guidelines were these: First, the ESB should be superior to individual ministries in policy making; second, it should be a temporary agency; third, it should maintain continuity without being influenced by political changes in the government; fourth, its director should have the authority to issue orders to cabinet ministers. At the news conference on May 31 regarding the establishment of the ESB, a GHQ official stated that

> the crisis of the Japanese economy, which was caused by the shortage of coal, food, and fertilizers and the difficulty of obtaining resources for the textile industry, necessitated a sound planned economy. In order to end this crisis, we strongly urge the Japanese state bureaucracies to abandon the tradition of sectionalism, and to cooperate on the important policy issues. The Economic Stabilization Board is designed for this purpose, and it integrates economic policies by individual ministries at the cabinet level. (Keizai Kikakuchō 1964:12)

The establishment of the ESB, however, did not immediately improve the state's capacity for policy integration. Between August 1946 and June 1947, the ESB failed to exercise its power effectively in controlling resource allocation because of the sectionalism in the state bureaucracy. The "Emergency Measures to Break the Coal Crisis in the Second Half of 1946" prepared by the ESB, for example, failed to integrate the ministries into a policy package; it simply listed the responsibilities of each ministry (Nakamura and Miyazaki 1990:12). In October 1946, the monthly output of coal was only about 1.8 million tons. Because the ESB under the leadership of Zen Keinosuke did not take strong action to implement the priority production program, Yoshida had to depend on the Coal Committee, headed by Arisawa Hiromi, to search for solutions (Nakamura and Miyazaki 1990:237). The Coal Committee, however, was not an official body, and it did not possess the power to control the actions of individual ministries. Besides, the committee's goal of producing 30 millon tons of coal by 1947 was much higher than the goal of producing 23 millon tons for 1946 and 27 million tons for 1947 set by the Ministry of Commerce and Industry. State bureaucracies reacted strongly to the fact that a private brain trust to the prime minister intended to rewrite the plans they had previously made (Miyazaki Masayasu 1990:16–17). Arisawa, Inaba Hidezō, and Ōkita Saburō were worried about this situation. In the "Special Measure to Improve Coal Production" (*sekitan zosan tokubetsu taisaku*) prepared by the Coal Committee on 18 October 1946, they stated that "the confusion and inefficiency of the bureaucracy must be prevented." To promote production, the state needed to "establish a cooperative system for coal production which integrates all relevant bureaucracies." In particular, the state should "establish a Coal Committee in the Economic Stabilization Board and put it under the direct control of the Prime Minister in order to take charge of the bureaucracies." On the issue of the state's capacity to control society, this document declared that if the private coal mines failed to achieve the goals of production set by the government, "the government should change their managers or even finally buy up ownership." To promote production, the coal industry would not have to be managed according to the principles of capitalism. If private ownership restricted production, it should be changed to public management (Nakamura and Miyazaki 1990:161).

An easy money policy

The implementation of the priority production program was constrained not only by the institutional structure of the decentralized administration in the Japanese state, but also by the ideology of liberal capitalism held by the leading politicians. The first two directors of the ESB, Zen Keinosuke and Ishibashi Tanzan, as well as Prime Minister Yoshida Shigeru, were famous conservative politicians. They were skeptical about direct bureaucratic control over resource allocation and favored the forces of the market. At the time, Yoshida himself concentrated on political and diplomatic issues and left his economic policy to Ishibashi Tanzan. Yoshida once recalled:

> Ishibashi's idea of abolishing economic control was the same as mine. We believed that we should get rid of economic control as soon as possible, letting the economy run vigorously by itself. . . . Ishibashi held that the first priority was to end the shortage of materials and to stimulate production. This was a fundamental way to prevent inflation. If we could manage financial and monetary policies at a suitable level, there would be no major problems. Since it was a difficult time, I entrusted him with everything. I believed that I should trust Ishibashi, letting him do as he thought. *Entrust* was the word to describe my position, I had no other alternative." (Yoshida 1957, vol. 3:182–3)

As minister of finance and then director of the ESB, Ishibashi Tanzan was the most important politician in charge of state economic policy at that time. Ishibashi had been a famous liberal (*jiyū shugisha*) in Japan since the late 1920s, and his perspective on the economy was a mixture of Keynesian macroeconomic policy and laissez-faire doctrine. On policy issues, Ishibashi called himself a Keynesian and often asked himself, "What kind of policy would Keynes adopt if he were in Japan at this moment?" He was regarded as the first Japanese politician who deliberately employed Keynesian theory in Japanese financial policy, though the practice of Minister of Finance Takahashi in the early 1930s is often perceived as resonating with Keynesian theory (Chō 1974b:18). In the famous speech that he delivered to the Diet on 25 July 1946, Ishibashi ([1946] 1970:194–6) agreed with Arisawa on the necessity of state intervention and the importance of leadership by the state. He also believed that the promotion of coal production was the top priority in Japan's postwar economic reconstruction and that the Japanese state should adopt some epochal measures. Nevertheless, his policy proposal and his vision for the Japanese economy differed significantly from Arisawa's on two major issues.

First, in contrast to Arisawa's emphasis on bureaucratic control, Ishibashi advocated the function of the market in carrying out priority production. Ishibashi believed that the state should stimulate the dynamics of the market rather than restraining its function. In Arisawa's idea of priority production, the state was the major actor, and its control over the distribution of materials was the major instrument for sustaining the priority production program. In contrast, Ishibashi ([1951] 1972:207–10) opposed state control and held that business freedom was a better way for a poor country such as Japan to proceed with postwar economic reconstruction. He believed that the managed economy had failed during the war because the state controlled everything. At present, Ishibashi argued, the state might try to control the distribution of minerals, timber, food, and even miners' underground socks in an effort to promote the production of coal. It would be very difficult, however, for the government to guarantee the supply of those materials. As a result, miners might lose their enthusiasm for coal production. In short, he intended to let the market mechanism increase production. He argued that although the state would intervene when the market did not work well, this intervention was intended only to create effective demand. Unlike Arisawa, who took the failure of the market for granted and derived his solution from that failure, Ishibashi believed firmly in the dynamics of the market and the creativity of the private sector, and wanted state intervention only as a supplementary factor. In Ishibashi's view, the market forces would rationalize Japanese industries at the company level. This was not only an indispensable way to promote production in key industries, it also had strategic implications for increasing the income of the working class and improving the standard of living. Because the rationalization of production in companies would produce layoffs, and because numerous Japanese had been sent back to Japan from overseas after Japan's defeat in the war, Ishibashi further suggested that it was very important for the state to establish a social security system to combat the problem of unemployment.

Second, although Ishibashi advocated state intervention, he emphasized macroeconomic policy rather than direct bureaucratic control as the instrument of state intervention. In this sense, Ishibashi's vision of priority production reflected an adaptation of the postwar environment. To promote production in strategic industries while keeping the consumer market stable, Ishibashi suggested that consumer prices should be controlled at the current level and producer prices increased significantly. The government should provide subsidiaries to make up the difference. In the meantime, Ishibashi argued, the state should provide capital to the private sector through the Reconstruction Finance Bank (RFB) because individual companies no longer had any financial resources. In 1946 Ishibashi argued that "the most urgent task of the government finance, especially under the current circumstances in Japan, is to create business opportunities for people, to revive industries, and to develop a national economy with full employment." Whether or not the state had a budget deficit was not Ishibashi's major concern. He believed that "the government may have a seemingly balanced budget. As long as domestic unemployment increases and production equipment is not being run at full capacity, however, this budget cannot be regarded as truly healthy" (Ishibashi [1946] 1970:190). According to Ishibashi, when unemployment and idle production elements exist, the top priority of the state's financial policy should be to mobilize those elements for economic reconstruction. "For this goal," Ishibashi argued, "additional currency must be issued, even when a deficit [then] arises in the finances of the government" (Ishibashi [1946] 1970:192). It was clear that Ishibashi's idea was based on the assumption of the existence of a fully functioning market.

Arisawa and his fellow Marxists, especially Ōuchi Hyōe, held that inflation was the biggest danger to the Japanese economy. Therefore they strongly opposed any easy money policy and urged the Japanese state to adopt a tight money policy (Ōuchi, Arisawa, Wakimura, Takahashi, and Minobe 1946, 1949). In their criticism of Ishibashi's financial policy, they repeatedly cited the case of Germany after World War I. Ishibashi, however, drawing on the Keynesian definition, argued that true inflation did not exist at all. Although some phenomena, such as the issuing of a great deal of currency and the soaring prices and salaries, resembled inflation, true inflation would appear only when purchasing power was increased after full employment had been achieved and when all production elements, including both labor and materials, were fully employed. Ishibashi further argued that the real problems in the Japanese economy at present were unemployment, idle production capacity, and low productivity. These conditions signified not full employment but underemployment; thus there was no inflation at all (Ishibashi [1946] 1970).

Under Ishibashi's leadership, the RFB was established and charged with providing state capital for priority production. To prevent his easy money policy from being revised by those who believed in classical economics, Ishibashi several times opposed GHQ over the selection of a director of the RFB from the Bank of Japan, where many classical economists were employed (Yoshino 1975:116–17). Ishibashi's easy money policies left an enduring controversy in studies of Japan's postwar economic history. They were often criticized as being responsible for accelerating inflation. Many RFB officials disagreed, however. They argued that whenever people spoke of postwar inflation, they believed that the RFB was guilty. Yet the RFB was the only means to stimulate production at that time. Inflation could not be eliminated without an increase in production; history has proved this point. The officials admitted that the financial policies of the RFB exacerbated inflation, but they contended that capital was extremely short in those days. New capital had to be created in order to replace industrial equipment quickly. Even though the RFB caused some short-term inflation, it played a critical role in the postwar recovery by stimulating production. The proportion of loans provided by the RFB to all financial agencies was only 4.2% in March 1947, but this figure increased to 17.6% by September 1947. From March 1948 to March 1949, it remained between 24.0% and 24.6%. Most loans provided by the RFB were guaranteed by the Bank of Japan: 94% at the end of March 1947, 76% at the end of March 1948, and 64% at the end of March 1949 (Shikagui 1979:161). Forty percent of the new currency issued by the Bank of Japan went to the RFB. The loans from the RFB were a powerful instrument in strengthening production power. In 1946 the reconstruction funds were spent mainly on the daily operation of private firms and on salary subsidies. Once the RFB was established, it immediately began to provide loans to private firms to upgrade or replace damaged production equipment. Of the total loans provided by the RFB, the proportion spent for production equipment was 47.7% in March 1947, 59.0% in March 1948, and 69.1% in March 1949 (Shimura 1976:646–7).

Despite the differences, both Arisawa's and Ishibashi's ideas were implemented in the priority production program, and both strongly influenced Japan's industrial policy later on. Arisawa's idea that the state should adopt a discriminatory policy in resource allocation ensured that the state policy agenda was adopted again in the 1950s, as the next chapter shows, to nurture Japan's strategic industries. Ishibashi's idea of depending on an aggressive financial policy to promote the national power of production was repeated in the mid-1950s when he became the prime minister, and was implemented again to a much greater degree by Ikeda Hayato, Ishibashi's deputy at the Ministry of Finance in the late 1940s and his minister of finance in the mid-1950s, who became prime minister himself in 1960. In this sense, Ishibashi was a pioneer in applying Keynesian economics to promote the industrial structure of the economy, which has been a key component of Japanese developmentalism in the postwar period.

Wada Hiroo's ESB

By mid-1947, the Ministry of Finance, led by Ishibashi Tanzan, was able to carry out the easy money policy effectively because the ministry had complete control in this domain and Ishibashi's authority in financial policy was backed by Prime Minister Yoshida, who shared this policy orientation. In contrast, the ESB, headed by Zen Keinosuke, failed to integrate state bureaucracies successfully in priority production.

As Sherwood M. Fine, chief of the Government Division of the Civil Affairs Section (G-5) at GHQ, pointed out:

> The failure of a more satisfactory recovery to materialize through 1947 was due not in small degree to the Japanese government's understandable disorganization. Despite requests by ESS [Economic and Scientific Section] that an economic coordinating organization be created no response was forthcoming. Instead, such agencies as the Ministry of Finance, Ministry of International Trade and Industry and Ministry of Agriculture and Forestry frequently pursued mutually inconsistent or antagonistic policies. After extended persuasion had failed, SCAP directed the Prime Minister to establish a cabinet level organization to formulate basic economic policy and coordinate the activities of the various governmental agencies concerned. Accordingly, there was organized a new agency, the Economic Stabilization Board, established under the immediate jurisdiction of the prime minister, in August 1946. The ESB was made responsible for the formulation of production, distribution, price and financial policies. The various competing ministries were enabled to issue orders pursuant to plans and policies formulated by the ESB. However, despite the creation of this central economic authority, the Japanese government chose not to utilize the new board in the fashion contemplated. The concept of governmental economic planning and the use of publicly directed as opposed to private controls was foreign to the party in power. It was not until June 1947 with the formation of the Social Democratic led cabinet that the ESB made a serious effort to perform as a planning body, a move viewed with ill concealed hostility by the business community." (Fine 1952:193–4)

Constrained by bureaucratic inefficiency and the politicians' beliefs in laissez faire, the Japanese state failed to control the situation, and

the economic situation deteriorated quickly. Inaba Hidezō even predicted that by the end of March, the Japanese economy would collapse
when it ran out of materials.

The GHQ decided to push the Japanese government to strengthen its
policy-integrating capacity to an unprecedented level. On 6 February
the Economic and Scientific Section at the GHQ sent an informal memorandum to the Japanese government suggesting that the government
transfer all planning functions and all personnel related to economic
administration from individual ministries to the ESB. The ESB had the
authority to make plans for all kinds of economic policies, and the
individual ministries were to ensure their implementation. The ESB
could recruit its staff from both bureaucrats and civilians and could
increase its size in order to ensure its function (Keizai Kikakuchō
1964:47–8). On 22 March 1947, General MacArthur sent a letter to
Japanese Prime Minister Yoshida Shigeru saying that

> the Allied Powers, of course, are under no obligation to maintain or
> to have maintained any particular standard of living in Japan, nor is
> there any responsibility to import foodstuffs to meet deficits arising
> from the failure of Japan to assure the just and efficient distribution of
> its own food supplies . . . it is essential that the Japanese Government,
> through the Economic Stabilization Board which was created for this
> purpose, takes early and vigorous steps to develop and implement the
> integrated series of economic and financial controls which the current
> situation demands. (MacArthur [1947] 1982, vol. 20:518–19)

Under strong pressure from the GHQ and the economic situation,
the Yoshida cabinet abandoned the laissez-faire ideology that had influenced its policy for a year and admitted that the ESB, as the core of state
leadership in economic reconstruction, had to be given greater weight
in the state bureaucracy (Keizai Kikakuchō 1964:46). This was an
unprecedented reform in the institutional arrangement of Japanese
state bureaucracies; during the war years, the reform bureaucrats had
tried hard to achieve this goal but had failed.

After Katayama Tetsu became prime minister in May 1947, he appointed Wada Hiroo director of the ESB. Wada had been deeply involved in conducting the managed economy in the late 1930s and early
1940s. Thus, after he became director of the ESB, the personnel of this
agency reflected more strongly the wartime legacy. Wada appointed to
high-ranking posts many former bureaucrats who had served at the
CSB, the CPA, and the CPB and were arrested with him in 1941 for the

CPB incident. Katsumata Seiichi became secretary to Wada, Sada Tadataka became the director of the Financial and Monetary Bureau, and Inaba Hidezō became the deputy secretary-general of the minister's secretariat. These men had shared the experience of operating the managed economy in wartime, so they strongly supported the idea of priority production. Besides the Wada group, two other government economists who are important to this study also obtained important posts in this agency: Ōkita Saburō became the director of the Planning Division and Shimomura Osamu the director of the Price Division.

The ESB under Wada Hiroo's leadership was regarded as the most powerful economic bureaucracy in Japanese history. It had strong autonomy in policy making not only from societal demands, but also from the leadership of the prime minister. At that time, Inaba Hidezō was an important go-between in politics. Before encouraging Wada to assume the directorship of the ESB, he sought two conditions from Katayama. First, as prime minister, Katayama had to accept whatever policy decisions the ESB made. If he disagreed with this condition, Wada would not accept the appointment. Also, the ESB should hire some nonprofessional bureaucrats for its high-ranking posts, including representatives from both business and labor. Katayama accepted both conditions (Inaba 1988:58–9).

As mentioned earlier, Wada had a very close relationship with Arisawa, Nakayama, and Tōbata. Even before the Wada ESB came into being, Arisawa had often spoken with some of the future core members of this board about how to implement the priority production program, and they had reached a consensus. After the Coal Committee stopped functioning as a private brain trust to Yoshida Shigeru in early 1947, its members still met frequently to discuss policy issues. Their activities were first shifted to the Planning Division of the Ministry of Commerce and Industry (MCI), where MCI bureaucrats Yamamoto Takayuki, Tokunaga Hisatsugu, and Satō Naokuni were involved in discussions. In April they moved to Inaba Hidezō's Research Association for the National Economy, where Wada himself attended the discussions. At that time, Wada was the president of this association; he had quit his position as minister of agriculture in the Yoshida cabinet (Sugita 1989:139–40). Several economists were directly involved in the personnel arrangements for the Wada ESB. In fact, appointments to major posts were initially decided by Arisawa, Inaba Hidezō, Tsuru Shigeto, and Ōkita Saburō because at that time Arisawa was still considering accepting the directorship of the ESB (Tsuru 1988b:227). Katayama himself, however, did not prefer Arisawa; Yoshida Shigeru also recommended Wada to Katayama, so eventually this position was given to Wada, despite opposition by Inaba and Wada himself.

Although the state's capacity was strengthened greatly, it was sustained primarily by external forces. In fact, the GHQ intervened directly at several critical points, which sustained the development of the priority production program. The influence of the GHQ was reflected most clearly in its pressure to strengthen bureaucratic control and to eliminate sectionalism in the state bureaucracy. Without the support and initiative of the GHQ, the Japanese state might have remained reluctant to tighten its bureaucratic control and might have failed to centralize its power in policy making and implementation. The ESB might not have come into being. At that time, many GHQ officials were influenced by the American New Deal policy. They believed that state intervention would be an effective way for the Japanese to survive the economic crisis. When the Japanese government failed to do its job, the GHQ intervened directly. In this sense, the occupation policy implemented by the GHQ was important in explaining both the discontinuities and continuities of the wartime system in the postwar period.

Production versus economic equality

Tsuru Shigeto became the chairman of the Comprehensive Policy Integration Committee, with the status of deputy minister in charge of final integration of macroeconomic policy at the ESB, directed by Wada Hiroo. He was in a powerful position to influence policy making. Tsuru was a Harvard-trained economist who returned to Japan after the Pacific war broke out. He went to the United States for his college education because he had been involved in the student movement in the early 1930s and was expelled from high school. Thus, from the beginning, Tsuru, as a left-wing thinker, did not belong to the mainstream of Japanese society. His major plan in returning to Japan was to witness Japan's defeat in World War II as a social scientist in order to develop a vision for rebuilding a new Japan. Tsuru firmly believed that Japan had an opportunity to reform its wartime economic system.

Tsuru's major concern was how to achieve economic equality by breaking up the state–big business complex that had been built up during the war. In contrast to Arisawa Hiromi, who emphasized production and regarded the recovery of the national economy as the most important task, Tsuru Shigeto, who was influenced by the American New Deal policy, paid more attention to the equal distribution of economic welfare among different social classes (Miyazaki 1985:42; Ōtake 1981:472; Tsuru 1947b:16). In the wartime managed economy, the state, in order to support the war, channeled the major resources to the munitions industries, which were dominated by big companies. Because of the discriminatory policy of the state in resource allocation, these companies occupied a monopoly position in the market and made huge profits from participating in the state-sponsored programs. This mechanism continued to work in early postwar Japan. When the Japanese state started its priority production program, the big companies received the most favorable treatment in resource allocation, both in priority financing through the RFB and in the distribution of production materials by the state bureaucracies. They made huge profits in the black market because of their position in the distribution system.

Tsuru opposed the reliance on big businesses to carry out the priority production program. The big companies' profits, he argued, had a series of effects on income and then on consumer prices. The harmful cycle involving income and consumer prices was the major source of inflation. The corporations, which continued their wartime function of controlling the distribution of materials, often became the major sites of corruption. Tsuru believed that this situation was not fair to ordinary, hard-working people. He asserted that even if priority production could improve productivity, as long as the state tolerated profits made by companies in monopoly positions or through black markets, Japan had to face the sad reality of "honest people being regarded as foolish and hard-working people suffering losses."

Although Tsuru did not assert the need for a revolution to overthrow the whole capitalist system immediately, he advocated a gradual institutional reform. Tsuru supported the idea of priority production, but not by a managed economy. He stated that it was a mistake to think that increasing police and government regulations and raising penalties would suppress the black market. A tougher policy on black market and monopoly profits or institutional reform of monopoly capitalism was needed to stabilize the economic situation. He argued that "in order to establish an institution in which those who worked would be benefitted in the long run, we have to start with this urgent and difficult problem as our current goal" (Keizai Antei Honbu [1947] 1965:185).

Because one-third of the GDP was distributed by government finance, the government should not buy any goods on the black market. As Miyazaki Yoshikazu (1985:29) points out, "To regard the impact of black market profits in distribution on prices and income as the culprit in the vicious salary–price cycle, to call for their elimination, and to pursue a simultaneous determination of salaries and prices did not simply aim at establishing order in distribution, but implied a policy direction against the nature of monopoly capitalism. It raised an institutional issue."

Under Tsuru's leadership, the *Policies for Economic Emergency* was made public by the ESB on 11 June 1947. In this document, the government made a strong commitment to improving the distribution system by eliminating black markets and enforcing control over food and transportation. Meanwhile, the schedules for prices and wages were revised in an effort to raise the standard of living (Tsusanshō 1954:48–9). In the public pricing system, the state set 1,800 yen as the standard average monthly salary. On the basis of this estimate, it set public prices for basic materials such as iron-steel, fertilizers, and soda at 65 times higher, and coal at 48 times higher, than their prices in 1934–6. The consumer prices for other goods were calculated according to the prices of these basic materials. The government provided subsidies for any market price higher than the public price. The subsidies constituted 21% of the government expenditure in the general account in 1947 and 24% in 1948.

Tsuru's focus on economic equality clashed with the production orientation of the priority production program. Therefore, it was seriously criticized by Arisawa. Arisawa argued that a focus on equality would not solve Japan's problem for several reasons. First, it was impossible to establish order in distribution and realize equality at a time of high inflation. Also, even if these goals were realized, they would not increase the amount of materials available for equal distribution: "Even if the effect of measures such as the distribution order could be realized one hundred percent, the savings in consumption realized by those measures would be only about five to seven percent" (1948f:93). In an article written in November 1947, Arisawa further stated:

> The first policy adopted by the new cabinet was to establish order in distribution and a new system of salaries and prices. It also asked people for tolerance of material shortages. . . . To my understanding, the government has recognized the necessity of promoting production. Since it is almost impossible to conduct priority production with

full speed due to the severe shortage of materials, the government has given up all hopes of increasing production quickly. . . . Instead of choosing a difficult change, it chose an easy covering shot. (1948f:88)

Arisawa concluded that even if the government had not gone in a totally wrong direction, it was not achieving the major goal.

In his vision, Tsuru intended to base the priority production program on the foundation of democracy, replacing bureaucratic control with mass participation. In the first government white paper on the economy, titled *The Report on the Economic Situation* (*keizai jisson hokokusho*), which he drafted for the government in July 1947, Tsuru called for national endurance to overcome the economic hardship, as well as cooperation between the working class, management, and the state. This white paper asserted that the success of the priority production program would depend on mass participation by the Japanese people. It also stated, "It is the responsibility of a democratic government to report on the situation without hiding any facts, no matter how critical the situation is." Only by doing so would the state be able to obtain support from the general public. The white paper opposed bureaucratic control of people's lives by coercion. It argued that the Japanese people had been controlled by the state during the war. When this control was abolished in the postwar reform, the public lost the consensus about the future and became fragmented. "In democratic Japan the instrument for mobilizing the fragmented public for economic recovery is neither the whip nor the carrot – the whip is not allowed to be used, while the carrot is not available due to the poor conditions. Good cooperation is based on the spontaneous consent of eighty million citizens" (Gaimushō 1947:1). Following this logic, the white paper stated, "Since the Japanese people are the very essence of the national economy, they should be the masters of countermeasures themselves. They should encourage the government, which is elected by them, to pursue the success of countermeasures as its own business" (Keizai Antei Honbu [1947] 1965:178). The paper held that the Japanese should regard their endurance of temporary material shortages as something they had to do for themselves in an effort to carry out the mission of economic recovery.

Class interest or national interest?

The call for national endurance and cooperation between the state, management, and labor in the white paper stimulated a heated debate on whose interest should be the first priority: that of the nation or that of the working class.

At that time, Japanese ideologies had undergone profound changes. Japan's defeat in World War II caused a vacuum in intellectual authority. The subsequent collapse of the old emperor system significantly weakened the impact of nationalism. During the democratic reform, state control over thought was abolished; the basic values of Western societies, such as democracy, freedom, equality, and esteem for human beings, were introduced to Japan forcefully by the occupation authority, with the goal of ensuring that Japan would not again become a military threat to the world peace (Maruyama in Umemoto, Satō, and Maruyama 1966:10–13). Under such circumstances, the legitimacy of using the nation-state as the unit of analysis in policy debates became problematic. As a reaction to the wartime state control over civilians' freedom, calls to share national burdens did not easily gain legitimacy. A major contender to the wartime type of assertion of the national interest came from Marxism, which regained popularity in Japan in 1946–9. When a group of political prisoners who refused to convert to the emperor system were released, they were regarded as the only heroes who had resisted fascism. In a self-reexamination, many left-wing liberals and Marxists felt that they were responsible and guilty for not organizing to resist fascism in 1931–45. One of the major reasons, they believed, was that Japanese intellectuals as a social group had been too close to the state and had long been isolated from the ordinary people. To assume their responsibility as intellectuals in the Western sense – that is, to represent the interests of civil society – they believed, they should take a strong antistate position and draw a clear line with regard to state policy. This was the only way to prevent the return of the dark period (Takeuchi 1980:88–90). In this period, many former communists who had renounced their belief in Marxism reconverted to Marxism, causing a new wave of *tenkō* in Japanese intellectual history.

These Marxists rejected the notion of national interest. They took a conflict approach in the policy debates, emphasizing ways to protect the interest of the working class in the priority production program and rejecting the goal of cooperation. To Marxists who believed in class struggle, the call for cooperation between the state and society sounded like wartime psychology. They argued that since the Meiji Restoration, the Japanese people had been told that the will of the state and the national interest were more important than the interests of society and of individuals. After state control of civilian life was eliminated during the postwar reforms, they contended, the interest of society was no longer inferior to that of the state. According to one Marxist critic, "The call for national endurance and national unity had greatly polluted Japanese society and economy"; the white paper was "simply some dregs of the wartime ideology. . . . The present issue is not national endurance, but a fair distribution of materials among the Japanese people. . . . [T]he real task is to eliminate injustice, which should not be overshadowed by the slogan of national endurance" (Kishimoto 1947:12).

The Marxists believed that the cooperation with the state suggested by the white paper was "mainly designed for labor": "Throughout its content, the white paper kept asking labor to support the policy of freezing salaries. In exchange, what the government promised them was simply to eliminate the black market. . . . In the last analysis, only labor would bear the cost, though the white paper claimed that the priority production program would serve all the people" (Ōuchi 1947:2). According to Marxist analyses, although the white paper enumerated many phenomena of the economic crisis, it did not touch on the nature of the crisis at all (Kawasaki 1947:4). The huge deficit had resulted from spending on munitions during the war, followed by skyrocketing prices. "Focusing on the black market without touching those important issues simply reflects a perspective of pure laissez-faire economics or naive equilibrium theory" (Ōuchi 1947:3). "If the government really intends to plan the economic recovery based on the stability of daily life of ordinary people, the question would not be how to rebuild capital but how to abandon the capitalist mode of production" (Kawasaki 1947:5). As the first socialist cabinet in postwar Japan, the Katayama cabinet was the target of high expectations from Marxists. They stated that "The Socialist Party . . . should represent the interests of labor. Although sometimes political compromise is necessary, abstaining from the position of labor is equal to suicide" (Kishimoto 1947:12). In such an intellectual environment, the priority production program was perceived as not designed simply to promote production. Rather, it was thought to strengthen the dominance of "state-monopoly capitalism" because it employed "coercion by the state" for the "original accumulation of capital" through governmental subsidies to big business, state control over the distribution of materials, and favorable financing for big businesses by the RFB.

These sweeping criticisms angered those who were involved in state policy making. To those who regarded the survival of the nation as the top priority in state industrial policy, class as the unit of analysis was somewhat like an enlarged individual. According to Arisawa, class interest was still secondary to economic reconstruction because the working class would not be able to secure its own interests without successful economic reconstruction. He argued that "the struggle for class liberation today has to be conducted in the form of a struggle for production" (1948e:99). Nakayama Ichiro criticized the labor movement influenced by Marxism for representing "group egoism." Labor unions, according to his analysis, were not a constructive actor in the economic reconstruction because they had adopted the strike as the only strategy and did not care about the interests of others. Nakayama (1948b:14) held that

> it is understandable that labor adopted an aggressive strategy, especially in the antilabor atmosphere of capitalist society, because the labor union is an organization to protect group interests. Nonetheless, as the representative of new workers and the master of economic reconstruction, it is not a right attitude at all. . . . When the economy was disintegrated by the defeat and not reorganized as an organic whole, group egoism was the biggest artificially imposed obstacle to the reconstruction.

Ōtake Keisuke (1981:474) once noted that commentators on economic issues in the early postwar period were often "irresponsible" and "lopsided." "What they said was nothing but sharp and caustic abuse. Such characteristics of critics in the Japanese mass media were formed in the special environment of the postwar period and have lasted even until today." Tsuru Shigeto (1965:7) also pointed out that because the progressive forces did not have a realistic perspective, they had lost an opportunity to make real change.

Economic growth versus stability

By the end of 1947, the Japanese state had basically achieved the goal of producing 3 million tons of coal annually. At around that time, Arisawa Hiromi, Tsuru Shigeto, and several ESB bureaucrats discussed whether the state should take action to stabilize inflation immediately. Their conclusion was that it was still too early. As mentioned before, Arisawa asserted that the state would not act to eliminate inflation until production had recovered to 60% of the prewar level. His major concern was the reconstruction of the economy. According to this logic, reconstruction was the business of the Japanese themselves; to achieve this goal, they should not depend on foreign aid but rather on themselves. Organized labor had to work harder. According to Arisawa (1948e:99), participation in the struggle for production did not serve only the interests of capital but also those of the working class. By participating in this struggle, the working class would gain the power to influence the patterns of business management.

The Marxist Kimura Kihachirō delivered another attack on the priority production program in late 1947 by demanding that the state act to dampen inflation immediately. In Kimura's view, stability was more important than production to economic reconstruction because inflation would accelerate underproduction by forcing people to spend money on consumption immediately rather than directing their savings to production. Before inflation was controlled, it would be impossible to revive the economy because even after production was increased, reproduction and ultimate consumption would not increase immediately.

Kimura (1947) also asserted that the current policy adopted by the state to strengthen priority production served the interests of the capitalist class. He argued that because inflation was created by the floating capital that formed during the war and by the unfair profits made during the implementation of the priority production program, it was necessary for the state to levy a heavy tax on this money. In other words, inflation had to be eliminated at the expense of business interests. In this sense, the overemphasis on production had simply provided an excuse for capitalists to avoid taking this burden.

Kimura also asserted that the intensification of work in the priority production program was not in the interest of the working class. He pointed out:

> The output of coal in Japan reached its peak at 50 million tons in 1940. The well-known condition enabling Japan to keep the output of coal at the 50 million-ton level in 1941, 1942, and 1943 was the employment of foreign labor in terrible working conditions by cruel coercion. Now, such labor is no longer available. It has been replaced by Japanese workers who have the same rights and freedom as we do, liberated by democracy. In such a radically changed situation, in order to encourage workers' creativity and determination to strengthen production, the coal mining equipment, which was not initially in good condition and then was damaged further during the war, must

be improved. Any Japanese who once visited a mine must ask the question: "Who would like to work here under this kind of working conditions?" (1948:22)

Arisawa defended his production orientation in the debate. Because his major concern was the economic reconstruction of the national economy rather than the interest of a particular social class, he opposed immediate stabilization. Although he was well known for his anti-inflation policy and was strongly opposed to Ishibashi's Keynesian financial view, he disagreed with the idea that the Japanese state should adopt a tight money policy immediately. He asserted that underproduction was the major problem for the Japanese economy. According to Arisawa (1948d:77–8), the Japanese economy faced a major dilemma. On the one hand, the black market and the speculative behavior of economic actors were nurturing a severe crisis for the economy: "The longer the underproduction continues, the more severe the inflation will become. The larger the black market is, the more the short-term behavior in production will crop up. . . . Even if the economy could be sustained for a while by inflation and black markets, sooner or later the day will come when the economy will collapse." On the other hand, the existence of the black market and speculation at least were "protecting enterprises from bankruptcy and delaying the explosion of underproduction." If the state adopts tough measures to stabilize inflation at this moment, he said, there will be a "stabilization panic" in which "the elimination of inflation and the black market may result in many bankruptcies. Even if we have done this, production may still decline and streets will be full of the unemployed. Their damages to the entire economy will be terrible, and we will have no means at all to control the situation" (1948d:77–8). To minimize the impact of stabilization on the economy, Arisawa asserted that production must be increased to at least 60% of the prewar level before a tight money policy could be adopted.

The production orientation reflected in Arisawa Hiromi's idea of priority production had been a central theme in the policy paradigm of the managed economy. As the critics pointed out, Arisawa might have contributed greatly to identifying the direction of Japan's postwar economic reconstruction and development, but he failed to stress the necessity of establishing institutions that distributed income more equitably. The implementation of the priority production program exerted a strong impact on the state's industrial policy and the future pattern of

Japan's economic development (Hayasaka, Masamura, Takeyama, Hamaguchi, Shibata, and Hoshino 1974:58). As mentioned earlier, the moral and ethical criticisms of the priority production program reflected a rapidly changing ideological environment in early postwar Japan. As a result of democratic reforms, the demand for economic equality and the consciousness of social class, which had been suppressed in the ideology of the managed economy during 1931–45, revived, challenging the assertions for production and national interest. Nevertheless, as history indicates, these challenges were not strong enough to block the continuity of the wartime ideology in postwar Japanese industrial policy.

Foreign capital or national independence?

In March 1948, the Democratic Party politician Ashida Hitoshi became prime minister. He intended to rely on foreign investment to revive the economy and reestablish Japan's international credit. He regarded the introduction of foreign capital as an important measure for the priority production program. His rationale was that because the elimination of inflation required the promotion of production and because production needed capital accumulation, foreign investment was an important source of capital. This resulted in a new policy debate on how Japan should define the role of foreign capital in its postwar economy, in which cosmopolitanism clashed with nationalism.

Japan's defeat in World War II resulted in the collapse of the spiritual pillar of nationalism, which had supported the Japanese worldview since the Meiji Restoration. When the myth of the "unmatched Imperial Army" was shattered and the emperor disowned his divinity, the national identity of the Japanese was weakened considerably. Meanwhile, cosmopolitanism regained popularity. It was believed that Japan would soon rejoin the international community. The progressive intellectuals, according to Maruyama Masao, neglected the reality of Japan's occupation by a foreign country and enjoyed the liberties granted by the occupation (Maruyama 1982:113–14). The defeat and the occupation were interpreted not as a threat to the country, but as the result of misconceived collective efforts during the 15-year war. As early as 1946, the report by the Special Survey Committee Regarding Economic Recovery by the Ministry of Foreign Affairs had argued that financial aid would be the first step toward postwar reconstruction because the Japanese economy had been seriously damaged by the war. Its future would be determined by whether Japan could return to the international economy. Before 1948, however, Japan was not allowed to engage again in international trade, so this idea sounded like idle theorizing. In 1947, when the United States changed its policy toward Japan from democratization to support for its recovery, some Japanese believed that the chance had come for Japan to pursue this strategy.

Classical and neoclassical economists, in particular, regarded foreign investment as the key factor in stabilizing the economic situation and stimulating postwar reconstruction. Because Japan had lost all of its colonies, the Japanese economy could not survive without capital, technology, markets, and resources from the international market. Nakayama Ichirō was an active advocate of foreign investment. Drawing on the Russian and German experiences of economic reconstruction after their defeat in World War I, Nakayama believed that the future of the Japanese economy lay in participation in the international economy for two important reasons. First, the Japanese economy needed to build a solid foundation by accumulating capital and by channeling resources to the development of production equipment and technology. This goal could not be achieved without trade and foreign investment. Second, Japan needed to feed its huge population; this was one of the biggest problems of the Japanese economy at the time. To achieve full employment, Japan had to participate in international trade and solve this problem outside its borders. Nakayama examined the great famine that occurred in Ireland and England in 1846, in which Ireland's population declined to one-tenth that of England. He concluded that the major difference was that Ireland depended primarily on its domestic crop, whereas England benefited greatly from international trade with its colonies (Nakayama 1948c:66–73). Nakayama also believed that foreign investment would help to stabilize exchange rates and enable Japan to survive economic hard times through international trade. The stabilization of the economy in an isolated environment would never create conditions for fixing the exchange rate (Nakayama 1948c). Participation in the division of labor in the international economy had been the most important reason for Japan to industrialize since the Meiji Restoration; the postwar reconstruction would be no different.

This cosmopolitan perspective, however, was criticized by those who held strong nationalist positions. They believed that introduction of foreign capital would allow the Japanese economy to be controlled by other countries and that Japan should prevent the dominance of foreign capital in its domestic economy. The Marxist economist Nawa Tōichi (1947:26) regarded the initiative of business circles in introducing foreign capital as a strategy of the capitalist class to avoid tough measures against inflation and to counter the domestic demands for institutional reform. When foreign capital was introduced before inflation was brought under control, domestic production would be replaced by a flood of cheap foreign products, the domestic economy would be dominated by foreign capital, and domestic capital would be directed to other countries in order to keep its market value. This situation would destroy the productivity and export capacity of the Japanese economy. In the Marxist framework, the introduction of foreign capital was not a purely economic issue; it also concerned the issue of political independence. Arisawa argued that "capital is not a philanthropic gift. The dominance of huge foreign capital and üeberfremdung [excessive foreignization] will lead to loss of economic independence." In Arisawa's understanding, the two alternatives before the Japanese working class at the time were either to reconstruct the economy by their own efforts or to depend on foreign capital. It was a trade-off. Arisawa preferred the first; he said:

> I have no intention of charging the working class with the responsibility of rebuilding the Japanese economy independently [with minimum foreign aid]. They can choose to do nothing if they want. Nonetheless, what I want to tell them is that if they do nothing, the Japanese working class then perhaps will fall into the fate of suffering double exploitation. . . . If the economic recovery depends only on foreign aid, the working class will lose its right to speak. (Ōuchi et al. 1949:266–7)

Arisawa asserted that it would be better for Japan to accomplish the economic recovery through its own efforts. Even if foreign aid was needed, the amount should be kept to a minimum. In his thinking, foreign investment was not a technical or economic issue of how to accumulate capital, but a political issue concerning national sovereignty and the interests of labor.

This debate on foreign investment, which occurred in the late 1940s, reflected the ideological conflict between the inward orientation that Japan shared with Germany and Italy in the 1930s in its managed economy and the outward orientation derived from the principle of free trade asserted by liberal capitalism. It had a lasting impact on the Japanese economy. In postwar Japan, many bureaucrats, business leaders, intellectuals, and commentators believed that keeping foreign capital at a minimum was the correct strategy for protecting their nation's interests. Foreign capital, as Chapter 6 shows, became a critical issue again in the 1960s when Japan was forced to liberalize capital investment. The long-term impact of the inward orientation became more evident in the 1980s, when many countries criticized Japan for erecting too many barriers to foreign companies attempting to enter the Japanese markets when the flood of Japanese investment had created much economic friction.

The strategy of developing heavy-chemical industries

By early 1948, the Japanese state had finalized its long-term vision for economic reconstruction in the Plan for Economic Reconstruction (*Keizai fukkō keikaku*) made by the ESB. In the ESB, Inaba Hidezō was in charge of developing this plan. Its finalization was supervised by a special committee chaired by Arisawa Hiromi. Despite strong opposition from Marxists, Arisawa's view prevailed. The plan held that the state would wait for another two years to stabilize inflation.

The most important part of this plan was the announcement that Japan's postwar economic reconstruction would be based on the heavy-chemical industries. In 1931–45, the development of these industries had been part of the fascist program of preparing for total war. In this plan, it was given new meaning for economic development in peacetime. Nevertheless, it was still part of the grand strategy of building national power, though the focus was shifted from the military forces to wealth.

The initial motivation behind the Plan for Economic Reconstruction pertained to war reparations. As a defeated nation, Japan faced huge demands for war reparations from countries it had invaded and occupied during the war. According to the proposal prepared by the Pauley delegation sent by the U.S. government, which was published on 22 September 1945, half of Japan's manufacturing capability, all of the factories for the army and the navy, all of the factories that made airplanes, all of the factories that made ball bearings, all of the equipment in factories that made airplanes engines, all of the equipment and supplementary equipment of 20 shipbuilding factories, the annual 2.5-million-ton iron and steel production capacity, half of the power stations, and many other manufacturing elements in Japan would be confiscated for war reparations. The proposal stated that "the peoples oppressed by Japan have the first priority while Japan has the last." In Pauley's opinion, in order to weaken Japan's capacity to wage another war, Japan's economic scale must be restricted. For example, the annual production of iron and steel should be less than 180 million tons, and chemical industries should not be allowed to develop. When Pauley's report was published at the end of 1945, the Japanese viewed it as a threat to their economy (Nakamura and Ōmori 1990:v). Japanese bureaucrats at the Ministry of Foreign Affairs, the Ministry of Commerce and Industry, the Ministry of Agriculture and Forestry, and the Ministry of Finance began a study of the future level of Japanese industry in order to develop a counterargument to Pauley's report (Keizai Kigakuchō 1964:79). In 1947 a policy proposal drafted by GHQ officials regarding the future of the Japanese economy was leaked to Japanese bureaucrats at the ESB. Wada Hiroo, the director of the ESB, and Inaba Hidezō, deputy director of the director's secretariat, decided to create an official plan for the Japanese government in order to counter the GHQ's proposal and to persuade the Occupation Authority to change its policy (Inaba 1988:58–9). Accordingly, the ESB established the Economic Planning Division, headed by Inaba, to draft the Plan for Economic Reconstruction.

In this plan, the development of heavy-chemical industries aimed at positioning the Japanese economy strategically in a changing international environment. The perception of the challenge to the Japanese economy from developing economies in Asia was an important reason why heavy-chemical industries continued to be the major objective in Japanese industrial policy. This plan argued that it was almost impossible for Japan to build a self-sufficient economy in the near future because of the limits on natural resources, the poor condition of the domestic infrastructure, the increasing population, the constraints on capital, the increase in marginal production costs, international competitiveness, and the difficulties of trade. Therefore "the Japanese economy should follow the trend of economic development demonstrated by history, and structure itself to the global economy with active participation" (Nakamura and Hara 1990:196). In the international division of labor, Asian countries would soon replace Japan in light industries, as they had much cheaper labor. On the basis of this understanding, the plan asserted that state industrial policy should emphasize heavy-chemical industries in order to shift the structure of exports from cotton and silk to machinery and chemical products, and at the same time to enable Japan to reduce the amount of imports by using its domestic resources more efficiently (Nakamura and Hara 1990:197).

Because this plan contradicted the Dodge Plan on the issue of inflation, it was not officially accepted. Nevertheless, the vision of developing heavy-chemical industries was inherited and became the central theme in Japanese industrial policy since the 1950s.

The end of the managed economy

Implementation of the priority production program was largely successful in promoting productivity in key industries. If the integral productivity index between 1934 and 1936 was rated at 100, it improved rapidly from 22.6 in March 1947 to 55.2 in March 1949. Annual production per miner jumped from 5.8 tons in April 1948 to 8 tons in March 1949. Nevertheless, the Japanese economy still did not rest on a solid foundation.

In 1948 the U.S. government changed its policy toward Japan. In the early stages of the occupation, the American policy toward Japan was "to insure that Japan will not again become a menace to the United States or to the peace and security of the world" (SWNCC-150/3 [1945] 1982). To achieve this goal, GHQ conducted a series of democratic reforms. Meanwhile, it did not engage in economic reconstruction, but left this task primarily in the hands of the Japanese government. At the same time, however, the U.S. government had to provide roughly $400 million a year in aid to Japan. On 6 January 1948, K. G. Royall, the secretary of the U.S. Army, delivered his famous speech in San Francisco. He declared that the U.S. government had realized that it "cannot forever continue to pour hundreds of millions of dollars annually into relief funds for occupied areas." The United States, he said, should help Japan "to promote recovery and thereby hasten the day when Japan will cease to be a financial burden to the United States" and be able to sustain "a self-sufficient democracy, strong enough and stable enough to support itself and at the same time to serve as [a] deterrent against any other totalitarian war threats which might hereafter arise in the Far East" (Royall [1948] 1982:185–6). In

October of that year, the U.S. government adopted new policies toward Japan, proposed by George F. Kennan and William H. Draper, Jr., including decreasing aid, eliminating state control of the private sector, stabilizing labor relations, controlling inflation, and adopting a balanced budget. In December 1948 the United States sent Joseph M. Dodge, president of the Detroit Bank and financial consultant to the U.S. government, as envoy to Japan. Dodge regarded the Japanese economy at that time as a "stilts" economy that stood on two feet: The private sector depended heavily on government subsidies, and the Japanese government depended heavily on financial aid from the United States. To end this situation, the Japanese state had to take effective measures to eliminate inflation immediately. Dodge designed a complete policy package for the Japanese government known as the *Dodge Plan*. The implementation of the Dodge Plan ended the era of the managed economy.

Conclusion

This chapter has shown that many institutions and ideologies of the managed economy, due to various structural factors, not only survived the political storm of democratization, but also influenced Japanese industrial policy in 1946–9 and were inherited as part of the foundation by postwar Japanese developmentalism.

The legacy of the managed economy shaped the way economic actors perceived their interest and devised their strategy. Some major policy makers who designed or implemented the priority production program had practiced the managed economy in 1931–45, and their policy orientation exerted a strong influence on Japanese industrial policy in 1946–9. Arisawa Hiromi, who was deeply involved in designing the economic new order for the Konoe cabinet, became the chief advisor to Prime Minister Yoshida Shigeru. Wada Hiroo, Inaba Hidezō, and several others, who had worked in the CSB, the CPA, and the CPB in the 1930s and early 1940s, occupied important positions in the state bureaucracy in 1946–9. It is not difficult to imagine why the Japanese state relied heavily on the policy instruments and institutions that had developed during the war. As mentioned before, these men had been arrested as communists in the late 1930s and early 1940s. For this reason, they were portrayed as progressive to the general public. This representation played down and even concealed their close connections with the wartime operation of the managed economy and provided legitimacy for their policy proposals.

The seriousness of the economic crisis and the perception of national isolation in the early postwar period also helped the developmental ideology to prevail in state industrial policy. Because of hyperinflation and the severe shortage of materials, production was perceived as the top priority in industrial policy, tight control over resource allocation was regarded as indispensable for national survival, and state intervention was believed to be the only way for Japan to overcome its economic crisis. In the midst of a great economic crisis, the pro-market policy could hardly convince the general public because the market was perceived as undermining economic order and social stability. Therefore, despite strong challenges from Western individualism and Marxist class analysis, the nation-state remained the unit of analysis in Japanese economic thinking and the state-centered ideology prevailed in policy debates. This pro-state orientation was strengthened by the perception of Japan's national isolation and by the distrust of the GHQ's policy concerning Japan's postwar reconstruction.

Nevertheless, after the defeat in World War II, Japanese capitalism was at a turning point. It confronted a major challenge from liberal capitalism and had an opportunity to depart from its wartime legacies. The democratic reforms profoundly changed the structure of the Japanese economy and society. In this new environment, the assertions for production, bureaucratic control, and national interest in the state industrial policy encountered strong resistance from various social groups. Although both 1931–45 and 1946–9 can be categorized as periods of managed economy, the political environments in these two eras differed considerably. In 1931–45, the unit of analysis in the policy debates was moving from the individual and the social class to the nation-state, influenced by the rise of fascism. In 1946–9, by contrast, it was moving away from the nation-state to the individual and the social class, influenced by the democratic reforms. This means that although the developmental orientation of the wartime legacies survived, it had to adapt to a new political environment.

The GHQ's policy toward Japan was one of the most important structural factors in explaining both the continuities and discontinuities of the wartime legacies in 1946–9. On the one hand, the GHQ was the major initiator of change. Its democratic reforms considerably changed Japan's economic and social structures. On the other hand, the

GHQ's policy also created a favorable environment for many elements of the wartime system to continue. It indeed demilitarized the Japanese economy by eliminating the military. At the same time, however, it strengthened the position of bureaucrats in policy making and enabled the state to break down the barriers of bureaucratic sectionalism. The dissolution of *zaibatsu* indeed contributed greatly to the economic democracy of postwar Japan, even if it was not carried out as initially planned. This also destroyed the foundation of the prewar company system, in which shareholders had strong power to monitor management.

In the managed economy in both 1931–45 and 1946–9, Japanese industrial policy emphasized the effectiveness of resource allocation by the state at the macro level rather than production efficiency at the micro level. Due to Japan's isolation from the international market, how to survive economically by making efficient use of limited domestic resources was a critical issue. Under such circumstances, the state made great efforts to constrain the market forces. It not only depended on direct bureaucratic intervention, but it also encouraged the development of nonmarket governance structures. In the ideology of the managed economy, the profit motive of private companies was thought to conflict with national goals. The state concentrated on how to make individual companies function better as part of the entire economic system under the guidance of the state, rather than on how to help them make profits.

The Japanese experience during the managed economy also indicates the complicated relationship between the decentralized administrative system and the Japanese perception of democracy. In Japan, decentralized administration was regarded as an indicator of liberal capitalism, whereas efforts to centralize state leadership were often considered planning or the sign of a socialist orientation. For this reason, both the occupation authority and the Japanese bureaucrats regarded the establishment of the ESB as a temporary measure to combat the economic crisis. Both sides failed to realize that in the long run, this perception would leave an unsolved problem regarding the leadership of the Japanese state.

5. Promoting exports

Promoting exports was the leading paradigm of Japanese industrial policy in the 1950s. This paradigm had a profound effect on the Japanese economic system. Unlike the 1946–9 period, in which the wartime legacies were either challenged or were simply inherited without much adaptation, Japanese developmentalism in the 1950s demonstrated a strong capacity for innovation in the new environment. It started the transformation from the military version to a trade version for peacetime.

Kenneth Pyle (1992:139–40) writes that the United States twice played an important role in transforming the organizing structure of regional politics in Asia after both world wars ended. The establishment of the Pax Americana after World War II shaped Japan's postwar order. "The extraordinary rise of Japan as an economic superpower is, to a considerable extent, the result of this special relationship [with the United States]" (Pyle 1992:141). Beginning at the end of the 1940s, the Pax Americana determined the external environment of the Japanese economy in two decisive ways. First, the implementation of the Dodge Plan in 1949 directly linked the Japanese economy with the international market. As discussed in Chapter 3, Japan's wartime economic system had a strong anticapitalist orientation, marked by restraints on market competition and the rejection of the profit principle. In 1946–9, due to various structural factors, the managed economy not only continued but was even enhanced. When Japan was again forced to survive international competition after more than one decade's isolation, competitiveness and efficiency became the top issues in Japanese industrial policy. Second, as the Korean War broke out, the huge amount of special procurement and the increasing pressure for rearmament from the U.S. government forced Japan to be integrated into the Cold War system. The nation faced the choice of continuing to build the economy on the basis of military production or searching for a new strategy.

173

The impact of the postwar democratic reforms on the economy remained largely structural. In contrast, the wartime legacies encountered serious challenges in the 1950s.

Responding to these two great challenges, two grand strategies were formulated. Prime Minister Yoshida Shigeru prescribed a political strategy to respond to the challenge of the Cold War. Yoshida argued that Japan should stand on the U.S. side politically in exchange for economic aid while limiting its defense expenditures to a minimum and concentrating all its resources on economic development. By doing so, Japan would be able to obtain economic advantages from the United States and meanwhile avoid the danger of direct involvement in military conflicts between the two blocs. In the 1950s, Japan was at a crossroads because different versions of nationalist ideologies clashed on the issues of rearmament and the revision of the constitution. As the Korean War broke out, some business leaders and former military officials asserted that Japan should be integrated into the Cold War system economically and militarily through rearmament and should build up its industrial structure based on the production of weapons. This stream of conservative political nationalism intended to restore Japan's former status as one of the great powers in the old way. In contrast, the progressive forces asserted the need for independent diplomacy and neutrality in international politics. They strongly opposed rearmament and regarded this policy as serving only the interests of business circles while making the whole nation risk the danger of involvement in military conflicts between the socialist bloc, headed by the Soviet Union, and the capitalist bloc, headed by the United States. Although the rearmament program was seriously undermined by conflicts among business leaders and among state bureaucracies, the dispute over the national purpose was not settled until the 1960s (Pyle 1992).

The other strategy was to build up Japan's comparative advantage in production technology in order to promote exports. The diffusion of Joseph A. Schumpeter's theory of innovation played a very important role in forming the Japanese strategy of promoting exports. This theory fundamentally changed the Japanese definition of comparative advantage in international trade. Foreseeing the fourth industrial revolution, Japanese economists turned Schumpeter's explanatory theory of long-term economic change based on innovation by entrepreneurs into a prescriptive strategy for international competition. According to the

Japanese understanding of Schumpeter's theory of innovation, a strategic position in future international competition would depend on comparative advantage in production technology. Unlike comparative advantages in cheap labor or raw materials, which are natural endowments to a country, comparative advantage in production technology must be built up by purposeful effort. To build such an advantage, the Japanese state must not only help private companies with government loans for aggressive investments in production equipment and technological transfer, but also must support or initiate institutional reforms at the company level, making the managerial environment supportive of the innovation effort. This new idea changed the way economic actors defined their interest and how they derived their responding strategy. Some progressive managers were enlightened by the German experience, which relied on nationalism to stabilize labor relations during the postwar reconstruction. They began to advocate the traditional value of harmony and of cooperation between labor and management. This action was designed to weaken the impact of both the Marxist claim of class struggle, which had dominated Japanese labor movements since the end of World War II, and the profit principle, which revived during the rationalization movement in the early 1950s. Nevertheless, these efforts did not obtain wide support from management and labor until the 1960s.

Under the policy paradigm of promoting exports, two conflicting trends occurred in the Japanese economic system. On the one hand, bureaucratic controls over the distribution of materials and prices, which had been practiced by the Japanese state in 1931–45 and were even strengthened in 1946–9, assumed a more sophisticated form. The focus of state industrial policy shifted from controlling resource allocation by bureaucrats to promoting the competitiveness of Japanese companies in strategic industries, and the principle of rejecting competition changed to restraining excessive competition. Although the market began to resume its function, the state still restrained competition considerably by controlling imports, credit, and foreign exchange in order to serve its policy objective. On the other hand, some components of developmentalism, such as business groups and labor relations, which were strongly challenged by the postwar democratic reforms, began to revive in new forms with state support. Japanese developmentalism began to transform itself from the military version to a trade version. The inward orientation that prevailed in the managed economy was replaced by an aggressive outward orientation. The Japanese industrial policy in this period, as Yonezawa Yoshie (1993:231) points out, was "very mercantilist, selective, and competition-constrained." These two strategies encountered strong resistance due to their competing agendas. Nevertheless, they prescribed the future course of the Japanese economy.

The revival of the wartime legacies did not simply repeat the practices themselves, but adapted to the new environment considerably. The reorganization of the former *zaibatsu* companies into *keiretsu* and the effort to stabilize labor relations were no longer governed simply by pressure for cooperation and unity in national crises such as the Great Depression and World War II. Now they were guided by the desire to build up national competitiveness in production technology. By shifting the concept of comparative advantage from cheap labor, which had often resulted in massive layoffs, to production technology, which required cooperation between management and labor, these institutional arrangements were regarded as new weapons for Japan to compete in the international market. In this new policy paradigm, the production orientation was no longer measured by how much companies should produce, but rather by how and what to produce. In other words, the focus of Japanese industrial policy shifted from the quantity of production, which had been a major concern in both the managed economy during World War II and the priority production program in the early postwar period, to the quality of production and production technology in strategic industries, which would add more value in the international market. This shift indicates a significant new development in the strategic view of the economy. According to many accounts, the adoption of the policy paradigm of promoting exports was a watershed in the postwar Japanese economy.

The pressures for economic independence

The implementation of the Dodge Plan was a great challenge to the managed economy, forcing the Japanese economic system to adapt to a new environment.

The operation of the Japanese economy in the early postwar period had been supported what Dodge called "two stilts": financial aid from the United States to the Japanese government and government subsidies to private companies. In this "stilts economy," 70% of consumer prices were supported by government subsidies, and about $400 million of the annual budget of the Japanese government was provided by the United States. The Dodge Plan aimed at placing the Japanese economy on a solid foundation while ending U.S. aid to Japan. On 11 December 1948, the Department of the Army of the U.S. government sent SCAP its "Nine-Part Interim Directive on Stabilization," which established two major principles for the Japanese economy. First, the Japanese government should stabilize the economy as soon as possible by taking whatever measures were necessary to eliminate inflation and achieve stability in financial and monetary system, prices, and wages. To attain this goal, the Japanese government should "achieve a true balance in the consolidated budget," "pursue maximum expansion in total government revenues," and "assure rigorous limitation in the extension of credit." Second, the Japanese economy would be linked with the international market by a fixed exchange rate, with 1 dollar equal to 360 yen. From then on, the Japanese had to balance their international payments by participating in trade. Japanese companies should no longer depend on government subsidies but should build up their own competitiveness in the international market. In other words, Japan had to achieve economic independence by promoting exports (Masamura 1985:359).

The implementation of the Dodge Plan created a completely new environment for the Japanese economy, which required a drastic change in Japanese industrial policy. In the managed economy, as Ōkita Saburō (1949) pointed out, industrial policy had been driven by the principle of resource mobilization, which regarded production as the top priority and treated cost as a secondary issue. Tight control over competition and rejection of the profit principle had made inefficiency the major problem in the economy. Now the economic institutions at the micro level had to be rationalized. Without promoting efficiency, Japanese companies would never be able to compete internationally. Without promoting exports, moreover, the Japanese economy could never balance its international payments because Japan, as a country with few natural resources, had to import massively.

The mission to ensure Japan's position in the international market, however, was constrained by a number of structural factors. First, in comparison with the prewar period, Japan's overseas markets had been reduced drastically, not only because its Western trading partners had instituted an economic embargo during the war but also because Japan had lost its colonies and occupied areas in Asia after the defeat. In terms of exports, Japan had fallen from 5th in the world in 1934 to 33rd in 1947. If the average level of Japanese exports between 1930 and 1934 was rated at 100, it was only 8.8 in 1946, 11.7 in 1947, and 16.2 in 1948 (Tsusanshō 1954:93). In addition, the structure of the international market constrained Japanese exports because most industrialized countries in the West were suffering from a shortage of dollars during the postwar reconstruction. To overcome this shortage, they all tried to restrict imports while promoting exports. Meanwhile, many developing countries began their industrialization programs after the war. This further increased the global shortage of dollars, which, in turn, restricted the imports of consumer goods in many countries.

Second, the structure of Japanese exports, which concentrated on labor-intensive industries, could not generate enough hard currency to balance its international payments. Despite the rapid development of heavy-chemical industries during World War II, Japanese exports in the early 1950s were still dominated by textile products, whose proportion of total exports was as high as 75.5% in 1947 and 61.1% in 1948. At that time, the use of cheap labor was the Japanese companies' major strategy for increasing exports. According to a survey, the average hourly salary in Japanese industries in May 1949 was 62.74 yen, whereas those in Britain and the United States were 221.20 yen and 494.28 yen, respectively; workers' salaries in Britain and the United States were 3.5 and 7.9 times higher, respectively, than those in Japan. This cheap labor policy was maintained particularly in the textile industry, where the hourly salary was only 21.55 yen, in comparison to 183.49 yen in Britain and 428.15 yen in the United States. In the spinning industry, the hourly salary was only 13.50 yen in Japan, in comparison to 156.24 yen in Britain and 387.36 yen in the United States. Japan's cheap labor policy caused strong reactions both internationally and domestically. Not only did Britain and the United States protest Japanese dumping practices, the labor unions in Japan also went on strike frequently and asked for salary increases (*Ekonomisuto* 1950b). Under such circumstances, it was impossible for Japanese companies to generate enough hard currency from their exports. Therefore the Japanese economy was always constrained by the bottleneck in foreign reserves.

Third, although the Japanese economy was forced to promote exports, it was in bad condition because of the poor competitiveness of

Japanese companies. The low quality of Japanese products was a major barrier preventing Japanese companies from competing with their foreign counterparts. In the early 1950s, Japanese products in the international market were still known for their low price but poor quality. From the end of World War II to April 1950, the Ministry of International Trade and Industry (MITI) received 634 claims from foreign consumers. Of these, 327 concerned the poor quality of products, and 366 came from the United States, Japan's largest trading partner. Before World War II, the government or an authorized agency had had the power to examine all major export products, but this system was abandoned during the democratic reforms after the war. In the new system, the government defined grades, standards, and conditions for export products, and private companies examined their own products according to these criteria. Poor quality resulting from the absence of competition became a life-and-death issue when Japan came under strong pressure to promote exports in the early 1950s (*Ekonomisuto* 1950a:23).

The program of promoting exports

The Dodge Plan was carried out immediately. At the end of 1948, the RFB stopped issuing loans. Meanwhile the budget deficit, which was 92.3 billion yen in 1946, 103.9 billion in 1947, and 141.9 billion in 1948, was eliminated dramatically. The government budget for fiscal year 1949 achieved a "super balance," 156.9 billion yen in the black (Masamura 1985:359). Business circles, however, influenced by the deflation policy, suffered a great shortage of capital. To lessen the impact of the stabilization panic on the economy, the Japanese state decided to adopt a disinflation policy by providing 92.1 billion yen in credit to the private sector.

How did the implementation of the Dodge Plan and the program of promoting exports influence the governance structure of the Japanese economy?

The Japanese state responded to this challenge aggressively by replacing the inward orientation that dominated the managed economy with an outward orientation toward international competition. Promoting exports was regarded as the top priority for state industrial policy. Within the state bureaucracy, the Ministry of Commerce and Industry and the Board of Trade were merged to form the Ministry of International Trade and Industry. The establishment of MITI signaled the rapid departure of Japanese industrial policy from the managed economy. To demonstrate its determination in promoting exports, MITI reorganized, attaching the prefix "international trade" to the name of each of its bureaus. As Chalmers Johnson (1982:191–2) points out, this transition in state policy orientation "probably had as great an impact on the Japanese and world economies as any of Dodge's measures."

The strategic view of the economy continued to influence the state industrial policy. The wartime focus on developing heavy-chemical industries was carried on in the 1950s but was given new meaning. It no longer aimed at producing weapons, but rather at optimizing the industrial structure of the economy in order to maximize Japan's gain from international trade. This policy creatively revised the orthodox definition of comparative advantage. It asserted that a nation's comparative advantage in international trade did not have to be based on given factors such as natural resources. It could also be built up strategically. In the global competition for wealth among nation-states, Japan's comparative advantage in cheap labor at the time could not generate much gains in the future because it would soon be replaced by developing countries. In order to build up its comparative advantage in production technology, the Japanese state had to allocate resources strategically. Facing a tough international environment, Japan decided to engage in international competition aggressively by pursuing the comparative advantage in production technology. This policy distinguished Japanese developmentalism clearly from those developing economies that focused on either exporting natural resources or substituting imports.

In order to build up a comparative advantage in production technology, the state established an industrial assistance system in its financial and monetary policies. This consisted of a low-interest-rate policy practiced by the Bank of Japan, government investment and finance, and tax deduction programs.

The state continued to control the interest rate. The Bank of Japan not only backed up the loans issued by private banks to manufacturers, but also provided loans directly to commercial banks. Even when it had to tighten the money supply for the sake of making international payments, the Bank of Japan did not raise the interest rate in general, but instead changed the quota of its loan to private banks on certain projects through the so-called window regulation (*madoguchi kisei*).

To promote exports and nurture strategic industries, the state, supported by the postal-saving system, established the Export Bank in 1950 (which was renamed the Export-Import Bank in 1952) to provide long-term export credit and the Development Bank in 1951 to provide capital to key industries, such as the electric and shipbuilding industries. Tax deductions and government subsidies were applied widely to encourage technological transfer and investment in heavy-chemical industries (Masamura 1985:366–72).

In the iron and steel industry, the private sector and MITI together devised a rationalization plan that set a 10% annual growth rate for capital investment. Because this level was far beyond the financial capacity of individual companies, the state provided 15% of the total capital for investments, whereas the companies' own capital accounted for less than 25% (Arisawa 1976:345). According to a 1957 MITI report, industrial investment in the 1950s "showed an orientation toward emphasizing the development of basic industries and catching up to the global trend of technological innovation by investing in new industrial fields and new technologies" (Tsūsanshō 1957). The aggressive investment in production equipment and technological transfer aimed not only to bridge the gap between Japan and the West, but also to occupy the future strategic industries. Between 1950 and 1966, Japan imported 4,135 technological patents, of which 77% were for machinery and chemical technologies. The United States, the biggest technological exporter to Japan in this period, sold 2,471 of the 4,135 patents imported by Japanese companies (Arisawa 1969:30–2).

Under the policy paradigm of promoting exports, the relationship between the state and the market changed significantly. The principle of rejecting competition in the managed economy was upgraded to rejecting excessive competition. The state no longer replaced the market but instead organized it. The state abolished bureaucratic controls over material distribution and prices but continued to practice a discriminatory policy concerning government credit and foreign currency exchange. With this transition, the state began to nurture the development of Japan's strategic industries by two means: First, as mentioned earlier, it provided some companies with favorable conditions in terms of market competition, rather than replacing competition with administrative means. Second, it prevented other companies from engaging in competition by enacting strict government regulations. In the managed economy, the function of the market was basically rejected. In the 1950s, in contrast, the state intended to use the market to promote the competitiveness of Japanese companies while trying to organize market competition to work for its policy objectives. In other words, although the function of the market was reintroduced, it was not left alone. Despite the fact that the state changed its method of intervention, the strategic nature of industrial policy remained. Beginning in the 1950s, the relationship between the state and the market in Japanese industrial policy was no longer exclusive but became supplementary in nature. The state capacity that developed in the managed economy underwent some important innovations in the 1950s. This characteristic distinguishes Japanese developmentalism from both liberal capitalism and socialism. Even in its early stage in the 1930s, as noted in Chapter 3, it was influenced by both an anticapitalist and an anticommunist orientation. The so-called the free economy in postwar Japan is considerably different from the laissez-faire Anglo-Saxon economies.

Although the market was reinstated, competition was still under strong constraints. MITI's 1957 White Paper on the Rationalization of Industry argued:

> Several conditions in the environment of a national economy and the market structure may constrain the role of competition. In a country where there are not abundant resources but a huge population, the freedom of economic activity itself is restricted and the competition often becomes inadequately excessive. Human beings sometimes do not behave according to economic rationalism. If a national economy depends heavily on the international market, it will be strongly influenced by the fluctuation of economic cycles, which often disturbs economic stability unnecessarily. Moreover, the modernization and rationalization of an economy in a comparatively late-developing country need active assistance from the state. Competition is never the best method. (Tsūsanshō 1957:287)

Laissez-faire competition indeed stimulated economic growth, according to this document. Nevertheless, as companies competed for capital in their investment in production equipment, crises often occurred in Japan's international payments, creating an obstacle to economic growth. To sustain long-term, stable economic growth, the Japanese economy had to organize industries and business organizations.

To balance its international payments, the state tightly controlled foreign exchange by enacting the Law Regarding Foreign Exchange and Foreign Trade. Under this law, all foreign currencies earned by private companies in exports must be submitted to the government, and the foreign currency needed for imports or other purposes was controlled by the quota established by the government. The government decided the quota of foreign currency according to its policy objective. This system existed until 1964, when Japan finally liberalized trade. This policy had two effects. First, it made efficient use of limited foreign currency. Second, by constraining imports, it protected domestic industries and gave them time to strengthen their international competitiveness. In 1951, Japan also started a tariff system characterized by low tariffs for raw materials and important production equipments and high tariffs for foreign products that competed with Japanese industries.

The Japanese state revised the antimonopoly law twice – in 1949 and 1953 – and dismissed the Shareholding Company Readjustment Committee in July 1951. Japan's antimonopoly law was enacted in 1947 under the pressure of the Occupation Authority. The revisions of this law aimed at encouraging the reorganization of former *zaibatsu* companies. Through these revisions of the antimonopoly law, the Japanese state ceased to prohibit common actions by multiple companies; cartels were allowed to operate to reduce the impact of economic recession and to rationalize the production process. Meanwhile, the state relaxed its control over intercompany shareholding and appointment of personnel, which formerly had been regarded as monopolistic behavior. In contrast to antitrust practice in the United States, whose primary goal was to ensure equality of business opportunity for individual companies and to protect the interests of individual consumers, the Japanese antimonopoly law aimed at strengthening the competitiveness of the nation by eliminating excessive competition (*kado kyōsō*), which was believed to dissipate Japan's limited capital and material resources, and by encouraging the concentration of capital and material resources in big companies in order to develop strategic industries (Arisawa 1976:351–2; Tsūsanshō 1989; Yamamura 1967). Arisawa Hiromi (Koizumi and Miyazaki 1967b:176–277) argued that big companies play a very important role in research and development. From the beginning of Japanese industrialization, he continued, it was the big companies that had commercialized various results of basic research. Because research and development in the 1950s were seriously constrained by the size and financial capacity of companies, Arisawa contended, Japan had to concentrate its limited financial resources on big businesses in order to support technological innovation.

Influenced by the state policy, former *zaibatsu* companies began to reorganize themselves into *keiretsu* in the 1950s. Big commercial banks became the center of business groups. Because Japanese companies suffered a great shortage of capital when they hurried to develop their heavy-chemical industries, banks became the major provider of business finance. During this process, banks became shareholders of the companies. The average proportion of stock held by banks in companies affiliated with Mitsui, Mitsubishi, and Sumitomo, for example, increased from 7.1% in 1952 to 11.5% in 1955. In the meantime, intercompany shareholding also developed rapidly. For example, shareholding by the Mitsubishi group jumped from 11.7% to 33.5% after the group was reunited in 1954. These *keiretsu*, especially Mitsubishi and Mitsui, also reorganized their trading companies, which had been dissolved during the occupation. A major difference between the prewar *zaibatsu* and the postwar *keiretsu*, however, was that *zaibatsu* were organized around the central holding companies, which were under the control of the *zaibatsu* families, whereas *keiretsu* were organized around banks but did not have a center of authority. As a major form of business integration, the famous presidents' meetings within the group became regular activities; the banks where these meetings were held functioned as the headquarters for each *keiretsu* organization (Arisawa 1976:341).

In the 1950s, the state enacted a series of industry laws: the Temporary Law Regarding the Rationalization of the Coal Industry in 1955, the Temporary Law Regarding the Promotion of Machine Tool Industry and the Temporary Law Regarding the Equipment in Fiber Industry in 1956, and the Temporary Law Regarding the Promotion of Electronic Industry and the Temporary Law Regarding the Production Equipment of Raw Silk in 1957. All of these industry laws allowed private companies to organize the market through cartels. They aimed at either promoting strategic industries with high growth potential or relieving sunset industries of structural declines and helping them in the transition (Masamura 1985:375–6).

With regard to the nature of the Japanese economic system in the 1950s, there is an interesting discrepancy in analysis. In the English literature, the 1950s is typically regarded as an extension period in which the state still exercised great control over the economy. In the Japanese literature, however, there is a clear distinction between the managed economy, which lasted until the implementation of the Dodge Plan in 1949, and the free economy (*jiyū keizai*), which started in the early 1950s. This discrepancy comes from the difference in conceptualization. Western scholars' conceptualization is centered on the state. Although one particular pattern of state intervention changed, the interventionist nature of state industrial policy still remained. In contrast, many Japanese scholars' conceptualizations are centered on the economy, in which two different patterns of state intervention refer to two completely different concepts. When the bureaucrats controlled the distribution of materials and prices, the economy was called the managed economy. When this control was abolished, it became the free economy. Combining the wisdom of both sides yields some insights for our analysis on the Japanese economy in the 1950s because it implies that although state intervention continued, it had changed profoundly, or that despite the profound changes in the pattern of state intervention, the nature of state industrial policy remained.

The rejection of the profit principle was inherited and bestowed with new meaning. During the war, the pursuit of shareholders' profit was regarded as conflicting with the national interest of surviving the war. In the 1950s, it was still regarded as conflicting with the national goal of building up competitiveness in strategic industries, which required companies to invest more and pay out less in dividends. According to Masamura Kimihiro (1985, Vol. 1:368), the taxation policy adopted by the state also hampered the profit principle by discouraging the development of the stock market. At the time, the dividends to shareholders were regarded as company profits, which were subject to tax, whereas the interest on loans paid to commercial banks was regarded as the cost of borrowing, which was tax free. Therefore, it was much cheaper for the companies to borrow money from banks than to issue stock. This, together with other factors, further weakened the power of shareholders in the management of the company while strengthening the autonomy of managers. As a result, the impact of the profit principle further declined.

An issue related to the profit principle was the problem of efficiency and its implication for labor relations. Although the profit principle never strongly challenged Japanese companies in the early postwar period, the issue of efficiency became a top concern after the implementation of the Dodge Plan. Business leaders argued as follows:

> The reconstruction and independence of the Japanese economy rely upon the promotion of exports. The promotion of exports is impossible without rationalizing companies . . . the goal of rationalizing companies is to produce, as much as possible, low-priced products with good quality . . . the rationalization of companies in the managed economy was controlled by the policy and administration of the state. As a result, irrationality and inefficiency were the biggest obstacles to the rationalization of companies. In order to make Japanese companies competitive internationally, we need to eliminate bureaucratic control and its major problems, such as unrealistic equality, and introduce the principles of free competition and efficiency. (Nikeiren [1948] 1966: 183)

Responding to the challenge of efficiency, Japanese companies began to introduce American managerial technologies in the 1950s, including industrial engineering, quality control, and top management. Industrial engineering was introduced in 1955 by the first delegation sent to the United States for the purpose of improving productivity in the iron and steel industry. Beginning at that time, industrial engineering boomed. Many American industrial engineering experts were invited to Japan to give seminars and advice. In 1959 the Japanese Association of Industrial Engineering was established and began to publish the first professional journal, *Industrial Engineering*. The well-known practice of quality control was introduced to Japan in the early 1950s. In the initial stage, this was primarily a managerial technique for engineers in firms. It was later extended to the famous concept of *total quality control*, which involved all employees. The Japan Science and Technology Federation began to organize seminars for managers at division and department levels in 1955 and for top managers in 1957. In the late 1950s, short-wave broadcasts and television were used to disseminate information about quality control nationwide. The new approach to top management centered on decision making. The CEOs' power in management was strengthened according to the American model, and from then on, the CEOs generally made decisions, which the boards of trustees approved. Meanwhile, the controller system was established to provide internal supervision (Tsūsanshō 1990a, vol. 6:389–91).

With regard to labor relations, the Japanese response to the challenge of efficiency was not linear. The rationalization program that started at the end of the 1940s was initially influenced by the orthodox practice of liberal capitalism – reducing production costs by layoff. From February 1949 to May 1950, 10,375 private firms fired 400,000 employees, while government and public agencies laid off 419,000 persons (Rekishigaku Kenkyūkai 1990:137). Meanwhile most firms froze hiring and began to use temporary and nonskilled workers, who earned much lower salaries than regular workers (Takajima 1953). As late as 1954, Japanese steel, coal, and chemical firms still used layoffs and increased working hours as the major means of rationalizing production, which resulted in a record high of 840,000 unemployed in March of that year (Ekonomisuto 1955, July 9). Between 1947 and 1956, manufacturing production increased by 650%, but employment increased by only 12%. In the mineral industry, production increased by nearly 200%, whereas employment decreased by 30% (Satō 1958). In the early postwar period, labor unions had gained much power in the struggle with management, supported by the prolabor policy of the Occupation Authority. The rise of the labor movement marked the end of the relatively stable labor relations that had been governed by nationalist ideology and state control during wartime. The new situation after the implementation of the Dodge Plan, however, enabled the companies to regain their power in management and to adopt an aggressive policy toward labor in the rationalization movement.

This strategy reached a dead end in the mid-1950s. Japanese bureaucrats and managers began to realize a dilemma: It was "difficult to mobilize high labor force commitment and adjust labor costs simultaneously [with] changing business conditions . . . the maximization of one generally results in minimizing the other" (Cole 1972:629). Thus management, supported by the state, changed its strategy toward labor from confrontation to cooperation by initiating the productivity movement in an effort to stabilize labor relations. With assistance from the United States, the Japanese state helped some progressive business leaders in establishing the Headquarters of Productivity (Nihon Seisansei Honbu). This agency, with representatives from management, labor unions, state bureaucracies, mass media, and academia, worked to develop a better relationship between management and labor. It became the center of the productivity movement. In the second half of the 1950s it sent delegations overseas; invited many experts to Japan to give lectures; conducted studies and investigations on management issues; and disseminated production, marketing, and personnel management technologies through training and consultation. The Headquarters systematically introduced the latest developments in managerial science from the West, especially the United States (Nihon Seisansei Honbu 1985). To pursue comparative advantage in production technology, these companies made a historical trade-off. They gave up allocative efficiency, as measured in short-term cost–benefit analysis (this had been their primary concern in the early 1950s, which had resulted in massive layoffs), in exchange for labor's cooperation in technological innovation and quality control (to do this, the companies were required to provide workers with job security and to increase their salaries). This was the beginning of the institutionalization of Japanese management, which is characterized by lifetime employment, the seniority-based wage system, and the company-based labor union in some big companies. It is worth noting that this effort did not gain wide support from management and labor until the 1960s. Nevertheless, it clearly marked a new trend that began to reverse a decade-long period of constant confrontations.

The paradigm of promoting exports in Japanese industrial policy is profoundly significant in the institutional evolution of Japanese developmentalism. It adapted effectively to the new environment and increased the competitiveness of the Japanese economy in a number of important ways. Under the managed economy in 1931–49, the state strengthened its capacity to control resource allocation. Nevertheless, the wartime system was characterized more by the initiative of state bureaucracy than by that of private companies. Although this system seemed quite rational when Japan confronted the urgent task of surviving the war, efficiency was a major problem; the system operated largely on the basis of coercive government planning rather than through entrepreneurship in the private sector. The paradigm of promoting exports paid great attention to the micro institutions: It emphasized ways to mobilize the private sector to participate in the development of strategic industries and promote trade planned by the state. By implementing its policy through organization of the market, the Japanese state gained new capacity to achieve its objectives in a democratic political environment. In the managed economy, the principal method of state industrial policy was bureaucratic control over resource allocation. In this new system, both bureaucratic initiative and entrepreneurship were mobilized. The state emphasized institutional reforms at the micro level and began to make use of the market forces.

This process was more suitable to competition in the international market.

The adoption of an aggressive strategy of promoting exports in strategic industries distinguished Japanese developmentalism from the Latin American experience. Although in both cases the course of economic development was defined by the structure of the world system, Japan emphasized the enabling side, whereas Latin American countries focused on the constraining side. As dependency theory argues, when latecomer countries began to be integrated into the world system, the division of labor in the international economy put them in an unfavorable position, heavily dependent on advanced countries for capital and technology (Cardoso and Faletto 1979). Instead of assuming that increased contact between core and periphery would foster more rapid development, dependency theory asserts that ties with developed countries were the problem, not the solution. Driven by these negative perceptions of the international order and the absence of confidence in their own countries, Latin American countries chose the import-substitution strategy.

International trade or domestic development?

For more than a decade the Japanese economy was isolated from the international market, and the state industrial policy was dominated by an inward orientation that emphasized effective mobilization of domestic resources through bureaucratic control. When the Japanese state was pushed to promote exports, it was inevitably involved in a conflict with the wartime legacy of the insular mentality, causing a heated debate in 1949–50 on the general direction of Japanese industrial policy after the implementation of the Dodge Plan between two competing visions: the Marxist approach, represented by Arisawa Hiromi and Tsuru Shigeto, which advocated the development of the domestic market in a threatening international environment, and the classical economic approach, represented by Nakayama Ichirō, which emphasized international trade. As Chapter 4 shows, all of these three men – especially Arisawa Hiromi, who was appointed as the advisor to the newly established MITI – were very influential in state policy making at the time.

This debate began as an internal discussion in 1949. At that time, Nakayama Ichirō, Arisawa Hiromi, and Tsuru Shigeto, along with

Ōuchi Hyōe and Tōbata Seiichi, were members of the advisory committee to Ichimada Naoto, then president of the Bank of Japan. They met monthly with Ichimada to discuss various policy issues. The Japanese emperor was also interested in economic issues, and Ichimada was asked to provide tutors to give him lectures. Ichimada recommended all of his five advisors. At each session one economist gave a lecture to the emperor, which was followed by a discussion involving all five advisors. During the discussions, these economists were divided on the future foundation of the Japanese economy. Soon this debate was extended to the mass media.

Nakayama Ichirō argued that the Japanese economy should open itself to the international economy and pursue prosperity by participating in the international division of labor because the international market could "solve one country's economic problems at the global level." Taking lessons from British history, Nakayama (1949) argued that promotion of trade and participation in the international division of labor would be the only way for Japan, which had little natural endowment but a huge population, to accumulate capital, to obtain new technology and markets, and to achieve full employment. Because Japan's industrialization depended heavily on imports and because the cost of imports must be paid by exports, Nakayama (1949:3–6) asserted, "the focus of postwar reconstruction must be on the promotion of trade" and "imports and exports are the two pillars supporting Japan's industrialization." He believed that "no country can solve its problem without applying this method. So long as capitalism exists, this principle will continue to function" (Nakayama [1950] 1970:11). As an economist trained in the classical tradition, Nakayama's perception of the world system apparently downplayed the political factors that concerned many Japanese at the time while emphasizing purely economic laws. He believed that "the questions concerning the economy have to be explained by economic logic." Drawing on Alfred Marshall's belief that economists must have "a warm heart and a cool brain," Nakayama argued that economists should not replace the rational attitude toward economic issues with personal emotion, or replace objective predictions about economic situations with wishful thinking. To Nakayama, this was not only a methodological issue but also had important policy implications. Although he admitted that the current situation in the international market was unstable and that some countries were practicing managed trade, he still believed that these were only temporary phenomena rather than a long-term trend. Sooner or later, a new order of the international economy would develop as a result of the establishment of the Bretton Woods system and of European treaties in the late 1940s (Nakayama 1949:12).

Although Nakayama emphasized the importance of international trade, this does not necessarily mean that he believed in laissez-faire. At that time, the policy debate between domestic development and international trade was interpreted by some people as a choice between socialism and capitalism because the former stressed the importance of government planning, whereas the latter emphasized the function of the international market. Nakayama, however, argued that international trade and domestic development did not have to correspond exactly to capitalism and socialism. He regarded them as two separate dichotomies. Nakayama argued that "to advocate building the future of the Japanese economy on the basis of multinational trade by no means suggests that Japan must stubbornly defend the old type of capitalist system. . . . In reality, there is an increasing possibility of combining new elements with the structure of the global market which is guided by the principle of trade, and with the establishment of domestic economic institutions" ([1950] 1970:13). According to his logic, basing the Japanese economy on trade did not mean that the role of the state would be replaced by the market. Rather, the state capacity that developed during the era of the managed economy could be reapplied in a different form to promote trade and to strengthen the competitiveness of Japanese companies in the international market.

In contrast, Arisawa Hiromi's and Tsuru Shigeto's support for the development of domestic markets was based on the perception that the link with the international market would have some negative effects on the Japanese economy and would harm the interests of the working class. Arisawa and Tsuru viewed the world system within a framework of political economy. They were highly skeptical about the prospects of international trade for a number of reasons. First, they anticipated that managed trade would persist for a long time, despite goodwill and various efforts to rebuild a new order in the world system. State intervention in the economy in Western countries during World War II would not be simply a temporary phenomenon but rather "economic arteriosclerosis," an inevitable development in the stage of monopoly capitalism. Although some people dreamed of returning to a free international market, such a dream would simply be a form of "nostalgia"

(Tsuru [1950] 1970:33–4). Also, because the world was divided into two blocs by the Cold War, the scope of the international market and the amount of global trade were seriously restricted. As manufacturing industries developed on the basis of advanced technologies, the demand of Western countries for primary products from East Asia would decrease. In the meantime, the developing countries also would decrease exports of their primary products because their domestic industrialization would create more demands for these products. Finally, because most wealth, production, and money were concentrated in the United States, the shortage of dollars would restrict the amount of international trade.

Influenced by the practice of separating the domestic economy from the international market in the 1930s, Arisawa and Tsuru argued, the Japanese economy might become vulnerable to external economic disturbance if it was connected with the international market. Because the purchasing power of Western countries in the early 1950s was based heavily on financial aid from the United States, whenever an economic recession occurred, this recession would be exported to all countries connected with the U.S. economy. By participating in the international economy through an alliance with the United States, Japan would risk becoming involved not only in the Cold War between the capitalist and socialist blocs, but also in the conflicts between capitalist countries for a share of the international market (Tsuru [1950] 1970). Furthermore, Arisawa and Tsuru believed, linking the Japanese economy with the world system would lower Japan's domestic standard of living. Before World War II, the Japanese comparative advantage in international competition had been based on cheap labor. Now, if Japan based its economy on exports, the state would have to continue its cheap labor policy. This would not only undermine the achievements of the postwar democratic reforms but also might be protested by the international community. If the Japanese state had to follow a cheap labor policy by coercion, the foundation of political democracy might be jeopardized (Tsuru [1950] 1975:100). For all these reasons, Arisawa and Tsuru believed, Japan would be better off if it stayed away from the world system.

In the state industrial policy, Nakayama's view prevailed. The shift from the inward orientation toward the outward orientation marked the beginning of the ideological transition of Japanese developmentalism from the managed economy toward the trade version.

The Korean War: Opportunity and challenge

The state industrial policy, however, was confronted a big challenge when the Korean War broke out in June 1950. This unexpected event provided Japan with both opportunities and challenges.

On the one hand, the Korean War brought unexpected fortune to the Japanese economy in the form of a huge amount of hard currency created by special procurement orders for military goods and services from the U.S. government when the Japanese economy suffered from the stabilization panic caused by the implementation of the Dodge Plan. This currency gave a timely shot in the arm to the Japanese economy. It not only stimulated the accumulation of capital that Japan needed badly for its postwar reconstruction, it also provided the Japanese economy with an abundance of dollars to balance its international payments. The amounts of the so-called special procurement, measured in U.S. dollars, were $149 million in 1950, $592 million in 1951, $824 million in 1952, $809 million in 1953, $596 million in 1954, and $557 million in 1955 (Economic Planning Agency 1990b:134). Sustained by these special procurement orders, Japanese exports increased from $510 million in 1949 to $820 million in 1950 and to $1.3 billion in 1951, at an annual growth rate of more than 60% (Masamura 1985:359). The economic boom also improved the capital return in manufacturing industries, whose rate jumped from 2.75% in the first half of 1950 to 5.07% in the second half of 1950 and to 10.56% in the first half of 1951. Employment also increased rapidly (Rekishigaku Kenkyūkai 1990, vol. 2:140–1). Japanese business leaders admitted that "U.S. military special procurement not only revived the defense industry but provided a foothold for the revival of related machinery industries" (cited in Samuels 1994:141) To be specific, the special procurement provided the material foundation for the program of promoting exports in two ways. First, as indicated previously, it provided a huge amount of capital to Japanese companies. Second, as Richard Samuels (1994:141, 150) points out, "Through licensed production and the demanding product specifications of the U.S. military, Japanese makers learned the fundamentals of standardized parts manufacture, testing standards, and quality control. . . . The Japanese negotiated skillfully to maximize the transfer of technology and, more important, their freedom to diffuse it to civilian applications." In this sense, the Korean War was a key factor in the postwar development of the Japanese economy. Many people from former socialist economies have visited Japan to learn how the Japanese succeeded in making the transition from a managed economy to a market economy. The special opportunity created by the Korean War, however, cannot be expected to happen again.

Kanamori Hisao (1985) points out that the Korean War and the implementation of the Dodge Plan constituted "a wonderful combination," sustaining the transition of the Japanese economy from the wartime managed economy to a peacetime market economy. The Dodge Plan was the driving force rationalizing the microeconomic institutions after the long period of managed economy; the war functioned as a blood transfusion that enabled the Japanese to survive the stabilization panic following the implementation of the Dodge Plan. Without the Korean War, the Japanese economy might have moved in a very different direction.

On the other hand, the Korean War also created a major challenge to the transition of Japanese developmentalism from the military version to the trade version because rearmament became an important issue. The pressure for rearmament came from the United States. When John Foster Dulles visited Japan in June 1950 as the advisor to the U.S. secretary of state, at the meeting with Yoshida Shigeru concerning the conclusion of the San Francisco Peace Treaty, he strongly urged the Japanese to proceed with rearmament. After the Korean War broke out, the U.S. government was even more eager to push Japan to begin rearmament and asked the Japanese to establish a national police reserve. General MacArthur held that because four divisions of the U.S. army in Japan had been sent to the Korean Peninsula, 250,000 dependents of U.S. military personnel who were in Japan needed protection. As a result, many former military officers who were released after the purge on 6 August 1951 joined the national police reserve (Rekishigaku Kenkyūkai 1990, vol. 2:93). In January 1952, the GHQ held several meetings with officials of the Japanese government, further demanding that Japan establish an army with 325,000 soldiers. The Japanese public had a rather positive response to this initiative because of concern for national security: Japan's closest neighbor, Korea, was involved in a large-scale military confrontation. According to a national survey conducted by *Asahi shinbun* in September 1950, 53.8% of the respondents supported rearmament, 27.6% opposed it, and

18.6% were undecided. This opinion was confirmed in December 1950 by another survey, conducted by the *Mainichi shinbun*, in which 23.1% of respondents supported full-scale rearmament and 42.6% supported some degree of rearmament. Only 16.5% wanted Japan to remain in its present condition, and 15.0% were undecided (Rekishigaku Kenkyūkai 1990, vol. 2:100).

Developmentalism at the crossroads

How could Japan pursue its economic development in the climate of international tension? Specifically, should Japan base its economy on rearmament? These were the key issues in the debate on rearmament.

Whereas the debate on international trade versus domestic development was still abstract, involving only the general principle of Japan's grand strategy for economic reconstruction, the debate on rearmament had direct policy implications. At the time and throughout the 1950s, the Japanese were puzzled by the competing interests of the economic and political agendas. The country was divided on how to locate Japan within the world system and how to deal with the conflict between the two blocs in East Asia. In the policy debates, the nation was not only divided into conservative and progressive factions; even within the conservative camp, political leaders held different perceptions of national interest and policy agenda. Although Prime Minister Yoshida Shigeru had established the orthodox version of economic nationalism for Japan, it was strongly challenged by two different versions of political nationalism: progressive political nationalism, which advocated complete Japanese neutrality in the Cold War, and conservative political nationalism, which supported the revision of the constitution, full-scale rearmament, and greater political independence from the United States in international affairs (Pyle 1992). This debate strongly affected the future direction of the Japanese economy: Japanese developmentalism made a decisive transition from the military version to the trade version at a historical crossroads.

The pro-rearmament argument represented conservative political nationalism, which implied continuing the military version of developmentalism with probably only minor adjustments. In this view, the production of weapons and munitions would remain the foundation of the economy. The economic fortune brought by the Korean War nurtured the idea of basing the Japanese economy on the defense industry because some business leaders, bureaucrats, and former military officers were deeply impressed by the effect of special procurement on the Japanese economy. "In the early 1950s it seemed the boom would never fizzle, and many believed that military production would be the center of Japanese industrial development" (Samuels 1994:142). However, as the United States, China, and Korea started negotiations to ease the military tension on the Korean Peninsula, special procurement orders to Japan from the U.S. government declined. The shortage of foreign currency reserves once again became a major problem and even caused an economic recession in 1954.

Under such circumstances, some Japanese bureaucrats and business leaders conceived the idea of reconstructing the Japanese economy by subcontracting the production of weapons and other industrial goods from the U.S. government and exporting them to Southeast Asian countries. At that time, the United States was providing a large amount of aid to its Asian allies for building up a security system to contain communism in the region. The financial aid took two forms: military aid to strengthen the defense capacity of these countries and developmental aid to promote their industrialization. These bureaucrats and business leaders held that this Cold War policy had strategic implications for the development of the Japanese economy. Japan could benefit by subcontracting from the United States the production of both weapons and industrial goods and then selling them to these Asian countries. As a broker between the United States and the Asian countries, it was believed, Japan could obtain both the hard currency that accompanied the contracts with the United States and the markets for Japanese products because these products would be the material form of U.S. aid to Asian countries. This was called the *new special procurement,* in contrast to the special procurement of the Korean War. As an important proposal prepared by the general office at the Keidanren (Federation of Economic Organization) in August 1952 argued:

> Because the special procurements during the Korean War were directly linked to the military actions, they were temporary, unstable, and urgent in nature. In contrast, [because] the new special procurement will be primarily connected with the security plan of the free countries in East Asia headed by the United States, they are more stable, less urgent, and thus are easy to plan. . . . It is possible [that they may] become long-term contracts. . . . It is also possible to establish a new weapons industry in Japan's industrial structure. . . . The weapons industry reflects the highest level of technology of each era.

By obtaining technology through converting to U.S. designs and standards in weapons production, it is possible to clear the way for Japan's industrialization and rationalization. . . . Weapons, moreover, can be used as a new commodity in trade. . . . They will help to improve the balance of the international payment, especially dollars (Keidanren 1952).

In November 1951, the Japanese government began internal discussions on how to persuade the GHQ to adopt the new plan. On 12 February 1952, ESB Director Shūtō Eiyū sent a letter to the director of the Economic and Scientific Section at the GHQ presenting a formal proposal. In particular, this letter suggested, Japan expected technological and financial aid from the United States to rebuild its defense industry and to contribute to the U.S. plan for Japan's rearmament. In this way, Japan could ensure a stable source of U.S. dollars. The most important areas in which Japan hoped to have long-term contracts from the United States were automobile production; the assembly, repair, and parts production of aircraft; and the building and repair of ships (Nakamura 1992:298–9).

The proposal for rearmament encountered strong criticism from Marxists and other left-wing liberals. When the Korean War began, Nakayama Ichirō withdrew from the debate on international trade; Arisawa Hiromi and Tsuru Shigeto, with many other progressive intellectuals, participated in the peace movement opposing rearmament. The peace movement was sustained by several streams of ideology, ranging from idealistic pacifism to economic and political nationalism.

The idealistic pacifists advocated "absolute peace." As Abe Yoshishige (1950:4) argued, "human beings and nations produce weapons to avoid wars, but it is undeniable that they wage wars because they have weapons. It is very difficult for nations who have weapons, especially strong weapons, to avoid wars. This can be proved easily by the fact that today, the choice between peace and war in the world is determined by the two nations who have the strongest weapons." By moving toward rearmament, Usami Seijirō (1952:20) warned, "the aggressive nature of Japanese capitalism may revive." Kenneth Pyle (1992:44) points out that this view of Japan's national purpose "proclaimed Japan as a nation transformed by its experience of war, atomic bombings, and defeat, dedicated to showing the way to a new world in which nations would exist free of weapons and not resort to war."

Others, in contrast, opposed rearmament, for it would hurt Japan's national interest, either political or economic. The economic argument asserted that rearmament would increase the unnecessary burden of government finance and would delay economic reconstruction. As Arisawa Hiromi (1953d:3) pointed out, the boom created by special procurement during the Korean War did not originate within, but was added to the Japanese economy from the outside. He further argued that rearmament would require a large amount of new investment, which inevitably would restrict the accumulation of capital. Because Japan's large population and weak competitive position in the international market remained the most urgent economic issues, Japan should not sacrifice capital accumulation for rearmament (Arisawa 1952a). Moreover, rearmament would further lower the Japanese people's standard of living, which was only 70% of the prewar level in the early 1950s. According to Arisawa's (1952a) calculation, if Japan spent 6% of its national income on rearmament, the living standard would decrease 10%. If the former were 10%, the latter would be 15%. Besides, as Tsuru Shigeto ([1950] 1970) points out, rearmament would result in a change in the distribution of wealth between the state and the working class because the purchasing power of the working class would be further reduced by the state in its rearmament program through taxation or inflation policy. The ordinary people would suffer from the shortage of butter because the resources for producing butter would be used to produce guns. In this sense, rearmament would do nothing for the working class or the nation but would benefit the capitalist class. The threat to the Japanese economy contained in the rearmament program, Arisawa (1952a) contended, would be invisible at the beginning; once it became visible, it would be too late to handle. Opposing full-scale rearmament for economic reasons was a position shared by both the economists involved in the peace movement and the Yoshida strategy to be discussed later.

The political independence of Japan was another major reason for the progressive forces to oppose rearmament. It was argued that developing the economy through rearmament would make Japan increasingly dependent on the United States. Rearmament would "strengthen the control and leadership of the United States" and "increase the economic difficulties" of Japan and the Western European countries, making these economies weaker. Rearmament was "an instrument of the United States to further curb its own financial burden while incorporating these countries more effectively into its global strategy and war economy" (Ikumi 1953:4–5; Tsuru [1953]

1976:111–12). If the Japanese economy continued to depend on military production, Japan would become "a colony of the United States," "under national suppression and imperialist exploitation even after the occupation ended" (Usami 1952:18). If this scenario came true, independence would be an illusion. Therefore, rearmament suited U.S. interests but not those of Japan. As in the 1930s, when the Marxist approach was applied to domestic analysis, it often suggested conflicts between the capitalists and the working class. When the Marxist approach was employed to analyze the international political economy, the concept of class was often replaced by the concept of the nation-state, and the dichotomy between the capitalist class and the working class was often replaced by a dichotomy between core and peripheral nations.

The Yoshida doctrine

The competing views of those for and against rearmament indicate the great dilemma confronted by Japanese developmentalism in the 1950s. Building Japan's economic foundation on rearmament and the production of weapons suggested the danger of reviving the military economy that had developed in 1931–45. In contrast, the policy implications of the peace movement, as indicated in Arisawa and Tsuru's earlier advocacy of domestic development, might result in continuing isolation from the international market. In the early 1950s, access to the international markets and participation in the Cold War were presented to Japan as seemingly inseparable parts of a package, and both the conservatives and the progressives emphasized only one part of this package. It was Prime Minister Yoshida Shigeru who formulated the grand strategy to solve this dilemma. This strategy was to stand on the U.S. side politically and militarily in exchange for economic advantages; meanwhile, Japan would keep its defense expenditures to a minimum in order to concentrate all its resources on the economy. Yoshida (1957, vol. 2:160–4) viewed the international environment as both threatening and enabling, and believed that Japan could seize the advantages while avoiding the disadvantages.

In the 1950s, the Japanese worldviews differed significantly along two dimensions: the structure of the world system and the relationship between international politics and the international economy. Yoshida's worldview was hierarchical yet monistic: He perceived the structure of the world system as characterized by a hierarchy in which the United States dominated. At the same time, he believed that the world system was integrated politically and economically; thus Japan must choose between political independence and economic growth, giving up one goal for the other. Yoshida argued that as a semi-peripheral country, Japan could benefit only when it connected itself politically to the United States as closely as possible, meanwhile concentrating on economic growth (Pyle 1992; Yoshida 1957, vol. 3).

Yoshida was well known as a conservative. He believed that Japan could not prosper without taking part in the world system, and he asserted that "the best medicine for the Japanese economy would be to open it up to the world economy and the discipline of international competition" (Johnson 1982:189). In his worldview, Yoshida perceived a close relationship between international politics and economic growth. Having served as a diplomat for most of his career since the end of the nineteenth century, Yoshida believed that the future of the Japanese economy would be determined by Japan's relationship with the United States and Great Britain. From the Meiji Restoration to the end of the 1920s, Yoshida (1957, vol. 4) believed, Japan was destined for economic prosperity because it cooperated closely with the United States and Britain in international politics. When the country abandoned this policy after the Manchuria Incident, it allied itself with Germany and Italy and became involved in a reckless war with the United States. Thus, Japan suffered greatly from the defeat in World War II. According to Yoshida's logic:

> The importance of Japan–U.S. relations can be understood not only from historical inevitability, but also from the fundamental nature of Japan's national economy. Japan is an island country and an ocean country. It has, by world standards, an exceptionally dense population in a small territory. In order to feed this population, the promotion of international trade is absolutely necessary. In order to pursue constant economic growth, the introduction of capital and technology from the advanced countries is indispensable. For either international trade or introduction of capital, Japan should associate itself with the countries that are the richest economically and the most advanced technologically in the world. It is not a question of ism or ideology, but the most convenient way to the most net profits. From this point of view, the United States and Britain deserve the most respect in the world from Japan. (Yoshida 1957, vol. 4:23–5)

In the 1930–4 period, 24% of Japanese imports came from the United States and 23% of its exports went there; 53% of Japanese imports came from Asia and 60% of its exports went there. This relationship changed dramatically in the postwar era. In 1947, 92% of Japanese imports came from the United States and only 6% from Asia. Meanwhile, Japan shipped only 12% of its exports to the United States and 66% to Asia (Cohen 1949:494). Given this pattern, Japan had to ensure its position in the international economy by becoming an ally of the United States.

At the same time, however, Yoshida strongly opposed the proposal for rearmament. He said that "to think about rearmament itself is stupid . . . and it is simply a dream of jerks who don't understand the international situation" (Yoshida 1957, vol. 2:160). Yoshida (1957, vol. 2:160–1) gave three reasons for not supporting rearmament. First, the military strength of the United States was supported by its incomparable wealth. No other country could bear such a financial burden. Second, there was no psychological reason for the Japanese people to support rearmament. Third, Japan had many other tasks to accomplish after the defeat. Yoshida (1957, vol. 2:181) believed that Japan had a more important task than rearmament. He stated, "Now the urgent problem is to build up economic power for the nation and to stabilize civilian life. Due to the defeat, Japan has lost its national strength and become a thin horse. If we put too heavy a burden on this thin horse, it will collapse."

Yoshida keenly recognized the danger of becoming involved in military conflicts between the two blocs created by the rearmament program, but he believed that Japan could avoid it by concentrating its financial resources on economic reconstruction rather than national defense. Although the United States might constantly exert pressure on Japan to rearm, it would also provide enormous support to the Japanese economy in the form of a market, capital, and technologies. As long as Japan did not spend too much money on defense and rearmament, the Cold War would not be a major threat to the Japanese economy. Yoshida acknowledged the conflict between political independence and economic reconstruction, but he was willing to make a trade-off between the two. General MacArthur ([1947] 1982:26) once told the Japanese that "there can be no political freedom so long as a people's livelihood is dependent upon the largesse of others." Yoshida turned this logic around; he believed that political independence must be given up for economic recovery when it was impossible to have both simultaneously. He believed that "just as the United States was once a colony of Great Britain but now stands as the stronger one, . . . if Japan becomes a colony of the United States, it will eventually become the stronger one!" (Masamura 1985:192).

The progressive forces saw the world system as consisting of two opposing blocs with a neutral area between, and they held that Japan should locate itself in that area. Meanwhile, even though this outlook shared Yoshida's monistic perspective, it suggested a completely different policy implication. The progressive forces believed that for political independence and national security, Japan must sever its ties with the United States. The conservatives also differed from Yoshida's worldview in two dimensions. On the one hand, they shared with the progressive forces the perception of the world system as divided into three parts, but they believed that Japan itself might become a leader, at least in Asia. On the other hand, they held a dualistic perspective regarding the relationship between international politics and economics, believing that Japan could simultaneously pursue its political independence and obtain economic benefits from the United States. Throughout the 1950s, the conflicts among these ideologies continued. The clash among these three different worldviews culminated in the well-known domestic turmoil regarding the extension of the U.S.–Japan security treaty in 1960.

History has shown that different perceptions of the world system resulted in differences between Japan and the Latin American countries concerning strategies of economic development, and that different strategies created different political outcomes. Although they both believed that a late-developing economy is often influenced by the structure of the world system, the Japanese held that such an economy could benefit by attaching itself to an economic superpower. Yoshida took for granted the unequal status among the nation-states in the world system. Although Japan could do nothing to change this situation, Yoshida believed, Japan also had enough maneuvering room in international politics to promote its economic interests. In contrast, Latin American countries were overwhelmed by the unfavorable external environment and regarded the international market as a threat to their political independence. Therefore they decided to stay away from the global market, instead choosing import substitution as their primary strategy for domestic economic development. In this sense, their position was very similar to that of Arisawa Hiromi and Tsuru Shigeto. If the Japanese state had focused on the development of domestic markets, as prescribed by Arisawa and Tsuru, the Japanese economy might not have become as competitive as it is today. If the Japanese state had submitted to pressure from the United States on the issue of rearmament, the Japanese economy might not have grown as strong as it is today, though Japan might have achieved a much stronger presence in international politics. In this sense, the Yoshida doctrine laid the foundation for the postwar development of the Japanese economy.

The politics of rearmament

Eventually, the rearmament program failed. This failure has several structural reasons.

In the transition from the managed economy to the free economy, policy making in the state again became decentralized. Yoshida initially intended to eliminate the ESB. Because of strong resistance, the ESB was transformed into the Economic Deliberation Agency (EDA). Although the ESB survived as a bureaucratic agency, the EDA was given only the duty of conducting surveys on economic matters for the government; planning functions were returned to the individual ministries. After the conclusion of the San Francisco Peace Treaty, the Occupation Authority was no longer an external check on bureaucratic sectionalism, and bureaucratic disputes again became the major obstacle to policy integration.

The conservative financial policy adopted by the Ministry of Finance was the biggest obstacle to the proposal of developing the defense industry in Japan. From the implementation of the Dodge Plan in 1949 to 1965, the Ministry of Finance was strongly influenced by classical economics, regarding a balanced budget as the top priority of the government. It was argued that the easy money policy adopted by the Ministry of Finance in the prewar period under pressure from the military had contributed not only to the economic panic but also eventually to the outbreak of the Pacific war. Therefore, the Ministry of Finance always blocked any demand to increase government expenditures for rearmament (Ōtake 1984). As Richard Samuels (1994:147) points out, "MOF battled successfully for a policy of 'minimum necessary defense,' thereby restricting the deployment and manufacture of arms. It influenced the National Safety Agency by controlling its budgetary and personnel decisions through seconded officials, a practice that continued into the 1980s."

The competition among different bureaucracies for administration of the rearmament was another reason to count the failure. The task of developing a defense industry involved three government bureaucracies: MITI, the Ministry of Transportation, and the Defense Agency. In the beginning, all three bureaucracies supported the proposal of rearmament and developing a defense industry. Soon, however, they began to disagree about who should have the administrative power to supervise that industry. MITI, which regarded the development of a defense industry as a strategy to promote exports and to sustain the economic reconstruction, fought enthusiastically and won this struggle. It first defeated the Ministry of Transportation in competition for administrative power over the aircraft industry and then successfully repulsed a challenge from the Defense Agency, which intended to claim its own authority in the defense industry. Ironically, although MITI emerged as the winner in these bureaucratic struggles, it also lost its major allies within the state bureaucracies in pursuing the development of a defense industry. After they lost the battles with MITI, the Ministry of Transportation and the Defense Agency changed their attitude toward this program. The bureaucrats at the Defense Agency initially had planned to nurture the defense industry and regarded it as the foundation of the national defense. In their view, the nationalization of military production was a long-term goal and an important step toward independence in national security from the United States, which was the major supplier of weapons at that time. After the Defense Agency lost the chance to supervise the defense industry, it also lost its incentive for supporting the nationalization of weapons production. Although MITI obtained the power to supervise production by the defense industry, it lost the major buyer for the products; the Defense Agency was no longer interested in purchasing domestically produced weapons (Ōtake 1984, 1988; Samuels 1994).

The divisions among business leaders, and especially the opposition by commercial banks, also undermined the rearmament program. Supporters of this program came largely from manufacturing industries. On 25 January 1951, the Keidanren and seven other national business associations delivered a statement to U.S. government envoy John Foster Dulles, suggesting that the United States sign a treaty with Japan to strengthen cooperation between the two countries. This proposal suggested that the United States provide financial assistance and military aid to its Asian allies to promote their economic development and to

strengthen their defense capacity. Japan, it continued, would subcontract the production of weapons and other industrial goods from
the U.S. program and sell them to Asian countries. To carry out this
mission, Japan urged the U.S. government to establish a bilateral organization, which would include representatives of the U.S. government, the Japanese government, and Japanese business circles. The
Keidanren later established an internal agency, the Committee of
Defense Production (*bōei seisan iinkai*). The major functions of this
committee were to conduct surveys and investigations concerning
defense production, to draft policy proposals, and to integrate related
industries and firms. Many former military officers intended to use this
opportunity to rebuild Japan's military force. They asserted that Japan
should build up its national defense more independently. According to
an ambitious proposal drafted by these former officers, who met in the
deliberation division of the Committee of Defense Production, Japan
would create an army of 300,000 persons (30% larger than the prewar
imperial army), a navy with 300,000-ton warships, and an air force
with 3,000 military aircraft (Kondo and Osanai 1978, vol. 3:215). If
this plan had been carried out, the defense expenditures would constitute as mcuh as 10 percent of Japan's national income. Even if 44%
of the total defense expenditures came from the financial aid provided
by the U.S. government, the Japanese government still would have to
spend 5% of Japan's national income for defense. This proposal by
former military officers was based on the assumption that the U.S.
government would provide Japan with $1 billion in financial aid for
rearmament. The critics, however, pointed out that the total annual
expenditures for mutual security assistance (MSA) permitted by the
U.S. Congress were only $100 million (Senga 1978:228–31).

This radical proposal caused a major dispute in business circles.
Many business leaders did not like the idea of basing the Japanese
economy on the defense industry. Not only were some manufacturers
reluctant to take this risk, many commercial banks also had a negative
attitude toward the rearmament program. These business leaders believed that the proposal paid too much attention to military production, and they stated that the independence of the Japanese economy
must depend on the promotion of trade rather than on special procurement and MSA aid. They even demanded that the Committee of Defense Production be separated from the Federation of Economic Organizations. The promotion of military production required large-scale

investment in production equipment, but the commercial banks refused to provide credit to manufacturers in defense industries. Horie Shigeo, the deputy director at the Bank of Tokyo, argued that in a country like Japan, where war was not present, it was simply a gamble to organize the industrial structure around defense. The resistance of commercial banks to the rearmament program was particularly evident in those firms that had belonged to the prewar *zaibatsu* and had just reorganized themselves into *keiretsu;* they were under close control by the banks, which constituted the center of each *keiretsu* (Ōtake 1984:22–3). As Richard Samuels (1994:145) points out, "The controversy proved decisive in Japanese industrial and political history, for it was the last time industry and the military would openly urge a return to prewar force levels. . . . Instead of returning to military technonationalism, Japan would spend the next several decades focusing on civilian markets, developing an alternative technomilitary paradigm."

The diffusion of Schumpeter's theory of innovation

These structural factors worked to prevent Japan from continuing the military version of developmentalism, but they did not offer alternative means of achieving the goal of economic independence. It was the diffusion of Joseph A. Schumpeter's idea of innovation that resulted in the grand strategy of basing Japan's national competitiveness on production technology.

During the Korean War, the special procurement from the U.S. government created an economic boom. Exports increased from $501 million to $802 million in 1950 and $1.3 billion in 1951. After the cease-fire talks started, Japanese exports decreased in 1952 in comparison with 1951 and stayed at the same level in 1953. It was clear that the Korean War had enabled Japan to overcome the stabilization panic, but it could not solve the nation's basic problem of developing economic independence. Because the expansion of exports during the Korean War was sustained by military relations with the United States, rather than by competitiveness in the international market, ensuring a share of the international market for Japanese products resurfaced as an important issue as the Korean War ended (Masamura 1985, vol. 1:359–60). Under the leadership of the Hatoyama Ichirō administration, the Economic Planning Agency was created to take charge of long-term economic planning. In 1955, the Japanese government announced the "Five Year Plan for Economic Independence." This plan had two major goals for state industrial policy: first, to achieve economic independence by achieving an increasing balance of international payment that no longer depended on aid and special procurement from the United States; second, to achieve full employment (Masamura 1985, vol. 1:410).

How would Japan achieve these two goals? Drawing on Schumpeter's theory of long-term economic growth, the 1956 government white paper on the economy prescribed a new strategy: to depend on technological innovation. *Innovation,* as Schumpeter used the term, refers to new ways of production; new production technologies; new products, services, and markets; and new types of business organization. Schumpeter regarded innovation as an important source of economic expansion and productivity.

Schumpeter had been influential in Japanese economics since the prewar period, and he played an important role in shaping the development of Japan's *kinkei* economics. In 1924 Schumpeter was even offered a professorship by the Imperial University of Tokyo. Although he declined, he trained several Japanese students, who became prominent economists and were very influential in postwar Japanese industrial policy: Nakayama Ichirō and Tōbata Seiichi at Bonn University in Germany and Tsuru Shigeto at Harvard University in the United States. During his visit to Japan in 1931, Schumpeter gave the famous presentation titled "Business Cycles" and important advice to Japanese economists on how to study modern economics. Schumpeter's impact on Japanese economics was further enhanced by the translation of his works into Japanese. *The Theory of Economic Development* was translated by Nakayama and Tōbata as early as 1937. After Schumpeter died in 1950, his works were translated systematically. Nakayama and Tōbata together translated *The History of Economics* in 1950 and *Capitalism, Socialism, and Democracy* in 1951–2. Tsuru translated *Imperialism and Social Class* in 1953; Tōbata translated *The History of Economic Analysis* in 1956–7. The diffusion of Schumpeter's theory of innovation was greatly promoted by these translations.

The impact of Schumpeter's theory of innovation on Japanese industrial policy was greatly enhanced by the publication of the 1956 government white paper on the economy. Gotō Yōnosuke, director of the Survey Division at the Economic Planning Agency, played a major role in promoting the policy agenda of technological innovation. During a research trip to the United States in 1954 sponsored by the Eisenhower Foundation, Gotō was deeply impressed by the effects of automation and the productivity movement on the U.S. economy. When drafting the 1956 white paper for the government, he conceived the idea of using Schumpeter's theory of innovation as a framework for understanding the Japanese economy (Sugita 1989).

This document provided the Japanese with a totally new explanation of the dynamics of economic growth whose policy implications were significantly different from those of the rearmament program. This document argued that the fourth industrial revolution was underway. The global economy had been in a boom in the postwar era despite small recessions in 1949 and 1953. This robust growth could not be explained solely by the postwar economic reconstruction and the impact of the Korean War. Technological innovation was the most important factor. In the past three centuries, the world economy had experienced three such revolutions: The first took place between 1788 and 1815, stimulated by the invention of the steam engine; the second occurred between 1843 and 1873, represented by the spread of railroads; the third appeared between 1897 and 1920, caused by the emergence of the electronic, chemical, automobile, and aircraft industries. The fourth industrial revolution, this document asserted, was due to the application of atomic power and automation to the production process. Moreover, in each industrial revolution, the global economy had experienced long-term growth. Even if a short-term recession occurred, it was simply a minor episode between two waves of economic cycles (Keizai Kikakuchō 1956:33–5). As the world experienced the fourth industrial revolution, Gotō suggested, innovation would not only intensify the competition for capital investment but would also enlarge the consumer market (Gotō 1956:10).

The 1956 white paper on the economy turned Schumpeter's idea of innovation from an academic concept explaining long-term economic growth into a practical strategy to upgrade the industrial structure of the Japanese economy and improve the nation's standing in international competition. Gotō Yōnosuke once explained the sense in which he introduced Schumpeter's idea of innovation in the 1956 white paper: "According to Schumpeter's definition, innovation refers to new technology, new products, new business organizations, and the creation of new markets. In this white paper on the economy, the meaning of innovation is further broadened. It suggests the modernization of

Japan's economic structure" (1956:14). "Modernization," wrote Gotō, "is a process for making economic resources, including human capital, in a given country interact with each other in order to sustain the process of promoting productivity" (1956:12). Gotō said that modernization would create economic growth and determine its tempo. In the modernization process, investment would be an important factor, determining the levels of employment and productivity. Gotō had been intellectually stimulated by a report submitted by a Swedish economist to the United Nations titled "The Growth and Stagnation of the European Economies." The author of this report stated that innovation changed not only production technology but also the direction of capital investment, the patterns of consumption, the structure of trade, and the division of labor among industries and professions. Based on these visions, the 1956 white paper argued that "It is no longer the postwar period. We are facing a new situation. The growth through recovery has ended. From now on, the [economic] growth has to be supported by modernization."

The 1956 white paper on the economy had a great impact on Japanese industrial policy. After it was published, Gotō was invited more than 50 times by private companies and mass media to lecture on innovation. His expressions "It is no longer the postwar era" and "innovation" became catchwords, which set the leading agendas in political discourse and were used widely to symbolize the beginning of a new era in the postwar Japanese economy. In the 1950s, because few Japanese could obtain the large data set that described the economic situation at the macro level, the views presented in the white papers strongly influenced how bureaucrats, business leaders, labor unions, academicians, and the general public perceived the economic situation. In 1957, based on the framework of innovation, MITI published its famous document "The White Paper on Industrial Rationalization," in which it translated the theme of innovation into detailed industrial policy.

Influenced by Schumpeter's theory of innovation, the concept of comparative advantage in international trade was creatively redefined in Japanese industrial policy. In the late 1940s and early 1950s, Japanese economic thinking on trade had been dominated by the classical school. An economic advisor at the GHQ suggested to Japanese bureaucrats that Japan would be better off basing its economy on exports of textile products, raising chickens and exporting eggs, and developing tourism because these things represented Japan's comparative advantage in trade (Nakamura and Ōmori 1990:115–16). Ichimada Naoto, president of the Bank of Japan, also argued that Japan should develop light industries. Although the Japanese state did not take this approach seriously, it was still constrained intellectually by the orthodox definition of comparative advantage, which emphasized the naturally given conditions of a nation's economy. Therefore, in the first half of the 1950s, state industrial policy still regarded cheap labor as Japan's comparative advantage and emphasized ways to reduce production costs by layoffs and cutting workers' wages. This efficiency-oriented strategy did not differ much from the practice in liberal capitalist economies.

After the 1956 white paper on the economy was published, the Japanese began to interpret comparative advantage differently. They now believed that a nation's comparative advantage did not have to be based on natural endowments. It could also be built up intentionally. A nation might find it necessary to begin by exporting textile products and eggs in order to accumulate capital, but it must make every effort to develop (for example) heavy-chemical industries because such industries created value-added products. As a result, they would give the nation a strategic position in international competition. Following this logic, the Japanese began to perceive the production efficiency of individual firms from a new perspective. According to the conventional notion of efficiency, companies produced more profits with less input, and efficiency was usually measured in a given short period, such as a quarter, a half-year, or a year. This idea conflicted seriously with the task of upgrading the industrial structure of the Japanese economy because technological innovation consumed time and capital. The results of the investments would not be evident in a short period. In light of the paradigm of technological innovation, the Japanese replaced this short-term approach to efficiency with a new approach involving strategic planning. This approach emphasized whether a company could win the competition for production technology in the long run and how much market share a firm could obtain, rather than how much profit it could make in one year. For purposes of innovation, efficiency in the Western sense often meant ineffectiveness. In this sense, the innovation paradigm changed the time span and the preference of end in Japanese economic thinking.

During World War II, many Japanese economists had already perceived these industries as the future direction of the Japanese economy. The Five Years' Economic Independence Plan, proposed in 1949 by a team headed by Inaba Hidezō at the Economic Stabilization Board, had reasserted their importance. The rationale underlying this perspective was that the industrialization of other Asian countries would soon remove the Japanese advantage in cheap labor in the international market; Japan needed to upgrade its industrial structure in order to survive in the international competition. Both sides in the debate between domestic development and international trade, despite their conflicting positions on other issues, shared the understanding that Japan had to upgrade its industrial structure and develop heavy-chemical industries. Tsuru Shigeto ([1950] 1975:98) argued that to obtain foreign currency for economic independence, Japan must export value-added manufactured goods. Nakayama Ichiro ([1953] 1972:78–80) elaborated this position from a historical point of view, commenting that the constant accumulation and efficient use of capital had contributed greatly in the past to expanding the Japanese position in the international market. So far, Japan had benefited from the latecomer effect. It had cost Western countries several hundred years to develop modern economic institutions, industrial machines, instruments, and equipment. By importing these Western creations, Japan did not have to pay the trial-and-error cost of independent development. From now on, however, Japan would not be able to sustain the efficiency of its capital without improving technology on its own because it had reached a level of development similar to that of European countries. Arisawa Hiromi ([1950] 1970:20–2), in his analysis, even linked the issue of technological development with the future of capitalism. He argued that Japan would not be able to accumulate capital by depending on the private sector alone. It must introduce state capital in order to sponsor a revolution in production technology and in the development of national resources. By doing so, Japan eventually would be able to abolish capitalism because the introduction of state capital would lead to the socialization of the economy.

In many ways, the 1956 white paper on the economy reflected a significant step in the ideological evolution of Japanese developmentalism in the 1950s. First, it presented a new worldview. In contrast to the rearmament program, which was primarily driven by the perception of the Cold War, the policy agenda of innovation presented in the 1956 white paper was based on the belief that the capitalist and socialist blocs could coexist in the era of the fourth industrial revolution, and that the international competition for power among nation-states would shift from military confrontation to a "peaceful race" – "a competition for the economic growth rate and the promotion of productivity" (Keizai Kikakuchō 1956:43). This was a decisive shift in Japanese economic ideology toward the trade version of developmentalism. Second, it supplemented Yoshida's political strategy. Although Yoshida clearly defined the relationship between Japan's economic development and its diplomatic policy, his idea was, after all, a political strategy to ensure financial aid from the United States. In comparison, the policy of technological innovation offered a new interpretation: that production technology was the most reliable comparative advantage for Japan to ensure a strategic position in the international competition. Third, it supplemented Nakayama Ichirō's international trade argument, which had set the general direction for the postwar development of the Japanese economy. The technological innovation argument prescribed a concrete strategy for Japanese companies to promote exports. Fourth, it gave the wartime legacy of emphasizing the development of heavy-chemical industries new meaning. Although the Japanese also took technology seriously in the early 1950s, investing heavily in production equipment and technological transfers, they were governed more by the need to replace damaged machinery. In light of innovation, the development of heavy-chemical industries would not only upgrade the industrial structure and promote exports, it would also reflect a long-term strategy that could locate the Japanese economy in the historical trend.

The dual structure of the economy and the issue of employment

At around the same time, Arisawa Hiromi and Gotō Yōnosuke together provided a new vision for a Japanese industrial policy of realizing full employment by reducing the gap in the *dual structure* (*Nijū kōzō*) that characterized the Japanese economy.

Arisawa first used the concept of the dual structure to address the relationship between employment and the promotion of industrial structure. Arisawa was a member of the Committee on Unemployment Measures, established in March 1949 to deal with the unemployment crisis created by the implementation of the Dodge Plan. In 1955 this committee submitted an important report to the Japanese government calling for the adoption of technological innovation from a different angle. This idea was developed by Arisawa in two influential articles. He argued that the increasing number of people who needed to work had created great pressure on the Japanese economy. The issue of employment would determine the future of Japanese capitalism. In his analysis of recent changes in Japanese employment, Arisawa (1956b, 1957) showed that the employment structure had worsened in the early 1950s even though employment had increased with economic growth. The reason was that most of these job opportunities had been created in small and medium-sized companies, where people either could work only less than 20 hours per week or had to work more than 60 hours per week because of their low salaries. This kind of work could not be regarded as full employment.

The dual structure of the economy in Japan had three implications in the 1950s, when this term was used for the first time. First, it meant that more than 40% of Japanese who had a job were self-employed, in contrast to Britain, where 90% of employees were working for others. Second, it implied a major gap in wages based on the size of firms. Third, it meant that there were two large groups of companies represented by big companies and by small, family-owned shops. The middle-sized companies were few in number (Masamura 1991:692).

Arisawa (1957:34–5) argued that "sustaining and increasing employment cannot depend simply on the expansion of the economy"; the state must change its policy focus from helping unemployed workers to creating new job opportunities – in his words, "from an *ex post facto* response to preventive measures." Arisawa believed that employment was connected closely to the structure of the economy. The Japanese economy, he added, was characterized by a dual structure: The modern structure was represented by the big companies and the premodern structure by numerous family-run shops and stores. In the 1950s, the modern sector in the Japanese economy was too small to absorb many workers, and the surplus labor force remained in the low-paying premodern sector.

To solve the employment problem, which was fatal to the Japanese economy, Arisawa contended that Japan must eliminate the gap between the two structures by modernizing the industrial structure. To do so, Japan needed to develop the energy industries, to introduce new industries, and to reform the existing industries. Arisawa believed that this goal could not be achieved within the framework of traditional capitalism, which was driven by the pursuit of profits. He argued that "In order to make what is impossible possible in a capitalist economy, non-capitalist measures must be adopted . . . we must build a system which increases employment by adopting policies to promote the industrial structure" (1956b:32). The development of manufacturing industries would be the only way for Japan to solve the employment problem (Arisawa 1989a:128–9). Some analysts argue that by defining the problem of the dual economy as solvable, Arisawa lost the central focus on democracy (Hein 1994:772). Arisawa's own writings, however, indicate that improving employment and creating a material basis for democracy by upgrading industrial structure were the starting points of his analysis.

Based on Arisawa's theory, Gotō Yōnosuke presented a policy agenda for the Japanese government in the 1957 white paper on the economy. He argued that in order to realize full employment by reducing the gap of the dual structure, Japan must sustain its economic growth at an annual rate of 6–7%. In the meantime, Japan should not only emphasize the development of big businesses, but also modernize the premodern sector, developing the small businesses into medium-sized companies. As Masamura Kimihiro (1985, vol. 1:417–18) points out, it was a significant step in the state industrial policy to shift from achieving economic independence to realizing full employment and to present the reduction of the gap in the dual structure as a concrete policy agenda to achieve full employment. This change provided the legitimacy and rationale for the imminent high-growth policy.

The debate on the productivity movement

After the Japanese were convinced by Schumpeter's ideas of innovation and entrepreneurship, how to embody them in institutional reforms became the top policy issue. Because Schumpeter's theory of innovation related economic growth to a broad social analysis, the adoption of this theory in Japanese industrial policy not only suggested the need for large-scale investment in production equipment and technological transfer, but also demanded institutional reforms. A key issue was how to mobilize labor in the effort to achieve technological innovation.

In the first decade of the postwar period, labor relations were characterized by constant confrontations. These conflicts were a strong reaction to the wartime legacy. Although labor unions were quite powerful in the early postwar period, supported by the GHQ's policy, business leaders soon regained their power in the political struggle. They adopted a confrontational strategy toward labor in the rationalization program of the early 1950s, making massive layoffs to promote efficiency. After the Korean War broke out, the state conducted the famous "red purge," in which many leaders of labor unions were arrested. Labor relations were tense. Management's strength in the struggle with labor was supported largely by the economic boom created by the special procurement during the Korean War. When the war ended, however, the special procurement declined and the international competitiveness of Japanese products became an urgent issue again.

When innovation was identified as the major strategy for sustaining Japan's economic growth, labor relations attracted great attention. Some business leaders gathered at the Japan Committee of Economic Development (JCED; Nihon Keizai Dōyūkai) formulated a new strategy aimed at promoting productivity by stabilizing labor relations. These managers, who emerged after the *zaibatsu* dissolution, had a progressive orientation. Opposing the state's policy and practice of rationalization, which focused on company profits, they regarded labor as one of the most important components of the company and argued that "respect for the human being" should not be neglected in fostering economic growth and technological progress. They asserted that Japanese companies should prevent conflicts between management and labor and promote labor relations. Scientific management in Japan, they argued, must be different from what Taylorism represented in the United States. A JCED document published in November 1955 stated:

> Japanese companies usually regard the maximization of profit for capital as their life, and emphasize short-term interest. Many of them do not have a high, wide vision, and forget the mission of contributing to the welfare of society. . . . The company neither is made up simply of capital, nor should be responsible solely to the interest of capital. Since both capital and the company need to continue their operation, they must satisfy the welfare of employees and must benefit the general public. The company is a place of production. . . . [I]t is also a place of employment and a provider of welfare. The scientific promotion of productivity is not only a necessary condition for its own survival, but also a way to lighten employees' hardship at work, to improve their standard of living, and to provide good, cheap products to society. (Nihon Seisansei Honbu 1985:137)

With this strategy, nationalist ideology revived.

The resurgence of nationalist ideology was also sustained by cross-national learning. A JCED delegation visiting West Germany in 1953 discovered that whereas the influence of the wartime nationalist ideology had declined quickly in Japan after its defeat in World War II, German management in the postwar reconstruction period depended heavily on the concept of the *blood tie* between managers and workers, which came from nationality. This blood tie not only made German managers and workers cooperate voluntarily for the sake of the nation in the postwar reconstruction. It also made German workers believe that their standard of living could not be improved without the promotion of production, and it made German managers strongly appreciate German labor unions' participation in the reconstruction of the late 1940s – the most difficult period in modern German history. Kōshi Kōhei, one of the visiting Japanese managers, believed that the blood tie between management and labor could be a medium of continuous communication, which could constitute the foundation of healthy labor relations in Japan (Nihon Seisan-Sei Honbu 1985:30–2). After his trip to West Germany, Kōhei began to emphasize to business leaders the necessity of improving labor relations. At the same time, to enhance the U.S. foreign aid policy, the American embassy in Japan contacted the JCED and persuaded Japanese managers to promote productivity. In March 1954, encouraged by the JCED, four major Japanese business organizations together established the Japan–United States Council for Promoting Productivity.

MITI supported this initiative enthusiastically. MITI had paid a great deal of attention to the development of the productivity movement in Western Europe since its early stages because that movement was closely related to MITI's policy on the rationalization of industry. Observing the impact of the productivity movement initiated by the private sector, MITI decided to transform it into a semiofficial program sponsored by the state. After a series of discussions with the U.S. government and Japanese business leaders, MITI approved the proposal for establishing the Headquarters of Productivity. On 14 February 1955 the Headquarters of Productivity was established as the agency for implementing the productivity movement. Nakayama Ichirō became its vice-president, with Arisawa Hiromi and Inaba Hidezō as its board members. A MITI document said that the rationalization movement in the past had emphasized only the modernization of production equipment. From now on, the comprehensive promotion of productivity in all fields, including production technology, materials, labor relations, managerial skill, and the distribution system, would be the overall strategy used to reduce costs, improve quality, promote exports, and increase the national income. To strengthen its effect, the productivity movement should obtain support not only from government agencies, managers, and workers, but also from the general public, thus becoming a national movement.

The productivity movement, however, encountered serious criticism from Marxists. It was argued that the promotion of productivity could not transcend class interests in society and benefit everybody. Strong production forces could not develop automatically without good production relations. The latter would shape the nature, direction, and speed of the development of the former (Horie 1955). Even if science and technology could transcend the class struggle, they would have to be applied in a capitalist society: "Automation itself may provide some benefits and happiness. Its capitalist application, however, will create many negative effects and much unhappiness in human society" (Kanbayashi 1958:53). Automation, believed the Marxists, would not only pose an even greater threat to workers' job security, which was already a major concern because of the pressure of overpopulation in the 1950s; it would also cause a decrease in male workers' wages because it would simplify the working process so that companies could depend more strongly on female and young workers (Ōkōchi 1957). Besides, technological innovation through automation would further increase the workload, creating more alienation among workers. As a whole, said the Marxists, technological innovation would only strengthen the power of capital and weaken the power of labor in the class struggle (Horie 1955; Kanbayashi 1958).

Here we can see an ideological revival of the wartime legacy in a new environment. In both situations, labor was asked to cooperate with management for reasons of nationalist ideology. The call for cooperation in the productivity movement simply for national interest, however, encountered criticisms because it was unbalanced even from the perspective of the wartime legacy. Reelaborating his position on social policy, Ōkōchi Kazuo (1957) argued that the benefits created by innovation and the promotion of productivity must be "distributed fairly in society." The state must adopt the minimum wage, improve the social security system, achieve full employment, and enlarge the domestic

market. Criticizing the strategy of cheap labor for its exclusive attention to wages and production costs and for its general neglect of the
human element, Nakayama Ichirō ([1956] 1972) addressed the same
issue. He argued that productivity could not be promoted unless the
problems of wages and employment were solved. What is productivity? Nakayama (1956:46–7) believed that productivity is the creative
combination of the elements of production, which will result in better
employment of these elements in the production process. Productivity
will strengthen production forces and stimulate economic growth. The
difference between the concept of rationalization and the concept of
productivity is that the former emphasizes only production equipment,
whereas the latter also includes the workers. Consequently, the productivity movement was not simply designed to promote the interest of the
company; it also had to improve the standard of living by reforming
capitalist institutions. Without an institutional framework to generate
and sustain mutual trust, workers would remain skeptical of managers'
intentions in the productivity movement. As the vice-president of the
Headquarters of Productivity, Nakayama presented his famous three
principles for the productivity movement. First, the ultimate purpose
of promoting productivity was to increase employment. Government
and business must make every effort to prevent unemployment. Second, management must consult with labor on how to promote productivity according to the conditions at each firm. Third, the benefits
created by the promotion of productivity must be distributed fairly
between the firm and labor. "The productivity movement would not
have any reason to be supported," said Nakayama, "unless it proved
empirically that its achievement will fit not only the interest of managers and capitalists but also the interest of labor and the general
public" (Nakayama [1956] 1972:337–44).

In this debate, nationalist ideology was employed by different actors
in different ways. Business leaders used it to demand cooperation from
labor; labor unions used it to demand more benefits and economic
welfare. Nakayama's three principles, however, helped the two parties
to reach a compromise by linking the demands from both sides. As a
result, the productivity movement was no longer simply a ritual confirmation of the traditional value of harmony. Rather, it was a realistic
rationalization of the relationship between management and workers
in an effort to overcome what Charles Sabel (1994:137) calls "the
central dilemma of growth": the dilemma between *learning* – "acquir-

ing the knowledge to make things valued in markets – and *monitoring* –
"the determination by the transacting parties that the gains from learning be distributed according to the standards agreed to between them,
as interpreted by each." In this way, the revival of nationalist ideology
was significantly adapted to the postwar environment. It was no longer
to support the military adventure, but rather to solve the modern problem confronted by the Japanese economy in peace.

The unsettled solution

Labor's response to the productivity movement, however, was divided.
The General Federation of Labor (Sōdōmei) ([1955] 1966), whose
membership included one-third of Japanese labor unions at the time,
made a conditional promise. It made a list of eight requirements for
management, including guarantees not to increase unemployment, not
to worsen working conditions, and to share the benefits of the productivity movement. After witnessing how Japanese firms had tried to
reduce production costs by laying off workers after the implementation
of the Dodge Plan, the labor unions' major concern was the negative
effect of the productivity movement on employment and wages. The
most powerful union, the General Council of Trade Unions (Sōhyō)
([1955] 1966), however, refused to cooperate with management.
Sōhyō's major concern was that the productivity movement would
further worsen working conditions in the factories, lower salaries, and
increase the ability of management to crack down on labor unions.
These concerns were unfounded.

The resistance of the labor unions was no surprise. In the first decade
of the postwar period, Japanese labor relations were characterized by a
strong ideological orientation and a confrontational strategy. Initially,
backed by the GHQ, the Japanese labor movement revived quickly as a
strong reaction to wartime conditions. The management councils
(*Keiei kyōgikai*), which were established in the early postwar era under
the slogan "Labor's participation in management," became the place
for collective bargaining based on power. Labor unions obtained the
power to negotiate with the company not only on the terms of welfare
such as salary, bonus, retirement allowance, working conditions, voca-
tions, and paid menstruation and maternity leave for female workers,
but also on production, management, organizational matter, promotion, and layoffs (Nishinarita 1994). During the democratic reforms,

management had to make compromises to satisfy the labor unions. Managerial power, in Nishinarita's (1994) word, was indeed "constrained." As a result, as a business leader pointed out, "shareholders' interest was completely neglected. The operation of the business was controlled by employees. It was exactly the opposite to what I saw in the Taishō period when I came back to Japan. The dividend and the price of stocks became secondary while employees' benefits became the top priority. No one thought how to strengthen the foundation of the company and how to accumulate capital" (cited in Okazaki 1993:99).

Later, however, management started a counteroffensive under the slogan "Getting managerial power back." In 1949, the Labor Union Law was revised. The representatives of shareholders' interests, financial aid from the company to labor unions, and the automatic extension of labor contracts were outlawed. As Nishinarita (1994:143–4) points out, this revision marked "a decisive change" in labor relations, which had been characterized by the increased power of labor and the constraints on managerial power. As a result, companies no longer consulted the labor unions on decisions regarding personnel and the general principle of company management.

The function of the Council of Management Consultation shifted from collective bargaining to preparatory discussion before collective bargaining, which often appeared in the form of strikes. Although labor consultation was practiced in the early occupation period on a wider basis in Japan than in Germany, it failed to take deep root in Japan in comparison with Germany. In contrast to Japan, where power shifted from labor to management at the end of the 1940s, Germany had continuing cooperation between labor and management (Nishinarita 1994).

Ideology played an important role in determining these two situations. Both Germany and Japan practiced the policy of stabilizing labor relations in which fascist ideology had a great impact. During the democratic reforms, the ideology concerning labor relations evolved in different ways in Japan and Germany. In Japan the influence of nationalism at the grass-roots level declined rapidly; in the meantime, class consciousness was strengthened. Influenced by the revival of Marxism, labor movements took an aggressive position. In Germany, in contrast, the concept of socialization (shakaika) became very influential, supported by the reviving belief in economic democracy that dominated the Weimar Republic. According to Nishinarita (1994:155–6), there are two types of ideologies concerning industrial democracy in the postwar era. One, the ideology of liberal capitalism, holds that democracy is reflected in the function of labor unions as an opposition force to management. This view prevailed in Britain and the United States. The other argues that democracy consists of the participation of labor unions in management and decision making. This view was dominant in Germany. Before the settlement of the Miike Strike of 1960, Japanese labor relation as a whole in the postwar period were basically influenced by the Anglo-Saxon belief in industrial democracy. Although some progressive business leaders recognized the strength of the German model and tried to promote the productivity movement, the effort failed to generate wide support from labor until the 1960s.

Labor's suspicion of the productivity movement was no surprise. As reported by *Ekonomisuto* (1955, July 9:50), "The rationalization in 1954 in most industries was characterized by reducing the number of staff, lengthening the working hours, and increasing the production per worker . . . besides, according to the official statistics, the promotion of productivity not only barely improved the quality of workers' lives, but even resulted in unprecedented unemployment – 840,000 in March. It created a hell of unemployment." The Headquarters of Productivity also pointed out that "the attitude of cooperation between management and labor for the same goal was not nurtured in this period. Because labor relations still had a confrontational atmosphere in 1955, it is understandable that neither labor nor management immediately accepted the idea that the productivity movement was a national movement with the participation of labor unions" (Nihon Seisansei Honbu 1985:5).

The productivity movement had some positive effects. Unlike the rationalization movement, it did not create widespread unemployment because new technologies were introduced primarily in the frontier industries. Even when the reduction of the labor force became inevitable in a sunset industry, many companies transferred workers to other fields rather than letting them go. According to a survey conducted at the end of the 1950s, in 91% of the 409 firms that made technological innovations, only 2 actually laid off workers; 71% of these firms avoided layoffs through job transfers (Nihon Seisansei Honbu 1960).

Conclusion

This chapter demonstrates that Japanese developmentalism underwent a drastic transition in the 1950s in the new environment defined by liberal capitalism. In this transition, two dynamic forces were at work. On the one hand, the Dodge Plan ended the era of the managed economy. It raised the issue of efficiency, forcing Japanese industrial policy to change the wartime version of direct bureaucratic control over the distribution of materials and prices to a new form of state intervention that could not only allocate resources strategically, but also strengthen the production efficiency of Japanese companies to survive in the international competition. On the other hand, the Korean War not only provided the Japanese with an opportunity to survive the stabilization panic caused by the Dodge Plan and to accumulate capital, it also demonstrated the possibility of continuing the military version of developmentalism in one way or another. Japan was overwhelmed by the choice between these two alternatives in the 1950s, which made these 10 years what Nakamura Masanori calls a "political decade."

In response to these challenges, two grand strategies were formulated. Prime Minister Yoshida Shigeru presented a political strategy. By allying with the United States, Japan would not only receive economic benefits but also military protection. This would enable Japan to minimize its defence expenditure and concentrate on economic reconstruction. Economists presented Japan with an economic strategy. Schumpeter's theory of innovation changed the way Japanese economists understood the dynamics of long-term economic growth; it also reformulated the Japanese definition of comparative advantage in international trade in terms of production technology. Under this new definition, the wartime focus on the development of heavy-chemical industries obtained new significance in state industrial policy. It was no longer to support military expansion, but rather to build up a strategic position for Japan in international trade.

To adapt to the new international environment, two reverse trends appeared in the Japanese economic system. On the one hand, the state, whose capacity was strengthened greatly and reached its peak during the occupation, changed its means of economic intervention. To promote exports, the state shifted its policy objective from effective bureaucratic control over the distribution of materials and prices at the macro level to production efficiency of individual firms at the micro level. From the 1950s on, the state and the market were no longer mutually exclusive in Japanese industrial policy. The Japanese state began to use the market to promote the competitiveness of Japanese companies, meanwhile putting the scope of market competition under its control by issuing government regulations and implementing a discriminatory policy concerning credit and foreign currency controls. Although the Japanese state reinstated the functions of the market, this was not the same as the market in liberal capitalist economies. On the other hand, other, nonmarket institutions, which had been strongly challenged by the postwar democratic reforms, revived to serve the new national purpose. After the state revised the antimonopoly law twice, former *zaibatsu* companies began to organize themselves into *keiretsu*. The business groups, sustained by the main bank system, began to dominate the market again. Meanwhile, cartels also became legal again to combat the economic recession and to rationalize the industrial structure.

In labor relations, a new vision of replacing confrontation with co-operation also emerged. Business leaders started to stabilize the labor relations by initiating the productivity movement. They strategically asserted the nationalist ideology. Some labor unions began to partici-pate in the movement. Although the most powerful union still rejected the idea, there was a significant change in its general strategy, which shifted the focus from political issues such as rearmament to economic issues such as how to obtain more welfare through the organized an-nual spring strike. The shifting course of Japanese industrial policy in the early 1950s indicates the strong dependence of indigenous values on context. It shows that business leaders affirmed indigenous values of harmony and collective welfare only when the Korean War ended, when they realized that they could no longer depend on special pro-curement to obtain foreign currency; instead they had to depend on the promotion of production technology, which required the cooperation of labor. Such values were never affirmed for their own sake, but only for utilitarian purposes. During the rationalization movement of the early 1950s, in which Japanese firms conducted massive layoffs, none of the indigenous values were present. Instead the conflict approach of Marxism seemed more attractive to labor unions. A return to harmony and cooperation became a welcome alternative only when every party's interest was addressed and every party could benefit.

Despite these changes, the transformation of Japanese developmentalism from the military version to a trade version remained unsettled in the 1950s, as the country was still deeply divided on some important issues. Although Prime Minister Yoshida Shigeru presented the grand strategy for the trade version of developmentalism, it was constantly challenged by both the conservatives, who intended to rebuild the military, and those who emphasized political independence from the United States. The advocacy of technological innovation demonstrated a great vision for Japanese industrial policy. In the 1950s, labor and management still had not worked out a mutually agreed upon institutional solution that embodied this vision, and the impact of the confrontational strategy remained strong on both sides. Finally, although the state changed the means of intervention, the economy was still heavily controlled. Market forces began to improve the competitiveness of Japanese companies, but foreign products had not joined the competition in Japan's domestic markets. In this sense, the real test was still to come. These three issues continued to generate tensions and conflicts. By the beginning of the next decade, they would cause major eruptions that led to new changes.

6. High growth and liberalization

High growth and liberalization was the leading paradigm in Japanese industrial policy during the 1960s. Under this paradigm, Japanese developmentalism accomplished its transition to the trade version, and both the ideologies and institutions of the contemporary Japanese economic system were patterned.

The 1950s was still an early stage in the transition of Japanese developmentalism to the trade version for three reasons. First, the Yoshida strategy was resisted by both conservatives and progressives, and the country was deeply divided on the issue of rearmament. Second, both management and labor still remained skeptical about the productivity movement, and the agenda of technological innovation had not received full support. Third, although Japan began to engage in international trade, the Japanese economy was still operated in a semi-open international environment because Japan's domestic markets were still extremely protected and the bureaucratic control over the economy was still quite strong.

Japanese developmentalism in the 1960s was driven by the Pax Americana in two significant ways. First, the extension of the Japan–U.S. security treaty greatly escalated the political tension between the conservatives and the progressives, creating a major political crisis in Japan in 1960. After this crisis, however, the Japanese changed "political season" to "economic reason." From then on, as Sasaki Takashi (1991:2) points out, Japan ended its attempts to redefine its position in the world system dominated by the United States; the nation "turned inward and made economic growth and the pursuit of affluence its highest priorities." The progressive forces, which in the 1950s had demonstrated great strength in the struggle with the conservatives on the issues of rearmament and the Japan–U.S. security treaty, were effectively demobilized because they presented no alternative policy proposal to counter the conservative Liberal-Democratic Party's (LDP's) theme of high growth. The LDP had maintained its administration successfully until the early 1990s. The shift to this strong commitment to economic growth indicates a profound change. In the military version of developmentalism, the economy was regarded as the means for the nation-state to achieve its goals in international politics. Now the means became the goal itself. Even though the potentially negative impact of high growth had drawn some attention, the nation as a whole was dominated by concerns about the GNP and liberalization. Japan has concentrated on the economy so singlemindedly that Western observers repeatedly wonder "what purpose this [economic] power will be put [to] in the future and what role Japan will play in the international system" (Pyle 1992:3).

Second, leading the emerging free trade regime, the United States pressured Japan to start the liberalization of trade and capital investment. At the time, liberalization was perceived as the arrival of the second black ship, a strong challenge to the survival of Japanese industries. It implied that Japan must end protectionist measures such as high tariffs and let foreign products enter Japanese markets. Because many areas of the Japanese economy had been under strong protection, the efficiency of companies in these areas was a major concern in state policy making. In addition, the promotion of domestic industrial structure and the national mobilization of both material and human resources through the "new industrial system" were believed to be crucial in determining the fate of the Japanese economy. According to the conventional understanding, liberalization means a further release of market forces and an increase in competition because it eliminates protective tariffs. The Japanese strategy, however, indicates that even after the tariffs are eliminated, domestic markets can still be effectively protected from foreign companies by organizing competition privately.

Another major conflict of the 1950s, the one between labor and management, was also settled after a major confrontation at the national level during the Miike strike in 1960. Although this crisis ended with labor's failure, all the parties involved changed their strategies from then on. In the 1950s, the LDP had regarded labor policy as an issue of public security in dealing with confrontations between labor and management. In the 1960s, however, it began to treat this issue as a social policy, recognizing the importance of cooperation by labor in promoting productivity. Management recognized the hugh cost of the confrontational strategy. The changing labor market situation also forced Japanese companies to try to maintain labor forces in the high-growth paradigm. Labor unions, after years of reluctance, were finally organized into the productivity movement. As a result, the wartime legacy, after more than one decade's interruption, began to take root in the new democratic political environment, addressing contemporary concerns.

The strategic view of the economy in Japanese industrial policy developed to a new level. In the 1960s, the interpretation of national power of production in Japanese economic ideology was extended from *strategic industries* (though the industrial level still remained very important to state policy) to *comprehensive national power* (*sōgō kokuryoku*). The Japanese state began to adopt an aggressive financial policy whose objectives were no longer limited to countering the effect of the business cycle when the economy suffered a recession or to sustaining the pace of economic growth in general. The state became an important instrument for upgrading the industrial structure of the Japanese economy and strengthening national competitiveness in both international and domestic markets. In December 1960 the state adopted the famous National Income Doubling Plan (NIDP) under the leadership of the Ikeda Hayato cabinet. The NIDP set a goal for the Japanese economy: to double the actual national income within 10 years. To achieve this goal, the state made a strong commitment to increase public spending for developing infrastructure, improving social security and social welfare, promoting human capital, and eliminating the dual structure in the economy.

Following the model of the wartime national mobilization, MITI's bureaucrats initiated the *new industrial system* (*shinsangyō taisei*), which aimed at organizing industries nationwide to compete with foreign companies after the liberalization of trade. To mobilize the nation to meet the challenge of liberalizing the economy, the Japanese state proposed the program of *reorganizing industries* (*sangyō saihensei*) by building a *new industrial system*. According to MITI's proposal, the state would work with the private sector to select a number of industries strategic to the national economy. Then the state would ensure financial credit and provide tax breaks to these industries. It would also supervise each loan that the commercial banks issued, in agreement with this blueprint for optimal industrial structure. Although the Diet did not pass this bill, its general principles were adopted in the later development of *keiretsu*. In comparison with the policy paradigm of innovation, the state in the high-growth paradigm played a much more direct role in sustaining economic growth through the public sector. In contrast to the managed economy, however, state intervention in the economy in the 1960s transcended direct bureaucratic control over distributing materials or setting market prices, partially because of resistance by the private sector, whose political power increased during the postwar reconstruction period. The state began to influence the behavior of the private sector through various policy instruments. One of the major methods was administrative guidance, which has lasted until the present.

The rejection of excessive competition was another major concern in this policy paradigm. The Japanese state bureaucracy lost its most important leverage in controlling private companies during the liberalization of trade and foreign currency exchange. As a result, the effort to revive the wartime system according to its original model (by enacting the Special Measures Law for the Promotion of Designated Industries) lost its material foundation and the Keidanren's proposal for *independent integration (jijū chōsei)* eventually prevailed over MITI's proposal of *state–private sector coordination (kanmin chōsei)*. Nevertheless, liberalization of trade and capital investment does not necessarily mean that the market became dominant. The principle of reorganization of industries designed to strengthen the economy of scale of Japanese companies in the era of liberalization, was still supported by various nonmarket governance structures: MITI relied on administrative guidance to implement its industrial policy rather than on direct bureaucratic control; the *keiretsu*, which integrated private firms both vertically and horizontally in the form of business groups, became the major pattern by which the Japanese economy organized market competition.

The rejection of the profit principle, especially its implication for labor relations, became wide spread under the pressure of liberalization and of the labor shortage that occurred in the mid-1960s as a result of high growth. It led to the institutionalization of Japanese management among big companies, characterized by lifetime employment, the seniority-based wage, and the company-based labor union. The assertion of cultural traditions such as harmony became the leading tone in labor relations. High growth itself provided this nationalist ideology with a material foundation. It created a strong demand for young workers, which forced the big companies to compete with each other to ensure the stability of their labor forces by offering permanent employment and seniority-based wages. By the mid-1960s, the principle of keeping labor relations stable, which had originated in World War II to mobilize workers in the struggle for national survival in total war, took root in a new environment. Now this principle served to mobilize workers in the competition for the survival of Japanese companies in both international and domestic markets.

The diffusion of Keynesian economics, the legacy of the managed economy, and the European experiences with a mixed economy played an important role in shaping the Japanese strategies. Economists such as Shimomura Osamu, Nakayama Ichiro, and Ōkita Saburō exercised intellectual leadership in forming Japanese industrial policy in the 1960s. They strongly influenced the formation of the idea of high growth and, as a concrete policy proposal, transformed it into the NIDP. Their influence, especially that of Shimomura, was strongly sustained by the close link with the leading politician Ikeda Hayato. This was crucial in explaining why the idea of high growth obtained political currency. At the same time, Arisawa Hiromi based his experience on the managed economy; MITI bureaucrat Morozumi Yoshihiko, who had witnessed a mixed economy at work when he served in the Japanese embassy in France, proposed a policy of building a new industrial system for the Japanese economy. On the basis of their ideas, MITI drafted the Tokushinhō (Special Measures Law for the Promotion of Designated Industries) bill. Although the effort to build the state–private sector coordination system eventually failed, the principles they presented remained in the independent integration system.

A turning point in Japan's postwar history

The Japanese economy had developed rapidly during the 1950s. Between 1950 and 1955, the average annual growth rate of Japan's GNP was 8.9%, the rate of private investment in production equipment was 10.2%, and the rate of exports was 13.9% (Kōsai 1989:285). Various economic indexes reached record levels: total GNP in 1954, industrial production in 1955, consumption per capita in 1956, and GNP per capita in 1957. As mentioned in Chapter 5, Japanese companies accumulated a huge amount of capital through the special procurement of military goods and services for the U.S. government during the Korean War. They began to invest heavily in production equipment and technological transfer. Driven by the high rate of private capital investment in the second half of the 1950s, the Japanese economy experienced two unprecedented booms. The economy underwent a consumption revolution marked by the possession of the "three sacred treasures": the TV set, the washing machine, and the refrigerator.

At the end of the 1950s, however, the Japanese economy confronted several structural problems. The first was the strong international pressure to liberalize trade and foreign currency exchange. The postwar reconstructions in Western Europe and Japan depended strongly on U.S. dollars. To balance their international payments, these countries continued to practice managed trade. As their economies revived, however, the U.S. share in world exports of industrial products declined from 38% in 1948 to 22% in 1959. Consequently the outflow of dollars worsened the international payments of the United States. Therefore, the U.S. government urged Western European countries and Japan to abolish their discriminatory restrictions on imports from the United States. In response, Britain, France, and Italy rescinded many restrictions on the imports of American products; meanwhile, in 1958, they resumed convertibility between the U.S. dollar and their own currencies (Keizai Kikakuchō 1976). Japan, as a member of the International Monetary Fund (IMF) and the General Agreement on Trade and Tariffs (GATT), was required to cooperate with the liberalization of trade and foreign currency exchange. At that time, Japan's domestic market was still tightly protected. At the end of August 1959, only 26% of Japanese imports faced no government-imposed restrictions (Economic Planning Agency 1990b:102). In 1959, for the first time in postwar history, Japanese exports to the United States exceeded imports, ending $113 million in the black (Arisawa 1976:440). At the GATT conference held in Tokyo in 1959, the U.S. representative warned that if Japan did not quickly rescind restrictions on imports from the dollar areas, the United States might restrict imports of Japanese products (Masamura 1985). It seemed clear that if Japan did not respond to these pressures, its economic interests in the international market would be jeopardized.

The second problem was the constraint on economic growth imposed by an underdeveloped infrastructure. Beginning in 1953, the Japanese economy surpassed its prewar level. Yet despite the rapid growth of the economy, the construction of infrastructure had lagged, and the operation of the Japanese economy had depended primarily on accomplishments in the prewar period. By the end of the 1950s, infrastructure became a major obstacle to further economic development. Although four industrial centers had emerged – the Tokyo–Yokohama area, the Ōsaka–Kōbe area, the Nagoya area, and the northern Kyūshū area – the highways, railroads, sewers, industrial water, and housing in metropolitan areas were still inadequate. At that time, Japanese transportation in major metropolitan areas was considered the worst in the world; many people in the urban areas lived in houses that had no sewer system; the number of telephones per 100 persons was only 4.7; and the airports and seaports were unable to support the rapidly expanding trade with other countries. Besides, Japan's standard of living remained low. Japan's living environment, educational institutions, and recreational facilities required an abrupt infusion of funds to catch up to other industrialized countries.

The third problem was the inefficiency in many sectors. Under the pressure of liberalization, there was an urgent need to further upgrade the industrial structure and to enhance the competitiveness of the economy. According to a survey conducted by the Finance and Monetary Association, the liberalization of trade would strongly affect the industries based on domestic resources, such as coal and raw metals, as well as the industries that did not have large domestic markets but nevertheless competed with foreign companies in international markets through cheap labor; these included special steel products, machine tools, chemical machinery, and construction machinery. More important, trade liberalization would also influence industries regarded as highly value-added in the international market, such as automobiles and petrochemical products (Yoshimura 1961:81–5). To promote competitiveness in these industries, the NIDP stated that Japanese firms must further upgrade their production equipment, establish a base of mass production, promote specialization, standardize the production of commercial goods, and build an industrial complex. The promotion of human capital and the development of science and technology would be essential in achieving these goals (Ōkita 1960). Without upgrading of the industrial structure, the traditional labor-intensive products could not generate enough hard currency; the imbalance in international payments often appeared to be the bottleneck restricting the further growth of the Japanese economy. Besides, the changing structure of the population indicated that although unemployment was still a concern in policy making, a comprehensive shortage of labor would occur in the Japanese economy in the second half of the 1960s because the fertility rate in Japan was declining rapidly.

The fourth problem was the existence of a dual structure in the economy and inequality in the distribution of economic welfare. When the economic situation improved in 1955 and 1956, employment indeed increased at a rate of 150,000 hires per month. Nevertheless, most of this hiring occurred in firms with 20 or fewer employees; that is, it entailed low-paid or part-time work. In contrast, large firms recruited far fewer workers. In the mid-1950s, large firms were still reluctant to recruit regular workers because they had to provide such workers with permanent employment and seniority-based wages. As Arisawa (1957:40) explained, "The reason why managers at big firms have a negative attitude is that they do not believe that the Japanese economy will grow at a high rate. They regard the high rate of economic growth in the early 1950s as a casual and exogenous phenomenon, which will soon go to the downside of the economic cycle." In regard to the liberalization of trade, the dual structure seemed to be a major disadvantage to the Japanese economy because it was believed that the small and medium-sized firms would scatter the limited capital and material resources; thus Japanese competitiveness would suffer because of economies of scale. The differences in size, technology, and degree of concentration of capital and labor caused a large gap in income and economic welfare between employees in big firms and those in small and medium-sized firms. This inequality not only created concern within Japan but also frequently became the target of international criticism. When the economic minister of West Germany visited Japan in 1958, he severely criticized Japan's cheap labor policy and poor social welfare measures (Tanaka 1959).

In the second half of the 1950s, in fact, the development of the Japanese economy reached an impasse: Further development of production technology was constrained by the poor condition of the infrastructure, human capital, and social welfare, and the market forces themselves could not overcome these difficulties. In these circumstances Arisawa Hiromi, one of the major advisors to the Japanese government, argued that "the government must plan and set up the domestic foundation for technological innovation. It is an extremely urgent task for the state to solve the problem of employment in Japan in the long run" (Arisawa 1957:42).

The program of high growth and liberalization

In response to these challenges, the Japanese government started to liberalize trade in 1959 and adopted the NIDP in 1961. High growth and demand management became new policy agendas, transcending the previous practices of simple countercyclical adjustment and promotion of the supply capability. In the meantime, the Japanese state changed its strategy of protecting domestic markets by tariffs to organizing Japanese companies into a new industrial system to compete with foreign companies in the home markets.

In the 1960s, the Japanese state successfully reduced the nation's political divide by shifting public attention away from sensitive issues such as the revision of the constitution and the Japan–U.S. security treaty to the optimistic prediction of high growth and the urgency of national unity in the process of economic liberalization. The encounter of Japanese developmentalism with liberal capitalism in the form of liberalization provided a strong impetus in finalizing the transformation of developmentalism to a trade version after two decades of evolution in the postwar era. In terms of concrete institutional arrangements, the economic system of the 1960s was not a simple reproduction of the wartime model. Rather, it was a creative reproduction reflecting adjustments in many areas, especially in state intervention and the state–business relationship, of the original format of the managed economy, and reflected the changing structure of the Japanese political economy. The basic economic principles for governing the economy were also upgraded.

The strategic view of the economy was further extended. In this new policy paradigm, the understanding of the national power of production shifted from the comparative advantage in production technology in the 1950s to the high growth of the entire economy in the 1960s. The whole nation once again was mobilized to concentrate its energy on a single goal; at this time, the GNP became the top priority. To sustain the high growth, the Japanese state adopted the NIDP. In this plan, it made a strong commitment to economic growth by rapidly increasing public expenditures in constructing infrastructure, including roads, harbors, railways, airports, transportation equipment, telephone and telegraph exchanges, residential houses, water supply lines, hospitals, social welfare establishments, and educational institutions. The total amount of investment over a 10-year period was 16.1 trillion yen.

In the NIDP the Japanese government adopted Keynesian policy innovatively, expanding the function of public spending through government financing from adjusting to the economic situation to stimulating economic growth. It regarded the money supply as a means to sustain such growth and viewed the appropriate distribution of these funds as the most important task of state finance. In 1965, when the Japanese economy fell into recession, the government abandoned its long-standing practice of balancing the budget, which it had followed since the implementation of the Dodge Plan in 1949, and began to issue public debt to sustain economic growth. In the 1960s, the Japanese state innovatively linked the Keynesian theory of demand management with its industrial policy. It made the increase in public spending not only an instrument for adjusting fluctuations in the business cycle or sustaining economic growth, but also a means for upgrading the industrial structure of the Japanese economy by emphasizing capital-intensive industries such as manufacturing and chemicals. In the 1960s the general machine tool, electrical engineering, automobile, high-polymer chemical, and raw metal industries were identified as the major strategic industries in which Japan would build its competitiveness.

The NIDP was adopted in December 1960 and had a powerful psychological and political impact on Japanese society. One day after its announcement, the average price on the Tokyo stock market jumped to a record high (Kobayashi 1989). The state commitment to high growth stimulated massive investments by the private sector, and the Japanese economy entered an era in which investments brought new investments. With the implementation of the NIDP, the average annual growth rate of the GNP in the 1960s was kept at 11.6% and the increase in national income at 11.5%. The annual growth rate in salaries jumped about 11% in contrast to 6–7% in the 1950s. The growth rate of exports was 16.8%, and the share of heavy and chemical products in total exports jumped to 62% in 1965, in contrast to 38% in 1955 (Economic Planning Agency 1990b). The goal of doubling the national income was realized within six years. By 1968, Japan had become an economic superpower in terms of GNP, second only to the United States.

At the same time, the concept of human capital was incorporated for the first time into the Japanese perception of the national power of production. In the NIDP, the Japanese state made a strong commitment to promote education, science, and technology based on the prediction that future competition in the global market would be determined by technological innovation and by a comparative advantage in the knowledge-intensive industries. The state greatly increased public expenditures in sponsoring research and development in strategic industries; it promised that by fiscal year 1970, the end of the period covered by the NIDP, the proportion of research funding in the total national income would have increased from 0.9% to 2%. In the educational system, the state sponsored the establishment of middle-level vocational education in order to train a new generation for the labor force. The enrollment rate in general high schools was also planned to increase from 59.8% in 1960 to 72.0% in 1970.

Under the pressure of liberalization, the strategic view of the economy was reflected in the state's effort to incorporate the country in the new industrial system. It was asserted that establishing a new industrial order as a means to strengthen international competitiveness had become an indispensable condition for economic growth. In the 1960s, the concept of reorganization of industries, which had originated in 1931–45, developed further. In the 1950s, this policy had emphasized either individual firms, as indicated by the concept of rationalization early in this decade, or individual industries, as indicated by the concern about production technology in strategic industries later in the decade. In the 1960s, in contrast, the concept of reorganization of industries was interpreted at the national level and became dynamic. The new industrial system, according to the definition given by the Subcommittee on Industrial System (SIS) headed by Arisawa Hiromi within the Investigation Committee on Industrial Structure (ICIS), is an institutional arrangement coordinating the behavior of individual companies, the interorganizational relationship among private companies, and the roles and responsibility of both the state and the private sector in economic activities (cited by Tsūsanshō 1990b, vol. 10:49). Theoretically speaking, once a consensus on optimal industrial structure is achieved, this industrial system should be able to integrate its various components and move to make the theory a reality.

The concept of the industrial system had direct implications for the role of the state. Because industrial structure was a macro issue, it could not be promoted without state intervention. In reality, the effort to build the new industrial system caused a serious struggle between the state and the private sector on the issue of leadership. The independent integration advocated by the private sector eventually prevailed over

MITI's state–private sector coordination. Nevertheless, as Tsuruta Toshimasa (1984:63) correctly points out, independent integration reflects the three basic understandings offered by the vision of state–private sector coordination. First, the major problems confronting the Japanese economy in the liberalization of trade were underscaled business operations and excessive competition. Second, the international competitiveness of Japanese companies had to be strengthened by encouraging mergers and coordination and by enlarging the scope of companies' business operations. Third, the state should allow cartels and mergers by relaxing the antimonopoly law. Equally important, the failure of MITI in the political struggle with the private sector over leadership in the new industrial system did not prevent it from supporting big business in obtaining more favorable treatment for the purpose of strengthening national capital (*minzoku shihon*). To mention this point only briefly here, in the late 1960s, in responding to the liberalization of capital investment, MITI strongly supported mergers among big companies. In light of comparative capitalism, however, it does not matter much whether the state or the private sector was more important in determining the fate of the Tokushinhō: Even though the private sector succeeded in pushing the new industrial system toward independent integration, this outcome did not mean that the Japanese *keiretsu* would behave the same way as their American counterparts in market competition.

The rejection of excessive competition also developed to a new level. According to the conventional understanding, liberalization would naturally lead to more competition. In reality, however, it was argued that because of liberalization, excessive competition was no longer acceptable. The reason was that the underscaled business operation was perceived as the major disadvantage of Japanese companies in competition with Western companies. To promote the economies of scale of Japanese companies, the state tried to limit the scope and degree of competition by enhancing government regulations and by encouraging cartels and *keiretsu* in an effort to promote cooperation among individual firms in research and development and investment.

Although MITI failed to induce the Diet to pass the *Tokushinhō*, it succeeded in enacting the Oil Industry Law. Back in 1952, after the abolition of the quota system for distributing oil, which began during the war, state control over the oil industry had taken the form of control over foreign currency, which was needed to purchase oil. In

July 1961, in preparing for the liberalization of the oil industry (which the Japanese state had promised would take place in October 1962), MITI established the Council on Energy, chaired by Arisawa Hiromi. After Arisawa led a delegation to Western Europe to investigate oil policy in Britain, West Germany, France, and Italy, the council submitted a report to MITI suggesting that the supply of cheap energy and the stability of the supply should be the two major principles in industrial policy. To ensure the energy supply, Japanese companies must engage in the development of oil fields, either domestically or internationally. In oil refining and sales, Japan must control at least 30% of the total capital. A certain level of domestic oil production must be safeguarded by the state's subsidies and by long-term transactions among refining companies. To secure the supply of special oil, a national policy company (*kokusaku kaisha,* the same term used during World War II) should be established by state capital or by the capital of the major users of oil, such as the oil refineries, the electric companies, and the iron and steel companies. In May 1962 the Japanese Diet passed the Oil Industry Law, which was drafted by MITI according to the principles suggested by the Council on Energy. Later this law became an important weapon used by big oil companies to form cartels and by the state to establish the Public Oil Corporation. The enactment of the Oil Industry Law created many problems for the Japanese economy, as it seriously restrained competition. During the first oil shock, major oil companies raised their oil prices rapidly; this increase became the target of strong criticism by the general public and led to the Japanese government's tightening of the antimonopoly law in 1977. When this law was still under development by the Council on Energy, only Wakimura Yoshitarō, a professor of economics at the University of Tokyo, opposed it. He argued that "against the global trend of internationalization, the rigid distinction between foreign capital and national capital, the fear of foreign capital, and the rejection of foreign capital are anachronisms, and the purpose of the Oil Industry Law, to reject foreign capital, is a problem of the state" (Tsūsanshō 1990b, vol 10:522).

In the 1960s, the rejection of the profit principle was also given new meaning. The practice of stabilizing labor relations in order to promote productivity, which was asserted by the progressive managers in the 1950s, began to receive wide recognition. After the Miike dispute, in conjunction with the changing labor market situation, big Japanese companies institutionalized the practice of lifetime employment and the seniority-based wage system. Labor unions, who were demobilized by their failure in the Miike dispute, also changed their position on the productivity movement. The ideology of Japanese corporatism emerged. It replaced the emphasis on efficiency, measured by the short-term profit of the company, with a focus on cooperation between management and labor, sustained by a strategic assertion of the traditional value of harmony.

The ideas of high growth

The high-growth policy was sustained by the idea that the Japanese economy had entered an era of high growth and that the state should sustain this trend by practicing a Keynesian financial policy. This idea, which directly contradicted the orthodox theory of business cycles, resulted in a cognitive revolution in Japanese economic thinking. In the late 1950s, most Japanese bureaucrats and businessmen still believed that the two economic booms in the second half of the 1950s would be followed by a recession and that the state should adopt a tight-money policy to slow economic growth.

Three economists contributed most to formulating the high-growth agenda for Japanese industrial policy. Shimomura Osamu, a government economist who worked at the Ministry of Finance, first presented the idea that the Japanese economy had entered an era of high growth. Nakayama Ichirō argued that doubling the income would be a direct means for Japan to develop a welfare state and to sustain economic development. Ōkita Saburō, the director of the Comprehensive Policy Bureau at the Economic Planning Agency (EPA) in charge of drafting the NIDP, transformed Shimomura's and Nakayama's ideas into concrete policy proposals.

Shimomura's thesis of high growth was derived intellectually from the ideas of Schumpeter, Keynes, and Harrod-Domar, as well as from empirical data on the Japanese economy. According to Shimomura, two factors determined economic growth. One was supply capacity, including both production capacity and import capacity; the other was effective demand, measured by industrial investment, government expenditure, exports, and consumption. To initiate and sustain economic growth, both supply capacity and effective demand were important. Shimomura argued that Japanese companies' heavy investments in production equipment in the 1950s had strengthened the productivity and import capacity of the Japanese economy and had provided it with great potential for high growth. To sustain economic growth, he asserted, the Japanese state should create effective demand by increasing public expenditures (Shimomura 1958, 1959a, 1959b, 1962).

Keynesian economics constituted a very important part of Shimomura's thesis of high growth. That thesis, however, incorporated various sources. The basic assumption of Shimomura's idea was Schumpeter's theory of innovation. When he changed Keynesian theory from a short-term theory of economic fluctuation to a long-term theory of economic growth, Shimomura also incorporated the Harrod-Domar model of economic dynamics, which emphasized *effective output*. He stressed the role of the state in economic growth but opposed efforts by MITI or the private sector to constrain the dynamics of the market through either state–private sector coordination or independent adjustment. Shimomura valued the function of market competition but rejected the laissez-faire doctrine. He believed that "when the process of innovation has just begun, the government and the central bank must assume leadership to provide the appropriate conditions in order to sustain economic growth. This is the responsibility of the government" (Kanamori 1985:151).

Shimomura had begun to study Keynesian economics in 1936 after he purchased a copy of Keynes's newly published *Theory of Employment, Money and Interest* in New York City, where he worked at a branch office of Japan's Ministry of Finance. In 1952, after long study, Shimomura sent an article he had written on Keynesian economics to Professor Yasui Takuma, an authority on Keynesian economics, who taught at Tōhoku University, for comments. Yasui was deeply impressed by the quality of the article and recommended that Tōhoku University award Shimomura a doctorate in economics. This was a major event in the Ministry of Finance; it also led to Shimomura's becoming the chief advisor to Ikeda Hayato, who had been the deputy minister of finance and became prime minister in 1960.

The Keynesian economics advocated by Shimomura in his high-growth thesis contradicted the orthodox economic thinking of the time, and it led to heated debates in the late 1950s. On the issue of how to perceive the strength of the Japanese economy in the late 1950s, Gotō Yōnosuke (1957) and Tsuru Shigeto (1959) were skeptical about Shimomura's judgment and warned about the impact of business cycles. Shimomura (1958), in contrast, made a clear distinction between business cycles and economic growth. He argued that the business cycle is determined by investments responding to fluctuations in the market, whereas economic growth is governed by entrepreneurs' investments in innovation. The business cycle approach assumes that an economic boom will be followed by a recession. In contrast, the economic growth approach predicts that despite short-term fluctuations, the economy will grow constantly over the long run. For this reason, Shimomura was extremely optimistic about the future of the Japanese economy, believing that it had entered a golden era of high growth.

The philosophical difference in preference between economic growth and stability was a major issue in the debate. Shimomura, believing in the Schumpeterian approach, argued that economic growth was a process in which innovation would constantly create bottlenecks and then break them. Therefore the recession after a boom was not a threat to the economy and could be left alone. In contrast, Gotō Yōnosuke, took a narrowly defined Keynesian approach and argued that the state should intervene when the economy experienced a recession; he believed that economic growth could be achieved by minimizing the scope of economic fluctuations (Kanamori 1985). On the policy implications for the state, Gotō stressed the necessity of government planning. Educated as an electrical engineer, he believed that the economy was controllable, and that state intervention would sustain the balance of international payments and break the bottleneck in economic growth. Shimomura, who spent his long bureaucratic career at the Ministry of Finance, where Adam Smith's view of the economy was quite influential, took a "natural" approach to the economy. He strongly objected to state control over people's economic activities. Instead, Shimomura focused on liberalizing the conditions under which people's creativity could be encouraged because he believed that "the very dynamic of economic growth lies in the free creativity of entrepreneurs" (Sawa 1984; Shimomura 1962:295).

Whereas Shimomura's thesis only offered a prediction on the future of the Japanese economy, Nakayama Ichirō's (1959) support of the NIDP further confirmed the policy targets of the Japanese state from the viewpoint of welfare economics. As vice-president of the Headquarters of Productivity and as president of the Central Council of Labor, whose major task was to improve labor relations through arbitration, Nakayama stated in a 1959 article titled "Advocate Doubling Monthly Salary" that the future of the Japanese economy lay in the construction of a welfare state; doubling monthly salaries would be a concrete step toward this goal. According to his analysis, Japan's production and exports had to depend on a low standard of living because of low productivity. To promote productivity, business should not only ask for cooperation from labor but should also increase salaries. Because the doubling of monthly salaries was based on the conditions of promoting productivity, accumulating capital, introducing new technology, and ensuring an international market, it would be in the interest of both business and labor and should be a national policy for Japan's future.

The idea of high growth reflected the impact of modernism on Japanese economic thinking. In the 1960s, the popularity of rationalism and social engineering swept the Western social sciences (Sawa 1984:4–5, 62). Japanese economists, like economists in many other countries, embraced the idea that the economy could be controlled by human rationality. They dreamed about endless growth and progress, succumbing to the fantasy that the increase in the GNP was the only basis of human happiness. Behind the NIDP stood strong beliefs in continuous economic growth and progress, and in the omnipotence of science and technology. As critics have pointed out, the high-growth policy focused on increasing the GNP and pursuing economic growth for its own sake. This emphasis, in turn, delayed responses to various social problems such as rapid increases in consumer prices, soaring land prices, and environmental pollution (Masamura 1974:31).

Brain trusts in policy making

The influence of Japanese economists on state policy making reached a new peak in the late 1950s and early 1960s. Members of the older generation, such as Arisawa Hiromi, Nakayama Ichirō, and Inaba Hidezō, remained very influential; the younger generation, especially government economists such as Shimomura Osamu, Ōkita Saburō, and Morozumi Yoshihiko, also played an important role in shaping Japanese industrial policy.

In the late 1950s, government economics (*kanchō ekonomikusu*) emerged as a distinctive school in Japanese economic thinking, and it changed the intellectual environment of Japanese industrial policy considerably. Methodologically, government economics derived its propositions from empirical data. According to Kanamori Hasao (1985), this realistic approach strongly influenced Shimomura. Drawing on statistical data from the Japanese economy, Shimomura always raised timely issues. He was interested in theory but sought a theory that would help explain reality. When the theoretical framework did not fit reality, he always altered the doctrine and developed new perspectives. With regard to research methodology, government economics appeared as a challenge to both Marxist and neoclassical economics. Although most economics departments in Japanese universities were dominated by the Marxist perspective at the time, Marxist economists were unfamiliar with even the elementary applications of econometrics. In the late 1950s there were only about 300 classical or neoclassical economists in Japan, and most of them, according to Sawa Takamitsu (1984:26), were busy learning theories that depended heavily on mathematics and had no time to conduct empirical studies of the Japanese economy. Meanwhile, "Western economic theories, which were based on thorough individualism and quantitative methodology, might be an effective analytical tool for understanding Western Europe and North America. For comprehending the Japanese economy in the second half of the 1950s, however, they were simply what Schumpeter called a 'toy gun'" (1984:14). In the 1950s, only a few academicians, such as Nakayama, Tsuru, and Ōkawa Kazushi, had employed quantitative methods to analyze empirical data on the Japanese economy. At the end of the 1950s, a new generation of neoclassical economists began to challenge the deductive methodology, asserting the importance of empirical data in economic analysis. At the 1959 annual meeting of the Japanese Association of Theoretical Economics, Komiya Ryūtarō, an associate professor of economics at the University of Tokyo, made a sensational speech. Drawing on his recent experiences while studying in the United States, he said that

> the fact that most Japanese economists devote their attention to pure theory and mathematical modeling reflects the backwardness of Japanese economics. No positivist science will be able to progress without an empirical foundation. To further develop economics in Japan, the majority of economists must engage in empirical research and deal with the practical issues. (Komiya [1959] 1971:219)

Peter A. Gourevitch (1989:87) once commented, "To become policy, ideas must link to politics – the mobilization of consent for policy." As had happened before, the diffusion of economic ideas in state policy making in the 1960s was sustained strongly by the connection between economists and the leading politicians. In the 1950s, as mentioned above, few Japanese bureaucrats held a doctorate in economics. Shimomura and Ōkita were among the exceptions. After Shimomura received his degree, he came to the attention of Tanaka Ikuo, the director of the general office at the Kōchikai, an association for the support of the politician Ikeda Hayato. Ikeda intended to compete for the post of prime minister, and Tanaka was eager to find policy proposals that might enhance Ikeda's political position. For this reason, Tanaka organized a private brain trust for Ikeda, which included seven members. They met once a week to hear Shimomura discuss his idea of high growth.

Ikeda himself was also a Keynesian, and he accepted Shimomura's idea without reservation. In his career as a politician, Ikeda was strongly affected by two men. In politics and international relations he was influenced by Yoshida Shigeru; he was "one of the best students at the 'Yoshida school'" (Kobayashi 1989:22). The Yoshida school was the group of ex-bureaucrat politicians whose careers were sponsored by Yoshida. In the early postwar period, many prewar party politicians were purged by the Occupation Authority for their connection with the military during the war. Prime Minister Yoshida thus selected a group of ex-bureaucrats to fill the vacuum. They later became the so-called conservative mainstream. These politicians committed themselves to Yoshida's grand strategy, holding that economic reconstruction was Japan's top priority and that Japan should concentrate all of its financial resources on economic development. In contrast to party politicians, who emphasized political affairs and ideologies, these ex-bureaucrats gave their primary attention to economic affairs because they had a strong background in economic administration. In economic affairs, Ikeda was influenced strongly by Ishibashi Tanzan, who called himself a Keynesian. As a bureaucrat at the Ministry of Finance in the early postwar era, Ikeda was promoted to vice-minister by Ishibashi, who was the minister of finance at the time. Later, when Ikeda himself became minister of finance and implemented the "Dodge line" in the third Yoshida cabinet, he changed Dodge's *deflation policy* to a *disinflation policy*, issuing many loans to protect firms from bankruptcy. In 1955, when Ishibashi became prime minister, Ikeda served as his minister of finance. The two men coauthored the policy titled "100 Billion Yen Public Expenditure and 100 Billion Yen Tax Reduction" in an effort to sustain growth. It was not implemented, however; Ishibashi had to quit because of ill health after holding office for only four months (Kobayashi 1989).

Ikeda supported Shimomura's high-growth thesis for political as well as intellectual reasons. In 1958, as the head of the second largest faction among the eight within the Liberal-Democratic Party, he sought to become prime minister, though he was in a relatively weak position in terms of seniority in the party. Ikeda intended to employ economic policy as a major weapon in the political competition within the LDP. Deeply impressed by Shimomura's idea of high growth, he decided to use it to challenge party politicians who had no attractive policy proposal regarding the economy. Ikeda's sponsorship of Shimomura's idea shows that ideas must be advocated by political agents within the state in order to influence policy. These ideas become influential only when they fit the interests of leading politicians and are supported by the political leaders. In this sense, the policy orientation of the leading political party is a key factor in the fate of economic ideas.

The EPA played a leading role in transforming the idea of high growth into a detailed policy proposal for the NIDP. Ōkita Saburō contributed greatly to this process. Unlike Shimomura, who emphasized the possibility of high growth, Ōkita focused on how to close the gap in the dual structure of the Japanese economy. Ōkita and his colleagues at the EPA envisioned the implications of high growth for the Japanese economy, such as improving the infrastructure, promoting trade, developing human capital, and reducing the gaps between the agricultural and industrial sectors, between big firms and small or medium-sized firms, and between various regions. As mentioned in Chapter 3, Ōkita developed a close relationship with the *gosanke,* namely, Arisawa Hiromi, Nakayama Ichirō, and Tōbata Seiichi, in the early postwar period, when he was involved in the priority production program. He continued to seek intellectual stimulation from the *gosanke* when he was in charge of drafting the long-term government economic plan. In 1958, sponsored by the Rockfeller Foundation in the United States, Ōkita visited more than 20 countries to investigate how they conducted long-term economic prediction and government planning. After he returned to Japan, his vision for a national income plan was initially stimulated by the Subcommittee on Long-term Prediction (*Chōki tenbō bukai*), headed by Tōbata Seiichi. This group within the Economic Council (*Keizai shingikai*) was the leading agency opposing the Japanese government on economic policy. Arisawa and Nakayama were also members of this subcommittee. When Ōkita began officially to develop the plan, he worked closely with four subcommittees at the Economic Council: the Subcommittee on Comprehensive Policy, headed by Nakayama Ichirō; the Subcommittee on Econometrics, headed by Yamada Yūzō; the Subcommittee on the Public Sector, headed by Inaba Hidezo; and the Subcommittee on the Private Sector, headed by Takahashi Kamekichi. The whole deliberation process involved more than 2,000 persons (Ōkita 1981b).

Becoming a first-class nation

The negative self-image was a major barrier to the high-growth policy at the time. Economic growth was not new to the Japanese; the economics of development pioneered by Arthur Lewis had already been introduced to Japan. Making high growth the top priority in state industrial policy, however, was alien to most Japanese because no country had ever followed such a policy. In the late 1950s, Japan was still perceived as an economically backward country. It was argued that because the average annual growth rate between 1948 and 1958 was 3.0% in the United States, 2.4% in Britain, 5.8% in France, and 3.5% in Sweden, the normal growth rate of the Japanese economy could not be very high (Ōkita 1959b:45; Shimomura 1959b:188). Shimomura's vision for the Japanese economy met strong resistance. In the policy debates, he fought almost in isolation. He was criticized by both bureaucrats, who regarded the outstanding performance of the Japanese economy in the 1950s as a result of the economic reconstruction, and by left-wing intellectuals, who regarded Japan as heavily dependent on or even as a colony of the United States. Thus, high growth would be unlikely without systematic institutional reform (Masamura 1985:168). The negative self-image was enhanced by Marxists during the debate on rearmament issues in the early 1950s. At that time, many Japanese intellectuals were sympathetic to the Marxist criticism, which objected to the dependence of the Japanese economy on the Cold War system. This dependency theory was very similar to the theory that appeared in Latin America in the 1960s and to the world system theory that emerged in the United States in the 1970s. This argument had a strong impact on the Japanese perception of their own economy: Many Japanese intellectuals had a negative-self image, assuming that Japan was economically backward and that the Japanese economy could not have a bright future.

Shimomura argued that the factors determining economic growth varied among nations. It would not be appropriate to draw a conclusion about the Japanese economy based on the economic situation in the United States and Western Europe (Shimomura 1959b:188–9). Komiya Ryūtarō (1960:6–7) also pointed out that the Japanese understanding, among intellectuals in general and economists in particular, was far from the reality; the intellectuals had been overwhelmed by pessimistic assessments of the Japanese economy and had underestimated the development of the international economy. According to Komiya, Marxism had caused the lag in the Japanese vision of the economy. He argued that the great merit of the high-growth policy was that it confirmed the ongoing reality of high economic growth in Japan.

In the broader intellectual environment, a growing consciousness of national identity helped to overcome the psychological barrier to the high-growth policy. A group of scholars began to present a brighter prediction for the future of the Japanese economy, demonstrating increasing confidence in their country. The negative self-image was challenged by scholars from both the *marukei* and the *kinkei*. The Marxist Kono Yoshihiko recognized that the Japanese economy had become much stronger by the end of the 1950s. He argued that although Japan had depended heavily on the United States, this dependence was only temporary because Japan's monopoly capital initially might need aid from the United States for its own recovery. Now it was trying to achieve economic independence by enforcing compulsory saving, enlarging the domestic market, and exploiting the working class. Once Japanese monopoly capital rebuilt its domestic foundation, it would regain the power to exercise imperialism by large-scale investment in production equipment and by promoting competitiveness. Sooner or later, a conflict between Japan and the United States would erupt (Kojima [1976] 1978:71–2). The *kinkei* economist Sakamoto Jirō searched for the national identity of the Japanese economy from a different viewpoint. He argued that in the view of many Japanese intellectuals, industrialization was equal to Westernization. Their point of reference was either the United States, Britain, or the Soviet Union. Because these intellectuals used other countries' values and ways of thinking to examine the reality of the Japanese economy, they had always emphasized the discrepancy between Japan and industrialized

Western countries and had attacked the backwardness of the Japanese economy. Sakamoto asserted that although Japan was not an advanced nation (*senshinkoku*), it was not a backward nation. Even though its consumption level was still low, as in many developing countries, its level of industrial production had reached that of industrialized nations (Sakamoto 1954:24, 41).

Even with Western economies as the reference, Umezao Tadao, a junior historian at Ōsaka City University, was quite confident about the Japanese economy. Contrary to the orthodox view that Japan's industrialization was an outcome of international pressure in the mid-nineteenth century, he argued that Japanese industrialization had resulted from a process of independent development in which Japanese society had accumulated enough modern elements to industrialize. Even if Western powers had not knocked on Japan's door in the nineteenth century, Japan would have moved naturally toward industrialization because of its internal dynamics. According to Umezao, Japan not only had a parallel history with Europe, which its Asian neighbors did not share, Japan had fared much better than Britain and France in balancing the conflict between cultural tradition and industrialization since the nineteenth century. In the 1950s, among industrialized countries, only Japan and West Germany achieved economic growth without colonies. In this sense, Japan was on the historical frontier, without the burden of the past, and was headed toward the future (Umezao, Takeyama, Hayashi, and Suzugi, 1957). Kono, Sakamoto, and Umezao held one belief in common: After a decade of economic reconstruction, the Japanese economy was no longer weak; therefore the Japanese should be confident about their future.

From "political season" to "economic season"

The acceptance of the high-growth thesis in state industrial policy was driven by the LDP's strategy of shifting people's attention from politics to the economy after the political crisis caused by the extension of the Japan–U.S. security treaty. Economic reconstruction was the top priority that Yoshida Shigeru set for Japan in the early 1950s. This priority, however, had encountered strong challenges from other competing agendas. Yoshida's successors, especially Hatoyama Ichirō and Kishi Nobusuke, emphasized political rather than economic issues. Kishi's efforts to renew the Japan–U.S. security treaty reflected the pro-politics orientation of the LDP in the late 1950s. The deep national division on the treaty resulted in a weariness with politics after the Anpō movement (opposing the Japan–U.S. security treaty). Under such circumstances, then Prime Minister Ikeda Hayato formulated a new strategy, using high growth to shift the nation's attention away from politics.

To be sure, economic interest was also an important motivation in the extension of the Japan–U.S. security treaty. Because of the contribution of the U.S. government's special procurement program to Japan's capital accumulation and international payments during the Korean War, the LDP and the business leaders were keenly aware of the economic benefits created by the military tie between Japan and the United States. The original treaty signed by the two countries in 1951 contained no provision regarding economic relations; thus the LDP intended to use the renewal of the treaty as an opportunity to make it clear that the treaty would also benefit the Japanese economy by promoting bilateral economic relations. As the LDP proposal pointed out, the renewal of this treaty was intended to "clarify the bilateral relationship of cooperation in various fields"; it "should be regarded as a step toward more cooperation between the two countries in politics and the economy" (Jimintō [1959] 1966a:139). "Following the example of NATO, Japan–U.S. relations will not be limited to security, but also will be extended to the common foundation of democratic liberalism in politics, and to large-scale exchange and interdependence in the economies" (Jimintō [1959] 1966b:140).

In fact, the extension of the treaty was also opposed in part by economic considerations. In the debates, some socialists contended that the Japanese economy had been dependent on the United States for more than 10 years, and that during this period the dependence promoted the interest of monopoly capital but victimized the Japanese people (Shakaitō undated; Tsuji 1966:146). In contrast, Ōuchi Hyōe, Arisawa Hiromi, and Tsuru Shigeto continued to perceive this issue from the economic perspective, consistent with their position in the peace movement of the early 1950s. They argued that renewal of the treaty might further stimulate Japan's defense expenditures. As a result, an important part of Japanese industry might be transferred to defense. This would constrain spending on the real welfare of the Japanese people in areas such as education, culture, the infrastructure, and social security. More important, they contended, as history had often shown, the establishment of a defense industry in the private sector would inject a dangerous element into Japanese society because some interest groups would prefer international tension. This would further hurt the economy (Heiwa Mondai Danwakai [1959] 17 December 1966:144; also see Hein 1994).

Nevertheless, the struggle over extension of the treaty was largely perceived as political, and most of the opposition concerned Japan's political independence. The division on this issue created a major political crisis. On 16 January 1960, when Prime Minister Kishi left for the United States to sign the treaty, 700 radical students attempted to stop him at the airport but were removed by 5,000 police officers. The treaty was signed on 19 January and was approved on 20 May by the 233 Diet members of the LDP who were present, 1 person less than half of the total house membership of 467. All of the Diet members affiliated with opposition parties were forcibly ejected by the police from the voting area by order of Prime Minister Kishi. Beginning at that time, an anti-Kishi movement emerged nationwide, which strongly demanded the resignation of the Kishi cabinet. Japan experienced an unprecedented political unrest. Eventually, U.S. President Dwight D. Eisenhower was forced to cancel his planned trip to Japan. Although the Japan–U.S. security treaty was renewed, it caused the Kishi cabinet to resign. The LDP fell into a crisis.

After the Anpō movement, rebuilding a political coalition for conservative politics became the top priority among LDP politicians. Newly elected Prime Minister Ikeda Hayato believed that the major cause of the chaos was the disappointment of the Japanese people with poor living conditions; this situation could be ameliorated by a policy that promised to improve Japan's standard of living. According to his assistant, Ōhira Masayoshi (who himself became prime minister in the late 1970s), when the Japanese finally had recovered from the long period of war and the severe shortage of materials that followed the defeat, they began to have a spiritual thirst. They were not satisfied with the conservative politics that was perceived as a legacy of the postwar occupation or were even repelled. Their anger came either from the reaction to the conservative legacy or from weariness with this legacy (Yoshimura 1985:31). Under such circumstances, Ikeda believed, a wise political strategy for the LDP at this moment was to return to the Yoshida doctrine, changing the barometer of domestic politics from the "political season" to the "economic season." He decided to use the

NIDP to appeal to the general public. In the meantime, he adopted the low-profile political slogan "tolerance and patience."

The adoption of the high-growth policy effectively shifted the nation's attention from politics to the economy, and this shift had a profound effect on Japanese developmentalism. The 1950s was a "political decade" (Nakamura 1995b:4). In these 10 years, according to Sasaki (1991:4), Japan faced a difficult international situation that caused severe clashes of opinion over foreign and security policies, making the political situation very unstable. A fairly large number of conservatives, including the leading politicians Hatoyama Ichirō and Kishi Nobusuke, insisted that "Japan should revise the Constitution written under the supervision of the Occupation Authority and should promote a more independent policy for national security." As a result, the economic agenda had been challenged by political agendas. After the failure of the Anpō movement, the leadership of the LDP shifted from the politically oriented Kishi to the economically oriented Ikeda. From then on, Japan abandoned all efforts at political and military self-assertion and devoted itself instead to increasing its national economic strength. The Japanese began to believe that the security treaty, for all of its faults, had the merit of keeping the country's military burden to a minimum, thereby facilitating economic growth. They came to accept the coexistence of two seemingly disparate elements in the international order – a united political-military front of Western countries headed by the United States and an international economy sustained by GATT and the IMF. Once the Yoshida doctrine was institutionalized, it went beyond being simply an alternative chosen at a certain point in time; it became part and parcel of Japan's identity.

The transition from the political season to the economic season ensured support for conservative politics by effectively demobilizing the progressive forces. After the Ikeda cabinet adopted the NIDP, even the Socialist Party began to advocate structural reform, demonstrating a revisionist orientation. Unlike their previous doctrine, which emphasized the dependent nature of Japanese capitalism and asserted that Japan should be liberated from the control of "American imperialism," the structural reform approach held by both the Socialist Party and the Communist Party in the 1960s focused on the need for partial reform of Japanese capitalism rather than revolution. Their major target shifted from American imperialism to Japan's monopoly capital. "The partial reform of production relations means changes in the economic policy of the state and the participation of labor in management. Its purpose is to control monopoly capital and to reform the work place by restricting profits, prices, and investments, and to democratize various economic institutions through workers' effective participation" (Shakaitō [1 January 1961] 1966:178). Nevertheless, as the former head of the Socialist Party, Katsumata Seiichi, once admitted, the response of his party to the era of high growth was immature. This was a major reason explaining its decline (cited in Nakamura 1995b:55–6). After all, the two LDP prime ministers, Ikeda Hayato and Satō Eisaku, who rebuilt conservative politics based on the Yoshida doctrine in the 1960s, were former economic bureaucrats. By emphasizing the economic priority, the LDP forced the progressive forces to compete in a policy area in which the latter did not have enough expertise. Nakamura Masanori and others point out that the so-called 1955 system, characterized by long dominance of the Conservative Party LDP, can be hardly regarded as a stabilized power structure before the Anpō movement. Only after Ikeda shifted national attention from politics to the economy, the progressive forces were demobilized and the LDP succeeded in maintaining its dominance until the early 1990s (Nakamura 1995b:17–18).

Political action and bureaucratic constraints

Chalmers Johnson (1982) once observed that because the operation of the Japanese state depended on the existence of a widely agreed upon set of overarching goals, it was cast adrift when confusion or conflict over those goals occurred and was incapable of coming to grips with basic problems. The adoption of the high-growth policy was a good example. It encountered strong resistance from both state bureaucracies and business circles. It was Ikeda's strong leadership that changed the views of these political actors and caused the idea of high growth to be officially accepted as a state policy.

On 27 December 1958, along with two other ministers, Ikeda resigned his position as minister of state in the Kishi cabinet to oppose Kishi's sending a bill to the Diet strengthening the power of the police. In January 1959, after Ikeda learned of Nakayama Ichirō's idea of doubling monthly salaries, he decided to use it as his political slogan for the coming election of the House of Councilors in June. Because Shimomura's thesis of high growth was too abstract for the general public, Ikeda borrowed Nakayama's popular phrase "doubling monthly salaries" to build a political coalition. On 22 February 1959, he gave his first public speech on this subject at a regional conference of the LDP in Hiroshima, his hometown. One day later, he repeated it in Ōsaka in a meeting with business leaders from the Kansai region. Business leaders had held that the major problem in the Japanese economy was that the pie was too small and that the Japanese had to work to make the pie larger. Labor unions had asserted that before the pie was made larger, it should be decided how to divide it more equitably. Ikeda's proposal of doubling monthly salaries provided a third position by asserting that the pie could be enlarged by changing the way it was cut.

Contrary to Ikeda's expectation, his new vision found no support but instead provoked much criticism from both business and labor. Business leaders contended that the destiny of the Japanese economy lay in manufacturing and trade. Effective demand could be created only by exports. To improve international payments, Japan had to promote exports, reduce costs, accumulate capital, and control salaries. Ikeda's proposal of creating domestic demand by increasing salaries placed too much weight on the domestic market and miscalculated the significance of exports to the Japanese economy. A strategy of economic growth that neglected exports was not acceptable. Labor unions, in principle, did not oppose the idea of doubling the monthly income and regarded Ikeda's proposal as a progressive contrast to the Japanese government's current practice of promoting exports by depending on a cheap-labor policy. Nevertheless, they held that the idea of doubling monthly salaries was too good to believe and was unlikely to happen. Enacting a minimum wage law and establishing a social security system and a national pension system were more realistic policy measures (Tanaka 1959).

Under such circumstances, Ikeda decided to make compromises in order to win the support of business leaders for his high-growth policy. On 9 March 1959, he published an article in *Nihon Keizai Shinbun* in which he ingeniously shifted his position. He wrote that he did not suggest the position that monthly salaries be doubled immediately. Rather, doubling would result naturally from the promotion of productivity and the increase in the GNP and national income. Meanwhile he reasserted that further development of the national economy was constrained by the shortage of effective demand, and that the state should increase public expenditures to sustain growth (Ikeda 1959). Ikeda's new position was different from that expressed in his speeches in February. By accommodating to the position taken by business, Ikeda began to gain support for his high-growth agenda in discussions of policy (Tanaka 1959).

Ikeda's proposal changed the focus of Japanese politics. In May 1959 Kishi Nobusuke decided to take over Ikeda's proposal as a proposal of the LDP in the June election for the House of Councilors; he announced that the government would begin to make a long-term economic plan to double the scale of the Japanese economy. In November 1959 Kishi asked the Economic Council, the major advisory agency to the Japanese state on economic policy, to devise a plan. The Council established 4 departments and 17 subcommittees involving more than 2,000 scholars, business leaders, representatives of labor unions, and bureaucrats in related research. The EPA served as the Council's office of general affairs in charge of drafting the NIDP. This action, however, did not save Kishi's political career after the extension of the Japan–U.S. security treaty. The strong support for the high-growth policy enabled Ikeda to win the competition within the LDP, and he became prime minister in July 1960. Business leaders liked Ikeda's idea of active government spending to sustain economic growth. They donated a large amount of money to ensure his victory in the election. A survey showed that the Ikeda cabinet obtained 51% of public support, one of the highest support rates in postwar Japanese politics, second only to that for the Yoshida cabinet after the San Francisco Peace Treaty was concluded.

Within the Japanese state bureaucracies, however, the implementation of the high-growth policy still faced strong resistance. Among the economic bureaucracies, MITI was Ikeda's major supporter. MITI bureaucrats held that because Japan had to liberalize trade, Japanese companies would confront strong challenges from foreign products in Japan's domestic markets. Therefore they were eager to upgrade Japan's industrial structure in order to meet the challenge. Two major bureaucratic opponents of Shimomura's version of the high-growth policy were the Ministry of Finance and the EPA. Shimomura had set the annual growth rate for the Japanese economy at 11%, much higher than the 7.2% predicted by the EPA. The Ministry of Finance, especially its Planning Bureau, had a strongly institutionalized belief in balanced government budget. "The orientation of this bureau was a personalized principle of finance, namely to keep expenditures within the limits of income. They have a strong commitment to social justice, avoiding any waste of public finances gained from taxes." The Ministry of Finance constantly opposed the NIDP throughout the policy-making process (Itō Daiichi 1967).

After Ikeda became prime minister, the Ministry of Finance gradually shifted its position because Ikeda had enough resources to induce the ministry's bureaucrats to change their minds. Ikeda himself had worked at the ministry for 27 years and eventually became its vice-minister, the highest position attained by a professional bureaucrat in the Japanese government. Even after he became a politician, he served twice as minister of finance. As a result, he had a strong personal network within the ministry. This network could exert a strong influence on promotions within the ministry, as well as on the arrangement of careers for bureaucrats after they left the ministry. In Japan, every bureaucrat must eventually leave the bureaucracy if he can no longer be promoted along with his entering cohort. Every ministry takes care of its "old boys," seeking positions for them in its peripheral organizations or in the private sector. Many bureaucrats become CEOs in big businesses immediately after they leave government service. In terms of social status and economic well-being, life after leaving the bureaucracy is important to Japanese bureaucrats. Thus Ikeda's influence exerted an invisible pressure on opponents, even when he no longer headed the Ministry of Finance. The bureaucrats at the ministry were clever enough to shift their attitude toward the NIDP from a purely economic policy judgment to a political judgment with reference to Ikeda's high-growth policy orientation (Itō Daiichi 1967).

The EPA was in charge of drafting the NIDP but favored stable growth at an annual rate of 7.2%. The EPA's view had gained broad support, not only from leading economists but also from business leaders, labor unions, and the mass media, because it mobilized more than 2,000 persons to draft the NIDP. Shimomura Osamu believed that a growth rate of 7.2% would harm the economy because once a low growth rate was established as the goal for state policy, higher growth could be restricted: The government would adopt a tight-money policy when the real growth rate outperformed the plan (Shimomura 1981a:84). Although Ikeda preferred Shimomura's prediction, he knew that the EPA's view was more acceptable to the majority of the Japanese, both in the state bureaucracies and in the society at large. When his economic beliefs countered his political considerations, and when the need to use high growth to rebuild the political coalition opposed the need to stabilize popular feeling, Ikeda decided to compromise again. Instead of adopting an annual growth rate of 11%, he chose 9%, halfway between Shimomura's 11% and the EPA's 7.2%, as the goal for the next three years. He believed that 9% was high enough to advertise his high-growth policy; meanwhile, it would help him to alter more easily the structural constraints within the state bureaucracies. A delicate position of the EPA in the larger context of bureaucratic struggles enabled Ikeda eventually to alter the EPA's position on this issue. The EPA had been staffed by bureaucrats transferred from various agencies. The Japanese bureaucracy has a temporary transfer system by which each ministry sends its own bureaucrats to work temporarily at other bureaucracies. The kinds of posts that the temporarily transferred individuals receive depend on the relative strength of their ministry in the bureaucratic world. For this reason, many EPA major posts had been under the control of MITI, and until 1960 this agency had never produced its own vice-minister. Therefore the EPA was given a nickname: a "branch office" of MITI. The EPA's bureaucrats had been attempting to establish their own domain within the bureaucratic world, depending on their "cultural capital" in the knowledge of the economy and their skill in using quantitative analysis to make long-term government plans. For this reason, the EPA could not resist Ikeda's proposed 9% growth rate because the adoption of the NIDP would afford it a critical opportunity to strengthen its domain. If the EPA had opposed the plan stubbornly, it would have had to sacrifice its own interests (Itō Daiichi 1967).

High growth versus stable growth

Shimomura's high-growth thesis demonstrated a strong production orientation, a major characteristic of Japanese developmentalism since the 1930s. Shimomura emphasized the promotion of production forces in the form of creating effective demand, assuming that the increase in productivity would foster economic welfare and improve the standard of living. In Shimomura's logic, the unit of analysis was the national economy as a whole. He was concerned with the growth of the economy rather than with the interests of certain social classes. Accordingly, he emphasized the creation of wealth rather than the distribution of wealth. He believed that it would be much easier and more constructive to discuss how to achieve full employment, raise the national standard of living, and increase social welfare than how to distribute the gains created by high growth among different social groups (Shimomura, Yamamoto, Imai, and Aoba, 1960:60).

Shimomura's high-growth thesis reflected both the rationalist perspective that predominated worldwide at the time and the wartime legacy of a production orientation. In the 1960s, economic thinking in Japan, as in many other industrialized countries, concentrated on technological innovation and economic growth; people assumed that human beings could control economic variables such as the growth rate, international payments, and prices, and economic growth eventually would help solve all problems confronting human societies. Many government officials and their economic advisors trusted macroeconomic policy excessively, expecting that economic growth would bring the greatest happiness to the majority of Japanese people (Sawa 1984). Similar to the wartime economic thinking, the high-growth policy of the 1960s excluded other concerns: It focused on promoting the national power of production and on organizing all of the national resources to achieve this goal. This was apparently an extension of the wartime legacy of production priority.

For these reasons, Shimomura's high-growth thesis was criticized by many economists at that time. The Marxist economist Nagasu Kazuji argued that in the high-growth paradigm "everything is mobilized and organized to realize the 9 percent growth rate. The whole national economy is brought into the framework to serve this 9 percent, no matter what it costs. The NIDP starts with the predetermined 9 percent growth rate and determines other numbers. It is very dangerous" (Arisawa, Minobe, Nagasu, Itō, and Miyazaki 1960:26). The major concerns raised by critics were economic stability and equality. The EPA had constantly advocated stable growth as a competing agenda to Shimomura's high-growth thesis. Although Ōkita Saburō was well known for his confidence in the potential of the Japanese economy and his support for an active government policy to sustain economic growth, he was worried about the trade-off between growth and stability. He argued that if the government adopted an active policy to sustain economic growth, inflation might occur. On the other hand, if the government tried to control inflation, growth would slow down and unemployment would become a problem. If the state's policy was too aggressive and created too much growth for the economy to absorb, there would be a strong reaction after the economic boom; this would eliminate many medium-sized and small companies and increase social stress. In view of these considerations, Ōkita suggested that the Japanese state support "stable economic growth without disturbance" (1959b:46–7). Accordingly, Ōkita set the growth rate at 7.2% in the NIDP, a far more moderate figure than Shimomura's 11%. Tsuru Shigeto (1959:135–6) also supported Ōkita's position, asserting that it was extremely important for the Japanese government to control economic fluctuation through its policies in order to reduce the social conflicts created by unstable economic growth.

Equality was another major issue. Marxists and left-wing intellectuals directly questioned the nature of economic growth within the institutional framework of capitalism. The question of the dual structure, raised by Arisawa Hiromi in the 1950s, remained a major concern in the policy debate on high growth in the 1960s. Itō Mitsuharu argued that high growth would create further inequality because it would bring high profits and high wages to the modern industrial sector while low profits and low wages continued in the promodern sector (Arisawa, Minobe, Nagasu, Itō, and Miyazaki, 1960). Arisawa also pointed out that the transition of the labor force from the premodern to the modern sector would cause problems. Young college graduates would have no problem entering any new industries. Because of the seniority-based wage system, however, middle-aged workers would find it difficult to enter the new job market. Under such circumstances, although the per capita GNP might increase rapidly, some social groups still could be left behind in the process of economic development (Arisawa, Minobe, Nagasu, Itoō, and Miyazaki, 1960). Some neoclassical economists also were concerned with the issue of equality. To stimulate and sustain high growth, the Japanese state had decided to reduce taxes by 100 billion yen, as requested by business leaders. Some economists argued that this redistribution of national income was unfair to those who worked hard. Komiya Ryūtarō (1960:10) stated that only one-fourth to one-third of Japanese could benefit from the tax reduction. Rather than reducing taxes, he argued, the government should promote social security and the public sector (Imai in Shimomura et al. 1960:62). Moreover, Komiya believed that the high-growth policy would create a favorable environment for big business, but that Japan's late-developing agriculture and the premodern sector would be victimized. Because Japan's antimonopoly policy was far from appropriate, it might increase the gap between the big companies and the medium-sized and small companies (Komiya 1960:11).

The progressive views represented by the structural reform approach, as exemplified by the so-called Eta vision, regarded the equal distribution of economic welfare as a major concern. In July 1962 Eta Saburō, the general secretary of the Socialist Party, presented his new ideas on the future direction of the socialist movement in the high-growth era. Eta argued that the major achievements of human societies so far were the high standard of living in the United States, the complete social welfare system in the Soviet Union, the parliamentary democratic institutions in Britain, and the peace constitution in Japan. Therefore the Socialist Party should make a comprehensive adjustment in its policy, incorporating all of these elements in order to achieve socialism in Japan (Kojima [1976] 1978:84). The Marxist economist Takahashi Masao (1981:87) pointed out, two decades later, that both the conservatives and progressives were unaware of the possibility that high growth would have a "poisonous impact" on Japanese society. It would result not only in economic friction with other countries, but also in the "Japanese disease," characterized by environmental pollution and by the coexistence of overpopulated urban areas and underpopulated rural areas. Moreover, consumer prices rose rapidly between 1961 and 1963, with an average annual growth rate of 6.5%. Meanwhile, the living environment was deteriorating and industrial pollution was becoming a major problem. Under these circumstances, business encountered strong criticism from the general public.

The high-growth thesis enforced the GNP's orientation in Japanese industrial policy. Increasing the GNP remained the top priority until the 1970s, when the first oil shock forced the Japanese economy to enter an era of slow growth. Even though Shimomura's original position was not extreme in this regard, the social atmosphere induced by his idea achieved a momentum of its own, which sustained, expanded, enhanced, and reproduced the GNP orientation (Masamura 1974:42).

Issuing public debt

The stable-growth approach, which had lost the battle against the high-growth thesis in the late 1950s, began to attract public support in the 1960s. The high-growth policy encountered strong criticism. After Satō Eisaku became prime minister in late 1964, he decided to shift from the high-growth policy to a stable-growth policy. The shift, however, was soon replaced by a setback.

After the Tokyo Olympics in 1964, the Japanese economy suffered a recession. In March 1965, the Sanyō Special Steel Company announced bankruptcy, with 50 billion yen in debt. In May of that year, one of the four major stock companies, the Sanichi Stock Company, was facing bankruptcy, and many investors canceled their contracts. This event shook the Japanese financial institution profoundly. Financial Minister Tanaka Kakuei called for an emergency press conference, announcing that the Bank of Japan, for the third time in the twentieth century since the big earthquake in 1923 and the financial crisis in 1927, would provide special loans to private companies (Nakamura 1995b:54).

At the same time, a heated debate on whether the government should issue national bonds was held. Since the implementation of the Dodge Plan, the Japanese government had adhered to a balanced budget. Under the pressure of this recession, however, the business circles asserted that the government should reduce taxes and issue national bonds in order to modify the economic situation. Kawai Yoshinari, president of the Tomatsu Company, argued that the major reason why business financing was tight, companies could not accumulate capital, and loans kept increasing was that the state had taxed the private firms too heavily. Now the state should return the excess tax money to the firms by reducing taxes in the future. In the meantime, it should issue national bonds to fulfill the need for public spending (Hayashi 1965).

After Satō Eisaku reshuffled his cabinet in June 1965, Fukuda Hamakazu became the financial minister. Fukuda had formerly advocated the stable growth approach. This time he changed his position. Enlightened by Takahashi Korekiyo's practice of issuing national debt to combat the Great Depression, Fukuda argued that issuing national bonds would not only make up for overlending by banks and overborrowing by companies, but would also increase public spending to promote the infrastructure. As neither private companies nor households had much money, new construction projects, roads, and ports had to depend on government financing. To sustain economic growth, the Japanese state had to reduce taxes. As a result, however, the internal revenue would not be sufficient to support the big projects; thus the government would have to issue national bonds (Nakamura 1995b:54).

Shimomura Osamu ([1965] 1971:476–8) strongly urged the Japanese government to issue national bonds. He argued that a balanced budget represented a static perspective. According to this perspective, when the equilibrium was disturbed, the government would adopt policy measures to return the economy to the original equilibrium. When the balance of international payments was upset, the government would reduce imports by repressing domestic demand, production, and investment. Such a policy might be suitable to an economy that did not grow. Because such an economy would not change, it could be pushed back to the position it had held before it lost its balance. In the Japanese case, however, the economy was growing rapidly and was in a dynamic situation. Under such circumstances, when the equilibrium in international payments was upset, the government should not reduce imports, control domestic demand, or decrease production, but should balance the imports by increasing exports. By upgrading the industrial structure, Japan could promote competitiveness in international markets and increase exports. When the economy was in a recession, Shimomura contended, the government must lower the interest rate, reduce taxes, and issue national bonds.

Eventually, the Japanese government issued 260 billion yen in national bonds through the supplementary budget of the 1965 general account and 740 billion yen in construction bonds in the 1966 budget to sustain economic growth. Stimulated by public spending, private investment in production equipment increased at an average rate of 21.1% in 1965–70.

The Miike dispute and the aftermath

In the 1960s, the conflict between management and labor was also settled. The Miike dispute in 1960 was a turning point at which all major political actors – the state, the LDP, the conservative business leaders, and the labor unions – changed their positions on labor relations and the productivity movement. This change created a political foundation for institutionalizing Japanese management.

The Miike dispute occurred in 1960 as a conservative response to the structural change in Japanese industry from coal-based to oil-based energy. The Mitsui Company intended to lay off 6,000 workers at its Miike coal mine. This was the first step in a series of large-scale layoffs, estimated at 110,000 throughout the industry. The initiative was supported strongly by both the government and business circles. Labor unions resisted strongly, with nationwide support, and engaged in violent conflicts with the police. At the time, it was called a "general confrontation between entire management and entire labor." After a 313-day strike, the Mitsui dispute ended with the failure of the labor unions. As Nakamura Masanori (1995b:30) points out, "the end of the Miike dispute marked the end of the confrontational labor movements in postwar Japan." From then on, most labor unions changed their strategy and became supporters of the productivity movement.

Although the government and management won the dispute, they were shook by the scope and impact of this event on politics and the economy. The conservative Liberal-Democratic Party had adopted a pro-business policy, treating the labor dispute as a matter of public security. After the Miike dispute, it began to take the treatment of workers in sunset industries as a serious matter that directly concerned social stability. When Minister of Labor Ishida Hiroe negotiated the resolution with the president of Mitsui, all of the major business leaders who had been invited to attend expressed their concern about labor relations. In 1963 Ishida published an influential article in which he stated, "It is an urgent task for the conservatives to shift the policy toward protecting the interest of employees by adopting a labor charter." As the chairman of the National Organizational Committee of the LDP, Ishida argued that the party should "take a neutral position on the issues concerning labor relations and should represent the interest of the nation by mediating the competing interests" (Rekishi Kenkyūkai 1990:13–4).

In 1963, demand exceeded supply in the Japanese labor market for the first time in history. Beginning at that time, the shortage of labor became a major problem; starting salaries for young workers increased at an annual average of more than 13% in the early 1960s, in comparison with less than 5% in 1954–8. In such circumstances, the introduction of lifetime employment and the seniority-based wage system in large Japanese firms was no longer simply a way to divide economic welfare between the firm and labor, but also a necessary strategy for preserving the skilled labor force.

Under such circumstances, Japanese business leaders changed their view of labor relations. In the resolution issued at the 1963 national meeting of the Japan Federation of Employers Associations, it was argued that in the past 18 years of the postwar era, management and labor have experienced together how much turmoil the class confrontation between management and labor, the political struggle, and the prejudice toward labor unions could bring to labor relations and social order. . . . In order to pursue the mission of promoting stability and social welfare, we must reexamine frankly the mistakes we have made. Management and labor should recognize the values of democracy and independence, and take their responsibility. We should cooperate with each other to pursue peace between management and labor, the prosperity of the company, and the development of the national economy in order to meet the demands of the era. (Nikeiren [1963] 1966a:461)

At the same meeting, in his keynote speech, the deputy director of the Nikeiren spoke particularly about lifetime employment and the seniority-based wage. He argued that there were only two ways to bring about peace between management and labor. One was a long-term, stable wage policy; the other was continuous communication between management and labor within the company. He also pointed out that

we have had the practice of lifetime employment in Japan and the seniority-based wage which supports it. Of course, there are some shortcomings in both practices. However, they were born and nurtured in the Japanese culture. This is an advantage. We should make good use of Japanese tradition. Japan's lifetime employment is completely opposite to the short-term contracts practiced in Europe and North America. Behind the perspective of lifetime employment, there exists a long-lasting custom or style of the company, which is indivisible by money or any economic forces. An important issue for the future is how to balance, arrange, and combine the style, goodness, and advantage of the seniority-based wage, which is based on lifetime employment, with the service-based allowance, which has a modern taste. Speaking of Japanese management, we must devise a Japanese style of wage system and employment systems." (Nikeiren [1963] 1966b:462)

As a MITI official points out, the productivity movement had the power to penetrate the daily operation of the company and to induce mass participation in innovation. The major reason the productivity movement succeeded is that the introduction of lifetime employment and seniority-based wages demonstrated a great vision: It concerned not only the interests of the company, but also the interests of labor (Nihon Seisansei Honbu 1985:124). In the productivity movement, the wartime ideology of rejecting shareholders' profit revived in a new form of corporatism that asserted the sovereignty of employees. This ideology was institutionally sustained by Japanese management in big companies, which provided 30% of the labor force with lifetime employment and the seniority-based wage as an incentive to participate in technological innovations. Organized labor forced Japanese managers to reexamine their principles: They came to believe that the interest of the company was not in short-term profits but in long-term international competitiveness. Even if the company could win the struggle with labor, its gains would still be very small in comparison with what it could gain from the international market. In these circumstances, management must "get rid of the arbitrariness of the old capitalism, which follows the instinct to pursue profits, according to the new wisdom of management" (Nihon Seisansei Honbu 1985:35). This new wisdom held that managers had to establish autonomy from shareholders; the "arbitrariness of capital" should be restricted and revised; the social function, mission, and responsibility of the company should be stressed; management should transcend the self-centered approach and recognize labor as one of the most important components of the company; and respect for human beings had to be recognized during the process of economic growth and technological progress.

The pressure for liberalization

The evolution of Japanese developmentalism in the 1960s was driven by more than high growth, the transition from international politics to domestic economy, and the settlement of labor relations. More important, it was also driven by the challenge of liberalization of trade and capital investment.

By the end of the 1950s, liberalization of the economy had become an irresistible trend in the major industrialized countries. In the early postwar era, Western European nations and Japan had placed many restrictions on imports and foreign currency exchange because of the unstable economic situation and the shortage of dollars. This practice was allowed by Article 14 of the IMF. The liberalization process started with the OECD's resolution in 1949, which was established to carry out the Marshall Plan for Europe's postwar economic reconstruction. This resolution aimed at building a united European market by establishing a multinational trade system and an international payment system and by eliminating the restrictions on trade. It required the member countries of the OECD to be responsible for liberalizing trade by at least 90% in Europe by the end of June 1959. This goal was largely achieved by 1955. The liberalization of trade with the dollar areas was much slower, however. Countries such as West Germany and Switzerland, whose currencies were strong in exchange with the dollar, took the initiative, whereas countries such as France, Italy, and Britain, where currencies were weak or a shortage of dollars prevailed, did not reach the same level as West Germany and Switzerland until 1958. Under pressure by the United States, Western European countries began to restore the convertibility of their currencies and to withdraw their restrictions on imports of U.S. products in the late 1950s. They moved toward Article 8 status in the IMF, which prohibited any restriction on foreign currency to balance international payments. At the end of the 1950s, a free trade regime sustained by the Pax Americana was emerging in the international economy.

In mid-1959, Japan became the target of criticism from Western countries on the issue of liberalization. When Prime Minister Kishi Nobusuke visited the United States to renew the U.S.–Japan security treaty, the U.S. government demanded that Japan proceed with the liberalization of trade. At the annual meetings of both the IMF and GATT, U.S. representatives strongly criticized Japan for its restrictions on imports.

This situation stirred a heated debate in Japan. Horie Shigeto, a leading authority on international finance, who had represented an international perspective in domestic debates concerning economic policy, argued that Japan must catch up with its trading partners and competitors. Because Japan depended heavily on trade, it could not afford to be left behind. Just as major industrialized countries in Western Europe had obtained Article 8 status, sooner or later Japan had to do the same (Imai 1977:170–1; see Johnson 1982:250). According to Horie's perception, a new regime in the international economy was being institutionalized by the IMF and GATT, which was designed to stimulate worldwide economic growth by achieving nondiscriminatory and multinational free trade. Horie (1967) believed that the international economy would change profoundly because the convertibility of Western European currencies would create many new international markets, both "material" and "financial." The establishment of this new regime would bring long-term prosperity to the global economy. Drawing on history, Horie argued that the Great Depression of 1929–

33 resulted from the policy of pauperizing one's neighbors adopted by many countries in the 1920s. In the early postwar era, many countries continued to control foreign currency exchange when they placed a priority on domestic employment and economic growth. Although this policy helped the economic reconstruction, it also constrained the international division of labor and the efficiency of the global economy as a whole. Because Japan now belonged to the group of industrialized nations, it had to assume responsibility for sustaining the free trade regime and prosperity of the world economy.

Komiya Ryūtarō wrote a series of articles for the *Nihon Keizai Shinbun* (*The Japan Economic Journal*) arguing that "a free and competitive market mechanism ought to function smoothly by itself and produce the optimum allocation of resources." Japan's participation in the liberalization of trade and foreign currency exchange would increase the efficiency of Japanese firms and benefit the Japanese people (Komiya 1986). Komiya represented a new generation of Japanese economists who had studied neoclassical economics in the United States after the war. He suggested that to understand the importance of liberalization, Japanese bureaucrats and economists should adhere to economic principles such as welfare economics, the theory of the most appropriate tariffs, and the second best theory (Komiya [1959] 1971:222).

Horie's and Komiya's pro-liberalization position was shared by Ikeda Hayato, then the minister of MITI, who soon became prime minister. Ikeda believed that Horie understood the international trend and that Japan had to respond quickly to this new situation (Johnson 1982:250). At the time, Ikeda's effort to liberalize trade encountered strong resistance. "Young officials thought that liberalization would mean the end of their jobs, senior officials in the vertical bureaus were worried about the structural weaknesses of their industries, and politicians feared for their election" (Johnson 1982:251). Exercising his power as MITI minister, Ikeda succeeded in persuading MITI bureaucrats to shift Japan to the IMF's Article 8 status (Johnson 1982). In promoting the liberalization of trade, Ikeda laid a solid foundation for his future actions; he mobilized MITI bureaucrats to support his high-growth policy by making them believe that high growth was the only way for Japan to counter the effects of the liberalization (Tanaka 1959).

Under Ikeda's leadership, the Japanese government decided to begin liberalizing trade in 1960 despite anxiety, criticism, and opposition from many interest groups. In June 1960, the Japanese government announced its "Outline of the Plan for the Liberalization of Trade and Foreign Currency Exchange." This document argued that liberalization would "eliminate the inefficiency and irrationality created by the present management and control, increase free access to cheaply priced materials in overseas markets, lower production costs, require companies to behave rationally in the international market, improve living standards, and promote the interest of the whole economy" (Arisawa and Inaba 1966:370). According to this plan, Japan would liberalize trade to 80% of the total in three years. If coal and oil were included, the proportion would be 90%. In 1964, yielding to pressure by the IMF and the OECD, Japan also ended its restrictions on foreign currency exchange.

State–private sector coordination versus independent integration

Although the Japanese economy was reconnected with international markets after the implementation of the Dodge Plan at the end of the 1940s, Japanese companies had competed with foreign companies only overseas because Japan's domestic markets were tightly protected in the 1950s. As liberalization would create an open environment for the Japanese economy, how to respond to this challenge became a key issue in Japanese industrial policy of the 1960s. In a series of heated debates on the new industrial system between the demand for state–private sector coordination and the demand for independent integration by the private sector, the ideology of Japanese developmentalism regarding organized competition entered its sophisticated stage.

The necessity of building a new industrial system was first raised officially in the NIDP from two perspectives. First, because the Japanese economy was moving toward the heavy-chemical industries, a further rationalization of the industrial order was needed. Second, after the liberalization of trade, Japanese companies would have to compete with big foreign companies, and it would be difficult for Japanese companies to establish a dominant share in Japan's domestic markets. Under such circumstances, the conventional concepts such as competition and monopoly deserved rethinking, and Japan's strategy must take the competition with foreign companies as the precondition. Not only would Japanese companies need to enlarge in order to adopt the newest technologies, reduce production costs, improve the quality of their products, and pursue economies of scale; a new industrial system would also be the foundation for strengthening the competitiveness of Japanese companies.

To MITI bureaucrats, liberalization did not necessarily mean free competition, and the new industrial system should be based on the state–private sector coordination. Morozumi Yoshihiko, director of the First Enterprise Division at the Enterprise Bureau, argued that orthodox laissez-faire had never existed in the history of any major industrialized country; it was simply a utopian economic principle. In a complicated industrial society, complete freedom was impossible. To strengthen the economy through free competition would be time-consuming and cause a great deal of friction. In an emergency situation such as liberalization, Japan could not wait for such a slow process. When Japan was being forced to participate in the international division of labor, waiting would force the country into the labor-intensive industries. It was necessary for the Japanese economy to have a clear orientation. The role of the state in the new industrial system would not be limited to administration of licensing and determining quotas; it also would be an important player in financial, monetary, and managerial activities (Morozumi 1962a:12).

In October 1961 MITI established the Investigation Committee on Industrial Structure (ICIS), headed by Kojima Shinichi, former deputy minister of MITI and currently the president of the Hatsumi Iron Company. This committee was supervised by the Survey Division on Industrial Structure at the Minister Secretariat. The subcommittees within this committee were supervised directly by bureaus according to their administrative sphere. The Subcommittee on Industrial System was established in December 1961 and was chaired by Arisawa Hiromi. It worked directly with the First Enterprise Division at the Enterprise Bureau of MITI to plan the state–private sector coordination by drafting the bill for the Special Measures Law for the Promotion of Designated Industries (tokutei sangyō shinkō rinji sōchihō). Unlike many committees and councils in Japan, whose function was to provide symbolic authorization to bureaucrats' policy proposals, the Subcommittee on Industrial System played an important role. As Tsuruta Toshimasa points out, this subcommittee contained no representative of present businessmen, even though it included the chairman of the Keidanren (Tsuruta 1984:63–5).

The excessive competition, the lack of economies of scale, and the bottleneck of international payments were three major concerns of MITI bureaucrats. Excessive competition, according to these bureaucrats, had resulted in an unnecessary increase in costs and a waste of resources. It occurred not only in sales, in the form of advertisements, rebates, and price reductions, but also in investment in production equipment and technological transfer. It often caused a disturbance in the economy. The lack of economies of scale was indicated by the dual structure of the Japanese economy. In this structure, there were numerous medium-sized and small companies that were inefficient not only in the competition with foreign products in domestic markets, but also in the international competition in heavy-chemical industries. So far, their survival had depended greatly on the proximity of Japanese markets, low wages, and strong ties with financial institutions. During the liberalization process, however, they would face a strong challenge from foreign firms. The bottleneck of international payments had already created great disturbance in the Japanese economy, and it had often affected the stability of economic growth in Japan. For these reasons, the state had to play a leading role in the new industrial system. MITI's bureaucrats repeatedly stressed that this coordination would be based on mutual consent between the state and the private sector, and that bureaucratic participation would not be authoritative. They argued that the purpose of the coordination was to sustain a market economy without laissez-faire, to maintain order without direct control, and to pursue a collectively shared goal without depending on totalitarianism (Morozumi 1962a:17).

The proposal for state–private sector coordination had two intellectual sources. One was the wartime legacy. As mentioned in Chapter 2, Sahashi Shigeru, director of the Enterprise Bureau, envisioned the new industrial system as developing directly from the wartime practice of national general mobilization. Arisawa Hiromi also carried forward his theory of the managed economy in the design for the new industrial system.

Many people were concerned about the impact of the wartime system on the proposed new industrial system. Amaya Naohiro, a young MITI bureaucrat, pointed out:

The present industrial system has to be traced back to 1935. What was the wartime system? It was a complete rejection of price mechanism, and a centralized managed economy. . . . This system was accomplished during the war and was left as it was after Japan's defeat. Although SCAP brought the ideology of free economy to Japan, it allowed this system to continue to exist in place of the military with some organizational adjustments because, in reality, 10 million people might die due to the severe shortage of food. For this reason, the major components of the managed economy were maintained. As the Japanese economy and private firms accumulated strength during the Korean War, there was a movement to make the ideology of free economy into a reality in the economy. The managed economy was abolished in 1952 . . . only the bureaucratic control of foreign currency exchange and trade was left. From then on, however, the Japanese economy was neither a free economy nor a managed economy, but [followed] a compromised pattern. Therefore even though business circles, especially the Kendanren, held the ideology of free economy, they still regarded bureaucratic control as a necessary evil. At MITI, some bureaucrats, who might be too bureaucratic, thought that free economy was harmful. . . . [They] even took the extreme view that Japan should continue the managed economy by practicing the quota system for foreign currency exchange, and that free economy could be accepted only to some extent within government planning. . . . During the liberalization, the foundation that supported the economic order will disappear. How to search for a new order is a big issue. . . . The new industrial order should be [based on] neither traditional bureaucratic control nor the optimistic doctrine of laissez-faire asserted by the Keidanren, but on a third position. (Amaya, Komiya, and Sakamoto 1962:71–2.

In contrast to the wartime legacy, Morozumi regarded the European experience of a mixed economy as the model. Morozumi had worked for three and a half years at the Japanese embassy in France. During his stay, he intensively studied the relationship between the state bureaucracy and the private sector in the French type of mixed economy. Morozumi argued that government planning in France was unique because it was neither simply an economic forecast nor socialist. Rather, it was a mixture of the will of the state, which represented the public interest, and the judgment of the private sector. It combined order and freedom. The process of making such a plan provided an opportunity for coordination between the state and the private sector at the level of the national economy through discussion, exchange of information, and examination of the economic prospects. The agreement achieved in this process was based on mutual consent.

Private companies would voluntarily behave according to this agreement; meanwhile, the state would provide various benefits to support their activities through taxation and financial credits. In other words, from the viewpoint of private companies, the agreement was a voluntary pledge to link business activity with the public purpose. From the viewpoint of the state, it was a public contract to provide conditions beneficial to private interests. A dynamic give-and-take relationship would arise in the process of achieving the goal on which both sides had agreed. This goal, moreover, would often be designed from the viewpoint of the national economy as a whole (Morozumi 1962b:61).

Although most Japanese business leaders admitted that the liberalization of trade and foreign currency exchange was necessary, and although they agreed with MITI on the necessity of organizing the market in light of liberalization, they strongly advocated independent integration, aiming at preventing the revival of wartime-type bureaucratic control.

The private sector argued that the Japanese economy consisted of both the industries that had economies of scale and were internationally competitive and the industries that were too weak to compete with foreign producers. It did not oppose MITI's initiative for building a cooperative system in the automobile and petrochemical industries, as these industries would need to accumulate capital and promote competitiveness to meet the international challenge. The private sector, however, strongly objected to MITI's proposal of building an industrial system based on bureaucratic guidance to cover the entire economy. The reason was that the so-called collective goal or national interest declared by MITI was not self-evident. It might be acceptable on an abstract level when discussing Japanese competitiveness. As soon as the collective goal was discussed in concrete terms such as the adequate scale and form of production, however, many conflicts would arise. The Keidanren argued that MITI's claim of an equal position for each party in this cooperative system was self-contradictory because the proposal for state–private sector cooperation itself was based on the belief that independent integration would not work. If MITI believed that independent integration would not work, it would have to involve itself as the ultimate authority in this system. Therefore, insofar as the state was involved, no matter what form the system took initially, in the end it would lead to nothing but bureaucratic control. If this happened, bureaucratic control would call for more bureaucratic control, as indicated by the history of the managed economy, and all industries would be overwhelmed (Keizai Dantai Rengōkai 1978).

Rejecting MITI's proposal for state–private sector coordination, business leaders regarded independent integration by the private sector as an effective means to compete with foreign products in Japan's domestic markets. They suggested that Japanese companies reduce excessive competition and increase the economies of scale by encouraging mergers and acquisitions. They also demanded the revision of the antimonopoly law. According to Horikoshi Teizō (1962), director of the General Office of the Keidanren, Japan's antimonopoly law made the cartel sound like an evil in a country where numerous small, weak companies needed to be integrated. The antimonopoly law had resulted in excessive competition. To change this situation, the law had to be revised comprehensively, with a fundamental reorientation. In the Kendanren's proposal, independent integration meant autonomy in business activities without control by state bureaucracies, which would give private companies the power to organize their activities in preferred patterns such as mergers, cartels, and *dangō* (insiders' deal) without being restrained by the antimonopoly law. Kotō Rikuzō (1963), deputy manager of the Keidanren, argued that Japan had the "strictest antimonopoly law in the world." Even after being revised in 1949 and again in 1953, it was still stricter than the antimonopoly laws of European countries. Japan's antimonopoly law was designed to prohibit actions that might interfere with the public interest and damage consumers by constraining competition. This concern would no longer be necessary once trade and foreign currency were liberalized. In a closed market, it was at least reasonable to worry that cartels and mergers might constrain competition, even if they were not contrary to the public interest. In an open market, even after domestic producers and dealers organized cartels, actual constraints on competition would not appear because foreign companies would always offer strong competitive pressure. Kotō argued that for these reasons, the antimonopoly law should be revised. It should relax the requirement for cartels during recessions, allow joint actions to prevent excessive competition, enlarge the range of rationalization cartels, permit cartels that promoted exports, liberalize interfirm stockholding and exchange of managers, relax the regulations on mergers, and allow the existence of holding companies.

The struggle over the special measures law for the promotion of designated industries

In August 1962, the Subcommittee on the Industrial System headed by Arisawa Hiromi began to draft the bill for the Tokushinhō based on the proposal made by the Enterprise Bureau. In March 1963, the bill was submitted to the Diet. This bill identified the special steel, automobile, and petrochemical industries as special. It also left space for the designation of other special industries. According to this bill, once the special industries were identified, the minister of MITI, the related industrial associations, and the banks that financed these industries would develop guidelines for the industries regarding scale, specialization, proper investment in production equipment, efficient use of equipment, general behavior, mergers, and change of business direction (the minister of finance would also participate in the discussion concerning tax and finances). Commercial banks were to refer to these guidelines in issuing loans. The government financial institutions would ensure credit for these industries. The state would reduce the corporate tax and the registration tax for companies in the special industries. In addition, those firms would be exempted from the antimonopoly law by permission of the Fair Trade Commission regarding restrictions on variety, method, and quantity of production, production equipment, the purchase of parts, facilities for production, storage, and transportation, and the financial adjustments accompanying the change of business direction. The Fair Trade Commission would consult with the MITI minister in making decisions about the application of antimonopoly law in these industries (Miyasaka, Kaneko, and Takahashi 1979:175–8). The Tokushinhō bill was put aside, however, without being discussed in the Diet. MITI resubmitted it twice but could not pass it because of resistance by the LDP, the opposition parties, the private sector, and MITI's rivals in the state bureaucracies.

The Keidanren's position on this issue reflected a dilemma. On the one hand, it hoped the government would be involved in the integration process in case independent integration did not work. On the other hand, it feared that strong government involvement might lead to increased bureaucratic control, which would end the freedom of the private sector in business activities. In addition, business leaders had become more confident about the international competitiveness of Japanese companies because they believed that the heavy investment in production equipment and technological transfers had already greatly strengthened Japanese industries. Although liberalization might have some negative effects on the automobile, petrochemical, and special steel industries, the Japanese economy in general had reached a stage at which private companies could compete with foreign products in domestic markets. Thus the Keidanren intended to relax the antimonopoly law in the name of the national interest. It preferred to have more freedom to organize cartels and conduct mergers without much intervention from the state while preventing bureaucrats from reducing their own power in business activities (Sahashi 1977). To protect the private sector from bureaucratic control, the Keidanren also demanded legalization of the new industrial system, expecting a law to clarify the boundaries of bureaucratic involvement (Tsūsanshō 1990b, vol. 10:64).

MITI supported the Keidanren's initiative in relaxing the antimonopoly law but did not favor a comprehensive revision of that law. Because of their failure to revise the antimonopoly law in 1958, MITI's bureaucrats believed that it would be too risky to pursue a new industrial system through such a revision because the Keidanren's proposal encountered strong criticism from academia and the general public. Therefore they preferred to depend on the exemption laws to circumvent the antimonopoly law. MITI's wanted not only to survive the risk of losing its influence during the liberalization process, but also to mobilize the national resources for international competition. It supported big businesses for the purpose of upgrading the economies of scale of Japanese firms and eliminating excessive competition, but meanwhile, it also tried to link medium-sized and small companies with big companies in order to mobilize more resources, to maintain employment, and to reduce bankruptcy. There were two alternatives for legalizing the new industrial system: a general law supported by the Enterprise Bureau at MITI and industry-based special laws, such as the Oil Industry Law, supported by other administrative bureaus at MITI. Because the Oil Industry Law was strongly opposed by the Keidanren on account of bureaucratic control, MITI decided to support the Special Measures Law for the Promotion of Designated Industries.

Because MITI's proposal involved the administration of the Fair Trade Commission and the Ministry of Finance, it had to obtain the support of these two bureaucracies. Initially the Fair Trade Commission asserted that the exemption proposed by MITI was possible within the present antimonopoly law and that it was not necessary to enact a new law. Although the Fair Trade Commission in the end agreed to allow the rationalization cartels, it still strongly opposed the merger. The Ministry of Finance agreed with MITI about the tax break, but opposed MITI's original proposal to provide favorable tariffs to the special industries and to ensure financing. It feared that the former might cause international criticism, as well as creating a chain reaction in other laws, and that the latter might result in overlending by the Japan Development Bank, an important government financial institution. The Ministry of Finance also opposed MITI's proposal to allow financial institutions to participate in the coordination because that step might weaken its own control of these institutions. On 11 February, Prime Minister Ikeda asked to discuss the Tokushinhō bill at the economic ministers' meeting. The Fair Trade Commission continued to resist MITI's proposals on rationalization cartels and mergers. Eventually, however, under pressure from other state bureaucracies, the Commission accepted MITI's proposal for the Tokushinhō; in exchange it obtained the power to license the rationalization cartels. Minister of Finance Tanaka Kakuei asked for coadministration of the Tokushinhō with MITI; MITI refused. The National Bank Association then refused to participate in the integration.

Eventually the National Bank Association agreed with the compromise proposal offered by EPA Director Miyazawa Kiichi: The MITI minister and the representative of the manufacturing industries would decide on the guidelines for coordination in the special industries according to discussions by the MITI minister, the representative of the manufacturing industries, the representative of the financial institutions, and the minister of finance, but they would be required to consult with the minister of finance again after the guidelines were determined. If the interest of any commercial bank or firm was damaged, the guidelines could be changed by the consensus of the parties concerned. Ironically, MITI's practice of controlling credit and foreign exchange through banks in the 1950s strengthened the power of commercial banks. By the 1960s, they had become a strong competitor to MITI in making policy for the new industrial system. When commercial banks functioned as the instruments of MITI in credit and exchange control, they also became the centers of various business groups, obtaining great power in the *keiretsu*. The growing strength of Japanese banks forged a special interest group in politics, which became quite powerful in the 1960s.

MITI's Tokushinhō bill was never discussed by the Diet. Nevertheless, the coordination mechanisms, as represented by system finance (*taisei yūshi*) and by the state–private sector coordination forum (*kanmin kyōchō kontankai*), were established informally. On 29 June 1964, MITI Minister Fukuta Hajime stated in a cabinet meeting:

> The Special Measures Law for the Promotion of Designated Industries cannot be enacted by the Diet. Nevertheless, in regard to liberalization, the principles represented by this bill – namely, the establishment of a rational production system and the promotion of international competitiveness by strengthening management in Japan's strategic industries – must be realized. . . . To support the efforts of business circles in the agreed-upon direction, the government will have priority in using government capital, such as financing by . . . Japan's Development Bank and the Financial Trust for Medium-Sized and Small Firms, and will ask for the available support from commercial banks. Regarding the common behavior for rationalization, such as the integration of standards and the specialization of production, MITI will try its best to help [those industries] obtain exemption from the antimonopoly law. (Tsūsanshō 1990b, vol. 10:82–3)

Indeed, MITI later practiced system finance, though the scale was much smaller than that proposed by the Tokushinhō. The forum on state–private sector coordination was established in several industries, mostly in those that had suffered a recession, as well as in the petrochemical industry, but the representatives of commercial banks did not participate.

In 1967 the Subcommittee on Industrial System headed by Arisawa Hiromi submitted a report to the Japanese government titled "On the Formation of New Industrial Order." This report supported MITI's earlier proposal for state–private sector cooperation in the reorganization of Japanese industries but prescribed a new strategy. It held that in capital-intensive industries such as iron and steel, petrochemicals, fertilizers, and oil, reorganization should achieve the economies of scale through business linkups, investment adjustments, and rotating or cooperative investments. Eventually these would lead to the establishment of an industrial system through mergers that could compete effectively on an international scale. In the technology-intensive industries, more attention should be paid to increasing research and development and to concentrating on research capacity. In consumer products industries, economies of scale as well as the division of labor in product lines, the standardization of products, and cooperation in marketing also deserved attention (Arisawa and Tsuchiya 1967:12–13).

The settlement of private ordering in the governance structure of the Japanese economy in the 1960s marked the successful transition of Japanese developmentalism from the military version to a trade version. The transition from the managed economy to a market economy in the 1950s was driven primarily by the pressure of promoting exports rather than by domestic politics. At that time, the state, well aware of the importance of the competitiveness of private companies, voluntarily changed its pattern of economic intervention. In the 1960s, in contrast, MITI failed to maintain strong control in the new industrial system, even though it tried hard. This time, private ordering was shaped by the structure of state–business relations. Through two decades of economic growth, the private sector had grown strong and had become a contender to MITI's power in governing the economy. By doing so, Japanese developmentalism had moved further away from the socialist model of the economy; in the meantime, it had become more distinctive from liberal capitalism.

Conclusion

This chapter has described the transformation of Japanese developmentalism into a trade version. It has shown that after two decades of interaction between the wartime legacy and liberal capitalism, the contemporary Japanese economic system incorporated elements from both sides.

Liberal capitalism in the form of the Pax Americana changed Japan's national purpose from military conquest to the attainment of wealth. An opened international economy forced Japanese industrial policy to adapt to the market. In the meantime, however, the general principles that had emerged in the 15-year war remained and were reproduced to solve new problems confronted by the Japanese economy. As Komiya Ryūtarō pointed out in the 1960s, the will of the state in economic intervention did not change at all. The only difference was that the goal of building a "rich nation, strong army" was replaced by "heavy-chemical industrialization" or "being the champion in iron-steel production in the world." Consumers' interests were not given major attention. The state policy sustained the interests of big business in the name of the national interest.

The nation-state as the unit of analysis was deeply institutionalized in Japanese economic thinking under the pressure of a constantly perceived external threat. From the general mobilization for total war in 1931–45 to the effort to promote exports in the 1950s and meet the challenge of liberalization of trade and capital investment in the 1960s, the concern for the national interest had always been the driving force in Japanese industrial policy. Japan has been divided on the issues of rearmament and Japan–U.S. relations in the 1950s. The strong concern for the national interest under the pressure of liberalization, however, soon replaced the concern for political agendas and united the country on the goal of high growth.

The production orientation, which originated in the managed economy to ensure the munitions supply during the war, was drastically upgraded to production technology in strategic industries of the 1950s, influenced by Schumpeter's idea of innovation. By the 1960s, it was further extended to the high growth of the entire economy, promoting national competitiveness through infrastructure, human capital, education, and science.

The three general principles, whose rise was strongly influenced by fascist ideology in the managed economy, were also upgraded effectively in the new democratic political environment and the open international economic environment. These principles were adjusted to the postwar changes in both the domestic and international political economies.

The strategic view of the economy was once the foundation supporting the total war in 1931–45. Although the military nature was eliminated by the postwar democratic reforms, the principle of treating the economy as an object of social engineering was maintained to combat the economic crisis in the late 1940s, to promote exports in the 1950s, and to sustain high growth and meet the challenge of liberalization of trade and capital investment in the 1960s. Responding to the changing external environment – from closed in 1931–49 to semiclosed in the 1950s and then to open in the 1960s – the Japanese organization of the economy was also often modified by the politics of industrial policy, in which the balance of power between the state and the private sector was constantly changing. Direct bureaucratic control over the distribution of materials and prices in the managed economy was first shifted to control over credit and foreign exchange in the 1950s and then to administrative guidance in the 1960s. The process of moving toward an opened economy weakened the power of bureaucrats. In the meantime, it also increased the sophistication of state intervention in the economy. Throughout this process, the function of government regulations remained. By the late 1960s, a new industrial system aimed at sustaining economic growth had matured. This system linked the Keynesian theory of effective demand with the policy objective of promoting industrial structure. Despite the fact that the Japanese state still intervened more actively than any of its counterparts in liberal capitalist economies, increasing private ordering appeared in the governance of the economy. This characteristic of the economic system clearly distinguished Japanese developmentalism from a socialist economy.

Nevertheless, in this economy, the market still did not work according to its own laws, but was constrained by both government regulations and nonmarket governance structures. In contrast to the managed economy, in which market function was largely replaced by state control, the governance of the Japanese economy since 1950 had been gradually shifted to nonstate institutions. Of course, administrative guidance by the state and government regulation remained important components in this economic system even after the 1960s. Beginning with the new industrial system of the 1960s, however, the functions of maintaining order and restraining excessive competition were privatized. The cartels and trade associations had been applied systematically to combat the Great Depression and to support the war in 1931–45. In light of liberalization of trade, they were endowed with new meaning: to promote national competitiveness. *Keiretsu* and trade associations began to take over many coordinating functions formerly carried out by MITI. In the 1960s, the state and the market were institutionally linked in the Japanese economy; each assumed its role by working with the other through the mediation of nonmarket/nonstate mechanisms. The strategy of restraining excessive competition and promoting economies of scale through coordination of private companies also distinguished the Japanese economy from orthodox liberal capitalism.

According to the ideology of Japanese developmentalism of the 1960s, the meaning of business organization must be understood at the macro level. Because Japan had limited capital and a bottleneck in international payments, greater coordination was perceived as more rational than laissez-faire competition. When the country was under strong pressure to liberalize trade and capital investment, a more highly organized market, as measured by greater coordination and less competition, was believed to be more effective to meet the challenge. History has proved that the Japanese achieved what they sought from independent integration. Even today, few foreign companies can surpass Japanese companies in Japanese domestic markets. Meanwhile, as MITI has repeatedly shown in recent negotiations with the United States, the Japanese state can no longer be responsible for changing these organized markets.

By the 1960s, the concept of productivity had also become sophisticated and was deeply institutionalized in the Japanese management system. The rejection of the profit principle had originated in 1931–45 to ensure the national mobilization for war. Although the profit principle never became predominant again in postwar Japan, management and labor fought intensively over a related issue, efficiency, which often caused massive layoffs. Although some progressive managers proposed to stabilize labor relations through the productivity movement in the 1950s, both management and labor were still under the strong influence of the confrontational strategies they had adopted at the end of the war. Immediately after the implementation of the Dodge Plan, the Japanese managerial ideology was strongly influenced by Western economic theories. By the 1960s, however, the significance of the rejection of the profit principle was connected not only with the efforts to build up the comparative advantage in production technology, but also national mobilization to meet the challenge of liberalization of trade and capital investment. The harmful impact of the confrontational labor relations on domestic politics and national competitiveness, as displayed by the Miike dispute, profoundly changed the Japanese perception of this issue. This cognitive change resulted in the institutionalization of Japanese management in big companies. In this process, Japanese developmentalism transcended liberal capitalism and socialism, which both interpreted labor relations in class terms.

7. The institutional environment of economic reasoning

I began my analysis by showing the static characteristics of Japanese developmentalism, which emerged in 1931–45 and was developed further in the postwar period. After examining the dynamic process by which this ideology shaped three paradigms of Japanese industrial policy, I am convinced that Japanese developmentalism was a product of special historical circumstances. The constantly perceived international threats, either of total war with other nation-states or of external pressure to liberalize trade and capital investment, often set the policy agenda. Cross-national learning had been the major source of new economic ideas. Because of the traditional ties between Japan and Europe, especially Germany, in the prewar period, these ideas often came from Europe rather than the United States. To influence policy, economic ideas had to confront three different factors. First, the nationalist ideology that emerged in response to the perceived external threats often rejected the lower-level unit of analysis in the policy debates while providing legitimacy and generating public support for economic nationalism. Second, the structure of the state and state–business relations strongly influenced the means chosen to implement the new policy paradigm because the means directly redefined and influenced interest. Third, in this process, the strong link between economists and leading politicians often helped ideas to gain political power. In this chapter, I discuss further the significance of the Japanese case for our understanding of several theoretical issues.

The world system, nationalism, and Japanese developmentalism

In contrast to explanations that emphasize domestic sources of economic development in Japan, this book portrays the emergence of modern Japanese industrial policy in relation to the international environment. I argue here that the changing structure of the world system and Japan's nationalistic response were two major factors explaining the rise of Japanese developmentalism. As the expansion of the world economy has involved various nation-states in an international division of labor, each nation has had to define its own position in this system to pursue prosperity. This is particularly true in Japan, which has few natural resources and depends heavily on trade. In modern Japanese history, each major transformation of the world system has been perceived as a great challenge to national survival. Japan's domestic response to these changes often were accompanied by the rise of a nationalist movement, which influenced the institutional evolution of Japanese capitalism.

Between the 1930s and the 1960s, the rise of Japanese developmentalism can be attributed largely to three transformations in the structure of the world system, each of which was perceived as a great challenge to the nation. The first two came at the end of wars, and all three were driven by the United States.

The first transformation came after what Kenneth Pyle (1992:140) calls "the destruction by World War I of the imperialist balance of power in East Asia." When the failure of the self-regulated market described by Karl Polanyi resulted in disorder in the international economy, the United States intended to establish an order in Asia based on the Wilsonian principle of self-determination, replacing the Anglo-Japanese alliance with multilateral treaties upholding the open door in China. Japan, however, responded to the Great Depression in a different way. Perceiving itself as unfairly constrained by a Western-dominated international order, Japan chose to challenge the status quo with military confrontation. A national crisis occurred in the 1930s driven by the increasing tension between Japan and the Western powers after the Manchuria Incident. Because the nation's fate and dignity would be determined by total war, the national general mobilization gave rise to developmentalism. The profound changes in both ideologies and institutions during the practice of the managed economy marked a great departure of the Japanese economy from its pre-1930 practice.

The second transformation took place after World War II. The rise of the Pax Americana became the dominant factor in shaping the external environment of the Japanese economy. In the 1950s, Japan was confronted with the military conflict between the socialist and capitalist blocs on the Korean Peninsula. Although Japan was eager to emphasize its economic reconstruction, the Cold War forced the country to deal with two competing agendas. Politically, Japan had difficulties fitting into the new order in international politics dominated by the United States, and the country was deeply divided throughout the 1950s. Economically, however, the components of the economic system that had been reformed during the occupation, such as business groups, cartels, and labor relations, began to reconsolidate themselves in combination with components that were untouched in the postwar democratic reforms, such as the state and the financial system. Facing the challenge of achieving economic independence by promoting exports, the Japanese believed that these legacies, after certain adaptations, were essential in building the country's comparative advantage in production technology.

The third transformation came at the end of the 1950s and the early 1960s, when a free trade regime was emerging in the international economy under the leadership of the United States. Since the 1930s, Japanese markets had been protected from foreign products and investment. Because the Japanese economy could not survive without international markets, liberalization was regarded as the price Japan had to pay, and the Japanese emphasized ways to respond strategically to this new situation. Perceiving liberalization as the coming of the second black ship, the Japanese settled their domestic division on the issue of Japan–U.S. relations after extending the bilateral security treaty and stabilizing labor relations after the Miike dispute. In the meantime, it moved toward a new industrial system for mobilizing the whole country to meet this challenge. By the end of the 1960s, all the contemporary characteristics of the Japanese economic system were patterned and Japanese developmentalism had been transformed from the military version to a trade version.

Nationalism guided each domestic adjustment in Japanese industrial policy to respond to the transformations in the world system. Because these transformations were perceived as a challenge to national survival, the level of analysis in Japanese economic thinking shifted inevitably to the nation-state. Nationalist ideology sustained not only the emergence of the managed economy, but also the continuation of national mobilization in the postwar era. It created an environment that favored the collective welfare while suppressing claims for the interests of individuals and social classes. Under the pressure of collective survival, the assertion of national power of production constantly denied other concerns. The perceived national crisis often supported the assertion that the Japanese had to make sacrifices in order to sustain their nation, and that individuals would enjoy more material comfort only when the nation becomes rich. Not until the 1990s did the Japanese realize that even after Japan had become a rich nation, they had remained relatively poor as individuals. This result confirms that in a challenging situation, the sense of belonging to a nation creates a feeling of security, homogeneity, and conformity for individuals (Degenaar 1982:12), and loyalty to the nation-state overrides loyalty to a social class (Smith 1971:21).

The nationalist nature of Japanese developmentalism led inevitably to state intervention. According to nationalist ideology, the state is the "ideal form of political organization," and nationality is the "source of all creative cultural energy and of economic well-being" (Degenaar 1982:9–10). Nationalism often leads to a socialist orientation in economic thinking because socialism is a program to further the welfare of the whole community (Davis 1967:xi). Because Japan is a homogeneous country, it was easy for the state to establish national solidarity based on the nation-state. Under the influence of nationalism, the divisions on economic issues between communists and capitalists, and between liberals and conservatives, were often suppressed. The intensive interaction between the world system and Japanese nationalism during Japan's economic development confirms the argument that external factors, such as international threats and competition, contribute greatly to the construction of a strong state apparatus (Thomas and Meyer 1984; Tilly 1975). In the Japanese case, as Chalmers Johnson points out, "the role of the government and its degree of reliance on authoritarian intervention are enlarged by actual or anticipated crisis conditions in the environment. . . . When crisis conditions abate, the balance of initiatives in the systems may once again shift from the public sector toward the private sector" (1987:145)

In response to the external threat, the economy was viewed strategically. Under strong pressure to survive, obtaining the greatest benefits for the nation at the lowest cost stood at the center of Japanese economic thinking on industrial policy and presented a great intellectual challenge to the Japanese state. To the *Jissen-ha* economists, the international environment was enabling as well as constraining, though often threatening. The Japanese had no choice but to maneuver among limited alternatives in order to obtain capital, resources, markets, and technology from the international markets; to speed the adoption of advanced forms of organization; and to avoid the "penalty for taking the lead" in technological development and surpass the early-developing countries through the "merits of borrowing" (Gerschenkron [1952] 1992; Rostow [1960] 1979; Veblen [1915] 1939; 1919). For the same reason, the anticompetition policy was intended to allocate resources more effectively within the national boundary; the concept of productivity referred to the effort to mobilize human resources as fully as possible. Both means demanded "devotion to the interests of a particular community" (Davis 1967:x) and "bind[ing] together people in a particular territory" (Breuilly 1982:365).

This quality of Japanese developmentalism moved the country closer to its peers in East Asia while distancing it sharply from its counterparts in Latin America. Although the Japanese have an enduring sense of weakness, they have been less concerned with the sources of weakness and more concerned about discrepancies between the standard of living in their own country and that of Western countries. They have been eager to catch up, and to do so quickly. "The greater the lag, the more radical and exalted were the theories which fired the effort at catching up" (Hirschman 1971:271). Driven by a strong will to catch up with the West, the Japanese economy experienced constant unbalanced growth. This growth was sustained by a strong will to promote the national power of production because catching up was the most urgent task facing the Japanese in order to promote their position in the world system. Even when the Cold War situation in East Asia seriously constrained opportunities for international trade, Japan, Korea, and Taiwan used the American presence in the region to negotiate their access to the U.S. market by arranging a trade-off between economic gain and political and military dependence (Cumings 1984).

Influenced by nationalist ideology, Japanese economists did not share belief in the neoclassical assumption. Those who were involved in policy making in 1931–65 displayed the psychological condition of what Mary Matossian ([1958] 1971) called the *assaulted* intellectuals in late-developing countries. Although they were overwhelmed by the contrast between the degree of development in their own country compared to Western countries and supported the effort to catch up with the West, they often resented the West and tried hard to identify "a 'true self'" in order to be equal with that part of the world. This condition often caused them to "merge fact and value, to superimpose upon things as they are the things that are desired in economic thinking," and to stand as the representatives of collective interests, advocating the conquest of the difficulties created by domestic class conflicts and power struggles.

Neoclassical economics assumes that human behavior in a modern economy is motivated solely by instrumental rationality. Even if social norms still have some influence, they are marginal and can be neglected in economic theorizing. The Japanese case, in contrast, demonstrates that even in a modern economy, subjectivity is not destroyed by commodification and still shapes material life (Zelizer 1988:627–8). Non-instrumental value systems still set limits to instrumental rationality by proscribing market exchange in sacred objects and relationships (Granovetter 1985; Zukin and DiMaggio 1990). In this sense, moral and ethical imperatives in the form of values or norms in economic analysis cannot be reduced to utilities, and group identity often motivates individual behavior (Etzioni 1988; Sen 1987). In an oriental country such as Japan, indigenous values have always been in tension with the industrialization process. It is not only that the indigenous values permeate industrialization; in addition, industrialization selects some indigenous values over others that cannot stay current with the increasing complexity of modern life. These revivals of indigenous values are not mere repetitions of the past; they constitute a process of spiral development. As an outcome of this process, the collectively shared meanings of social order and national interests have been distilled in Japan's modern economic institutions.

Institutionalized beliefs and cross-national learning

This book demonstrates that the institutionalized beliefs about how a latecomer country industrializes exerted a great impact on Japanese industrial policy and economic institutions. The ideology of Japanese developmentalism has created a distinctive *industrial culture* – "the economic customs that structure industries and economies, and simultaneously . . . the means–ends designations that are socially constructed in the process of the enactment of those customs" (Dobbin 1993:5; also see Dyson 1983). The nation-state as the unit of analysis, the strong production orientation, the strategic view of the economy, the organized competition, and the concept of productivity, taken together, contrast sharply with Western mainstream economic theories and present a competing model of industrialization.

The ideology of Japanese developmentalism evolved in a process of interaction between institutionalized beliefs about how a latecomer country industrializes and the challenge of new situations in the environment. The Japanese case reconfirms Hugh Heclo's (1974:305) argument that governments not only "power"; they also puzzle. Policy making entails both deciding and knowing. With regard to knowing, cross-national learning plays an important role. When economic theories were credited with creating successful industrialization in some countries, other countries sought to emulate these experiences, driven by international competition, the expectation of rewards for political achievement, and the ritual ceremony of the state (DiMaggio and Powell 1983; Hall 1989; Ikenberry 1990; Meyer and Rowan 1977). In this sense, economic thinking in a late-industrializing country such as Japan was constrained intellectually at the beginning by Western economic ideas, which stood as rationalized myths. The Japanese case also shows that institutionalized beliefs are not sustained in a static manner. Rather, they are achieved in a dynamic process in which many peripheral elements can be refined and transcended in an effort to sustain the deeply rooted principles in a new environment. In comparison with their original formats, all of the major principles demonstrated in this study had developed to a considerable extent by the 1960s. Sometimes, as in the diffusion of Keynesian theory in Japanese financial policy making in the early postwar period, "misconceptions could be as effective a stimulus as accurate reports" (Heclo 1974:310).

This study indicates that those ideas that fit the industrial culture of a given country are more likely to be accepted and diffused because the "logic" of the particular industrial culture underlying current practice has an enduring effect on future choices. According to Frank Dobbin (1993, 1994), when nations face a new policy dilemma they design new institutions around the logic of existing institutions; policy approaches are reproduced because state institutions provide cause–effect logic that policymakers apply to new problems. Robert Wuthnow (1989:552) states, "Ideas become embedded in concrete communities of discourse rather than floating freely in the creative minds of their investors." As Peter Hall (1989:393) remarks, this discourse will "provide a language in which policy can be described within the political arena and the terms in which policies are judged . . . work to the advantage or disadvantage of new policy proposals . . . [and] have a major impact on the likelihood that a new set of policy ideas will be accepted."

The ideology of Japanese developmentalism demonstrated a strong German impact. Although the German impact on the Meiji state was documented by Kenneth Pyle (1974) more than 20 years ago, it did not attract much attention until very recently. In light of comparative capitalism, the German economic theories, as an intellectual alternative to orthodox liberal capitalism, have attracted great attention (Fallows 1994; Williams 1994). As James Fallows (1994:182) points out, "The Germans deserve emphasis because many of their philosophies endured. They did not take root in England or America, but they were carefully studied, adapted, and applied in parts of continental Europe and in Asia, notably in Japan. In place of Rousseau and Locke, the Germans offered Hegel. In place of Adam Smith, they had Friedrich List." Behind List's *National System of Political Economy,* says David Williams (1994:122–3),

> stands the long and profound German meditation on the practical problems of turning the state into a war machine, on how to achieve bureaucratic rationality and efficiency, on the principles of national identity in an era of fierce ethnic conflicts, on the economics of national competition, and on revolutions "from above" to achieve such policy ends.

It was similar historical experiences in industrialization and the international environment that made the Japanese not only embrace the German historical school in the Meiji and Taishō periods, but also follow the German theory of total war in the national mobilization for World War II. In the 1950s, the German experience of relying on nationalist ideology to unite labor and management during the postwar economic reconstruction once again provided intellectual stimulus to the transition of Japanese labor relations.

The influence of Marxism on Japanese economic ideology also deserves attention. Marxism became a new cornerstone of Japanese economic thinking after World War I. When the German historical school was challenged strongly by the new situation in Japanese industrialization, the institutionalization of Marxism in Japanese academia indicated another departure of Japanese economists from the classical tradition: After the German historical school failed to cope with the increasing social conflicts that resulted from rapid industrialization,

Japanese economists searched for a radical solution that was not acceptable to classical economics. In the 1930s, however, Japanese Marxism underwent a radical twist in the *tenkō* movement. As a result, some crucial elements of Marxism, such as its assertions of class struggle and cosmopolitanism, were eliminated, and the principle of the planned economy remained. The production force theory advocated by Ōkōchi Kazuo, together with the German theory of total war, the New Deal, and the Soviet five-year plans, served Japan's national mobilization for war. In the postwar era, the version of the Marxist perspective asserted by Arisawa Hiromi shared this characteristic. It emphasized government planning, but stressed the importance of national unity and national interest rather than class struggle and cosmopolitanism.

In the reception of foreign economic ideas, there are two distinctive patterns: wholesale and retail. In the wholesale pattern, ideas become doctrine; their propositions function more as constraining than as enabling factors. In the retail pattern, ideas are accepted with conditions; their propositions remain legitimate insofar as they fit economic reality. By retailing, elements of different ideas can be borrowed to form a new variation, making the best use of different ideas according to local conditions. The wholesale pattern had often been evident in Japan's academic economics, both *marukei* and *kinkei*. *Jissen-ha* economics, however, had constantly shown the retail pattern. In the 1930s, the German theory of total war was well received in Japan. At the same time, however, Marxism was refined: Although some of its radical elements were eliminated, the concept of the planned economy remained. To strengthen state intervention in the managed economy, the Japanese looked for advice simultaneously from Germany, the Soviet Union, and the United States. These diverse sources of economic ideology together supported the departure of Japanese capitalism from its liberal tradition. The creative applications of Schumpeter's theory of innovation and Keynes's theory of demand management also demonstrate the retailing pattern of cross-national learning in Japan. The Japanese transformed Schumpeter's idea of innovation from a theory that explained the dynamics of long-term economic growth into a business strategy that aimed at promoting exports. In Japan, Keynes's idea of demand management was also applied creatively: It was converted from a theory about short-term market fluctuation to an instrument of state industrial policy promoting Japan's industrial structure in the long run.

More important, during the evolution of Japanese developmentalism, institutionalized beliefs did not develop in a linear fashion. The old applications were refined and transcended, and the general principles remained. The impact of institutionalized beliefs on Japanese industrial policy, this study shows, did not always appear as simple inheritance, but rather in the form of reproduction through interactions with competing beliefs. In the Japanese case, developmentalism could not perpetuate itself indefinitely because the German and Anglo-Saxon traditions had been in competition for a long time, and the wartime legacies often encountered strong challenges from orthodox liberal capitalism. In many cases, these challenges forced Japanese developmentalism to adapt, upgrade, or even transcend itself. Nevertheless, the general principles that emerged in 1931–45 survived through constant reproductions in the postwar era. For example, the implementation of the Dodge Plan and the liberalization of trade forced the Japanese state to change its methods in economic intervention, but the leading role of the state in economic development remained.

Ideas and interests

In demonstrating the strong impact of institutionalized beliefs on Japanese industrial policy, I also show that the fate of ideas and ideology in state policy making is not preordained, and it faces challenges from special interests. Although "economic ideas are explicitly programmatic about the organization of production and the distribution of its benefits and burdens," they do not explain their own acceptance because "economic ideas are always contested and ultimately are never settled" (Jacobsen 1995:286–7, 289). Economic ideas do prescribe rational actions, but state industrial policy is not determined solely by the need for efficiency; the demands for legitimacy, the goals of internal control and predictable order held by state bureaucracies, and the business leaders' desire to protect their economic freedom are almost as important as the market mechanism (DiMaggio and Powell 1983; Meyer and Scott 1983; Weber 1968). The role of ideas cannot be understood properly unless ideas are linked to material interests because, as Judith Goldstein and Robert Keohane (1993:26) argue, "ideas and interests are not phenomenologically separate."

John K. Jacobsen (1995) raised an important question in his critique of recent literature on the impact of ideas on policy making: Do ideas have independent effects on policy, apart from the interests of the actors who defend them? My answer is that it depends on which interest is used as the reference for judging the independent impact of ideas. The independent effects of ideas on policy making are reflected not by prevailing over the interests of actors, but by the fact that ideas have the power "to change the perceptions a group had of its own interests" and "possible new courses of action that changed the material world itself" (Hall 1989:369). If the old definition of interests held by actors is taken as the reference, the impact of ideas on policy making is independent because the political outcome is inconsistent with these interests. When we take the actors' new definition of interests as the reference, in contrast, the effect of ideas on the policy outcome can hardly be separated from the interests because no ideas can produce any change in policy making without support from political actors. In this sense, the power of economic ideas is reflected in their success in generating enough political support from actors who want to use them as weapons.

This study shows that the policy innovations and institutional reforms in Japan often required the redefinition of actors' interests as the precondition for success; the ideology of developmentalism exerted great impact on the process of redefinition. The ideas of the managed economy, technological innovation, high growth, and the new industrial system profoundly changed the way Japanese bureaucrats, business leaders, and workers defined their interests, perceived the situation, and formulated their responding strategies. In Chapter 5, for example, I stated that efficiency was regarded as the top priority in the rationalization movement of the early 1950s. With this perception, Japanese companies defined their interests in terms of low production costs and high capital return. This strategy led to massive layoffs, which generated great tension between management and labor. When Japanese managers were enlightened by the new idea of technological innovation, they no longer defined their companies' interests in short-term profits, but rather in long-term market share and comparative advantage in production technology. As a result, they changed their strategy toward labor from confrontation to cooperation by institutionalizing the Japanese management system. This was a historical trade-off between efficiency and the cooperation of labor. Economic ideas indeed have political power, as reflected in the fact that they changed the ways Japanese companies defined their interests.

Moreover, the impact of ideas on policy making, under the constraints of special interests, often appears as a driving force to change previously held perceptions, rather than determining the future course of action exclusively. This is particularly true when political actors refuse to accept the new definition of interests prescribed by ideas. Under such circumstances, ideas cannot exert significant influence on policy outcomes unless the actors who support them are willing to compromise. In the Japanese case, we have seen repeatedly that actors reached agreement relatively easily on the goals prescribed by economic ideas but had difficulty reaching a consensus on the means of realizing the goals. As I mentioned earlier, nationalism was important in shaping Japanese industrial policy. Under external pressure, bureaucrats, business leaders, and workers agreed on the urgent necessity of building up the national power of production. All major political actors, however, are concerned with protecting and even promoting their own interests through the means suggested by policy innovations and institutional reforms. Thus "most major decisions are made on the basis of a complicated process of confrontation, conflict, dialogue and political compromise" (Martinelli and Smelser 1990:31). In the 1930s, for example, even business leaders supported the state program of the managed economy. They agreed that given its limited resources, Japan could not survive the military undertaking without allocating resources more efficiently at the macro level. Nevertheless, when the reform bureaucrats intended to separate management from ownership and to bestow official status on managers, the business leaders fought strenuously. Eventually the state had to modify its program. The Japanese case reconfirms Margaret Weir and Theda Skocpol's (1985:118) argument that "if a given state structure provides no existing, or readily foreseeable, 'policy instrument' for implementing a given line of action, government officials are not likely to pursue it, and politicians aspiring to office are not likely to propose it."

This study also shows that ideas that "define cooperative solutions or act as coalitional glue" have a better chance of influencing policy outcomes when interests conflict with each other. When competing interests become a major obstacle to reaching a simple solution in an agent's favor, "the agent may forgo short-term benefits in order to realize long-term benefits . . . collective actors may subordinate special interests to common interests" (Windhoff-Heritier 1991:31). Especially when the international environment seems threatening, even behavior motivated by self-interest can lead to cooperation and pursuit of the collective welfare (Elster [1979] 1984). The three principles of the productivity movement suggested by Nakayama Ichirō are a good example. Addressing the interests of both management and labor in the innovation program, these three principles gradually won political support from both sides. The policy favoring large companies is another example. In the United States, such a policy would certainly violate antitrust law because small and medium-sized firms are perceived as having equal status in regard to state policy. In Japan, although the antimonopoly policy favored large companies, the development of *keiretsu* also encouraged associations between small and medium-sized companies and large companies in a hierarchical order. In short, this policy aimed not at eliminating small and medium-sized companies, but rather their survival under unequal conditions. The state achieved both goals simultaneously.

Because ideas cannot be separated from interests in influencing state policy making, the connection between political and academic elites is an important factor in explaining why certain economic ideas, such as the managed economy, priority production, and high growth, obtained political currency. *Social learning* – the diffusion of foreign ideas – as John Ikenberry (1990) points out, is different from *policy wagoning* – the adoption of foreign experiences by policy makers. The former does not necessarily result in the latter. This study demonstrates that the transition from social learning to policy wagoning is often supported by the link between academia and the state. As this study shows, the close ties between the SRA and Prime Minister Konoe Fumimaro, between Arisawa Hiromi and Prime Minister Yoshida Shigeru, and between Shimomura Osamu and Prime Minister Ikeda Hayato worked strongly in favor of the new order in 1939 and 1940, the priority production program in the late 1940s, and the high-growth thesis in the 1960s, respectively. Moreover, the direct involvement in government office by Ishibashi Tanzan, Tsuru Shigeto, and Inaba Hidezō explains the conditions in which their ideas influenced policy. In addition, when Nakayama Ichirō helped to establish Japanese-style management in the 1950s, he was not only a senior advisor to the Japanese state; he also became vice-president of the Headquarters of Productivity, directly in charge of labor relations. Through these special channels between the state and academia, the ideas of a small number of economists acquired political power and enabled an academic agenda to permeate the policy-making process.

Conflicts and the institutional coherence of developmentalism

This study argues that the conflict approach in studies of Japanese industrial policy needs to be supported by an institutional approach in order to reveal more clearly the nature of Japanese developmentalism. I have not only analyzed the conflicts in the politics of industrial policy, but have also demonstrated how economic institutions evolved in these conflicts.

The conflict approach has been an influential perspective in studying the Japanese political economy since the early 1980s. It emerged in reaction to the earlier interpretation of Japanese politics as a process of consensual decision making that is sustained by the social harmony. This approach is powerful in demonstrating the process and dynamics of change. It served to transcend the simplistic version of the "Japan, Inc." argument and has greatly enriched our understanding of the Japanese political economy. In the same time, however, the conflict approach has overlooked the impact of nationalist ideology on conflict resolution in the country confronted crises, as well as how the institutions that developed in these conflicts have served to reduce conflicts.

Two typical dichotomies derived from the conflict approach have been questioned by the reality of Japanese political economy in the 1990s.

The first dichotomy is the one between the conservatives and the progressives in the 1955 system. The *1955 system* refers to Japan's postwar political structure, in which the LDP, backed by major corporations, medium-sized and small companies, and farmers, ruled the country for almost 40 years. This one-party government was opposed by the Japan Socialist Party (JSP). As Fukunaga Hiroshi (1995:3) points out:

> To date, analysis of the 1955 system has emphasized the confrontational aspects of this relationship [on issues of international diplomacy and defense policy] and failed to cast enough light on the discreet cooperation between the two big parties . . . a close look at the present coalition government shows that the two parties are in virtual agreement about many of Japan's basic policies, such as the

protection of weak industries, continuation of government regulations, and giving priority to producers rather than consumers. . . .
While this system has been the foundation of Japan's political structure over the past four decades, it is not the source of its industrial
policies, bureaucratic regulations, and popular attitudes toward progress. These stem from something older, the development of a basic
system of controlling the economy that was set in place at least 15
years before the 1955 system.

The second dichotomy is the one between the state and the private
sector in the analysis of policy making. Since Chalmers Johnson presented the *developmental state* argument in 1982, this dichotomy has
been widely employed to either refine or challenge his argument. As a
result, Johnson's original dichotomy between the developmental state
in Japan and the regulatory state in the United States was replaced by a
dichotomy between the state and the private sector in Japan, and the
debate has focused on one of the subthemes in Johnson's developmental state argument – bureaucratic dominance or autonomy in policy
making. On the one hand, our understanding of Japanese politics has
been complicated, as many analysts have found that political, business,
and bureaucratic elites in Japan have cooperated closely with each
other, and that state policies were also influenced by societal forces
(Calder 1988; Samuels 1987). On the other hand, few studies, if not
none, have successfully falsified Johnson's main theme: that the Japanese state is a developmental state. If this main theme is overlooked, the
conflict approach has difficulties in explaining several major economic
phenomena in Japan. For examples, although the nation has the highest consumer prices in the world, a powerful consumer movement is
absent in Japan. Although bureaucrats, politicians, and big businesses
often conflict with each other, they also engage in an *iron triangle* or the
official–business adhesion (kanzai yuchaku). By Western standards,
Japanese workers work longer hours and receive less pay when they are
young, but there are no confrontational labor movements today.

As Daniel Okimoto (1989:230) points out, "the secret to Japan's
apparent success lies in the overall system within which industrial policy functions. It is the dynamic combination of factors, interacting
within the structure of an integrated system, that gives shape to the
apparent effectiveness of Japanese industrial policy." Many new studies published in Japan in the 1990s also take this institutional perspective. They focus on the "mutual supplement of institutions" and argue
that the Japanese economic system consists of multiple institutions,

including the state, business groups, trade associations, and the Japanese management system. Each of these institutions works in relation to others. Analytically, when one institution is under examination, the impact of others must be taken into account (Noguchi 1995; Okazaki and Okuno 1993b).

From the perspective of comparative capitalism, the real issue about the Japanese state is not whether bureaucrats dominated (they did in many cases but failed in others: nevertheless, they did have much more autonomy than their counterparts in the United States), but whether the economic system was developmental and how its programs were carried out. A developmental state may be well embedded in society (Evans 1995), and the Japanese state has been able to achieve its policy objectives through nonstate institutions (Tilton 1996). This study shows that the development of many economic institutions that are usually labeled as private has in fact been driven by the industrial policy of the Japanese state. The role played by the developmental state in Japan consisted not only of formulating industrial policy (this is a very important role), but also of creating an economy system with multiple institutions (many of which are nonstate) that aimed at mobilizing the whole country for the national mission of economic growth and maintaining political stability by making the competing interests interdependent.

Developmentalism is sustained by nationalist ideology. Nationalism plays a very important role in conflict resolution. The conflict approach assumes that the interests and goals of different actors are incompatible, and therefore they are the prime sources of conflict. In Japanese developmental politics, however, economic actors have clashed more often on the means to sustain economic growth (which have direct implications for the distribution of economic welfare and political interest) than on the goal itself. The conflicts basically concerned how to balance competing interests to achieve the goal. More important, when the country was facing a strong external challenge, such as total war, economic survival, or liberalization, national interest was often asserted strategically to reduce domestic conflicts. The shared sense of national crisis had been an important political foundation allowing competing parties to work out a solution to their domestic disputes. Influenced by nationalism, some dichotomies used by social scientists do not appear in developmental politics in the same manner as in the politics of liberal capitalism. For example, the private sector in the 1930s could not reject the idea of the managed economy in general, given the pressures of the Great Depression and war, but it did oppose a radical version of bureaucratic control. Similarly, the state bureaucracy in the early 1950s abolished its tight control over the distribution of materials and prices after its capacity for economic control was greatly strengthened in the priority production program, even when no political forces at the time could challenge its power. We cannot explain developmental politics fully without recognizing the impact of nationalism.

On the issue of equality, a key difference between developmentalism and liberal capitalism is that the former focuses on the outcome, whereas the latter emphasizes opportunity. In liberal capitalism, members of society need to compete with each other according to defined rules for their share of economic welfare. This may result in more inequality and generate more social conflicts. Developmentalism is sustained by nationalism. Nationalism will not work if it fails to address the issue of equality because a deep gap in the distribution of economic welfare among citizens can dampen their enthusiasm for the national mission. Under the pressures of maintaining social order during rapid industrialization and mobilizing the whole country to respond to the external challenge, the politics of Japanese industrial policy have often resulted in the development of governance mechanisms aimed at reducing domestic conflicts by ensuring a relatively fair share of the pie by major economic actors at several critical moments in modern Japanese history. As a result, although the production orientation made the Japanese suffer by paying high prices as domestic consumers, it also enabled them to enjoy status as international producers whose employment and income ensured a material basis to sustain the high-priced consumption, and a huge majority of the Japanese perceive themselves as middle class. The development of *keiretsu* not only restrained competition, reduced the production cost of big companies, and made their products competitive by sacrificing the interests of their subordinates, it also brought business opportunities to medium-sized and small companies, which otherwise would have more difficulty surviving the market competition. The Japanese management system not only served the interest of the company, it also provided Japanese workers with more job security and steady increases in salary. These relations are certainly unequal; nevertheless, they work for both sides. For this reason, they served to effectively demobilize political opposition. Conflicts always occur in economic development, but they may not be repeated at the same level because economic actors are able to develop institutions to resolve them. As a result, despite the existence of disadvantaged groups or the dissatisfaction of individual Japanese when their burdens were greater than their benefits at a given moment, the political opposition to developmentalism in Japan has not been strong enough to change the course of history.

Such institutional development, as repeatedly shown in the Japanese case, was achieved most frequently during crises. In order to respond to these external challenges unanimously, economic actors in Japan have often compromised on domestic issues. The emergence of this characteristic in the 1930s was not accidental. In order to mobilize the whole country for total war, industrialized countries all adopted policy measures to improve equality (Yamanouchi 1995a). What made fascism distinctive was its rejection of the democratic principle in politics and its policy of compulsory equalization. National crises, such as the urgent need to promote exports and the liberalization of trade and capital investment, have been the primary driving forces behind the transformation of the governance of the Japanese economy. As Japan responded to each of these external challenges between the 1930s and the 1960s, its economic system increasingly tied up the whole country in the same wagon. This system is not as harmonious as the Japan, Inc., argument has assumed. It is full of conflicts. Nevertheless, economic actors within the system were able to find common ground on the issues involving international competition (which has sometimes resulted in a new balance of power and interests within the system) while continuing to differ on domestic issues.

I do not reject the conflict approach. Rather, I suggest that in order to reveal the coherence of Japanese developmentalism, we need to pay attention to the institutional outcomes resulting from the conflicts in the politics of industrial policy. In the 1980s, the focus of the debate was on who made the industrial policy or whether this succeeded. In the 1990s, the focus has shifted to what kind of governance structures were derived for the economy from the politics of industrial policy, how these structures protect Japan's national interest in international competition, and what kinds of problems these structures have created for Japan lately (Kobayashi et al. 1995; Noguchi 1995; Okazaki and Okumo 1993b). Conflicts and disputes always exist in the politics of industrial policy, but they often result in institutional development that reduces these conflicts. It is these institutions, not the conflicts in the past, that have a direct implication for the present. By incorporating the conflict approach, which is powerful in demonstrating the dynamics of change, with the institutional approach, which is powerful in explaining where these conflicts have led, we will gain a better understanding of the politics of Japanese industrial policy.

Epilogue: Japanese developmentalism in historical perspective

Japanese developmentalism, which emerged in 1931–45 to combat the Great Depression and to sustain total war, was transformed from the military version to a trade version in the postwar period through several encounters with liberal capitalism, including the democratic reforms, the implementation of the Dodge Plan, and the liberalization of trade and capital investment. By the end of the 1960s, the contemporary Japanese economic system was largely patterned. During the transformation, many components of the wartime legacies were reformed, upgraded, and even transcended. Nevertheless, the focus on the national economy, the strong production orientation, the strategic view of the economy, the restraints on market forces, and the rejection of the profit principle remained as the basic ideological framework of Japanese industrial policy and were institutionalized in the governance mechanisms of the economy.

How does the later history shed light on these debates in 1931–65 documented in this book?

Between the first oil shock in 1973 and the end of the Cold War in 1989, Japanese developmentalism, exemplified by these debates, demonstrated great strength in international competition. It enabled the Japanese economy not only to respond successfully to two oil shocks in the 1970s, but also to cope effectively with the rapid appreciation of the yen resulting from the Plaza Agreement in 1985. Bypassing Britain and France in 1967 and West Germany in 1968 in total GNP, Japan has become an economic superpower, second only to the United States. In 1975, for the first time in the postwar period, Japan was invited to attend the summit meeting of major industrialized countries. By the end of the 1980s, Japan, with its strong economic competitiveness, had not only built up a huge trade surplus, but had also become the biggest international investor, creditor, and official development aid provider in the world. By concentrating on building national wealth, the trade version of developmentalism allowed the country to achieve what it intended to achieve with the military version in 1931–45 but failed.

Japanese developmentalism was given a tough test during the first oil shock. However, it survived and further strengthened the capacity to reproduce itself.

After the fourth Middle East war broke out in 1973, the OPEC countries used oil as a weapon to punish the industrialized countries that supported Israel. In less than three months, the price of oil in the international market jumped nearly 400%. At the time, oil constituted 77% of Japan's energy; 99.7% of the oil consumed by Japan was imported; and most of the oil came from the Middle East.

The oil shock strongly challenged the Japanese perception of the optimal industrial structure centered on heavy-chemical industries. MITI started two important projects aimed at reducing the dependence of the Japanese economy on oil. It started the Sunshine Plan in 1974, which focused on developing a substitute for oil, and the Moonlight Plan in 1978, which emphasized energy-saving technology. In the meantime, the Japanese quickly shifted their industrial structure to high-tech industries. As a result, the energy dependence of the Japanese economy on oil was reduced from 77% in 1973 to 56% in 1985 (Hara 1995a:101). The Japanese economy was sustained by competitiveness in energy saving, pollution control, high performance, and technologies with a high density of information, and Japanese automobiles and home electronics came to dominate the international markets since the 1980s (Mitsuhashi and Uchida 1994:87). Although the capacity for bureaucratic control over the economy, in comparison with the pre-1970 period, was weakened as the business activities of Japanese companies went far beyond the national border, administrative guidance and government regulations had still been important instruments for state intervention in the economy in 1973–89.

The private ordering of the economy encountered a big crisis during the first oil shock. At the time, oil companies regarded the oil shock as a golden opportunity to make money; as a result, they raised the oil price together through black cartels. This caused a price snowball throughout all industries, and housewives rushed to the stores to buy toilet papers, salt, soap, and lamp oil. In the debate on the new industrial system in the 1960s, private ordering was believed to be effective enough to promote the national interest in international competition. This time, however, it backfired, endangering the stability of the entire economy. Even MITI's bureaucrats, who had always been pro-business, denounced the speculative behavior of the oil industry as the "root of all evils." The government even discussed a proposal to revive wartime bureaucratic control over consumer prices. Although this proposal was not adopted, Prime Minister Tanaka Kakuei warned business leaders that if the private sector failed to cooperate with the state and continue to raise oil prices disproportionately, the state would have no choice but to return to direct control. The Fair Trade Commission also announced that the price cartels adopted by 12 oil companies violated the antimonopoly law and had to be abrogated. To control the economic situation, the state established a price system, suggesting a price for each item within the major product categories. After this confrontation, the private ordering worked under strong supervision by the state (Mitsuhashi and Uchida 1994:22–9).

Efficiency, which was related to the rejection of the profit principle, also became an issue again. Responding to the oil shock, 75% of the companies surveyed in the first quarter of 1975 had adjusted their employment policies by cutting back on recruitment, reducing the number of temporary and part-time workers, reassignment and transfers, early retirement, and designated dismissals (Dore 1986:95–9). In the meantime, labor unions fought hard for a big raise in salaries to cope with the rapidly rising consumer prices caused by the oil shock. Although the annual growth rate of productivity turned out to be negative in 1974, salaries rose on average by 26.1% that year. This salary increase stimulated inflation. To stabilize the situation, the Japanese government made a great effort to control wholesale and food prices, and in the meantime asked the labor unions to soften their demand for annual raises. The Japanese state, business leaders, and labor unions learned a great lesson in the first oil shock. When the second oil shock came, the Japanese economic system coped with it effectively. Japanese companies avoided layoffs, and labor unions restrained their demand for annual salary raises. As a result, the Japanese economy achieved a growth rate higher than that of any major industrialized country. When the Japanese yen appreciated rapidly in 1985, Japanese companies showed little change in their employment policy.

Reflecting the expanding power of the Japanese economy, there was a boom in the *Nihonjin-ron* (the theory of the Japanese). The Japanese economic system, which had often been perceived as premodern before the late 1970s, received wide appraisal, and its origin was often traced back to the traditions of the Kamakura and Edo eras, samurai ethics, and the household and village systems. This perspective assumes implicitly that economic actors in Japanese society internalize indigenous values unconsciously and obey the norms of institutional settings voluntarily. In other words, indigenous values shape Japanese behavior in economic activities mechanically by insinuating themselves into the minds and bodies of individual Japanese. This approach largely failed to show under what conditions and through what processes the orientation toward harmony and cooperation was eventually institutionalized in the Japanese economic system. In contrast, other investigators discovered universally valid economic principles, such as the internal labor market and X-efficiency. Rather than conceptualizing the historical contingencies that led to the institutionalization of Japan's economic system, this approach focused on the rational element in the system after it had been institutionalized, on the assumption that the surviving institution must be efficient. It never addressed the critical issues of why and under what conditions Japanese companies preferred X-efficiency, and why Japanese companies did not pursue efficiency in the same way as American firms did. These two perspectives may be powerful in explaining the rationale of institutional reproduction, but they hardly explain the dynamics that gave rise to the institutions in the first place and why these institutions changed over time.

History is full of ironies. Japan lost the 15-year war but came out of the Cold War that followed as the biggest winner. As soon as the Cold War ended, however, the Japanese economy was immediately hit by the worst economic stagnation in the postwar period. The economic system had brought prosperity and triumph to the country. Many problems contained in this system had been overshadowed by its dazzling achievement. These problems now cloud the country's future. It is clear that the Japanese economic system is confronting a major challenge.

The nation-state perspective in Japanese economic thinking has encountered increasing difficulties in the interdependent international economy. Japan's industrial policy in the past, in Ushio Jirō's (1995:31) words, was for "one nation's economic prosperity," "one nation's peace," "one nation's security," and "one nation's value." The success of developmentalism in one country depended on the existence of a developmental state that made a great effort to ensure political stability during economic growth by equalizing economic welfare among different social groups through industrial policy. At the international level, however, such a state does not exist. The practice of developmentalism by one or several countries would inevitably create economic inequality cross-nationally, and generate tensions and conflicts (Murakami 1992). During the Cold War, the success of Japanese developmentalism depended on the capacity and willingness of the United States to absorb Japan's huge exports of manufactured goods without strongly demanding a balance of trade in exchange for Japan's support in containing communism. Now the United States no longer wishes to absorb Japan's huge exports without balancing trade. In addition, the transition within industrialized countries from heavy-chemical to information industries has changed the structure of the economy and resulted in rapid development of multinational corporations. This fundamentally challenges the nation-state perspective that emphasizes national competitiveness in all manufacturing industries (Yamanouchi, Narita, and Ōuchi 1996:18). The economic nationalism of Japanese industrial policy not only received strong criticism from Western countries. After it was introduced to developing countries as an alternative model of industrialization, ironically, Japan also had to face the consequences, such as the "national car" policy adopted by Brazil and some Southeast Asian countries that directly threatens the interests of Japanese automobile makers.

The strategic view of the economy now also needs upgrading. The Japanese economic system evolved primarily to cope with mass production. It was characterized by manufacturing technology, homogeneity, and mass production of a qualified labor force. In the new era of the information revolution, the Japanese economy is required to make its "second industrial divide" between developing the *technologies of manufacturing things* and the *technologies of using things,* which has high density of information and knowledge, and functions not as a final product but as a system that will enable users to meet their various requirements. The former is exemplified by the automobile and home electronics industries, in which Japan has a strong comparative advantage. The latter is exemplified by the information superhighway, in which the United States dominates the global competition. The technologies of using things not only have redefined the comparative advantage in international competition, but also have had a profound impact on the future of economic institutions (Imai 1993; Uchihashi and Yakushiji 1993). Competition in the technologies of using things requires flexibility of individual companies and high creativity of employees, which are closely associated with market dynamics, individualism, high job mobility, and a merit-based wage system. Under such circumstances, state intervention, which was institutionalized in the past, not only protected some industries even after these industries exhausted their growth potential created by the decline in marginal costs, but also created many problems, such as the recent crisis in the Japanese financial system, as indicated by the housing loan industry. As a result, the dynamics of the economy were restrained by government regulations. The slow response of the Japanese state in the recent recession is a good example.

The practice of restraining competition through nonmarket governance structures is also facing a major crisis. Intensive government regulation not only prolonged the economic recovery from the recession, it also created great tension between Japan and other countries. In the 1980s, the expanding power of the Japanese economy intensified frictions in international trade, and *keiretsu* and antimonopoly issues became two major concerns among policy makers in the United States. In the Structural Impediment Initiative, the enhancement and enforcement of antimonopoly laws were regarded as a measure not only to eliminate exclusionary business practices, but also to promote Japan's imports and improve the investment environment for foreign companies in Japan. In bilateral negotiations on automobiles in 1995 between Japan and the United States, the *keiretsu* practice of Japanese auto makers, who buy parts exclusively from their subsidiaries, was also a major issue. In Japan, reducing state regulations and strengthening the antimonopoly law were regarded by the Hosokawa cabinet as two important policy goals. According to the proposal of the Hiraiwa commission, a strict antimonopoly law would help to strengthen the effects of deregulation, break the state–big business complex, and address more effectively the issues of fair competition and economic equality. Because of the lack of competition, Japanese consumers have suffered from much higher prices than consumers in all major industrialized countries. Although Japan's GNP per capita has become number one in the world, the actual purchasing power of Japanese consumers is disproportionately low. Furthermore, private companies, constrained by state regulations, cannot compete innovatively. This problem is especially visible when the economy needs entrepreneurship to recover from a recession. Without deregulation, Japanese firms have to keep their headquarters in Tokyo; the resulting overconcentration of population causes major social problems.

Efficiency, which has been closely related to the rejection of the profit principle, has also become an urgent issue again. The practices of lifetime employment and the seniority-based wage have encountered a great challenge. Two major factors that sustained Japanese management in the past have disappeared. One is the exchange rate. The fixed exchange rate of 1 dollar to 360 yen, established by Joseph Dodge in 1949, lasted until 1971. From then on, the yen has continued to appreciate. At one point in 1995, the exchange rate even reached 1 dollar to 79 yen. In the past, the favorable exchange rate had been one of the most important factors supporting lifetime employment and the seniority-based wage. With such a low rate, Japanese companies could absorb the inefficiency hidden in their oversized work forces. In the 1990s, the issue of high production costs due to surplus personnel has become a major concern among Japanese companies. In 1992, for example, at an exchange rate of 1 dollar to 110 yen, the average annual incomes (including salary and bonus) of college-educated white-collar Japanese employees aged 50 to 54 who worked at firms employing more than 1,000 workers were $109,700, $102,000, and $122,200 in the manufacturing, wholesale/retail, and finance industries, respectively. The 1992 average annual income for male blue-collar workers in the same age group, who worked in the same firms, was $64,222. When they retired at age 55, white-collar employees received $245,454 on average as a one-time retirement allowance; the blue-collar employees received $181,818 (Kamiyo 1994:23).

The other problem is the structure of the labor force. In the seniority-based wage system, younger employees are paid less, even though their productivity is higher, whereas older but less productive employees are paid more. In this sense, the system plays an important role in redistributing employees' income from younger to older workers and in reducing total labor costs for Japanese companies because formerly, much lower salaries were paid to the majority of the labor force, as the younger generation was the major component of the Japanese labor force when these practices were institutionalized in large companies decades ago. Now Japan's labor force is aging in a low-growth era, and production costs have become a heavy burden to Japanese companies (Shimada 1994a). Besides, younger workers now prefer present income to future income, contrary to the principle of the seniority-based wage system. They also prefer an increase in free time to an increase in income. These workers have a much stronger orientation toward an ability-based system of promotions and wages. When the prospects of growth for both the firm and the economy were promising, the seniority-based wage system was acceptable to younger employees because the company could deliver high pay when the employees grew older. Now that the prospects are less promising, younger workers prefer a merit-based wage system so that they can cash in on what they have done for the firm (Keizai Kikakuchō 1994:246–7).

Reflecting these great challenges, the historical contingency of Japanese developmentalism has attracted great attention in recent debate on the country's economic system. As Noguchi Yukio (1995) points out, the origin of the contemporary Japanese economic system is not as old as the Nihonjin-ron has assumed; it was born in the national mobilization during World War II. Because this system was created to carry out the total war, it was peculiar in Japanese history and can be changed.

The Japanese economy has certainly entered a transitional stage. In what direction is it heading? Will it be converted to the Anglo-Saxon style of liberal capitalism? The pattern of interaction between the wartime legacies and new challenges in postwar Japan demonstrated in this book is suggestive for the future. It indicates that when the Japanese economy was facing a major challenge, the ideology of liberal capitalism often served to address the urgency of reform. The eventual solutions, however, often consisted of upgrading the legacies of the past. This pattern of response is likely to continue. As Yamanouchi Yasushi (Yamanouchi et al. 1996:11, 18–19) states, the assertion that the Japanese economic system will be converted to the Anglo-Saxon type of liberal capitalism fails to grasp the nature of the issue because the transformation Japanese capitalism experienced during World War II was irreversible, and was one pattern of the great transformation of modern capitalism in world history.

In his analysis of the impact of fascism on Germany's postwar prosperity, Simon Reich points out that studies of fascism have focused on its causes, to the neglect of questions about its consequences. During the Cold War period, the Western allies wanted the world to believe their victory had been complete and decisive. As a result, fascism was replaced by communism as the new totalitarian threat in studies on comparative politics (1990:303–4). For the same reason, the key differences in economic institutions and ideologies between Japan and the United States were deliberately neglected. The end of the Cold War provides us with an opportunity to reexamine the history of modern capitalism. Facing the same failure of the self-regulated market and the disorder of the international economy in the 1920s and 1930s, industrialized countries responded with three distinctive patterns, which together not only transformed modern capitalism but also laid the ideological and institutional foundations for its contemporary diversity. The wartime legacies of the German and Japanese economic systems, after adapting to a democratic political institution and a free trade regime, resulted in an alternative pattern of capitalism in the postwar era. As the Cold War ended, the conflicts and tensions generated from the diversity of capitalism resurfaced. The differences between liberal capitalism and developmentalism are a major challenge to the future order of the international economy. For this reason, Japanese developmentalism deserves serious study.

References in English

Abegglen, James C. 1958. *The Japanese Factory.* Glencoe: The Free Press.

Albert, Michel. 1993. *Capitalism versus Capitalism: How America's Obsession with Individual Achievement and Short-Term Profit Has Led It to the Brink.* New York: Four Walls Eight Windows.

The Advisory Group on Economic Structural Adjustment for International Harmony. 1986. "The Report of the Advisory Group on Economic Structural Adjustment for International Harmony." In U.S. Government Printing Office, *Hearings Before the Joint Economic Committee, Congress of the United States, Ninety-Ninth Congress, Second Session. December 11 and 12, 1986.*

Anesaki, Masaharu. 1921. "The War's Effect upon the Japanese Mind." In K. K. Kawakami, ed., *What Japan Thinks.* London: Macmillan, pp. 143–59.

Aoki, Masahiko. 1989. "The Japanese Firm in Transition." In Kozo Yamamura and Yasukichi Yasuba, eds., *The Political Economy of Japan, Vol. 1: The Domestic Transformation.* Stanford: Stanford University Press, pp. 263–88.

Apter, David E., ed. *Ideology and Discontent.* New York: The Free Press, pp. 93–127.

Ayusawa, Iwao F. 1940. "The New World Order: A Japanese View." *Contemporary Japan* 9(7): 791–810.

Barkai, Avraham. 1990. *Nazi Economics: Ideology, Theory, and Policy.* Oxford: Berg.

Barnhart, Michael A. 1987. *Japan Prepares for Total War.* Ithaca: Cornell University Press.

Bendix, Reinhard. 1960. *Max Weber: An Intellectual Portrait.* Garden City, New York: Doubleday.

Berger, Gordon Mark. 1977. *Parties Out of Power in Japan, 1931–1941.* Princeton: Princeton University Press.

Berger, Peter, and Thomas Luckmann. 1966. *The Social Construction of Reality: A Treatise in the Sociology of Knowledge.* Garden City, New York: Doubleday.

Biggart, Nicole Woolsey. 1991. "Explaining Asian Economic Organization." *Theory and Society* 20: 199–232.

Blaug, Mark. 1992. *The Methodology of Economics.* Cambridge: Cambridge University Press.

Blinder, Alan S. 1990. "There Are Capitalists, Then There Are the Japanese." *Business Week,* Oct. 8:21.

Block, Fred. 1990. *Postindustrial Possibilities.* Berkeley: University of California Press.

Block, Fred. 1994. "The Role of the State in the Economy." In Neil J. Smelser and Richard Swedberg, eds., *The Handbook of Economic Sociology.* Princeton: Princeton University Press, pp. 691–71.

Blomstrom, Magnus, and Bjorn Hettne. 1984. *Development Theory in Transition.* London: Zed Books.

Breuilly, John. 1982. *Nationalism and the State.* New York: St. Martin's Press.

309

Brinkly, Alan. 1989. "The New Deal and the Idea of the State." In Steve Fraser and Gary Gerstle, eds., *The Rise and Fall of the New Deal Order: 1930–1980*. Princeton: Princeton University, Press, pp. 85–121.

Brown, Delmer M. 1955. *Nationalism in Japan*. Berkeley: University of California Press.

Burns, James M. 1978. *Leadership*. New York: Harper & Row.

Burstein, Paul. 1991. "Policy Domains: Organization, Culture, and Policy Outcomes." *Annual Review of Sociology* 17: 327–50.

Business Week. 1994. Special Issue: 32.

Calder, Kent E. 1988. *Crisis and Compensation*. Princeton: Princeton University Press.

Calder, Kent E. 1994. *Strategic Capitalism*. Princeton: Princeton University Press.

Caldwell, Bruce J. 1982. *Beyond Positivism: Economic Methodology in the Twentieth Century*. London: Allen & Unwin.

Campbell,John L., J. Rogers Hollingsworth, and Leon N. Lindberg, eds. 1991. *Governance of the American Economy*. Cambridge: Cambridge University Press.

Campbell, John L., and Leon N. Lindberg. 1991. "The Evolution of Governance Regimes." In John L. Campbell, J. Rogers Hollingsworth, and Leon N. Lindberg, eds., *Governance of the American Economy*. Cambridge: Cambridge University Press, pp. 319–55.

Cardoso, Fernando Henrique, and Enzo Faletto. 1979. *Dependency and Development in Latin America*. Berkeley: University of California Press.

Cohen, Jerome B. 1949. *Japan's Economy in War and Reconstruction*. Minneapolis: University of Minnesota Press.

Cole, Robert E. 1972. "Permanent Employment in Japan: Facts and Fantasies." *Industrial and Labor Relations Review* 26:615–30.

Crowley, James B. 1966. *Japan's Quest for Autonomy*. Princeton: Princeton University Press.

Cumings, Bruce. 1984. "The Origins and Development of the Northeast Asian Political Economy: Industrial Sectors, Product Cycles, and Political Consequences." *International Organization* 38(1): 1–40.

Davis, Horace B. 1967. *Nationalism and Socialism*. New York: Monthly Review Press.

Degenaar, J. J. 1982. *The Roots of Nationalism*. Cape Town, South Africa: Academica Pretoria.

DiMaggio, Paul. 1988. "Interest and Agency in Institutional Theory." In Lynne G. Zucker, ed., *Institutional Patterns and Organizations*. Cambridge: Ballinger, pp. 3–21.

DiMaggio, Paul. 1990. "Cultural Aspects of Economic Action and Organization." In Roger Friedland and A. F. Robertson, eds., *Beyond the Marketplace: Rethinking Economy and Society*. New York: Aldine De Gruyter, pp. 113–36.

DiMaggio, Paul, and Walter R. Powell. 1983. "The Iron Cage Revisited: Institutional Isomorphism and Collective Rationality in Organizational Fields." *American Sociological Review* 83: 147–60.

DiMaggio, Paul J., and Walter W. Powell. 1991. "Introduction." In Paul J. DiMaggio and Walter W. Powell, eds., *The New Institutionalism in Organizational Analysis*. Chicago: University of Chicago Press, pp. 1–38.

Dimock, Marshal E. 1968. *The Japanese Technocracy: Management and Government in Japan*. New York: John Weatherhill.

Dobbin, Frank. 1993. "The Social Construction of the Great Depression." *Theory and Society* 22: 1–56.

Dobbin, Frank. 1994. *Forging Industrial Cultures*. Cambridge: Cambridge University Press.

Dore, Ronald. 1973. *British Factory, Japanese Factory: The Origins of National Diversity in Industrial Relations.* Berkeley: University of California Press.

Dore, Ronald. 1983. "Goodwill and the Spirit of Market Capitalism." *British Journal of Sociology* 34: 459–82.

Dore, Ronald. 1986. *Flexible Rigidities.* Stanford: Stanford University Press.

Dore, Ronald. 1987. *Taking Japan Seriously.* London: Athlone Press.

Dower, John W. 1988. *Empire and Aftermath.* Cambridge: Council on East Asian Studies, Harvard University.

Duus, Peter, and Daniel I. Okimoto. 1979. "Fascism and the History of Pre-war Japan: The Failure of a Concept." *Journal of Asian Studies* xxxix: pp.39–64.

Dyson, Kenneth. 1983. "The Cultural, Ideological and Structural Context." In Kenneth Dyson and Stephen Wilks, eds., *Industrial Crisis: A Comparative Study of the State and Industry.* Oxford: Martin Robinson, pp. 26–66.

Eccleston, Bernard. 1989. *State and Society in Post-War Japan.* Cambridge, U.K.: Polity Press.

Economic Planning Agency. 1990a. *The Japanese Economy, 1945–55.* Tokyo: Economic Planning Agency, Government of Japan.

Economic Planning Agency. 1990b. *The Japanese Economy, 1955–65.* Tokyo: Economic Planning Agency, Government of Japan.

The Economist. 1994. "Oriental Renaissance: A Survey of Japan." *The Economist* July 9: 3–18.

Elster, Jon. [1979] 1984. *Ulysses and the Sirens.* Cambridge: Cambridge University Press.

Elster, Jon. 1990a. "Marxism, Functionalism, and Game Theory." In Sharon Zukin and Paul DiMaggio, eds., *Structures of Capital: The Social Organization of the Economy.* Cambridge: Cambridge University Press, pp. 87–118.

Elster, Jon. 1990b. "Jon Elster." In Richard Swedberg, ed., *Economics and Sociology.* Princeton: Princeton University Press, pp. 233–48.

Entwestle, Basil. 1985. *Japan's Decisive Decade.* London: Grosvenor Books.

Erhard, Ludwig. 1963. *The Economics of Success.* Princeton: D. Van Nostrand.

Etzioni, Amitai. 1988. *The Moral Dimension: Toward a New Economics.* New York: The Free Press.

Evans, Peter B. 1995. *Embedded Autonomy: States and Industrial Transformation.* Princeton: Princeton University Press.

Evans, Peter B., and John D. Stephens. 1988. "Development and the World Economy." In Neil J. Smelser, ed., *Handbook of Sociology.* Newbury Park, California: Sage, pp 739–73.

Fallows, James. 1994. *Looking at the Sun.* New York: Pantheon Books.

Falt, Olavi K. 1985. *Fascism, Militarism or Japanism?* Rovaniemi, Finland: Pohjois-Suomen Historiallinen Yhdistys, Societas Historica Finlandiae Septentrionalis.

Fine, Sherwood M. 1952. "Japan's Postwar Industrial Recovery." *Contemporary Japan* 21(4–6): 165–216.

Flanagan, Scott C. 1983. "Prime Minister and Cabinet." In *Kodansha Encyclopedia of Japan, Vol. 6.* Tokyo: Kodansha, pp. 240–4.

Fletcher, William Miles, III. 1975. "Ideologies of Political and Economic Reform and Fascism in Prewar Japan: Ryū Shintarō, Rōyama Masamichi, and the Shōwa Research Association." Dissertation, Yale University.

Fletcher, William Miles, III. 1982. *The Search for a New Order: Intellectuals and Fascism in Prewar Japan.* Chapel Hill: University of North Carolina Press.

Fligstein, Neil. 1990. *The Transformation of Corporate Control.* Cambridge: Harvard University Press.

Francks, Penelope. 1992. *Japanese Economic Development: Theory and Practice*. London: Routledge.

Friedland, Roger, and A. F. Robertson, eds. 1990. *Beyond the Marketplace*. New York: Aldine de Gruyter.

Friedman, Milton. [1953] 1984. "The Methodology of Positive Economics." In Daniel M. Hausman, ed., *The Philosophy of Economics: An Anthology*. Cambridge: Cambridge University Press, pp. 210–44.

Friedman, David. 1988. *The Misunderstood Miracle*. Ithaca: Cornell University Press.

Fukunaga, Hiroshi. 1995. "Reform Is Possible." *Tokyo Business Roday* 63(9) Sept.: 3.

Fukuyama, Francis. 1989. "The End of History?" *The National Interest* Summer: 3–19.

Fujisawa, Chikao. 1932. "Japan versus Marxism." *Contemporary Japan* 1(3): 441–52.

Fujisawa Rikitaro. 1921. "The Monroe Doctrine and the League of Nations." In K. K. Kawakami, ed., *What Japan Thinks*. New York: Macmillan, pp. 21–48

Fukuyama, Francis. 1989. "The End of History?" *The National Interest* Summer: 3–18.

Fukuyama, Francis. 1995. *Trust: Social Virtues and the Creation of Prosperity*. New York: The Free Press.

Gao, Bai. 1994. "Arisawa Hiromi and His Theory for a Managed Economy." *Journal of Japanese Studies* 20(1): 115–53.

Garon, Sheldon. 1987. *The State and Labor in Modern Japan*. Berkeley: University of California Press.

Gereffi, Gary. 1990a. "Paths of Industrialization: An Overview." In Gary Gereffi and Donald L. Wyman, eds., *Manufacturing Miracles: Paths of Industrialization in Latin America and East Asia*. Princeton: Princeton University Press, pp. 3–31.

Gereffi, Gary. 1990b. "International Economics and Domestic Policies." In Alberto Martinelli and Neil J. Smelser, eds., *Economy and Society: Overviews in Economic Sociology*. London: Sage, pp. 231–58.

Gerschenkron, Alexander. 1962. *Economic Backwardness in Historical Perspective*. Cambridge: Harvard University Press.

Gerschenkron, Alexander. [1952] 1992. "Economic Backwardness in Historical Perspective." In Mark Granovetter and Richard Swedberg, eds., *The Sociology of Economic Life*. Boulder: Westview Press, pp. 111–32.

Giersch, Herbert, Karl-Heinz Paque, and Holger Schmieding. 1992. *The Fading Miracle: Four Decades of Market Economy in Germany*. Cambridge: Cambridge University Press.

Gisli, Palsson. 1991. *Coastal Economies, Cultural Accounts*. Manchester: Manchester University Press.

Gluck, Carol. 1985. *Japan's Modern Myths: Ideology in the Late Meiji Period*. Princeton: Princeton University Press.

Goldstein, Judith. 1993. *Ideas, Interests, and American Trade Policy*. Ithaca: Cornell University Press.

Goldstein, Judith, and Robert O. Keohane, eds. 1993. *Ideas and Foreign Policy: Beliefs, Institutions, and Political Change*. Ithaca: Cornell University Press.

Gordon, Andrew. 1985. *The Evolution of Labor Relations in Japan: Heavy Industry, 1853–1955*. Cambridge: Council on East Asian Studies, Harvard University.

Gordon, Andrew. 1991. *Labor and Imperial Democracy in Prewar Japan*. Berkeley: University of California Press.

Gotō, Fumihiro, Kazutomo Irie, and Akihiko Soyama. 1990. *The Current Situation and Prospects for Regional Economic Integration: Asia-Pacific Free Trade Area Proposals and Japan's Choice*. Tokyo: Research Institute of International Trade and Industry.

Gourevitch, Peter A. 1987. *Politics in Hard Times*. Ithaca: Cornell University Press.

Gourevitch, Peter A. 1989. "Keynesian Politics: The Political Sources of Economic Policy Choices." In P. A. Hall, ed., *The Political Power of Economic Ideas*. Princeton: Princeton University Press, pp. 87–106.

Granovetter, Mark. 1985. "Economic Action and Social Structure: The Problem of Embeddedness." *American Journal of Sociology*, 91: 481–510.

Granovetter, Mark. 1990. "Mark Granovetter." In Richard Swedberg, ed., *Economics and Sociology*. Princeton: Princeton University Press, pp. 96–115.

Gudeman, Stephen. 1986. *Economics as Culture: Models and Metaphors of Livelihood*. London: Routledge & Kegan Paul.

Hadley, Eleanor M. 1989. "The Diffusion of Keynesian Ideas in Japan." In Peter A. Hall, ed., *The Political Power of Economic Ideas: Keynesianism Across Nations*. Princeton: Princeton University Press.

Haley, John O. 1988. *Law and Society in Contemporary Japan*. Dubuque: Kendall Hunt.

Haley, John O. 1991. *Authority without Power: Law and the Japanese Paradox*. New York: Oxford University Press.

Hall, Peter A. 1989. *The Political Power of Economic Ideas: Keynesianism Across Nations*. Princeton: Princeton University Press.

Hamilton, Gary G., and Nicole Woolsey Biggart. 1988. "Market, Culture, and Authority: A Comparative Analysis of Management and Organization in the Far East." *American Journal of Sociology* 94: 52–94.

Harding, Thomas G., David Kaplan, Marshall D. Sahlins, and Elman R. Service, eds. 1970. *Evolution and Culture*. Ann Arbor: University of Michigan Press.

Hausman, Daniel M., ed. 1984. *The Philosophy of Economics: An Anthology*. Cambridge: Cambridge University Press.

Heclo, Hugh. 1974. *Modern Social Politics in Britain and Sweden*. New Haven: Yale University Press.

Hein, Laura E. 1990. *Fueling Growth*. Cambridge: Council on East Asian Studies, Harvard University.

Hein, Laura E. 1994. "In Search of Peace and Democracy: Japanese Economic Debate in Political Context." *The Journal of Asian Studies* 53(3): 752–78.

Hicks, John. 1969. *Theory of Economic History*. Oxford: Oxford University Press.

Hirschman, Albert O. 1958. *The Strategy of Economic Development*. New Haven: Yale University Press.

Hirschman, Albert O. 1971. *A Bias for Hope*. New Haven: Yale University Press.

Hirschman, Albert O. 1980. *Morality and the Social Sciences: A Durable Tension*. Memphis, Tennessee: P. K. Seidman Foundation.

Hirschman, Albert O. 1986. *Rival Views of Market Society*. New York: Viking Penguin.

Hirschman, Albert O. 1989. "How the Keynesian Revolution Was Exported from the United States, and Other Comments." In Peter A. Hall, ed., *The Political Power of Economic Ideas: Keynesianism Across Nations*. Princeton: Princeton University Press.

Hirschman, Albert O. 1990. "Albert O. Hirschman." In Richard Swedberg, ed., *Economics and Sociology*. Princeton: Princeton University Press, pp. 152–66.

Hoston, Germaine A. 1983. "Tenkō & Marxism in Prewar Japan." *Polity* 16(1): 96–118.

Huntington, Samuel P. 1993. "The Clash of Civilizations?" *Foreign Affairs* 72(3) Summer: 22–49.

Huppes, T. 1976. *Economics and Sociology: Towards an Integration*. Leiden: Martinus Nijhoff Social Sciences Division.

Hampden-Turner, Charles. 1993. *The Seven Cultures of Capitalism: Value Systems for Creating Wealth in the United States, Japan, Germany, France, Britain, Sweden, and Holland.* New York: Doubleday.

Ikenberry, John. 1990. "The International Spread of Privatization Policies: Inducements, Learning, and 'Policy Bandwagoning.'" In Ezra N. Suleiman and John Waterbury, eds., *Political Economy of Public Sector Reform and Privatization.* Boulder: Westview Press, pp. 88–110.

Isaac, Larry W., and Larry J. Griffin. "Ahistoricism in Time-Series Analyses of Historical Process." *American Sociological Review* 54(6): 873–90.

Ishihara, Shintaro. 1989. *The Japan That Can Say No.* New York: Simon & Schuster.

Ishii Ryōsuke. 1980. *A History of Political Institutions in Japan.* Tokyo: University of Tokyo Press.

Itō, Monoshige, Kiyono Kazuharu, Ōkuno Masahiro, and Suzumura Kōtarō, eds. 1991. *Economic Analysis of Industrial Policy.* San Diego: Academic Press.

Jacobsen, John K. 1995. "Much Ado About Ideas: The Cognitive Factor in Economic Policy." *World Politics* 47(2): 283–310.

Johnson, Chalmers. 1977. "MITI and Japanese International Economic Policy." In Robert Scalapino, ed., *The Foreign Policy of Modern Japan.* Berkeley: University of California Press, pp. 227–79.

Johnson, Chalmers. 1982. *MITI and the Japanese Miracle.* Stanford: Stanford University Press.

Johnson, Chalmers. 1987. "Political Institutions and Economic Performance: The Government–Business Relationship in Japan, South Korea, and Taiwan." In Prederic C. Deyo, ed., *The Political Economy of the New Asian Industrialism.* Ithaca: Cornell University Press, pp. 136–64.

Johnson, Chalmers. 1988. "Study of Japanese Political Economy: A Crisis in Theory." In The Japan Foundation, ed., *Japanese Studies in the United States: History and Present Condition,* Tokyo: Japan Foundation, pp. 95–113.

Johnson, Chalmers. 1990 [1964]. *An Instance of Treason: Ozaki Hotsumi and the Sorge Spy Ring.* Stanford: Stanford University Press.

Johnson, Chalmers. 1993. "Comparative Capitalism: The Japanese Difference." *California Management Review* 35(4) Summer: 51–67.

Johnson, Chalmers. 1995. *Japan: Who Governs? The Rise of the Developmental State.* New York: W. W. Norton.

Kaplan, Eugene J. 1972. *Japan: The Government–Business Relationship.* Washington, D.C.: U.S. Department of Commerce.

Keynes, John Neville. [1917] 1984. "The Scope and Method of Political Economy." In Daniel M. Hausman, ed., *The Philosophy of Economics: An Anthology.* Cambridge: Cambridge University Press, pp. 70–98.

Kinzley, William D. 1991. *Industrial Harmony in Modern Japan: The Invention of a Tradition.* London: Routledge.

Kohli, Atul. 1994. "Where do High Growth Political Economics Come From? The Japanese Lineage of Korea's 'Developmental State'." *World Development* 22(9) Sept.: 1269–93.

Kohn, Hans. 1985. *Nationalism: Its Meaning and History.* Malabar, Florida: Robert E. Krieger Publishing Co.

Komiya, Ryūtarō. 1986. "Industrial Policy's Generation Gap." *Economic Eye* 7: 22–4.

Komiya, Ryūtarō, ed. 1988. *Industrial Policy of Japan.* Orlando, Florida: Academic Press.

Komiya, Ryutaro and Kozo Yamamura. 1981. "Japan: The Officer in Charge of Economic Affairs." In A. W. Coats, ed., *Economists in Government, an International Comparative Study*. Durham: Duke University Press, pp. 262–90.

Krasner, Stephen D. 1984. "Approaches to the State: Alternative Conceptions and Historical Dynamics." *Comparative Politics* 16: 223–46.

Krauss, Ellis S., Thomas P. Rohlen, and Patricia G. Steinhoff, eds. 1984. *Conflict in Japan*. Honolulu: University of Hawaii Press.

Kuhn, Thomas S. 1970. *The Structure of Scientific Revolution*. Chicago: University of Chicago Press.

Lane, Robert E. 1991. *The Market Experience*. Cambridge: Cambridge University Press.

Lazonick, William. 1991. *Business Organization and the Myth of the Market Economy*. Cambridge: Cambridge University Press.

Lincoln, James R., Hanada Mitruyo, and Kerry McBride. 1986. "Organizational Structures in Japanese and U.S. Manufacturing." *Administrative Science Quarterly* 31: 338–64.

Lincoln, James R., and Kerry McBride. 1987. "Japanese Industrial Organization in Comparative Perspective." *Annual Review of Sociology* 13: 289–312.

Lindberg, Leon N., and John L. Campbell. 1991. "The State and the Organization of Economic Activity." In John L. Campbell, J. Rogers Hollingsworth, and Leon N. Lindberg, eds., *Governance of the American Economy*. Cambridge: Cambridge University Press, pp. 356–90.

Lindberg, Leon N., John L. Campbell, and J. Rogers Hollingsworth. 1991. "Economic Governance and the Analysis of Structural Change in the American Economy." In John L. Campbell, J. Rogers Hollingsworth, and Leon N. Lindberg, eds., *Governance of the American Economy*. Cambridge: Cambridge University Press, pp. 3–34.

List, Friedrich. [1841] 1985. *The National System of Political Economy*. London: Longmans, Green.

MacArthur, Douglas. [1947] 1982. "General MacArthur's Letter on the Food Situation and Economic Stabilization." In Ōkurashō Zaiseishitsu, ed., *Shōwa zaiseishi: shūsen kara kōwa made*. Tokyo: Keizai Shinpōsha, Vol. 20 pp. 518–19.

Marshall, Byron K. 1967. *Capitalism and Nationalism in Prewar Japan*. Stanford, California: Stanford University Press.

Martinelli, Alberto, and Neil J. Smelser, eds. 1990. *Economy and Society: Overviews in Economic Sociology*. Newbury Park, California: Sage.

Matossian, Mary. 1971. "Ideology of Delayed Industrialization." In Jason L. Finkle and Richard W. Gable, eds., *Political Development and Social Change*. New York: Wiley, pp. 113–22.

McCloskey, Donald N. 1985. *The Rhetoric of Economics*. Madison: University of Wisconsin Press.

McClosky, Donald N. 1990. *If You're So Smart*. Chicago: University of Chicago Press.

McMillan, Charles J. 1988. *The Japanese Industrial System*. Berlin: Walter de Gruyter.

Meyer, John W., and Brian Rowan. 1977. "Institutionalized Organizations: Formal Structure as Myth and Ceremony." *American Journal of Sociology* 83: 340–63.

Meyer, John W., and W. Richard Scott. 1983. *Organizational Environments: Ritual and Rationality*. Beverly Hills: Sage.

Moore, Barrington. 1966. *Social Origin of Democracy and Dictatorship*. Boston: Beacon Press.

Morris-Suzuki, Tessa. 1989. *A History of Japanese Economic Thought*. London: Routledge.

Morris-Suzuki, Tessa, and Seiyama Takuro. 1989. *Japanese Capitalism Since 1945*. Armonk, New York: M. E. Sharpe.

Murakami, Yasusuke. 1987. "The Japanese Model of Political Economy." In Kozo Yamamura and Yasukichi Yasuba, eds., *The Political Economy of Japan: Vol. 1 The Domestic Transformation*. Stanford: Stanford University Press.

Nakane, Chie. 1970. *Japanese Society*. Berkeley: University of California Press.

Neff, Robert. 1993. "Well, It's a Start: Japan Talks Deregulation at Last and More Changes May Be Coming." *Business Week*, 13 September: 48–9.

North, Douglass C. 1981. *Structure and Change in Economic History*. New York: W. W. Norton.

North, Douglass C. 1990. *Institutions, Institutional Change and Economic Performance*. Cambridge: Cambridge University Press.

Oberschall, Anthony, and Eric M. Leifer. 1986. "Efficiency and Social Institutions: Uses and Misuses of Economic Reasoning in Sociology." *Annual Review of Sociology* 12: 233–53.

Okada, Tadahiko. 1940. "On Japan's Position." *Contemporary Japan* IX(8): 968–71.

Okimoto, Daniel I. 1989. *Between MITI and the Market: Japanese Industrial Policy for High Technology*. Stanford: Stanford University Press.

Ōkita, Saburō. 1982. *Japan's Challenging Years: Reflections on My Lifetime*. Canberra: Australian National University Press.

Ōkita, Saburō. 1990. "The Role of the Economist in Government: Japan." In Ōkita Saburō, *Approaching the 21st Century: Japan's Role*. Tokyo: The Japan Times.

Okuma, Shigenobu. 1921. "Illusions of the White Race." In K. K. Kawakami, ed., *What Japan Thinks*. London: Macmillan, pp. 160–70.

Olson, Mancur. [1965] 1971. *The Logic of Collective Action*. Cambridge: Harvard University Press.

Olson, Mancur. 1982. *The Rise and Decline of Nations: Economic Growth, Stagflation, and Social Rigidities*. New Haven: Yale University Press.

Orru, Marco, Nicole Woolsey Biggart, and Gary G. Hamilton. 1991. "Organizational Isomorphism in East Asia: Broadening the New Institutionalism." In Walter Powell and Paul DiMaggio, eds., *The New Institutionalism in Organizational Analysis*. Chicago: University of Chicago Press.

Ouchi, William. 1981. *Theory Z*. Reading, Massachusetts: Addison-Wesley.

Ouchi, William. 1984. *The M-form Society*. Reading, Massachusetts: Addison-Wesley.

Ozaki, Robert S. 1988. "The Humanistic Enterprise System in Japan." *Asian Survey* 28(8): 830–48.

Patrick, Hugh. 1977. "The Future of the Japanese Economy: Output and Labor Productivity." *The Journal of Japanese Studies*. Summer: 239.

Peacock, Alan, and Hans Willgerodt, eds. 1989. *German Neo-Liberals and the Social Market Economy*. London: Macmillan.

Peacock, Alan, and Hans Willgerodt, eds. 1989. *Germany's Social Market Economy: Origins and Evolution*. London: Macmillan.

Peattie, Mark R. 1975. *Ishwara Kanji and Japan's Confrontation with the West*. Princeton: Princeton University Press.

Pempel, T. J. 1982. *Policy and Politics in Japan: Creative Conservatism*. Philadelphia: Temple University Press.

Pittau, Joseph. 1983. "Meiji Constitution." In *Kodansha Encyclopedia of Japan, Vol. 2*. Tokyo: Kodansha, pp. 1–3.

Polanyi, Karl. [1944] 1957. *The Great Transformation: The Political and Economic Origins of Our Time*. Boston: Beacon Press.

Popper, Karl R. 1959. *The Logic of Scientific Discovery*. London: Hutchinson of London.

Powell, Walter, and Paul DiMaggio, eds. 1991. *The New Institutionalism in Organizational Analysis*. Chicago: University of Chicago Press.

Preston, Nathaniel Stone. 1967. *Politics, Economics, and Power: Ideology and Practice under Capitalism, Socialism, Communism, and Fascism*. New York: Macmillan.

Pyle, Kenneth B. 1974. "Advantages of Followership: German Economics and Japanese Bureaucrats, 1890–1925." *The Journal of Japanese Studies* 1(1): 127–64.

Pyle, Kenneth B. 1989. "Meiji Conservatism." In Marius Jansen, ed., *The Cambridge History of Japan, Vol. 5, The Nineteenth Century*. Cambridge: Cambridge University Press.

Pyle, Kenneth B. 1990. "Japan, the World, and the Twenty-first Century." In Takashi Inoguchi and Danial I. Okimoto, eds., *The Political Economy of Japan, Vol. 2: The Changing International Context*. Stanford: Stanford University Press. pp. 446–86.

Pyle, Kenneth B. 1992. *The Japanese Question*. Washington, D.C.: AEI Press.

Quadagno, Jill, and Stan J. Knapp. 1992. "Have Historical Sociologists Forsaken Theory?" *Sociological Method & Research*, 20(4): 481–507.

Reddy, William M. 1984. *The Rise of Market Culture*. Cambridge: Cambridge University Press.

Reich, Simon. 1990. *The Fruits of Fascism: Postwar Prosperity in Historical Perspective*. Ithaca: Cornell University Press.

Reisman, Davis A. 1976. *Adam Smith's Sociological Economics*. London: Croom Helm.

Robbins, Lionel. 1935. *An Essay on the Nature and Significance of Economic Science*. London: Macmillan.

Rogers, Everett M. 1983. *Diffusion of Innovations*. New York: The Free Press.

Rohlen, Thomas P. 1974. *For Harmony and Strength*. Berkeley: University of California Press.

Rosovsky, Henry, ed. 1966. *Industrialization in Two Systems: Essays in Honor of Alexander Gerschenkron*. New York: Wiley.

Rostow, Walter. [1960] 1979. *The Stages of Economic Growth*. Cambridge: Cambridge University Press.

Royall, K. C. [1948] 1982. "Royall's Speech on American Policy Towards Japan." In Ōkurashō Zaiseishishitsu, ed., *Shōwa zaiseishi: shūsen kara kōwa made (The History of Finance of the Shōwa Period: From the End of the War to the Conclusion of the Peace Treaty)*. Tokyo: Tōyō Keizai Shinpōsha, Vol. 20, pp. 183–6.

Sabel, Charles. 1994. "Learning by Monitoring: The Institutions of Economic Development." In Neil J. Smelser and Richard Swedberg, eds., *The Handbook of Economic Sociology*. Princeton: Princeton University Press, pp. 137–65.

Sahlins, Marshall. 1976. *Culture and Practical Reason*. Chicago: University of Chicago Press.

Sahlins, Marshall, and Elman R. Service. 1970. *Evolution and Culture*. Ann Arbor: University of Michigan Press.

Sakakibara, Eisuke. 1993. *Beyond Capitalism: The Japanese Model of Market Economies*. Lanham, Maryland: University Press of America.

Samuels, Richard J. 1987. *The Business of the Japanese State*. Ithaca: Cornell University Press.

Samuels, Richard J. 1994. *"Rich Nation, Strong Army."* Ithaca: Cornell University Press.

Sasaki, Takeshi. 1991. "Postwar Japanese Politics at a Turning Point." *The Japan Foundation Newsletter* 18(5–6): 1–7.

Sasaki, Takeshi, Burumi Shunsuke, Tominaga Kenichi, Nakamura Masanori, Masamura Kimihiro, and Murakami Yōichirō, eds. 1991. *Encyclopedia of Postwar Japan, 1945–1990.* Tokyo: Sanseido.

Scalapino, Robert A. 1964. "Ideology and Modernization: The Japanese Case." In David E. Apter, ed., *Ideology and Discontent.* New York: The Free Press, pp. 93–127.

Schneider, H. K. 1974. *Economic Man.* New York: The Free Press.

Sen, Amartya. 1987. *On Ethics and Economics.* Oxford: Basic Blackwell.

Sen, Amartya. 1990. "Amartya Sen." In Richard Swedberg, ed., *Economics and Sociology.* Princeton: Princeton University Press, pp. 249–67.

Sewell, William H., Jr. 1991. "A Theory of Structure: Duality, Agency, and Transformation." Unpublished manuscript.

Shimada, Haruo. 1983. "Japanese Industrial Relations – A New General Model? A Survey of the English-Language Literature." In T. Shirai, ed., *Contemporary Industrial Relations in Japan.* Madison: University of Wisconsin Press, pp. 3–27.

Smith, Anthony D. 1971. *Theories of Nationalism.* London: Duckworth.

Steinhoff, Patricia. 1993. "Japanese Studies in the United States: The Loss of Irrelevance." In Internationa House of Japan, ed., *The Postwar Development of Japanese Studies in the United States – A Historical Review and Prospects for the Future.* Tokyo: International House, pp. 19–35.

Stepan, Alfred. 1978. *The State and Society: Peru in Comparative Perspective.* Princeton: Princeton University Press.

Stinchcombe, Arthur L. 1983. *Economic Sociology.* New York: Academic Press.

Stinchcombe, Arthur L. 1990a. *Information and Organizations.* Berkeley: University of California Press.

Stinchcombe, Arthur L. 1990b. "Arthur L. Stinchcombe." In Richard Swedberg, ed., *Economics and Sociology.* Princeton: Princeton University Press, pp. 285–302.

Sugimori, Kōjirō. 1940. "The European War and Its Effects." *Contemporary Japan* 9(7): 964–74.

Swedberg, Richard. 1987. "Economic Sociology: Past and Present." *Current Sociology* 35(1): 1–221.

Swedberg, Richard. 1990. *Economics and Sociology.* Princeton: Princeton University Press.

Swedberg, Richard. 1991a. "Major Traditions of Economic Sociology." *Annual Review of Sociology* 17: 251–76.

Swedberg, Richard. 1991b. *Joseph A. Schumpeter: The Economics and Sociology of Capitalism.* Princeton: Princeton University Press.

Swedberg, Richard, and Mark Granovetter. 1992a. *The Sociology of Economic Life.* Boulder, Colorado: Westview Press.

Swedberg, Richard, and Mark Granovetter. 1992b. "Introduction." In Mark Granovetter and Richard Swedberg, eds., *The Sociology of Economic Life.* Boulder, Colorado: Westview Press, pp. 1–26.

Swedberg, Richard, Ulf Himmelstrand, and Goran Brulin. 1990. "The Paradigm of Economic Sociology." In Sharon Zukin and Paul DiMaggio, eds., *Structures of Capital: The Social Organization of the Economy.* Cambridge: Cambridge University Press, pp. 57–86.

Swidler, Ann. 1986. "Culture in Actions: Symbols and Strategies." *American Sociological Review* 51(4): 273–86.

SWNCC 150/3. [1945] 1982. "United States Initial Post-Defeat Policy Relating to Japan: SWNCC 150/3." In Ōkurashō Zaiseishishitsu, ed., *Shōwa zaiseishi: vol. 20: Shūsen kara kōwa made.* Tokyo: Tōyō Keizai Shinpōsha, pp. 63–7.

Tachi, Sabutarō. 1934. "The Open Door in China and Manchuria." *Contemporary Japan* 2(4): 571–87.

Tai, Hung-chao, ed. 1989. *Confucianism and Economic Development*. Washington, D.C.: Washington Institute Press.

Tanaka, Tokichi. 1933. "Japan and America: Questions to Be Solved." *Contemporary Japan* 2(3): 375–81.

Thomas, George M., and John Meyer. 1984. "The Expansion of the State." *Annual Review of Sociology* 10: 461–82.

Thurow, Lester. 1980. *The Zero-Sum Society: Distribution and the Possibilities for Economic Change*. New York: Basic Books.

Thurow, Lester. 1983. *Dangerous Currents: The State of Economics*. New York: Random House.

Thurow, Lester. 1991. "Competing Games: Profit Maximization versus Strategic Conquest." In Richard M. Coughlin, ed., *Morality, Rationality, and Efficiency*. Armonk, New York: M. E. Sharpe, pp. 119–32.

Thurow, Lester. 1992. *Head to Head: The Coming Economic Battle Among Japan, Europe, and America*. New York: William Morrow.

Tilly, Charles. 1975. "Western State-Making and Theories of Political Transformation." In Charles Tilly, ed., *The Formation of National States in Western Europe*. Princeton: Princeton University, pp. 601–39.

Tilton, Mark. 1996. *Restrained Trade: Cartels in Japan's Basic Materials Industries*. Ithaca: Cornell University Press.

Tsurumi, Shunsuke. 1982 *An Intellectual History of Wartime Japan, 1931–1945*. London: KPI.

U.S. Government. 1982. "United States Initial Post-Defeat Policy Relating to Japan: SWNCC 150/3." In Ōkurashō Zaiseishishitsu, ed., *Shōwa zaiseishi: shūsen kara kōwa made*. Tokyo: Tōyō Keizai Shinpōsha, Vol. 20.

Veblen, Thorstein. [1899] 1934. *The Theory of the Leisure Class*. New York: Viking Press.

Veblen, Thorstein. [1915] 1939. *Imperial Germany and the Industrial Revolution*. New York: Viking Press.

Veblen, Thorstein. [1919] 1942. *The Place of Science in Modern Civilization*. New York: Viking Press.

Vogel, Ezra F., ed. 1975. *Modern Japanese Organization and Decision-Making*. Berkeley: University of California Press.

Vogel, Ezra F. 1979. *Japan as Number One: Lessons for America*. Cambridge: Harvard University Press.

Wade, Robert. 1989. "What Can Economics Learn from East Asian Success?" In Peter A. Gourevitch, ed., *The Annals of the American Academy of Political and Social Science, Vol. 505: The Pacific Region: Challenges to Policy and Theory*, Newbury Park, New York: Sage.

Wade, Robert. 1990a. "Industrial Policy in East Asia: Does It Lead or Follow the Market?" In Gary Gereffi and Donald L. Wyman, eds., *Manufacturing Miracles: Paths of Industrialization in Latin America and East Asia*. Princeton: Princeton University Press, pp. 231–66.

Wade, Robert. 1990b. *Governing the Market: Economic Theory and the Role of Government in East Asian Industrialization*. Princeton: Princeton University Press.

Wallerstein, Immanuel. 1974. *The Modern World-System*. New York: Academic Press.

Weber, Max. 1947. *The Theory of Social and Economic Organization*. New York: Oxford University Press.

Weber, Max. [1921] 1950. *General Economic History*. Glencoe: The Free Press.

Weber, Max. [1930] 1950. *The Protestant Ethic and the Spirit of Capitalism*.

Weber, Max. 1968. *Economy and Society*, Vol. 1. New York: Bedminster Press.

Weick, Karl. 1979. *The Social Psychology of Organizing*. Reading, Massachusetts: Addison-Wesley.

Weir, Margaret. 1989. "Ideas and Politics: The Acceptance of Keynesianism in Britain and the United States." In Peter A. Hall, ed., *The Political Power of Economic Ideas: Keynesianism Across Nations*. Princeton: Princeton University Press, pp. 53–86.

Weir, Margaret, and Theda Skocpol. 1985. "State Structures and the Possibilities for 'Keynesian' Responses to the Great Depression in Sweden, Britain, and the United States." In Peter B. Evans, Dietrich Rueschemeyer, and Theda Skocpol, eds., *Bringing the State Back In*. Cambridge: Cambridge University Press, pp. 103–67.

Williams, David. 1994. *Japan: Beyond the End of History*. London: Routledge.

Williamson, Oliver E. 1975. *Markets and Hierarchies: Analysis and Antitrust Implication*. New York: The Free Press.

Williamson, Oliver E. 1981. "The Economies of Organization: The Transaction Cost Approach." *American Journal of Sociology* 87(3): 548–77.

Windhoff-Heritier, Adrienne. 1991. "Institutions, Interests and Political Choice." In Roland M. Czada and Adrienne Windhoff-Heritier, eds., *Political Choice: Institutions, Rules, and the Limits of Rationality*. Frankfurt: Campus Verlag, pp. 27–52.

Wolferen, Karel Van. 1989. *The Enigma of Japanese Power*. London: Macmillan.

Woolf, S. J., ed. 1968. *The Nature of Fascism*. London: Weidenfeld & Nicolson.

Wrong, Dennis. 1961. "The Oversocialized Conception of Man in Modern Sociology." *American Sociological Review* 26(2): 183–93.

Wuthnow, Robert. 1989. *Communities of Discourse*. Cambridge: Harvard University Press.

Yamamura, Kozo. 1967. *Economic Policy in Postwar Japan: Growth versus Economic Democracy*. Berkeley: University of California Press.

Yanaga, Chitoshi. 1968. *Big Business in Japanese Politics*. New Haven: Yale University Press.

Zelizer, Viviana A. 1988. "Beyond the Polemics on the Market: Establishing a Theoretical and Empirical Agenda." *Sociological Forum* 3(4): 614–34.

Zelizer, Viviana A. 1989. "The Social Meaning of Money: 'Special Monies'." *American Journal of Sociology* 95(2): 342–77.

Zink, Harold. 1974. *The United States in Germany: 1944–1945*. Westport: Greenwood Press.

Zukin, Sharon, and DiMaggio, Paul. 1990. "Introduction." In Sharon Zukin and Paul DiMaggio, eds., *Structures of Capital: Social Organization of the Economy*. Cambridge: Cambridge University Press.

References in Japanese

Abe Yoshishige. 1950. "Nihon no saigunbi ni tsuite" (On the Japanese rearmament). *Asahi Hyōron* Nov: 2–9.

Akimaru Jirō. 1989. "Akimaru kikan no tenmatsu" (The Whole Story of the Akimaru Agency). In *Arisawa Hiromi no Shōwashi*, Hensan Iinkai, ed., *Kaisō*. Tōkyō: Tōkyō Daigaku Shuppankai, pp. 61–8.

Amaya Naoyasu, Komiya Ryūtarō, and Sakamoto Jirō. 1962. "Atarashii sangyō taisei to keizai seisaku" (New Industrial System and Economic Policy). *Keizai Hyōron* Aug.: 71–87.

Andō Yoshio, ed. 1966. *Shōwa keizaishi e no shōgen* (The Testimony of Showa Economic History). Tōkyō: Mainichi Shinbunsha.

Andō Yoshio. 1987. *Taiheiyō sensō no keizaishiteki kenkyū* (Studies on the Economic History of the Pacific War). Tōkyō: Tōkyō Daigaku Shuppankai.

Arisawa Hiromi. 1934. *Sangyō dōin keikaku* (Planning Industrial Mobilization). Tōkyō: Kaizōsha.

Arisawa Hiromi. 1937a. *Keizai tōseika no nihon* (Japan Under the Managed Economy). Tōkyō: Kaizōsha.

Arisawa Hiromi. 1937b. *Sensō to keizai* (War and Economy). Tōkyō: Nihon Hyōronsha.

Arisawa Hiromi. 1937c. *Nihon kōgyō tōsei-ron* (The Industrial Control in Japan). Tōkyō: Arikai Kaku.

Arisawa Hiromi. 1948a. "Fukahitekina mono" (An Inevitable Thing). In Arisawa Hiromi, *Infureishon to shakaika*. Tōkyō: Nihon Hyōronsha, pp. 3–30.

Arisawa Hiromi. 1948b. "Nihon infureishon no mondai" (The Problem of Inflation in Japan. In Arisawa Hiromi, *Infureishon to shakaika*. Tōkyō: Nihon Hyōronsha, pp. 33–51.

Arisawa Hiromi. 1948c. "Nihon keizai no hakkyoku o sukū mono" (The Strategy That Can Save Japan from Economic Collapse). In Arisawa Hiromi, *Infureishon to shakaika*. Tōkyō: Nihon Hyōronsha, pp. 53–69.

Arisawa Hiromi. 1948d. "Kiki toppa no shōten" (The Focal Point of Tiding Over the Crisis). In Arisawa Hiromi, *Infureishon to shakaika*. Tōkyō: Nihon Hyōronsha, pp. 70–9.

Arisawa Hiromi. 1948e. "Hitosuji no michi" (A Road). In Arisawa Hiromi, *Infureishon to shakaika*. Tōkyō: Nihon Hyōronsha, pp. 80–99.

Arisawa Hiromi. 1948f. "Shakaika no riron no tame ni" (For a Theory of Socialization). In Arisawa Hiromi, *Infureishon to shakaika*. Tōkyō: Nihon Hyōronsha, pp. 125–50.

Arisawa Hiromi. 1949a. "Genka no keizai jōsei ni tsuite" (On the Present Economic Situation). *Asahi hyōron* Oct.: 27–34.

Arisawa Hiromi. 1949b. "Kyūgensoku no jisshi wa bukka chingin ni dō hibiku ka" (How Do the Nine Principles Influence the Salary and the Price)? *Jitsugyō no nihon* Mar. 15: 2–5.

Arisawa Hiromi. 1949c. "Senji Sengo no Kōgyō oyobi Kōgyō Seisaku (Industries and Industrial Policies During and After the War). In Yanai Haratadao, ed., *Sengo nihon keizai no shomondai.* Tōkyō: Yūhikaku, pp. 57–139.

Arisawa Hiromi. 1949d. *Keizai seisaku no nōto* (Notes on Economic Policy). Tōkyō: Gakufū Shoin.

Arisawa Hiromi. 1951a. "Nihon keizai no saikentō" (A Reexamination of Japanese Economy). *Chūō kōron* Aug.: 4–12.

Arisawa Hiromi. 1951b. "Nihon shihonshugi to saigunbi" (The Japanese Capitalism and the Rearmament). *Sekai* Mar.: 26–36.

Arisawa Hiromi. 1952a. "Saigunbi no keizaigaku" (Economics of Rearmament). *Sekai* 78(June): 18–30.

Arisawa Hiromi. 1952b. "Sekaiteki gunkaku no naka ni aru nihon keizai no mujun" (The Contradiction of Japan's Economy in the Worldwide Military Expansion). *Shakaishugi* 1(June): 4–6.

Arisawa Hiromi. 1953a. "Heiwa no keizaiteki kiso" (The Economic Foundation of Peace). *Fuebian kenkyū* 4(May): 1–6.

Arisawa Hiromi. 1953b. "Heiki seisan to nihon keizai" (The Production of Weapons and the Japanese Economy). *Chūō Kōron* Jan.: 14–22.

Arisawa Hiromi. 1953c. "Tenki ni chokumen suru nihon keizai" (The Japanese Economy in Transition). *Fuebian kenkyū* June: 1–36.

Arisawa Hiromi. 1953d. "Nihon keizai to saigunbi ni mondai" (The Japanese Economy and the Issue of Rearmament). *Fuebian kenkyū* Nov.: 1–11.

Arisawa Hiromi. 1956a. "Shihonshugi no kunō" (The Trouble with Capitalism). *Fuebian kenkyū* 7(1): 1–13.

Arisawa Hiromi. 1956b. "Nihon shihonshugi to koyō" (The Japanese Capitalism and Employment). *Sekai* Jan.: 23–34.

Arisawa Hiromi. 1957. "Keizai kakudai wa koyō mondai o kaiketsu shiuru ka" (Is It Possible to Solve the Problem of Employment by Economic Expansion?). *Sekai* Mar: 34–44.

Arisawa Hiromi. 1960. *Gendai nihon sangyō kōza* (Lectures on Modern Japanese Industry). Tōkyō: Iwanami Shoten, Vol. 8.

Arisawa Hiromi. 1967. "Shakaishugi no rinen to keizai seisaku ni okeru riarizumu" (The Ideal of Socialism and the Realism in Economic Policies). In Koizumi Akira and Miyazaki Yoshikazu, eds., *Nihon keizai o miru gan.* Tōkyō: Tōyō Keizai Shinpōsha, pp. 267–300.

Arisawa Hiromi. 1969. *Seisansei to nihon keizai* (Productivity and the Japanese Economy). Tōkyō: Nihon Seisansei Honbu.

Arisawa Hiromi. [1950] 1970. "Nihon shihonshugi no unmei" (The Fate of Japanese Capitalism). In Kanamori Hisao, ed., *Bōeki to kokusai shūshi.* Tōkyō: Nihon Keizai Shinbunsha, pp. 20–2.

Arisawa Hiromi, ed. 1976. *Shōwa keizaishi* (The History of the Shōwa Economy). Tōkyō: Nihon Keizai Shinbunsha.

Arisawa Hiromi. 1978. "Seisaku to genjitsu no tanima" (In the Valley between Policy and Reality). In Kondō Kanichi and Osanai Hiroshi, eds., *Sengo sangyōshi e no shōgen.* Tōkyō: Mainichi Shinbunsha, Vol. 3, pp. 12–29.

Arisawa Hiromi. 1988. "Intabiū" (Interview). In Keizai kikakuchō, ed., *Sengo keizai fukkō to keizai antei honbu.* Tōkyō: Keizai Kikakuchō, pp. 79–99.

Arisawa Hiromi. [1957] 1989. *Gakumon to shisō to ningen to – wasurenu hitobito* (Scholarship, Theories, and Personalities – Unforgettable People). Tōkyō: Tōkyō Daigaku Shuppankai.

Arisawa Hiromi. 1989a. *Arisawa Hiromi sengo o kataru: Shōwashi e no shōgen* (Arisawa Hiromi's Talk on the Postwar Era: The Testimony of Showa History). Tōkyō: Tōkyō Daigaku Shuppankai.

Arisawa Hiromi. 1989b. *Rekishi no naka ni ikiru* (Living in History). Tōkyō: Tōkyō Daigaku Shuppankai.

Arisawa Hiromi. 1989c. "Ryakunenpo" (A Brief Resume). In Arisawa Hiromi no Shōwashi Hensan Iinkai, ed., *Rekishi no naka ni ikiru*. Tōkyō: Tōkyō Daigaku Shuppankai, pp. 295–316.

Arisawa Hiromi. 1989d. *Arisawa Hiromi kataru sengo keizai shi* (The History of the Showa Economy Told by Arisawa Hiromi). Tōkyō: Tōkyō Daigaku Shuppankai.

Arisawa Hiromi, Aihara Shigeru, and Ōkawa Kazushi. 1959. "Atarashii Furoncha: kijutsu kakushin" (New Frontier: Technological Innovation). *Ekonomisuto* Feb. 7: 54–9.

Arisawa Hiromi and Inaba Hidezō. 1966. *Shiryō sengo nijunenshi* (Literature on Twenty Years' Postwar History). Tōkyō: Nihon Hyōronsha, Vol. 2.

Arisawa Hiromi, Minobe Ryōkichi, Nagasu Kazuji, Itō Mitsuharu, and Miyazaki Isamu. 1960. "Kōseichō wa kokumin seikatsu o yūdaka ni suru ka?" (Does the High Growth Enrich the Japanese Life?). *Sekai* Nov.: 19–35.

Arisawa Hiromi and Ōkita Saburō. 1966. "Keizai saiken to keisha seisan" (Economic Recovery and Priority Production). In Andō Yoshio, ed., *Shōwa keizai shi e no shōgen*. Tōkyō: Mainichi Shinbunsha, Vol. 3, pp. 274–93.

Arisawa Hiromi, Ōuchi Hyōe, Naitō Katsu, and Minobe Ryōkichi. 1965. "Kōsai hakkōron o hihan suru" (Criticism of the Pro–Public Debt Approach). *Sekai* 241 (Dec.): 53–73.

Arisawa Hiromi, Ōuchi Hyōe, Wakimura Yoshitarō, Takahashi Masao, and Minobe Ryōkichi. 1946. *Nihon infureishon no kenkyū* (The Elimination of Inflation in Japan). Tōkyō: Kōdosha.

Arisawa Hiromi and Tamanoi Yoshirō. 1973. *Kindai nihon o kangaeru* (Thinking about Modern Japan). Tōkyō: Tōyō Keizai Shinpōsha.

Arisawa Hiromi, Tōbata Seiichi, and Nakayama Ichiro, eds. 1960. *Keizai schutaisei kōza* (On Economic Subjectivity). Tōkyō: Chūō Kōronsha, Vol. 7, *History* 2, pp. 248–84.

Arisawa Hiromi, Tōbata Seiichi, Nakayama Ichirō, Wakimura Yoshitarō, and Ōkita Saburō. 1960. "Keizai shutai kara mita nihon shihonshugi" (The Japanese Capitalism Seen in Economic Subjectivity). In Arisawa Hiromi, Tōbata Seiichi, and Nakayama Ichirō, eds., *Keizai shutaisei kōza*. Tōkyō: Chūō Kōronsha, Vol. 7, History 2, pp. 248–84.

Arisawa Hiromi and Tsuchiya Hiyoshi, eds. 1967. *Shihon jiyūka* (The Liberalization of Capital). Tōkyō: Shakai Shisōsha.

Arisawa Hiromi, Watanabe Takeshi, Tsuchiya Kiyoshi, Hotta Shōzō, and Wakimura Yoshitarō. 1949. "Keizai saiken no shomondai" (The Problems in the Economic Reconstruction). *Chūō kōron* Mar.: 4–15.

Arisawa Hiromi no Shōwashi Hensan Iinkai, ed. 1989. *Kaisō* (Recollection). Tōkyō: Tōkyō Daigaku Shuppankai.

Asahi Shinbunsha. 1967. *Nihon no hōei to keizai* (The Defense and the Economy in Japan). Tōkyō: Asahi Shinbunsha.

Baba Keinosuke. 1967. "Yutaka no chokkanryoku" (The Great Power of Intuition). In Koizumi Akira and Miyazaki Yoshikazu, eds., *Nihon keizai o miru gan*. Tōkyō: Tōyō Keizai Shinpōsha, pp. 223–32.

Baba Shūichi. 1969. "1930 nendai ni okeru nihon chishikijin no dōkō" (The Orientation of Japanese Intellectuals in 1930s). *Shakai kagaku kenkyū*, 21(1): 67–207.

Chō Yukio. 1974a. *Ishibashi: hito to shisō* (Ishibashi: The Man and His theory). Tōkyō: Tōyō Keizai Shinpōsha.

Chō Yukio. 1974b. *Shōwa Kyōkō* (The Showa Depression). Tōkyō: Iwanami Shoten.

Chō Yukio and Sumiya Kazuhiko, eds. 1971. *Kindai nihon keizai shisōshi* (The Modern History of Japanese Economic Thought). Tōkyō: Yūhikaku.

Ebata Kiyoshi, ed. 1969. *Kaisō Ryū Shintarō* (In Memory of Ryū Shintarō). Tōkyō: Asahi Shinbunsha.

Ekonomisuto. 1950a. "Yūshutsu sōshin o naigai yōin" (Internal and External Factors That Prevent Exports). July 21:19–26.

Ekonomisuto. 1950b. "Nihon teichingin to kokusai hikaku" (Japan's Low Wage and International Comparison). June 21: 31–2.

Ekonomisuto. 1955. "Seisansei undō no teikō to kyōryoku" (The Resistance and Cooperation in Productivity Movements). July 9: 50–2.

Ekonomisuto. 1961. "Kindai keizai gakkai no nūberu bagu" (The Nobel Bag Among Modern Economists). Jan. 3: 108–12.

Ekonomisuto. 1965. "Fukyō taisaku, yatō wa dō kaneru?" (Countermeasures to Depression, What Do the Nongovernment Parties Think?). Aug. 31: 40–4.

Fukuda Takeo. 1965. "Keizai fukyō to kōsai hakkō" (Economic Depression and the Issue of Public Debts). *Gendai no gan* 6(9): 45–52.

Gaimushō. 1947. *Seifu hakusho no hitsuyōsei* (The Necessity of the Government White Paper).

Gaimushō. [1946] 1990. "Kaitei nihon keizai saiken no kihon mondai (The Revised Version of "The Basic Problems of the Economic Reconstruction"). In Nakamura Takafusa and Ōmori Tokuko, eds., *Nihon keizai saiken no kihon mondai*. Tōkyō: Tōkyō Daigaku Shuppansha, pp. 143–263.

Gotō Ryūnosuke. [1966] 1993. "Konoe shintaisei" (Konoe's New Order). In Andō Yoshio, ed., *Shōwa keizaishi e no shōgen*. Tōkyō: Hara Shobō, Vol. 3, pp. 169–97.

Gotō Yōnosuke. 1956. "Gijutsu kakushin to wa nani zo ya?" (What Is Technological Innovation?). *Ekonomisuto*, Betsusatsu (separate volume) (Autumn): 9–24.

Gotō Yōnosuke. 1957. "Keiki dōkō to junkan kyokumen no rikai no tame ni" (For the Understanding of Economic Trend and Cycle). In Shimomura Osamu, ed., *Keizai seichō jitsugen no tame ni*. Tōkyō: Kōchikai, pp. 251–68.

Gotō Yonosuke and Shishido Toshio. 1958. "Gijutsu kakushin to nihon keizai" (Technological Innovation and Japanese Economy). *Ekonomisuto* Feb. 1: 52–5.

Hall, Ivan. 1990. "Nihon no chishikijin yo, motto yūki o" (Japanese Intellectuals, Be More Brave). *Chūō kōron* Apr.: 288–303.

Hara Akira. 1972. "Keisai shintaisei" (New Economic Order). In Nihon Seijigakukai, ed., *Konoe shintaisei" no kenkyū*. Tōkyō: Iwanami Shoten, pp. 71–133.

Hara Akira. 1982. "Mondai teiki" (Introduction of the Issues). In Shakai Keizaishi Gakkai, ed., *1930 nendai no nihon keizai*. Tōkyō: Tōkyō Daigaku Shuppankai, pp. 3–22.

Hara Akira. 1990. "Kaitai" (Introduction). In Nakamura Takafusa and Hara Akira, eds., *Keizai fukkō keikaku*. Tōkyō: Tōkyō Daigaku Shuppankai, pp. 3–15.

Hara Akira. 1995a. "Sengo gojūnen to nihon keizai" (The Fifty Years in the Postwar Era and the Japanese Economy). In *Nenpō nihon gendaishi 1995 – sengo gojūnen no shiteki kenshō*. Tōkyō: Higashi Shuppan, pp. 79–111.

Hara Akira, ed. 1995b. *Nihon no senji keizai* (Japan's Wartime Economy). Tōkyō: Tōkyō Daigaku Shuppankai.

Hara Akira. 1995c. "Nihon no senji keizai-kokusai hikaku no shiten kara" (Japan's

Wartime Economy – With a Comparative Perspective). In Hara Akira, ed., *Nihon no senji keizai*. Tōkyō: Tōkyō Daigaku Shuppankai, pp. 3–44.

Hara Akira and Miwa Ryōichi. 1992. "Keizai kaikaku-higunjika to keizai minshuka" (Economic Reforms – Demilitarization and Economic Democratization). In Sodei Rinjirō and Takemae Eiji, eds., *Sengo nihon no genten*. Tōkyō: Yūshisha, Vol. 1, pp. 355–426.

Hara Yūzō. 1940. *Nihon tōsei keizai-ron* (On Japanese Managed Economy). Tōkyō: Chikura Shobō.

Hata Ikuhiko. 1981. *Senzenki nihon kanryōsei no seido, sōshiki, jinji*. (The Institution of Bureaucracy in Prewar Japan, Organization and Personnel). Tōkyō: Tōkyō Daigaku Suppankai.

Hata Ikuhiko. 1982. *Shōwashi no gunjin tachi* (The Military Men in the Showa History). Tōkyō: Bungei Shunjū.

Hata Ikuhiko. 1983. *Kanryō no kenkyū* (Studies on Bureaucrats). Tōkyō: Kōdansha.

Hayasaka Tadashi, Masamura Kimihiro, Takeyama Morio, Hamaguchi Haruhiko, Shibata Toshio, and Hoshino Akiyoshi. 1974. *Sengo nihon no keizaigaku* (Economics in Postwar Japan). Tōkyō: Nihon Keizai Shinbunsha.

Hayashi Yoshinori. 1965. "Hanazakari ni kōsai hakkōron" (The Boom of the Pro-National Debt Argument). *Ekonomisuto* June 22: 30–4.

Heiwa Mondai Danwakai. [1959] 1966. "Heiwa mondai danwakai seimei" (The Public Statement of the Forum of Peace). In Tsuji Kiyoaki, ed., *Shiryō sengo nijūnenshi*. Tōkyō: Nihon Hyōronsha, pp. 142–4.

Hiwatari Nobuhiro. 1991. *Sengo nihon no shijō to seiji* (Postwar Japanese Market and Politics). Tōkyō: Tōkyō Daigaku Shuppankai.

Hooks, Gregory, and Raymond A. Jussaume, Jr. 1995. "Sensō kōi to kokka no hen'yō: dainiji sekai taisen ni okeru nihon to amerika" (The War and the Changes of the State: Japan and the United States in World War II). In Yamanouchi Yasushi, ed., *Sōryokusen to gendaika*. Tōkyō: Kashiwa Shobō, pp. 79–116.

Horie Masaki. 1952. "Jūzoku-teki gunju sangyō no honkakuka" (The Institutionalization of the Dependent Munitions Industries). *Keizai hyōron* Dec.: 61–71.

Horie Masaki. 1955. "Seisansei kōjō undō hihan" (Criticism on the Movement of Promoting Productivity). *Chūō kōron* Oct.: 144–55.

Horie Shigeo. 1967. "Sekaiteki kinritaka to shihonjiyūka e no taiōsaku" (Worldwide High Interests and Countermeasures to the Capitalist Liberalization). In Koizumi Akira and Miyazaki Yoshikazu, eds., *Nihon keizai o miru gan*. Tōkyō: Tōyō Keizai Shinpōsha, pp. 84–122.

Horikotshi Teizō. 1962. "Shinsangyō taisei wa dō aru beki ka" (What Kind of New Industrial System?). In Tōyō Keizai, ed., *Nihon keizai to shinsangyō taisei*. Tōyō Keizai Shinpōsha, pp. 3–32.

Hoshino Yoshirō. 1957. "Shinsangyō kakumei no tenbō" (The Outlook of New Industrial Revolution). *Sekai* 135 (Mar.): 63–77.

Ide Yoshinori. 1982. *Nihon kanryōsei to gyōsei bunka* (The Japanese Bureaucratic System and the Culture of Government Administration). Tōkyō: Tōkyō Daigaku Shuppankai.

Igarashi Takeshi. 1979. "Tainichi senryō seisaku no tenkan to reisen" (The Transition of the Occupation Policies Towards Japan and the Cold War). In Nakamura Takafusa, ed., *Senryōki nihon no keizai to seiji*. Tōkyō: Tōkyō Daigaku Shuppankai, pp. 25–57.

Iijima Banshi, 1941. *Shōwa Ishin* (The Showa Restoration). Tōkyō: Asahi Shinbunsha.

Iijima Tadashi, Arai Noriko, and Kawabata Hisashi. 1983. *Keizai bunseki no rekishi to riron* (History and Theory of Economic Analysis). Tōkyō: Bunka Shobō Hatsubunsha.

Ikeda Hayato. 1949. "Ikeda zaisei no hōkō" (The Direction of Ikeda Finance). *Jitsugyō no nihon* Mar. 15.: 18–19.

Ikeda Hayato. 1959. "Ikeda Hayato shi no gekkyū nibairon" (Ikeda Hayato's View on the Doubling of Income). *Ekonomisuto* Mar. 21: 6.

Ikuda, Tadakide. 1992. *Nippon kanryō yo doko e iku?* (Where Are Japanese Bureaucrats Heading?). Tōkyō: NHK Shuppan.

Ikumi Tashiichi. 1953. "Sensō keizai-ka ni okeru kyōkō" (The Recession in the War Economy). *Keizai Hyōron* Aug.: 2–12.

Imai Kenichi. 1993. "Nihon sangyō, saikōchiku shiron (On the Reconstruction of Japanese Industries)." *Ekonomisuto,* Nov. 16: 40–9.

Imai Seiichi and Itō Takashi. 1974. *Gendaishi shiryō: kokka sōdōin, 2* (Literature on Modern History: The National General Mobilization, 2). Tōkyō: Misuzu Shobō, Vol. 44.

Imai Zen'ei. 1977. "Jiyūka no suishin" (Promoting Liberalization). In Itō Mitsuharu, ed., *Sengo sangyōshi e no shōgen, Vol. 1: Sangyō seisaku.* Tōkyō: Mainichi Shinbunsha, pp. 159–79.

Inaba Hidezō. 1949. "Kyūgensoku wa ika ni susumerareru ka" (How to Carry Out the Nine Principles). *Ekonomisuto* Feb. 11: 146–51.

Inaba Hidezō. 1956. "Seisansei kōjō undō hihan" (Criticism of the Movement of Promoting Productivity). *Fuebian kenkyū* 7(Dec.): 6–24.

Inaba Hidezō. 1965. *Gekidō sanjūnen no nihon keizai* (The Exciting Thirty Years of Japanese Economy). Tōkyō: Jitsugyō no nihonsha.

Inaba Hidezō. 1975. "Keizai antei honbu no risō to keizai kikakuchō no 'genjitsu' " (The Ideal of Economic Stabilization Board and the Reality of Economic Planning Agency). *ESP* Sept.–Oct.: 52–68.

Inaba Hidezō. 1988. "Intabiū" (Interview). In Keizai kikakuchō, ed., *Sengo keizai fukkō to keizai antei honbu.* Tōkyō: Keizai Kikakuchō, pp. 45–75.

Inaba Hidezō. 1989. "Hyūmanisuchikku na shisō" (Humanistic Thought). In *Arisawa Hiromi no Shōwashi* Hensan Iinkai, ed., *Kaisō.* Tōkyō: Tōkyō Daigaku Shuppankai.

Inaba Hidezō, Aihara Shigeru, Ōuchi Tsutomu, Komiya Ryūtarō, Uchida Tatao, Ōuchiyama Kiyoshi, and Miyashita Buhei. 1960. "Shinpojiaumu" (Symposium). *Ekonomisuto* Nov. 15: 16–32.

Inaba Hidezō, Hirata Keiichirō, Mutō Seiichirō, and Yano Tomoo. 1985. "Sengo nihon keizai no genten o kaerimiru: (1) keizai antei honbu sōsetsu zengo" (A Reexamination of the Origin of the Postwar Japanese Economy: (1) Before and After the Establishment of the Economic Stabilization Board). *ESP* Aug.: 8–17.

Inaba Hidezō, Kojima Masaoki, Saeki Kiichi, and Yano Tomoo. 1986. "Sengo nihon keizai no genten o kaerumiru: (4) keizai fukkō keikaku no shūhen" (A Reexamination of the Origin of the Postwar Japanese Economy: (4) the Circumference Around the Plan of Economic Recovery). *ESP* Feb.: 82–91.

Iriye Tokurō, Furutani Anamasa, Yamazaki Hideo, and Takagi Keno. 1984. "Sano to katoyama no tenkō" (The Conversion of Sano and Katoyama). In Iriye Tokurō, Furutani Anamasa, Yamazaki Hideo, and Takagi Keno, eds., 1984. *Shinbun shūsei shōwashi shōgen.* Tōkyō: Honbō Shoseki Kabushiki Kaisha, Vol. 7, pp. 538–40.

Ishibashi Tanzan. [1946] 1970. "Shōwa nijūichi nendo shūgiin zaisei enjitsu" (The Speech on the Finance of 1946 at the House of Representatives). In *Ishibashi Tanzan zenshū.* Tōkyō: Tōyō Keizai Shinpōsha, Vol. 13, pp. 176–98.

Ishibashi Tanzan. [1951] 1972. *Tanzan kaisō* (Recollections of Tanzan). Tōkyō: Mainichi Shinbunsha.

Ishino Shinichi. 1981. "Zaisei kin'yū seisaku no yakuwari" (The Function of Financial and Monetary Policies). *Ekonomisuto* June 2: 92–9.

Itō Daiichi. 1967. "Keizai kanryō no kōdō yōshiki" (The Behavioral Pattern of Economic Bureaucrats). In Nihon Seiji Gakkai, ed., *Gendai nihon no seido to kanryō*. Tōkyō: Iwanami Shoten, pp. 78–104.

Itō Mitsuharu. 1967. "Wagamichi o iku 'kokō no hito': Tsuru Shigeto kyōjū" (The Erudite Person Who Goes His Own Way: Professor Tsuru Shigeto). In Koizumi Akira and Miyazaki Yoshikazu, eds., *Nihon keizai o miru gan*. Tōkyō: Tōyō Keizai Shinpōsha, pp. 255–65.

Itō Mitsuharu. [1966] 1970. *Hoshū to kukushin no nihonteki kōzō* (The Structure of Japanese Conservatism and Progressivism). Tōkyō: Tsukuma Shobō.

Itō Mitsuharu and Chō Yūkio. 1971. "Sengo keizai no shisō" (The Economic Theories in the Postwar Era). In Itō Mitsuharu and Chō Yūkio, eds., *Keizai no shisō*. Tōkyō: Tsukuma Shobō, pp. 3–36.

Itō Mitsuharu and Chō Yukio, eds. 1971. *Keizai no shisō* (Economic Thought). Tōkyō: Tsukuma Shobō.

Itō Monoshige, Kiyono Kazuharu, Okuno Masahiro, and Suzumura Kōtarō. 1988. *Sangyō seisaku no keizai bunseki* (The Economic Analysis of Industrial Policy). Tōkyō: Tōkyō Daigaku Shuppankai.

Itō Takashi. 1974a. " 'Kyōkoku icchi' naikakuki no seikai saihensei mondai" (The Reorganization of Political Circles During the Period of the Cabinet Supported by the Whole Nation). *Shakai kagaku kenkyū* 25(4): 59–147.

Itō Takashi. 1974b. "Shintaisei towa nanika?" (What Is the New Order Movement?). *Rekishi to jinbutsu* Apr.: 38–9.

Itō Takashi. 1974c. *Shōwa jūnenshi danshō* (The Episode of Ten Years' History of Showa). Tōkyō: Tōkyō Daigaku Shuppankai.

Itō Takashi. 1976. *Jūgonen sensō* (Fifty Years of War). Tōkyō: Shōgakukan.

Itō Zenichi. 1972. "Kōki" (Postscript). In Nakayama Ichirō, *Nakayama Ichirō zenshū*. Tōkyō: Kodansha, Vol. 11, pp. 512–21.

Jimintō. [1959] 1966a. "Jimintō kaitei yōkō" (The Outline of the Revision of the Liberal Democratic Party). In Tsuji Kiyoaki, ed., *Shiryō sengo nijūnenshi*. Tōkyō: Nihon Hyōronsha, pp. 139–40.

Jimintō. [1959] 1966b. "Jimintō shōinikai ketsuron" (The Conclusion of the Subcommittee of the Liberal Democratic Party). In Tsuji Kiyoaki, ed., *Shiryō sengo nijūnenshi*. Tōkyō: Nihon Hyōronsha, pp. 140–1.

Kamada Isao and Takamura Juichi, eds. 1988. *Shōgen sengo keizaishi* (The Testimony of the Postwar Economic History). Tōkyō: Nihon Keizai Shinbunsha.

Kaminishi Akio. 1985. *Burein seiji* (Brain Politics). Tōkyō: Kōdansha.

Kamiyo Wayoshi. 1994. "Nihonteki koyō kankō no meritto to demeritto" (The Merit and Demerit of the Japanese Employment Custom). *Rōdōjipō* June: 20–3.

Kanamori Hisao. 1985. *Taiken sengo keizai* (Experiencing the Postwar Economy). Tōkyō: Tōyō Keizai Shinpōsha.

Kanbayashi Teijirō. 1958. "Gijutsu kakushin no hyōka" (The Evaluation of Technological Innovation). *Ekonomisuto* Jan. 25: 50–4.

Katō Toshihiko. 1979. "Gunbu no keizai tōsei shisō" (The Military's Theory of Managed Economy). In Tōkyō Daigaku Shakai Kagaku Kenkyusho, ed., *Senji nihon keizai*. Tōkyō: Tōkyō Daigaku Shuppankai, pp. 67–110.

Katsumata Seiichi. 1981. "Fujūbun datta shakaitō no taiō" (The Incomplete Response of the Socialist Party). *Ekonomisuto* June 9: 82–9.

Kawahara Hiroshi and Asanuma Kazunori. 1979. *Nihon no fuashizumu* (Japan's Fascism). Tōkyō: Yūhikaku.

Kawai Saburō. 1989. "Tōkei kaizen no Arisawa sensei" (Professor Arisawa Who Has Improved Statistics). In *Arisawa Hiromi no Shōwa shi* Hensan Iinkai, ed., *Kaisō.* Tōkyō: Tōkyō Daigaku Shuppankai.

Kawasaki Misaburō. 1947. "Sōron ni tsuite (On the General Introduction)." *Sekai* Sept.: 4–8.

Kazami Akira. 1951. *Konoe naikaku* (The Konoe Cabinet). Tōkyō: Nihon Shuppan Kyōdō Kabushiki Kaisha.

Keidanren Jimukyoku. 1953. "Shintokuju no igi to keizai kyōryoku no kōsō ni tsuite" (On the Significance of New Special Procurements and the Proposal of Economic Cooperation). *Keizai Rengō* 2: 22–6.

Keizai Antei Honbu. [1947] 1965. "Keizai jitsusō hōkokusho" (The Report of Actual Economic Situation). *Keizai hyōron* Oct.: 178–204.

Keizai Dantai Rengōkai. 1978. *Keizai dantai rengōkai sanjūnenshi.* Tōkyō: Keizai Dantai Rengōkai.

Keizai Kikakuchō, ed. 1956. *Keizai hakusho: nihon keizai no seichō to kindaika* (The Economic White Paper: Japan's Economic Growth and Modernization). Tōkyō: Shiseidō.

Keizai Kikakuchō. 1960. "Kokumin shotoku baisō keikaku" (The National Income Doubling Plan). In Ōkita Saburō, ed., *Shotoku baisō keikaku no kaisetsu.* Tōkyō: Nihon Keizai Shinbunsha, pp. 167–244.

Keizai Kikakuchō. 1964. *Sengo keizaishi: keizai antei honbushi* (The History of Postwar Economy: The History of the Economic Stabilization Board). Tōkyō: Ōkurashō Insatsukyoku.

Keizai Kikakuchō. 1966. *Keizai kikakuchō nijūnen shōshi* (A Brief Twenty-year History of the Economic Planning Agency). Tōkyō: Ōkurashō Insatsukyoku.

Keizai Kikakuchō. 1976. *Gendai nihon keizai no tenkai: keizai kikakuchō sanjūnenshi* (The Development of Modern Japanese Economy: A Thirty Year History of the Economic Planning Agency). Tōkyō: Ōkurashō Insatsukyoku.

Keizai kikakuchō, ed. 1988. *Sengo keizai fukkō to keizai antei honbu* (The Postwar Economic Recovery and the Economic Stabilization Board). Tōkyō: Keizai Kikakuchō.

Keizai Kikakuchō. 1994. *1994 nendo nenji keizai hōkoku: kibishii chōsei o koete aratana furontia e* (The 1994 Annual Report of the Economy: Toward a New Frontier After a Difficult Adjustment). *Shūkan Tōyō Keizai* Aug. 13–20: 164–425.

Kimura Kihachirō. 1947. "Keizai saiken no zentei" (The Precondition of Economic Recovery). *Asahi hyōron* Nov.: 12–20.

Kimura Kihachirō. 1948. "Infureishon no shūsoku ni tsuite" (On the Elimination of Inflation). *Zenshin* Jan.: 20–5.

Kindai Nihon Kenkyū-kai, ed. 1982. *Taiheiyō sensō* (The Pacific War). Tōkyō: Yamakawa Shuppansha.

Kishimoto Seijirō. 1947. "'Keizai jitsusō hōkokusho' hihan" (A Critique on 'The Report on Economic Reality'). *Jiron* Aug.: 9–15.

Kita Iki. 1959. *Kita Iki chōsakushū,* Vol. 1: *Kokutairon oyobi junsui shakaishugi* (National Political System and Pure Socialism). Tōkyō: Misuzu Shobō.

Kiuchi Nobutane. 1948. "Arisawa, Kimura ronsō saihihan" (Further Criticism on the Controversy Between Arisawa and Kimura). *Ekonomisuto* May 21: 164–6.

Kobayashi Hideo. 1984. *Showa fuashisuto no gunzō* (A Group of Showa Fascists). Tōkyō: Kōsō Shobō.

Kobayashi Hideo. 1995. *"Nihon kabushiki kaisha" o tsukutta otoko-miyazaki masayoshi no shōgai* (The Man who Created the "Japan Inc." – Miyazaki Masayoshi's Career). Tōkyō: Shōgakukan.

Kobayashi Hideo, Okazaki Tetsuji, Yonekura Seiichirō, and NHK. 1995. *"Nihon kabushiki kaisha" no showashi* (The Showa History of Japan Inc.). Tōkyō: Sōgensha.

Kobayashi Kichiya. 1989. *Hana mo arashi mo* (Flower and Thunderstorm). Tōkyō: Kōdansha.

Koizumi Akira and Miyazaki Yoshikazu. 1967a. " 'Nihon keizai o miru gan' no kōzō" (The Structure of "The Eye on Japanese Economy"). In Koizumi Akira and Miyazaki Yoshikazu, eds., *Nihon keizai o miru gan*. Tōkyō: Tōyō Keizai Shinpōsha, pp. 302–18.

Koizumi Akira and Miyazaki Yoshikazu, eds. 1967b. *Nihon keizai o miru gan* (The Eye on Japanese Economy). Tōkyō: Tōyō Keizai Shinpōsha.

Kojima Seiichi. 1938. *Nachisu shintōsei keizai dokuhon* (Readings on Nazi's New Managed Economy). Tōkyō: Chikura Shobō.

Kojima Tsunehisa. [1976] 1978. *Nihon shihonsugi ronrōshi* (The History of the Debates on Japanese Capitalism). Tōkyō: Ariesu Shobō.

Komiya Ryūtarō. [1959] 1971. "Nihon ni okeru keizaigaku kenkyū ni tsuite" (On Economic Studies in Japan). In Itō Mitsuharu and Chō Yūkio, eds., *Keizai no shisō*. Tōkyō: Tsukuma Shobō, pp. 217–28.

Komiya Ryūtarō. 1960. "Yōsureba munaiyō" (In Short, It Is Meaningless). *Ekonomisuto* Nov. 15: 6–12.

Komiya, Ryūtarō, Ōkuno Masahiro, and Suzumura Kōtarō, eds. 1984. *Nihon no sangyo seisaku*. Tōkyō: Tōkyō Daigaku Shuppankai.

Kondō Kanichi and Osanai Hiroshi, eds. 1978. *Sengo sangyōshi no shōgen, Vol. 3: Enerugi kakumei bōei seisan no kiseki* (The Testimony of the History of Postwar Industry, Vol. 3: The Path Toward the Energy Revolution of Defense Production). Tōkyō: Mainichi Shinbunsha.

Kōsai Yotaka. 1989. "Kōdo seichō e no shuppatsu" (The Starting Point of High Growth). In Nakamura Takafusa, ed., *"Keikakuka" to "Minshuka."* Tōkyō: Iwanami Shoten, pp. 283–321.

Kotō Rikuzō. 1963. "Sangyō taiseiron" (On Industrial System). In Morozumi Yoshihiko, Minosō Hitoshi, Shōda. *Sangyō taisei no saihensei*. Tōkyō: Shunjūsha, pp. 107–36.

Kurokawa Toshio and Satake Gosaku. 1970. *Nihon seisansei honbu: sono jittai to yakuwari* (The Headquarters of Productivity: Its Entity and Function). Tōkyō: Aomi Shoten.

Kusayanagi Ōkura. 1975. *Kanryō ōkokuron* (On the Bureaucrats Who Harm the Country). Tōkyō: Bungeishunjū.

Maruyama Masao. 1951. "Sengo nihon no nashonarizumu no ippanteki kōsatsu" (General Examination on the Postwar Nationalism). In Nihon Taiheiyō Mondai Chōsakai, ed., *Ajia no minzokushugi*. Tōkyō: Iwanami Shoten, pp. 168–87.

Maruyama Masao. 1972. *Gendai seiji no shisō to kōdō* (Theory and Behavior of Modern Politics). Tōkyō: Miraisha.

Maruyama Masao. 1982. "Gendai nihon no chishikijin" (Intellectuals in Modern Japan). In Maruyama Masao, *Goei no ichi kara: "gendai seiji no shisō to kōdō" suihō*. Tōkyō: Miraisha, pp. 73–133.

Masamura Kimihiro. 1974. *Gendai nihon no keizai seisaku* (The Economic Policy in Modern Japan). Tōkyō: Tsukuma Shobō.

Masamura Kimihiro. 1985. *Sengoshi* (Postwar History). Tōkyō: Tsukuma Shobō, Vol. 1.

Masamura Kimihiro. 1991a. "Nijū kōzōron" (The Theory of Dual Structure). In Sasaki Takeshi, Tsurumi Shunsuke, Tominaga Ken'ichi, Nakamura Masanori, Masamura Kimihiro, and Murakami Yōichrō, eds. *Sengoshi daijiten.* Tōkyō: Sanseitō, p. 692.

Masamura Kimihiro. 1991b. "Sengo nihon no seiji gyōsei shisutamu" (The Political-Administrative System in Postwar Japan). *Tōyō Keizai* June 8: 182–91.

Masuda Hiroshi. 1988. *Ishibashi Tanzan: Senryō Seisaku e no Teikō* (Ishibashi Tanzan: The Resistance to the Occupation Policy). Tōkyō: Sōshisha.

Masumi Junnosuke. 1988. *Nihon seijishi* (The History of Japanese Politics). Tōkyō: Tōkyō Daigaku Shuppankai, Vols. 1, 2, 3.

Matsuda Michio. 1965. "Sensō to interigencha" (War and Intelligentsia). In Matsuda Michio, *Nihon chishikijin no shisō.* Tōkyō: Tsukuma Shobō, pp. 144–59.

Matsui Haruo. 1934. *Keizai sanbō honburon* (On the Economic General Staff). Tōkyō: Nihon Hyōronsha.

Matsui Haruo. 1938. *Nihon shigen seisaku* (The Japanese Policies of Resources). Tōkyō: Chikura Shobō.

Mikami Ryūzō. 1967. "Nihon ni okeru Keinzu keizaigaku no tōnyū" (The Diffusion of Keynesian Economics in Japan). In Itō Mitsuharu, ed., *Keinzu keizaigaku.* Tōkyō: Tōyō Keizai Shinpōsha. pp. 195–220.

Misonō Hitoshi. 1987. *Nihon no dokusen kinshi seisaku to sangyō soshiki* (Japanese Antitrust Policies and Industrial Organization). Tōkyō: Kawade Shobō Shinsha.

Mitsuhashi Tadahiro and Uchida Shigeo. 1994. *Shōwa keizaishi* (The Economic History of the Shōwa Era). Tōkyō: Nihon Keizai Shinbunsha.

Miwa Yoshirō. 1993. "Shūchū haijo seisaku no keizai kōka" (The Economic Effect of Deconcentration Policy). In Kōsai Yutaka and Teranishi Jurō, eds., *Sengo nihon no keizai kaikaku.* Tōkyō: Tōkyō Daigaku Shuppankai, pp. 109–30.

Miyajima Hideaki. 1987. "Senji tōsei keizai e no ikō to sangyō no soshikika" (Controlled Cartelization in the Early Stage of Wartime Economy). In Nihon Kindaishi Kenkyūkai, ed., *Senji keizai.* Tōkyō: Yamakawa Shuppansha, pp. 103–27.

Miyajima Hideaki. 1988. "Senji keizai tōsei no tenkai no sangyō soshiki hen'yō (1)" (The Development of Wartime Economic Control and the Changes of Industrial Organizations). *Shakai kagaku kenkyū* 39(6): 1–44.

Miyasaka Tominosuke, Kaneko Akira, and Takahashi Iwakazu, eds. 1979. *Dokusen kinshi hōrei shiryōshū* (Materials on Antimonopoly Law). Tōkyō: Seibuntō.

Miyazaki Masayasu. 1990. "Kaitai" (Introduction). In Nakamura Takafusa and Miyazaki Masayasu, eds., *Keisha Seisan Hōshiki to Sekitan Shōiinkai* (The Priority Production Program and the Coal Committee). Tōkyō: Tōkyō Daigaku Shuppankai.

Miyazaki Yoshikazu. 1985. *Nihon keizai no kōzō to kōdō* (The Structure and Behavior of the Japanese Economy). Tōkyō: Chikuma Shobō, Vol. 1.

Miyazawa Kiichi. 1981. "Anpo kara keizai e" (From the Security Treaty to the Economy). *Ekonomisuto* May 12: 130–7.

Mori Takeo. 1933. *Senji keizai tōseiron* (On the Wartime Economic Control). Tōkyō: Nihon Hyōronsha.

Morikawa Hidemasa, ed. 1977. *Sengo sangyōshi e no shōgen, Vol. 2: Kyodaika no jidai* (The Era of Giant Organization). Tōkyō: Mainichi Shinbunsha.

Morozumi Yoshihiko. 1962a. "Sangyō seisaku no kyōchōteki tenkai" (The Harmonious Development of Industrial Policy). *Tōyō Keizai.* Bessatsu, No. 3 Summer: 1 12–19.

Morozumi Yoshihiko. 1962b. "Furansu keizai ni okeru keikaku" (Planning In the French Economy). *Keizai Hyōron* Aug.: 53–62.

Morozumi Yoshihiko. 1966. *Sangyō seisaku no riron* (The Theory of Industrial Policy). Tōkyō: Nihon Keizai Shinbunsha.

Murakami Yasusuke. 1989. "Ikōki ni okeru chishikijin no yakuwari" (The Role of Intellectuals in the Period of Transition). *Chūō Kōron* Mar.: 188–207.

Murakami Yasusuke. 1992. Hankoten no seiji keizaigaku (Anticlassical Political Economy). Tōkyō: Chūō Kōronsha, Vols. 1 and 2.

Murakami Yasusuke. 1994. Hankoten no seiji keizaigaku yōkō (An Outline for Anticlassical Political Economy). Tōkyō: Chūō Kōronsha.

Murobuji Tetsurō. 1983. *Kōkyū kanryō* (High-Ranking Bureaucrats). Tōkyō: Sekai Shoin.

Muroga Sadanobu. 1978. *Shōwa juku* (The Showa School). Tōkyō: Nihon Keizai Shinbunsha.

Nagano Takeshi. 1993. "Kaisha ga abunaku nareba jinin seiri wa totsuzen da" (Layoff Is Inevitable When Companies Are in Trouble). *Ekonomisuto*, Apr. 24: 12.

Nagata Sadashi. 1957. "Gijutsu kakushin to nihon keizai no shinro" (The Course for Technological Innovation and Japan's Economy). *Chūō kōron* Nov.: 48–57.

Nakamura Masanori. 1994. "Nihon senryō no shodankai" (Different Stages in the Occupation of Japan). In Yui Daizaburō, Nakamura Masanori, and Toyoshita Narahiko, eds., *Senryō kaikaku no kokusai hikaku: nihon, ajia, yōroppa*. Tōkyō: Sanseitō, pp. 87–97.

Nakamura Masanori. 1995a. "Daikyōkō to dasshutsu e no mosaku" (The Great Depression and the Search for Escape). In Rekishigaku Kenkyūkai, ed., *Hisshi no daian: kitai to kiki no nijūnen*. Tōkyō: Tōkyō Daigaku Shuppankai, pp. 203–38.

Nakamura Masanori. 1995b. "1950–60 nendai no nihon" (Japan in the 1950s and 1960s). In Asano Naohiro, Amino Yoshihiko, Ishii Susumu, Kano Masanao, and Hayakawa Shōichi, *Iwanami kōza: nihon Tsūshi. Vol. 20. gidai I.* Tōkyō: Iwanami Shoten, pp. 3–68.

Nakamura Masanori. 1995c. "Sengo 50 nen to nihon gendaishi kenkyū" (Postwar 50 Years and the Studies on Modern Japanese History). *Shinnō*, 47(55, Dec.): 885–908.

Nakamura Seiji. 1959. "Sengo nihon no gijutsuteki hatten to sono seikaku" (Japan's Postwar Technological Development and Its Characteristics). *Ekonomisuto* Mar. 28: 44–50.

Nakamura Takafusa. 1967. "Tetteishita Jisshō Seishin: Arisawa Sensei" (A Strong Empirical Orientation: Professor Arisawa). In Koizumi Akira and Miyazaki Yoshikazu, eds., *Nihon keizai o miru gan*. Tōkyō: Tōyō Keizai Shinpōsha, pp. 290–300.

Nakamura Takafusa. 1974a. *Nihon no keizai tōsei* (The Japanese Managed Economy). Tōkyō: Nihon Keizai Shinbunsha.

Nakamura Takafusa. 1974b. "Ryū Shintarō to Tōsei Keizai" (Ryū Shintarō and the Managed Economy). *Rekishi to Jinbutsu* Apr.: 66–74.

Nakamura Takafusa. 1979a. "SCAP to nihon" (SCAP and Japan). In Nakamura Takafusa, ed., *Senryōki nihon no keizai to seiji*. Tōkyō: Tōkyō Daigaku Shuppankai, pp. 3–23.

Nakamura Takafusa. 1979b. *Senryōki nihon no keizai to seiji* (The Japanese Economy and Politics During the Occupation). Tōkyō: Tōkyō Daigaku Suppankai.

Nakamura Takafusa. 1982. "Nichibei 'keizai kyōryoku' kankei no keisei" (The Formation of Japan–U.S. Economic Cooperation). In Kindai Nihon Kenkyūkai, ed., *Taiheiyō sensō*. Tōkyō: Yamakawa Shuppansha, pp. 279–302.

Nakamura Takafusa. 1988. "Keizai keikaku no seikaku to igi" (The Characteristics and Significance of Economic Planning). In Nihon Keizai Seisaku Gakkai, ed., *Keizai seisakugaku no tanjō*. Tōkyō: Keisō Shobō, pp. 228–43.

Nakamura Takafusa. 1989. "Arisawa Sensei no gakufū" (The Scholarship of Professor Arisawa). In *Arisawa Hiromi no Shōwashi* Hensan Iinkai, ed., *Kaisō*. Tōkyō: Tōkyō Daigaku Shuppankai, pp. 156–63.

Nakamura Takafusa. 1990. "Shiryō: sengo nihon no keizai seisaku kōsō to sono jidai no haikei" (Materials: The Economic Policy Proposal in Postwar Japan and its Historical Background). In Nakamura Takafusa and Ōmori Tokuko, eds., *Nihon keizai saiken no kihon mondai*. Tōkyō: Tōkyō Daigaku Shuppankai, pp. i–xxi.

Nakamura Takafusa. [1978] 1993. *Nihon keizai: sono seichō to kōzō* (The Japanese Economy: Its Development and Structure), 3rd ed. Tōkyō: Tōkyō Daigaku Shuppankai.

Nakamura Takafusa and Hara Akira. 1972. "Keizai shintaisei" (The Economic New Order). In Nihon Seiji Gakkai, ed., *"Konoe shintaisei" no kenkyū*. Tōkyō: Iwanami Shoten, pp. 71–133.

Nakamura Takafusa and Hara Akira, eds. 1990. *Keizai fukkō keikaku* (The Plan of Economic Recovery). Tōkyō: Tōkyō Daigaku Shuppankai.

Nakamura Takafusa and Miyazaki Masayasu, eds. 1990. *Keisha Seisan Hōshiki to Sekitan Shōiinkai* (The Priority Production Program and the Coal Committee). Tōkyō: Tōkyō Daigaku Shuppankai.

Nakamura Takafusa and Ōmori Tokuko, eds. 1990. *Nihon keizai saiken no kihon mondai* (The Basic Problems Concerning the Japanese Economic Reconstruction). Tōkyō: Tōkyō Daigaku Shuppankai.

Nakamura Tetsu. 1948. "Tōsui to seiji to no kōsō" (The Conflict Between the Supreme Command and Politics). *Chōryū* Jan.: 5–16.

Nakasone Yasuhiro, Murakami Yasusuke, Satō Seisaburō, and Nishibe Susumu. 1992. *Kyōdō kenkyū: "reisen igo"* ("After the Cold War": A Joint Study). Tōkyō: Bungei Shunjū.

Nakayama Ichirō. 1948a. "Tōsei to jiyū to no aida" (Between Control and Freedom). *Asahi Hyōron* Dec.: 15–21.

Nakayama Ichirō. 1948b. "Sekai keizai e no sanka" (Participation in the World Economy). In Nakayama Ichirō, *Nihon saiken no kadai*. Tōkyō: Kamakura Shobō, pp. 66–83.

Nakayama Ichirō. 1948c. "Gaishi tōnyū to keizai no saiken" (Foreign Investment and Economic Reconstruction). In Nakayama Ichirō, *Nihon saiken no kadai*. Tōkyō: Kamakura Shobō, pp. 84–99.

Nakayama Ichirō. 1949. "Nihon keizai no kao" (The Look of the Japanese Economy). *Hyōron*, Dec.: 1–9.

Nakayama Ichirō. 1955. *Seisansei no riron to jissai* (The Theory of Productivity and Reality). Tōkyō: Nihon Seisansei Honbu.

Nakayama Ichirō. 1956. "Sensansei kōjō undō hihan o hanhihan suru" (A Reply to the Criticism on the Productivity Movement). *Chūō kōron* Jan.: 46–52.

Nakayama Ichirō. 1959. "Chingin nibai o teishō" (Doubling the Salary). *Yomiuri Shinbun* Jan. 3.: 1.

Nakayama Ichirō. 1967. "Nihon no kōgyōka to dentō shakai" (The Industrialization of Japan and the Traditional Society). In Koizumi Akira and Miyazaki Yoshikazu, eds., *Nihon keizai o miru gan*. Tōkyō: Tōyō Keizai Shinpōsha, pp. 6–40.

Nakayama Ichirō. 1969. "Wagamichi: keizaigaku" (My Journey: Economics).

Wagamichi. Tōkyō: Asahi Shinbunsha.

Nakayama Ichirō. [1950] 1970. "Sekai shijō to nihon keizai" (International Market and Japanese Economy). In Kanamori Hisao, ed., *Bōeki to kokusai shūshi.* Tōkyō: Nihon Keizai Shinbunsha, pp. 3–14.

Nakayama Ichirō. 1972a. "Keizai antei to jiritsu (Economic Stability and Independence). In Nakayama Ichirō, *Nakayama Ichirō zenshū.* Tōkyō: Kōdansha, Vol. 11, pp. 423–74.

Nakayama Ichirō. 1972b. "Sensansei no riron to jissai" (The Theory of Productivity and Reality). *Seisansei kōjō shirizu.* Tōkyō: Seisansei Honbu, pp. 331–44

Nakayama Ichirō. 1972c. "Bōeki to nihon keizai" (Japanese Economy and Trade). In Nakayama Ichirō, *Nakayama Ichirō zenshū.* Tōkyō: Kōdansha, Vol. 12, pp. 53–111.

Nakayama Ichirō. [1953] 1972. "Sekai keizai no naka no Nihon keizai" (The Japanese Economy in the World Economy). In Nakayama Ichirō, *Nakayama Ichirō zenshū.* Tōkyō: Kōdansha, Vol. 12, pp. 78–80.

Nakayama Ichirō. [1956] 1972. "Seisansei o meguru shomondai" (The Issues Concerning Productivity). In Nakayama Ichirō, *Nakayama Ichirō zenshū.* Tōkyō: Kōdansha, Vol. 14. pp. 253–382.

Nakayama Ichirō. 1973b. *Nakayama Ichirō zenshu* (The Complete Works of Nakayama Ichirō). Tōkyō: Kōdansha, Vols. 18, 19, 21.

Nakayama Ichiō. 1973a. "Watashi no nenpo" (My Resume). In Nakayama Ichirō, *Nakayama Ichirō zenshū.* Tōkyō: Kōdansha, bekken, pp. 3–19.

Nakayama Ichirō. 1978. "Nihon ni okeru kindai keizaigaku no shuppatsuten" (The Starting Point of Modern Economics in Japan). In Minoguchi Takeo and Hayasaka Tadashi, eds., *Kindai keizaigaku to nihon.* Tōkyō: Nihon Keizai Shinbunsha, pp. 23–57.

Nakayama Ichirō, Tōbata Seiichi, Yasui Takama, and Yamada Yūzō. 1973. "Kindai keizaigaku no tenkai to haikei" (The Development and Background of Modern Economics). In Nakayama Ichirō, *Nakayama Ichirō zenshū.* Tōkyō: Kodansha, bekken, pp. 24–49.

Namiki Nobuyoshi. 1993. "Keizai gakusha no tsumi to batsu" (Economists' Guilt and Punishment). *Shogun* 25(Jan.): 66–78.

Nawa Tōichi. 1947. "Shihonshugiteki antei to gaikoku shihon" (The Capitalist Stabilization and Foreign Capital). *Jiron* Sept.: 11–30.

Nihon Keizai Seisaku Gakkai, ed. 1988. *Keizai seisakugaku no tanjō* (The Birth of the Study of Economic Policy). Tōkyō: Keisō Shobō.

Nihon Seisansei Honbu, ed. 1960. *Gijutsu kakushin to nihon keizai* (Technological Innovation and Japan's Economy). Tōkyō: Nihon Seisan Honbu.

Nihon Seisansei Honbu. 1985. *Sensansei undō 30 nen shi* (A Thirty Year History of the Productivity Movement). Tōkyō: Nihon Seisansei Honbu.

Nihon Seisansei Honbu, ed. 1990. *Seisansei undō to wa nani ka?* (What Is the Productivity Movement?). Tōkyō: Nihon Seisansei Honbu.

Nikeiren. [1948] 1966. "Keieiken kakuhō ni kansuru ikensho" (A Statement Regarding the Protection of the Management Authority). In Ōkōchi Kazuo, ed., *Shiryō: sengo nijūnen shi.* Tokyo: Nihon Hyōronsha, pp. 102–4.

Nikeiren. [1963] 1966a. "Kongo no rōshi kankei to keieisha no kenkai" (Labor Relations from Now On and the Managers' Perspective). In Ōkōchi Kazuo, ed., *Shiryō: sengo nijūnen shi.* Tokyo: Nihon Hyōronsha, p. 461.

Nikeiren. [1963] 1966b. "Maeda senmu riji rōdō jōsei hōkoku 'nihonteki rōmu kanri o sodateyō'" (The Deputy Director Maeda's Keynote Report "Let's Foster the Japanese Style of Management"). In Ōkōchi Kazuo, ed., *Shiryō: sengo nijūnen shi*. Tōkyō: Nihon Hyōronsha, pp. 461–2.

Nishimura Tetsujirō. 1989. "Arisawa sensei to nihachikai" (Professor Arisawa and the 28th Meeting). In *Arisawa Hiromi no Shōwa shi* Hensan Iinkai, ed., *Kaisō*. Tōkyō: Tōkyō Daigaku Shuppankai, pp. 168–72.

Nishinarita Yutaka. 1994. "Sengo kiki to shihonshugi saiken katei no rōshi kankei: nihon to nishidoitsu no hikakushi" (The Postwar Crisis and Labor Relations in the Process of Capitalist Reconstruction: A Comparative History Between Japan and West Germany). In Yui Daizaburō, Nakamura Masanori, and Toyoshita Narahiko, eds., *Senryō kaikaku no kokusai hikaku: nihon, ajia, yōroppa*. Tōkyō: Sanseitō, pp. 132–61.

Noguchi Yukio. 1995. *1940-nen taisei* (The 1940 System). Tōkyō: Tōyō Keizai Shinpōsha.

Ogata Sadako. 1969. "Gaiko to seron" (Diplomacy and Public Opinion). In Nihon Kokusai Seiji Gakkai, ed., *Nihon gaikōshi kenkyū*. Tōkyō: Yūhikaku, pp. 40–55.

Ōishi Kaiichirō. 1974. "Sengo kaikaku to nihon shihonshugi no kōzō henka: sono renzokuseitsu to danzetsuseitsu" (The Postwar Reforms and the Structural Changes of Japanese Capitalism: The Continuity Argument and the Discontinuity Argument). In Tōkyō Daigaku Shakai Kagaku Kenkyūsho, ed., *Sengo kaikaku: kadai to shikaku*. Tōkyō: Tōkyō Daigaku Shuppankai, pp. 63–97.

Okazaki Tetsuji. 1988. "Dainiji sekai taisenki no nihon ni okeru senji keikaku keizai no kōzō to unkō" (The Structure and Operation of the Wartime Planned Economy in Japan During World War II). *Shakai kagaku kenkyū*, 40(4): 1–132.

Okazaki Tetsuji. 1993. "Kigyō shisutemu" (The Company System). In Okazaki Tetsuji and Okuno Masahiro, eds., *Gendai nihon keizai shisutemu no genryū*. Tōkyō: Nihon Keizai Shinbunsha, pp. 97–144.

Okazaki Tetsuji. 1995a. "Dainiji sekai taisenki no kin'yū seido kaikaku to kin'yū shisutemu no henka" (The Reform and Changes in the Financial System During World War II). In Hara Akira, ed., *Nihon no senji keizai*. Tōkyō: Tōkyō Daigaku Shuppankai, pp. 107–40.

Okazaki Tetsuji. 1995b. "Nihon no senji keizai to seifu-kigyōkan kankei no hatten" (The Development of State–Business Relations in Wartime Japan). In Yamanouchi Yasushi, ed., *Sōryokusen to gendaika* Tōkyō: Kashiwa Shobō, pp. 267–85.

Okazaki Tetsuji and Okuno Masahiro. 1993a. "Gendai nihon no keizai shisutemu to sono rekishiteki genryū" (Contemporary Japanese Economic System and Its Historical Origin). In Okazaki Tetsuji and Okuno Masahiro, eds., *Gendai nihon keizai shisutemu no genryū*. Tōkyō: Nihon Keizai Shibunsha, pp. 1–34.

Okazaki Tetsuji and Okuno Masahiro, eds. 1993b. *Gendai nihon keizai shisutemu no genryū* (The Origin of Japan's Contemporary Economic System). Tōkyō: Nihon Keizai Shibunsha.

Ōkita Saburō. 1949. "Kawase reito settei igo" (After Fixing the Exchange Rate). *Asahi hyōron* Apr.: 64–9.

Ōkita Saburō. 1959a. "Keizai seichōryoku to seichō jitsugen no seisakuron" (The Growth Power of the Economy and Policy to Realize Growth). In Kin'yū Zaisei Jijō Kenkyūkai, ed., *Nihon keizai no seichōryoku: Shimomura riron to sono hihan*. Tōkyō: Kin'yu Zaisei Jijō Kenkyūkai pp. 75–94.

Ōkita Saburō. 1959b. "Nihon keizai no seichōryoku to 'shinchōki keizai keikaku" (The Growth Power of the Japanese Economy and the "New Long-term Economic Plan"). In Kin'yū Zaisei Jijō Kenkyūkai, ed., *Nihon Keizai no Seichōry-*

oku: Shimomura riron to sono hihan Tōkyō: Kin'yu Zaisei Jijō Kenkyūkai, pp. 31–47.

Ōkita Saburō. 1960. *Shotoku baisō keikaku no kaisatsu* (The Introduction of the National Income Doubling Plan). Tōkyō: Nihon Keizai Shinbunsha.

Ōkita Saburō. 1961. *Keizai keikaku* (Economic Planning). Tōkyō: Shiseidō.

Ōkita Saburō. 1976. *Watashi no rirekisho* (My Resume). Tōkyō: Nihon Keizai Shinbunsha.

Ōkita Saburō. 1981a. *Tōbun seisō* (The Challenging Years of Japan). Tōkyō: Nihon Keizai Shinbunsha.

Ōkita Saburō. 1981b. "Itsutsu no seisaku mokuhyō ni chūten" (Emphasizing Five Policy Targets). *Ekonomisuto* Apr.: 84–91.

Ōkita Saburō. 1983. *Ekonomisto no yakuwari* (The Role of Economists). Tōkyō: Nihon Keizai Shinbunsha.

Ōkita Saburō. 1984. *Nihon kanryō jijō* (The Circumstances of Japanese Bureaucrats). Tōkyō: TBS Buridanika.

Ōkita Saburō. 1988. "Intabiū" (Interview). In Keizai Kikakuchō, ed., *Sengo keizai fukkō to keizai antei honbu*. Tōkyō: Keizai Kikakuchō, pp. 1–41.

Ōkita Saburō. 1989. "Keisha seisan kōsō" (The Idea of Priority Production). In *Arisawa Hiromi no Shōwa shi* Hensan Iinkai, ed., *Kaisō*. Tōkyō: Tōkyō Daigaku Shuppankai, pp. 83–6.

Ōkita Saburō, Tokunaga Hisatsugu, Mutō Seiichirō, and Yano Tomoo. 1985. "Sengo nihon keizai no genten o kaerimiru: (2) kunimo akaji, kigyōmo akaji, kakeimo akaji" (A Reexamination of the Origin of the Postwar Japanese Economy: All the Goverment, Firms and Household Are Having a Deficit). *ESP* Oct.: 94–103.

Ōkōchi Kazuo. 1941. *Senji shakai seisakuron* (On Wartime Social Policies). Tōkyō: Jichōsha.

Ōkōchi Kazuo. 1949. "Rōdō seisaku ni okeru senji to heiji" (Labor Policy in Wartime and Peace). In Yanai Haratadao, ed., *Sengo nihon keizai no shomondai*. Tōkyō: Yūhikaku, pp. 185–229.

Ōkōchi Kazuo. 1957. "Gijutsu kakushin to rōdō kaikyū" (Technological Innovation and the Working Class). *Sekai* 136(Mar.): 86–92.

Ōkōchi Kazuo. [1942] 1969a. *Sumisu to risuto* (Smith and List). Tōkyō: Aohayashi Shoinsha.

Ōkōchi Kazuo. 1969b. *Ōkōchi Kazuo chōsakushū* (Ōkōchi Kazuo's Works). Tōkyō: Aohayashi Shoin Shinsha.

Ōkōchi Kazuo. 1970. *Shakai seisaku yonjūnen* (Forty Years' Social Policies). Tōkyō: Tōkyō Daigaku Shuppankai.

Ōkōchi Kazuo. 1971. "Sangyō hōkokukai no zen to go to" (The Industrial Patriotic Association: From the Beginning to the End). In Chō Yukio and Sumiya Kazuhiko, eds., *Nihon kindai keizai shisō daikei*. Tokyo: Yūhikaku, Vol. 2, pp. 73–108.

Okumura Hiroshi and Ronald Dore. 1993. "Nihon no 'hōjin shihonshugi' wa hokorobi hajimetaka (Has Japanese Corporate Capitalism Begun to Collapse?). *Ekonomisuto* May 25: 28–33.

Okumura Kiwao. 1966. "Denryoku kokukan mondai" (The Issue of Nationalization of the Management of the Electric Industry). In Andō Yoshio, ed., *Shōwa keizai shi e no shōgen*. Tōkyō: Mainichi Shinbunsha, Vol. 2, pp. 198–209.

Okuno Masahiro. 1993. "Gendai nihon no keizai shisutemu: sono kōzō to kaikaku no kanōsei" (The Contemporary Japanese Economic System: Its Structure and the Possibility of Reform). In Okazaki Tetsuji and Okuno Masahiro, eds., *Gendai nihon keizai shisutemu no genryū*. Tōkyō: Nihon Keizai Shibunsha, pp. 273–91.

Ōkura Yukio. 1952. "Chōsen sensōka ni okeru kyōkō no shinka" (The Deepening Recession During the Korean War). *Keizai Hyōron* Dec.: 51–9.

Omae Kin'ichi. 1992. *Heisei ishin* (The Heisei Restoration). Tōkyō: Kōdansha.

Ōnishi Gongichi. 1975. *Keizai kikakuchō* (The Economic Planning Agency). Tōkyō: Kyōikusha.

Ōta Kaoru. 1953. "Gōrika tōsō o ikani kakatau ka" (How to Fight the Battle of Rationalization). *Shakaishugi* 27(Sept.): 2–5.

Otaka Kōnosuke. 1993. " 'Nihonteki' rōshi kankei" ("The Japanese-type" Labor Relations). In Okazaki Tetsuji and Okuno Masahiro, eds., *Gendai nihon keizai shisutemu no genryū*. Tōkyō: Nihon Keizai Shibunsha, pp. 145–82.

Ōtake Hideo. 1984. "Nihon ni okeru 'gunsankan fukugō' keisei no zasetsu" (The Failure of Establishing a Military–Business Circles–Bureaucracy System in Japan). In Ōtake Hideo, ed., *Nihon seiji no sōten*. Tōkyō: Sanichi Shobō, pp. 13–69.

Ōtake Hideo. 1988. *Saigunbi to nashonarizumu* (The Rearmament and Nationalism). Tōkyō: Chūō Kōronsha.

Ōtake Hideo. 1992. *Futatsu no sengo: doitsu to nihon* (Two Postwar Experiences: Germany and Japan). Tōkyō: Nihon Hōsō Shuppan Kyōkai.

Ōtake Keisuke. 1981. *Maboroshi no Hana* (The Phantom of Flowers). Tōkyō: Rakuyū Shobō, Vol. 1.

Ōuchi Hyōe. 1947. "Keizai hakusho no igi" (The Significance of the White Paper). *Sekai* Sept.: 1–4.

Ōuchi Hyōe. 1949. "Dojji rain wa antei o motarasu ka?" (Does the Dodge Line Bring About Stability?). *Hyōron* June: 2–13.

Ōuchi Hyōe. 1959. *Keizaigaku gojūnen* (The Fifty Years of Economics). Tōkyō: Tōkyō Daigaku Shuppankai.

Ōuchi Hyōe. 1967. "Infureishon no imashime" (A Lesson from Inflation). In Koizumi Akira and Miyazaki Yoshikazu, eds., *Nihon keizai o miru gan*. Tōkyō: Tōyō Keizai Shinpōsha, pp. 124–61.

Ōuchi Hyōe. [1952] 1975. "Kore kara no keizai kore kara no kyōiku" (The Economy and Education from Now On). In Ōuchi Hyōe, *Ōuchi Hyōe chōsakushū*. Tōkyō: Iwanami Shoten, Vol. 7, pp. 380–94.

Ōuchi Hyōe. [1953] 1975. "Nichibei kankei no shōrai" (The Future of Japan–U.S. Relation). In Ōuchi Hyōe, *Ōuchi Hyōe chōsakushū*. Tōkyō: Iwanami Shoten, Vol. 7, pp. 415–33.

Ōuchi Hyōe. [1965] 1975. "Nihon no zaisei" (Japanese Finance). In Ōuchi Hyōe, *Ōuchi Hyōe chōsakushū*. Tōkyō: Iwanami Shoten, Vol. 7, pp. 169–220.

Ōuchi Hyōe, Arisawa Hiromi, Wada Hiroo, and Takahashi Masao. 1954. "MSA to nihon" (MSA and Japan). *Shakaishugi* Mar.: 9–19.

Ōuchi Hyōe, Arisawa Hiromi, Wakimura Yoshitarō, Takahashi Masao, and Minobe Ryōkichi. 1946. *Nihon infureishon no kenkyū* (A Study on Japan's Inflation). Tōkyō: Kōdosha.

Ōuchi Hyōe, Arisawa Hiromi, Wakimura Yoshitarō, Takahashi Masao, and Minobe Ryōkichi. 1949. *Nihon keizai wa dō naru ka?* (Where Is the Japanese Economy Heading?). Tōkyō: Kōdosha.

Ōuchi Hyōe, Kawasaki Misaburō, Arisawa Hiromi, Kimura Kihachirō, Ōkita Saburō, and Tsuru Shigeto. 1947. "Keizai hakusho no igi" (The Significance of the Economic White Paper). *Sekai* Sept.: 1–18.

Peattie, Mark R. [1975] 1992. *Nichibe taiketsu to ishiwara kanji* (Ishiwara Kanji and Japan's Confrontation with the West). Translated by Ōtsuka Takehiro, Seki Shizuo, Ōtsuka Yūko, and David Askew. Daiwa, Shinagawa: Tamairabo.

Prinz, Michael. 1995. "Nachizumu to kindaika: doitsu ni okeru saikin no tōron" (Nazism and Modernization: Recent Discussions in Germany). In Yamanouchi Yasushi, ed., *Sōryokusen to gendaika*. Tōkyō: Kashiwa Shobō, pp. 57–77.

Rekishigaku Kenkyukai. 1990. *Nihon Dōjidaishi: Senryō Seisaku no Tenkan to Kōwa*. (The Contemporary History of Japan: The Transition of Occupation Policy and the Conclusion of Peace Treaty). p. 137. Tōkyō: Aoki Shoten.

Rengo Jōhōsha Henshūkyoku, ed. 1938. *Sensō keizai no zenshin* (The Progress of the War Economy). Tōkyō: Rengo Jōhōsha.

Rōyama Masamichi. [1934] 1965. "Kakoku ni okeru keizai kaigi no hikaku seido kenkyū" (The Comparative Study of the Institutions of Economic Council in Various Countries). In Rōyama Masamichi, *Gyōseigaku kenkyū ronbunshū*. Tōkyō: Keisō Shobō, pp. 56–96.

Rōyama Masamichi. [1936] 1965. "Dajōkan seido to naikaku seido" (The Dajōkan System and the Cabinet System). In Rōyama Masamichi, *Gyōseigaku kenkyū ronbunshū*. Tōkyō: Keisō Shobō, pp. 111–33.

Ryū Shintarō. 1939. *Nihon keizai no saihensei* (The Reorganization of the Japanese economy). Tōkyō: Chūō Kōronsha.

Saguchi Kazarō. 1995. "Sangyō hōkokukai no rekishiteki ichi: sōryokusen to nihon no rōshi kankei" (The Historical Status of the Industrial Patriotic Association: The Total War and Japanese Labor Relations). In Yamanouchi Yasushi, ed., *Sōryokusen to gendaika*. Tōkyō: Kashiwa Shobō, pp. 287–313.

Sahashi Shigeru. 1977. "Tokushinhō no ryūsan" (The Abortion of the Special Measures Law for the Promotion of Designated Industries). In Itō Mitsuharu, ed., *Sengo sangyōshi e no shōgen – sangyō seisaku*. Tōkyō: Mainichi Shinbunsha, pp. 123–58.

Sahashi Shigeru. 1988. "Jiūka taisaku ni fushin" (Working Hard on Countermeasures to the Liberalization). In Kamada Isao and Takamura Juichi, eds., *Shōgen sengo keizaishi*. Tōkyō: Nihon Keizai Shinbunsha, pp. 95–101.

Saitō Seiichirō. 1980. *Keizai Kanryō no Fukken* (The Rehabilitation of Economic Bureaucrats). Tōkyō: PHP Kenkyūsho.

Saitō Seiichirō. 1981. *Keizaigaku wa gendai o sueru ka?* (Can Economics Save Modernity?). Tōkyō: Bungei Shunjū.

Sakai Saburō. 1979. *Shōwa Kenkyūkai* (The Showa Research Association). Tōkyō: TBS Buritanika.

Sakakibara Eisuke. 1990. *Shihonsugi o koeta nihon* (Japan That Transcended Capitalism). Tōkyō: Tōyō Keizai Shinpōsha.

Sakakibara, Eisuke. 1995. "Nihon ishitsuron no ihhenshū: 40-nen taiseiron wa ideorogiteki rekishikan" (A Variant of Japanese Uniqueness Argument: The 1940 System Argument Is an Ideological Perspective of History). *Shūkan tōyō keizai*. July 8. pp. 40–3.

Sakamoto Jirō. 1954. "Nihon keizai no chūshinkokuteki tokushitsu" (The Characteristics of Japan's Economy as Late-Developed Country). In Nakayama Ichirō, ed., *Nihon keizai no kōzō bunseki*. Tōkyō: Tōyō Keizai Shinpōsha, pp. 23–139.

Sakamoto Jirō. 1967. "Shōhansuru mono o tōitsusuru sainō: Nakayama Hakashi" (The Ability to Integrate the Opposite: Dr. Nakayama). In Koizumi Akira and Miyazaki Yoshikazu, eds., *Nihon keizai o miru gan*. Tōkyō: Tōyō Keizai Shinpōsha, pp. 27–37.

Sakurada Takeshi. 1981. "Megumareta shojōken" (Various Advantages). *Ekonomisuto* May 19: 82–9.

Sakurada Takeshi and Shikanai Nobutaka. 1983. *Ima akirakasu sengo hishi* (The Newly Revealed Postwar Secret History). Tokyo: Sankei Shuppan, Vol. 1.

338   References in Japanese

Sakurai Tsuneji. 1947. "Shinkyōjū gurūpu no seikaku" (The Nature of New Professor Group). *Asahi Hyōron* Dec.: 38–43.
Satō Noboru. 1958. "Seisansei kōjō to chingin, koyō" (The Promotion of Productivity and Salary and Employment). *Ekonomisuto* Feb. 22: 50–5.
Sawa Takamitsu. 1984. *Kōdo seichō: rinen to seisaku no dōjidaishi* (High Growth: Histories of Both Ideology and Policy). Tōkyō: Nihon Hōsō Shuppankai.
Sawa Takamitsu. [1982] 1989. *Keizaigaku to wa nani darō ka?* (What Is Economics?). Tōkyō: Nihon Hōsō Shuppankai.
Sawa Takamitsu. 1991. *Kore kara no keizaigaku* (Economics in the Future). Tōkyō: Iwanami Shoten.
Sekitan Shōiinkai. [1946] 1990a. "Sekitan zōsan tokubetsu taisaku" (The Special Measures for Promoting Coal Production). In Nakamura Takafusa and Miyazaki Masayasu, eds., *Keisha seisan hōshiki to sekitan shōiinkai.* Tōkyō: Tōkyō Daigaku Shuppankai, pp. 87–90.
Sekitan Shōiinkai. [1946] 1990b. "Sekitan shōiinkai daiikkai gijiroku" (The Memorandum of the First Meeting of the Coal Committee). In Nakamura Takafusa and Miyazaki Masayasu, eds., *Keisha seisan hōshiki to sekitan shōiinkai.* Tōkyō: Tōkyō Daigaku Shuppankai, pp. 159–61.
Sekiya Reiji. 1989. "Kaisetsu" (Introduction). In Arisawa Hiromi, *Arisawa Hiromi sengo o kataru: Shōwashi e no shōgen.* Tōkyō: Tōkyō Daigaku Shuppankai, pp. 268–77.
Senga Tetsuya. 1978. "Yomigaeru gunju sangyō" (The Reviving Munitions Industries). In Kondō Kanichi and Osanai Hiroshi, eds., *Sengo sangyōshi e no shōgen.* Tōkyō: Mainichi Shinbunsha, Vol. 3, pp. 205–41.
Shakai Keizaishi Gakkai, ed. 1982. *1930 nendai no nihon keizai* (The Japanese Economy in the 1930s). Tōkyō: Tōkyō Daigaku Shuppansha.
Shakaitō. [1959] 1966. "Hata kokumu chōkan e no kōkai shitsumonshō" (The Public Inquiry to the State Secretary Parter). In Tsuji Kiyoaki, ed., *Shiryō sengo nijūnenshi.* Tōkyō: Nihon Hyōronsha, pp. 141–2.
Shakaitō. [undated] 1966. "Anpo iinkai ni okeru shingi jōkyō to kongo no wagatō no shitsumon yōkō" (The Hearing at the Security Committee and the Outline of Questioning by Our Party). In Tsuji Kiyoaki, ed., *Shiryō sengo nijūnenshi:* Vol. 1, *Seiji.* Tokyo: Nihon Hyōronsha, pp. 146–7.
Shakaitō. [1961] 1966. "Kōzō kaikaku no tatakai" (The Struggle of Structural Reform). In Tsuji Kiyoaki, ed., *Shiryō sengo nijūnenshi:* Vol. 1, *Seiji.* Tokyo: Nihon Hyōronsha, pp. 178–81.
Shakaishugi. 1953. "Teichingin sangyō no jittai" (The Reality of the Low Wage Industries). 27(Sept.): 58–61.
Shikagui Seiichi. 1979. "Fukkin to keisha seisan" (The Reconstruction Finance Bank and Priority Production). In Shimura Kaichi, ed., *Sengo sangyōshi e no shōgen, Vol. 5: Kigyō shūdan no keisei.* Tōkyō: Mainichi Shinbunsha, pp. 150–69.
Shimada Haruo. 1993a. "'Senshinkoku koyō' ni shifuto o isoge" (Pushing the Transition Toward the Advanced Countries' Style of Employment). *Ekonomisuto* Apr.: 22–4.
Shimada Haruō. 1993b. "'Senshinkoku gata koyō ni shifuto o isoge (Accelerating the Shift Toward the Employment Pattern of Advanced Countries)." *Shūkan Tōyō Keizai* Apr. 24: 22–4.
Shimada Haruo. 1994a. "'Shinsangyō, koyō sōshutsu kigaku' o isoge (Making Plans Quickly for the Creation of Employment: New Industries)." *Chūō Kōron* Jan.: 48–62.

Shimada Haruo. 1994b. "Kisei kanwa de shinkoyō no sōshutsu o (Creating New Employment by Deregulation)." *Shūkan Tōyō Keizai* Aug.: 13–20.

Shimazaki Miyoko. 1971. "Keisha seisan hōshiki" (The Priority Production). In Chō Yukio and Sumiya Kazuhiko, eds., *Nihon kindai keizai shisō daikei*. Tōkyō: Yūhikaku, Vol. 2, pp. 297–320.

Shimomura Osamu. 1958. *Keizai seichō jitsugen no tame ni* (To Achieve Economic Growth). Tōkyō: Kōchikai.

Shimomura Osamu. 1959a. "Nihon keizai no kichō to sono seichōryoku" (The Basic Condition of the Japanese Economy and Its Growth Power). In Kin'yū Zaisei Jijō Kenkyūkai, ed., *Shimomura riron to sono hihan*. Tōkyō: Kin'yū Zaisei Jijō Kenkyūkai, pp. 3–30.

Shimomura Osamu. 1959b. "Nihon keizai no seichōryoku to seichō riron" (The Growth Power of the Japanese Economy and the Growth Theory). In Kin'yū Zaisei Jijō Kenkyūkai, ed., *Shimomura riron to sono hihan*. Tōkyō: Kin'yū Zaisei Jijō Kenkyūkai, pp. 187–272.

Shimomura Osamu. 1962. *Nihon keizai seichōron* (On the Japanese Economic Growth). Tōkyō: Kin'yū Jijō Kenkyūkai.

Shimomura Osamu. 1967. "Naze seichō ni jishin o motsuka?" (Why Do I Have Confidence in Economic Growth?). In Koizumi Akira and Miyazaki Yoshikazu, eds., *Nihon keizai o miru gan*. Tōkyō: Tōyō Keizai Shinpōsha, pp. 164–202.

Shimomura Osamu. [1965] 1971. "Antei seichō ronsha wa yaburetari" (The Failure of Those who Asserted Stable Growth). In Shimomura Osamu, *Keizai taikoku nihon no sentaku*. Tōkyō: Tōyō Keizai Shinpōsha, pp. 440–507.

Shimomura Osamu. 1981a. "Seichō riron e no aporōchi" (The Approach to Growth Theory). *Ekonomisuto* Apr.: 80–7.

Shimomura Osamu. 1981b. "Rekishiteki bokkōki no imi" (The Implication of the Historical Rise). *Ekonomisuto* Apr: 80–7.

Shimomura Osamu. 1981c. "Seichō seisaku no seika" (The Outcome of the Growth Policy). *Ekonomisuto* Apr.: 82–91.

Shimomura Osamu, Yamamoto Masao, Imai Ichio, and Aoba Fumio. 1960. "Kōseichō seisaku no ronri" (The Logic of the High Growth Policy). *Ekonomisuto* Oct. 10: 58–64.

Shimura Kaichi. 1976. "Fukkō kin'yū kōko" (The Reconstruction Bank). In Ōkurashō Zaiseishishitsu, ed., *Showa zaiseishi: kyūsen kara shūsen made: Vol. 12*. Tōkyō: Tōyō Keizai Shinposha, pp. 623–854.

Shimura Kaichi, ed. 1979. *Sengo sangyōshi e no shōgen, Vol. 5: Kigyō shūdan no keisei* (The Formation of Business Groups). Tōkyō: Mainichi Shinbunsha.

Shioda Shio. 1991. "Shimomura Osamu to kōdō keizai seichō seisaku" (Shimomura Osamu and the High Growth Policy). *Purejidento* Aug.: 158–67.

Shishido Toshio. 1971. "Kanchō ekonomisuto nanatsu no kairitsu" (Seven Commandments of Government Economists). *Ekonomisuto* Apr. 25: 126–9.

Shisō no Kagaku Kenkyūkai, ed. 1959. *Tenkō* (The Conversion). Tōkyō: Heibonsha, Vol. 1.

Shisō no Kagaku Kenkyūkai, ed. 1960. *Tenkō* (The Conversion). Tōkyō: Heibonsha, Vol. 2.

Shōkō Gyōsei Kenkyukai. 1942. *Senjika no shōkō gyōsei* (The Administration of Commerce and Industry during the War). Tōkyō: Eiga Shuppansha.

Shōwa Dōjinkai. 1968. *Shōwa kenkyūkai* (The Showa Research Association). Tōkyō: Keizai Ōraisha.

Shōwa Dōjinkai, ed. 1968. "Nihon keizai no saihensei to Ryū Shintarō" (The Reorganization of the Japanese Economy and Ryū Shintarō). Tōkyō: Keizai Ōraisha, pp. 225–50.

Shōwa Kenkyūkai. 1939. *Burokku keizai ni kansuru kenkyū* (Study on the Bloc Economy). Tōkyō: Seikatsusha.

Shōwa Kenkyūkai Jimukyoku. 1974. "Seiji kikō kaishin taikō" (The Outline of the Reform of Political Institutions). In Imai Seiichi and Itō Takashi, eds., *Gendaishi shiryō, kokka sōdōin 2*. Tōkyō: Misuzu Shobō, Vol. 44, pp. 161–73.

Sōdōmei. [1955] 1966. "Dainikai chūō iinkai kettei: seisansei kōjō undō ni taisuru sōdōmei no taido" (The Decision by the Second Meeting of the Central Committee: Sōdōmei's Attitude Toward the Productivity Movement). In Ōkōchi Kazuo, ed., *Shiryō sengo nijūnenshi:* Vol. 4, *Rōdō*. Tōkyo: Nihon Hyōronsha, p. 308.

Sōhyō. [1955] 1966. "Seisansei zōkyō ni taisuru kihonteki taido" (The Basic Position on the Promotion of Productivity). In Ōkōchi Kazuo, ed., *Shiryō sengo nijūnenshi:* Vol. 4, *Rōdō*. Tōkyo: Nihon Hyōronsha, pp. 306–8.

Suetaka Shin. 1936. "Shinsangyō seisaku to tōseishugi" (New Industrial Policy and Economic Control). In Keizai Jōhōsha, ed., *Nihon keizai no saihensei, 3: sangyō oyobi bōekihen*. Tokyo: Keizai Jōhōsha, pp. 25–9.

Sugihara Shirō. 1984. *Nihon no Ekonomisuto* (Japan's Economists). Tōkyō: Nihon Hyōronsha.

Sugihara Shirō. 1990. *Nihon no keizai shisōka tachi* (Japan's Economic Theorists). Tōkyō: Nihon Keizai Hyōronsha.

Sugihara Shirō and Chō Yūkio. 1979. *Nihon keizai shisōshi dokuhon* (Readings in the History of Economic Theories in Japan). Tōkyō: Tōyō Keizai Shinbunsha.

Sugihara Shirō, Sakasai Takahito, Fujiwara Akio, and Fujii Takashi. 1990. *Nihon no keizai shisō yonbyakunen* (Four Hundred Years of Japanese Economic Thought). Tōkyō: Nihon Keizai Hyōronsha.

Sugita Hiroaki. 1989. *Shōwa no ekonomisuto* (Showa Economists). Tōkyō: Chūō Keizaisha.

Sumitani Mikio. 1986. "Sōron: keizaigaku kakubunya no hatten" (The Development of Economics in Various Fields). In Tōkyō Daigaku Keizai Gakubu, ed., *Tōkyō daigaku keizai gakubu gojūnenshi*. Tōkyō: Tōkyō Daigaku Shuppankai, pp. 111–42.

Suzuki Hideo. 1988. "IMF hachijōkoku ikō no koro" (When Moving Toward IMF Article 8 Country). In Kamada Isao and Takamura Juichi, eds., *Shōgen sengo keizaishi*. Tōkyō: Nihon Keizai Shinbunsha, pp. 101–10.

Suzuki Kōichirō. "Shihonron no hōyaku shōshi" (A Brief History of the Translation of "The Capital"). In Suzuki Kōichirō, *Shihonron to nihon*. Tōkyō: Kōbundū, pp. 8–39.

Suzuki Takeo. 1948a. "Arisawa, Kimura ronsō saihihan" (Further Criticism on the Controversy Between Arisawa and Kimura). *Ekonomisuto* Mar. 1: 226–9.

Suzuki Takeo. 1948b. "Chūkan anteiron hihan" (A Critique on Midway Stabilization). *Asahi hyōron* Aug.: 32–45.

Suzuki Takeo. 1949. "Keizai kyūgensoku to tanichi kawase reito" (Nine Economic Principles and Single Exchange Rate). *Hyōron* Apr.: 32–6.

Suzuki Takeo, Kimura Kihachirō, and Tsuru Shigeto. 1950. "Nihon keizai no hyōjō" (The Situation of Japan's Economy). *Hyōron* Jan.: 33–44.

Takabatake Michitoshi. 1960. "Seisanryoku riron" (The Theory of Production Force). In Shisō no Kagaku Kenkyūkai, ed., *Tenkō*. Tōkyō: Heibonsha, Vol. 2, pp. 201–47.

Takahashi Kamekichi. 1933. *Nihon keizai tōseiron* (On Japanese Economic Control). Tōkyō: Kaizōsha.

Takahashi Kamekichi. 1967. "Naze teikinri seisaku o shucchōsuru ka" (Why do I Suggest a Low Interest Rate Policy?). In Koizumi Akira and Miyazaki Yoshikazu, eds., *Nihon keizai o miru gan.* Tōkyō: Tōyō Keizai Shinpōsha, pp. 41–73.

Takahashi Makoto and Katō Saburō. 1974. "Kaizai fukkō to Ishibashi zaisei" (Economic Recovery and Ishibashi Finance). In Suzuki Takeo Kanrei Kinen Bunshū Iinkai, ed., *Keizai seichō to zaisei kin'yū.* Tōkyō: Shiseitō, pp. 31–45.

Takahashi Masao. 1981. "Keizai seichō wa mayaku datta" (Economic Growth as Poison). *Ekonomisuto* June 16: 80–7.

Takahashi Masao. 1989. "Daigaku no Uchi to Soto" (The Inside and the Outside of the University). In Arisawa Hiromi no Shōwashi Hensan Iinkai, ed., *Kaisō.* Tōkyō: Tōkyō Daigaku Shuppankai, pp. 36–43.

Takajima Kikuo. 1953. "Mujun no shūchūteki hyōgen – gōrika" (The Intensive Reflection of Contradiction – Rationalization). *Keizai hyōron* Aug.: 50–7.

Takana Shin'ichi. 1975. *Nihon sensō keizai hishi* (The Secret History of Japan's Wartime Economy). Tōkyō: Konpūtaeijisha.

Takawa Yawao. 1970. *Sengo nihon kakumei undōshi* (The Postwar History of the Japanese Revolutionary Movements). Tōkyō: Gendai shichōsha, Vol. 1.

Takemi Tarō. 1968. *Takemi Tarō kaisōroku* (Takemi Tarō's Recollection). Tōkyō: Nihon Keizai Shinbunsha.

Takeuchi Konomi. 1980. "Interiron" (On Intellectuals). In Takeuchi Konomi, *Takeuchi Konomi zenshū.* Tōkyō: Tsukuma Shobō, pp. 86–105.

Takita Minoru, Nagano Shigeru, Nakajima Tetsuzō, and Nakayama Ichirō. 1972. "Sengo nihon no rōshi kankei" (Labor Relations in Postwar Japan). In Nakayama Ichirō, *Nakayama Ichirō zenshū.* Tōkyō: Kodansha, pp. 82–106.

Tamanoi Yoshirō. 1971. *Nihon no keizaigaku* (Japan's Economics). Tōkyō: Chūō Kōronsha.

Tamanoi Yoshirō. 1975. *Tenkansuru keizaigaku* (Economics at a Turning Point). Tōkyō: Tōkyō Daigaku Shuppankai.

Tanaka Yonosuke. 1959. "Chingin nibairon o megutte" (Around the Issue of Doubling Salaries). *Ekonomisuto* Mar. 21: 6–11.

Teranishi Jūrō. 1993a. "Meinbanku shisutemu" (The Main Bank System). In Okazaki Tetsuji and Okuno Masahiro, eds., *Gendai nihon keizai shisutemu no genryū.* Tōkyō: Nihon Keizai Shibunsha, pp. 61–96.

Teranishi Jūrō. 1993b. "Shūsen chokugo ni okeru kinyū seido kaikaku" (The Reform of the Financial System in the Early Postwar Period). In Kōsai Yutaka and Teranishi Jūrō, eds., *Sengo nihon no keizai kaikaku.* Tōkyō: Tōkyō Daigaku Shuppankai, pp. 131–52.

Tōa Keizai Chōsakyoku. 1935. *Nachisu no keizai seisaku* (Nazi's economic policy). Tokyo: Tōa Keizai Chōsakyoku.

Tōbata Seiichi. 1967. "Keizai no shinpo to sono niraite" (The Progress of Economy and Its Agents). In Koizumi Akira and Miyazaki Yoshikazu, eds., *Nihon keizai o miru gan.* Tōkyō: Tōyō Keizai Shinpōsha, pp. 204–32.

Tōbata Seiichi. 1984. *Tōbata Seiichi wagashi wagatomo wagagakumon* (Tōbata Seiichi: My Teachers, My Friends and My Academic Career). Tōkyō: Kashiwa Shobō.

Tokunaga Hisatsugu. 1988. "Intabiu" (Interview). In Keizai kikakuchō, ed., *Sengo keizai fukkō to keizai antei honbu.* Tōkyō: Keizai Kikakuchō, pp. 125–45.

Tokyo Shōkō Kaigisho. 1941. *Gyōsei kikō kaikaku mondai ni kansuru shiryō* (The Literature Concerning the Issue of the Administrative System). Tōkyō: Tokyo Shōkō Kaigisho.

Tōyō Keizai. 1991. "Ronsōshi de tsūzuru sengo nihon keizai no rekishi" (The History of the Postwar Japanese Economy Seen from Debates). June 8: 40–55.

Tsuji Kiyoaki. 1966. *Shiryō sengo nijūnenshi* (Literature on Twenty Years' Postwar History). Tōkyō: Nihon Hyōronsha.

Tsuji Kiyoaki. [1969] 1981. *Nihon kanryōsei no kenkyū* (Studies on the Japanese Bureaucratic System). Tōkyō: Tōkyō Daigaku Shuppankai.

Tsujimura Kōtarō. 1984. *Nihon no keizai gakusha tachi* (The Japanese Economists). Tōkyō: Nihon Hyōronsha.

Tsuru Shigeto. 1947a. "Sonogo no shiunpeita" (Schumepter Since Then). *Sekai* May: 19–28.

Tsuru Shigeto. 1947b. "Kisōsha toshite" (As the Drafter of the Document). *Sekai* Sept.: 16–18.

Tsuru Shigeto. 1950. *Amerika Ryūgakuki* (Studying in America). Tōkyō: Iwanami Shoten.

Tsuru Shigeto. 1951. "Ichi keizai gakuto no hansei" (The Self-examination of a Student of Economics). *Sekai* Jan.: 9–18.

Tsuru Shigeto. 1959. "Nihon keizai no seichōryoku to keiki junkan" (The Growth Power and Business Cycle of the Japanese Economy). In Kin'yū Zaisei Jijō Kenkyūkai, ed., *Shimomura riron to sono hihan*. Tōkyō: Kin'yū Zaisei Jijō, pp. 97–136.

Tsuru Shigeto. 1965. "Nihon keizai no sengo nijūnen" (The Japanese Economy in the Twenty Years After the War). *Keizai hyōron, Nihon keizai – sengo nijūnen*, Oct., supplementary issue.

Tsuru Shigeto. 1967. "Ningen no fukushi to seiji keizaigaku no ninmu" (Human Welfare and the Task of Political Economy). In Koizumi Akira and Miyazaki Yoshikazu, eds., *Nihon keizai o miru gan*. Tōkyō: Tōyō Keizai Shinpōsha, pp. 234–65.

Tsuru Shigeto. [1950] 1970. "Kokusai keizai to nihon" (Japan and International Economy). In Kanamori Hisao, ed., *Bōeki to kokusai shūshi*. Tōkyō: Nihon Keizai Shinbunsha, pp. 26–45.

Tsuru Shigeto. [1950] 1975. "Nihon keizai no bunkiten" (The Turning Point of the Japanese Economy). In Tsuru Shigeto, *Tsuru Shigeto Chōsakushū*. Tōkyō: Kōdansha, Vol.5, pp. 78–104.

Tsuru Shigeto. [1954] 1975. "Nihon no keizai jiritsu to kokusai kankyō" (The Economic Independence of Japan and the International Environment). In Tsuru Shigeto, *Tsuru Shigeto Chōsakushū*. Tōkyō: Kōdansha, Vol. 5, pp. 42–62.

Tsuru Shigeto. [1955] 1975. "Nihon keizai to saigunbi" (The Japanese Economy and the Rearmament). In Tsuru Shigeto, *Tsuru Shigeto Chōsakushū*. Tōkyō: Kōdansha, Vol. 5, pp. 31–41.

Tsuru Shigeto. 1976. "'Keizaigaku no hitori aruki wa abunai" (The Danger of Going Alone in Economics). In Tsuru Shigeto, *Tsuru Shigeto chōsakushū*. Tōkyō: Kōdansha, Vol. 8, pp. 59–104.

Tsuru Shigeto. [1953] 1976. "MSA to nihon" (MSA and Japan). In Tsuru Shigeto, *Tsuru Shigeto Chōsakushū*. Tōkyō: Kōdansha, Vol. 6, pp. 103–21.

Tsuru Shigeto. [1954] 1976. "Sekai jōsei to nihon no shinrō" (The World Situation and the Course of Japan). In Tsuru Shigeto, *Tsuru Shigeto Chōsakushū*. Tōkyō: Kōdansha, Vol. 8, pp. 273–300.

Tsuru Shigeto. 1978. "Senkyūhyaku sanjūnendai igo no keizaigaku no hatten" (The Development of Economics After the 1930s). In Minoguchi Takeo and Hayasaka Tadashi, eds., *Kindai keizaigaku to nihon*. Tōkyō: Nihon Keizai Shinbunsha, pp. 119–47.

Tsuru Shigeto. 1983a. "Keizaigaku no sankyosei" (Three Superstars in Economics). *Asahi shinbun* Feb. 6: 1.

Tsuru Shigeto. 1983b. "Atarashii paradaimu no sōzōsha" (The Creators of New Paradigms). *Ekonomisuto,* Apr. 5: 112–22.

Tsuru Shigeto. 1983c. *Taisei henkaku no seiji keizaigaku* (The Political Economy of Institutional Reform). Tōkyō: Shinhyōron.

Tsuru Shigeto. 1988a. "Intabiu" (Interview). In Keizai kikakuchō, ed., *Sengo keizai fukkō to keizai antei honbu.* Tōkyō: Keizai Kikakuchō, pp. 103–22.

Tsuru Shigeto. 1988b. "Tsuru Shigeto nisshi" (Tsuru Shigeto's Diary). In Keizai kikakuchō, ed., *Sengo keizai fukkō to keizai antei honbu.* Tōkyō: Keizai Kikakuchō, pp. 209–410.

Tsurumi Shunsuke. 1960. "Yokusan undō no sekkeisha" (The Designer of the Movement of Imperial Assistance). In Shisō no Kagaku Kenkyūkai, ed., *Tenkō.* Tōkyō: Heibonsha, Vol. 2, pp. 53–120.

Tsurumi Shunsuke. 1976. *Tenkō kenkyū* (Studies on Conversion). Tōkyō: Tsukuma Shobō.

Tsurumi Shunsuke. 1982. *Senjiki nihon no seishinshi* (An Intellectual History of Wartime Japan: 1931–1945). Tōkyō: Iwanami Shoten.

Tsurumi Shunsuke, Hidaka Rokurō, Hariu Ichirō, and Kan Takaki. 1985. *Sengo towa nani ka?* (What Is the Postwar Era?). Tōkyō: Seikyōsha.

Tsuruta Toshimasa. 1984. "Kōdo seichōki" (The Period of High Growth). In Komiya Ryūtarō, Okuno Masahiro, and Suzumura Kōtarō, eds., *Nihon no sangyō seisaku.* Tokyo. Tokyo Daigaku Shuppankai, pp. 45–76.

Tsūsanshō. 1954. *Sengo keizai jūnenshi* (Ten Years' History of the Postwar Economy). Tokyo: Shōkō Kaikan Shuppanbu.

Tsūsanshō, ed. 1957. *Sangyō gōrika hakusho* (The White Paper of Industrial Rationalization). Tōkyō: Nikkan Kōgyō Shinbunsha.

Tsūsanshō. 1989. *Tsūshō sangyō seisakushi, Vol. 5: Jiritsu kiban kakuritsuki (1)* (The History of the Policies of Trade and Industry, Vol. 5: The Establishment of the Foundation of Economic Independence, 1). Tōkyō: Tsūshō Sangyō Chōsakai.

Tsūsanshō. 1990a. *Tsūshō sangyō seisakushi, Vol. 6: Jiritsu kiban kakuritsuki (2)* (The History of the Policies of Trade and Industry, Vol. 6: The Establishment of the Foundation of Economic Independence, 2). Tōkyō: Tsūshō Sangyō Chōsakai.

Tsūsanshō. 1990b. *Tsūshō sangyō seisakushi, Vol. 10: daisanki, kōdō seichōki (3)* (The History of the Policies of Trade and Industry, Vol. 10: the Period of High Growth, 3). Tōkyō: Tsūshō Sangyō Chōsakai.

Uchida Jōkichi. 1949. *Nihon shihonshugi ronsō* (The Debate on Japanese Capitalism). Tōkyō: Shinkō Shuppansha.

Uchida Yoshihiko. 1948. "Senji keizaigaku no mujun teki tenkai to keizai riron" (The Dilemma in the Development of Economics During the War and Economic Theories). *Chōryū* Jan.: 37–42.

Uchihashi Katsuto. 1993. "Nihon kei koyō chōsei no yūgami o tadase" (Fix the Problems in the Japanese Style of Employment Adjustment). *Ekonomisuto* Apr. 24: 18–20.

Uchihashi Katsuto and Yakushiji Taizō. 1993. "Mono zukuri ni shimei to hokoru o torimodose (Taking Back the Mission and the Pride in Making Things)." *Economisuto* Nov. 16: 34–8.

Uchino Tatsurō. 1975. "Sengo keizai seisaku sanjōnen shōshi" (A Brief Thirty Year History of Postwar Economic Policy). *ESP* July: 10–16.

Uchino Tatsurō. 1978. *Sengo nihon keizaishi* (Postwar Japanese Economic History). Tōkyō: Kōdansha.

Ueda Hirofumi. 1987. "Senji tōsei keizai to shitaukesei no tenkai" (Development of the Subcontract System Under the Wartime Controlled Economy). In Nihon Kindaishi Kenkyūkai, ed., *Senji keizai.* Tōkyō: Yamakawa Shuppansha, pp. 199–229.

Ueda Hirofumi. 1995. "Senji keizai ka no shitauke kyōryoku kōgyō seisaku no keisei" (Subcontracting in the Wartime Economy – the Formation of Cooperative Industrial Policy). In Hara Akira, ed., *Nihon no senji keizai.* Tōkyō: Tōkyō Daigaku Shuppankai, pp. 201–36.

Ueda Kazuo. 1993. "Kin'yū shisutemu-kisei" (The Financial System – Regulations). In Okazaki Tetsuji and Okuno Masahiro, eds., *Gendai nihon keizai shisutemu no genryū.* Tōkyō: Nihon Keizai Shibunsha, pp. 35–60.

Uemae Junichirō. 1985a. "Ikeda Burein Hajimeugokasu" (Initiated by 'Ikeda's Brain Trust'. *Gendai* July: 310–34.

Uemae Junichirō. 1985b. " 'Jinmu Keiki' no shikakarijin hashiru" (The Action of the Initiator of Jinmu Boom). *Gendai* Aug.: 334–57.

Uemae Junichirō. 1985c. "Shotoku baisō o jitsugen seyo" (Let's Double the National Income). *Gendai* Sept.: 312–36.

Uemae Junichirō. 1985d. "Nihon ga moeta hi" (The Day That Excited Japan). *Gendai* Oct.: 330–53.

Umemoto Katsu, Satō Noboru, and Maruyama Masao. 1966. *Gendai nihon no kakushin shisō* (Progressive Ideas in Modern Japan). Tōkyō: Kawade Shobō.

Umezao Tadao, Takeyama Michio, Hayashi Kentarō, and Suzuki Shigetaka. 1957. "Rekishi no okeru nihon no senshinsei" (The Advanced Nature of Japan in History). *Chūō Kōron* Nov.: 266–77.

Usami Seijirō. 1952. "Jūzoku taiseika ni okeru sangyō kōzō to dokusen" (Industrial Structure and Monopoly in a System of Dependence). *Keizai hyōron* Aug.: 17–29.

Ushikubo Hiroshi. 1988. "Sengo ni okeru rōdō kumiai no 'minshuka, kindaika' " (The Democratization and Modernization of Labor Unions in the Postwar Period). In Maeda Ai, Najita Tetsuo, and Kamishima Jirō, eds., *Sengo nihon seishinshi.* Tōkyō: Iwanami Shoten, pp. 468–83.

Wakimura Yoshitarō. 1970. "Kore de ii no ka: sekiyu seisaku" (Is the Present Policy on Oil OK?). *Tōyō Keizai* Jan. 17: 46–8.

Wakimura Yoshitarō. 1989. "Waimaru kyōwakoku jidai no Arisawa sensei" (Professor Arisawa in the Era of the Weimar Republic). In *Arisawa Hiromi no Shōwashi* Hensan Iinkai, ed., *Kaisō.* Tōkyō: Tōkyō Daigaku Shuppankai, pp. 9–36.

Watanabe Takeshi. 1983. *Watanabe Takeshi nikki* (The Diary of Watanabe Takeshi). Tōkyō: Tōyō Keizai Shinpōsha.

Wolferen, van Karel. 1990. "Naze nihon no chishikijin wa hitasura genryoku ni suiju suru ka?" (Why Do Japanese Intellectuals Follow Political Power So Earnestly?). *Chūō Kōron* Jan: 68–98.

Yamaguchi Yasushi. 1979. *Fuashizumu* (Fascism). Tokyo: Yūkikaku.

Yamakishi Akira. 1993. "21 seiki wa ōberyū no rōshi kankei ni tenkan" (The Transition Toward the European–American Style of Labor Relations in the 21st Century). *Ekonomisuto* Apr. 24: 13.

Yamamoto Yoshihito. 1989. *Senkanki nihon shihonshugi to keizai seisaku* (The Wartime Japanese Capitalism and Economic Policies). Tōkyō: Haku Shobō Kabushiki Kaisha.

Yamanouchi Yasushi. 1995a. "Hōhōteki joron: sōryokusen to shisutemu tōgō" (On Methodology: The Total War and the Integration of the System). In Yamanouchi Yasushi, ed., *Sōryokusen to gendaika.* Tōkyō: Kashiwa Shobō, pp. 9–56.

Yamanouchi Yasushi, ed. 1995b. *Sōryokusen to gendaika* (The Total War and Modernization). Tōkyō: Kashiwa Shobō.

Yamanouchi Yasushi, Narita Ryūichi, and Ōuchi Hirokazu. 1996. "Sōryokusen, kokumin kokka, shisutemu shakai" (The Total War, Civil State, System Society). *Gendai Shisō* 24(7): 8–33.

Yamazaki Hiroaki. 1995. "Gaisetsu" (Introduction). In Yamazaki Hiroaki and Kikkawa Takeo, eds., *"Nihonteki" keiei no renzoku to danzetsu*. Tōkyō: Iwanami Shoten, pp. 1–71.

Yamazaki Shirō. 1995. "Senji kōgyō dōin taisei" (The Industrial Mobilization System During the War). In Hara Akira, ed., *Nihon no senji keizai*. Tōkyō: Tōkyō Daigaku Shuppankai, pp. 45–106.

Yamazaki Tanshō. 1948. *Naikakuron* (On the Cabinet System). Tōkyō: Gakuyō Shobō.

Yano Tomoo, Shinohara Miyohei, and Yoda Susumu. 1975. "Nihon keizai sanjūnen no kaiko to hyōka" (Retrospection and Evaluation of Thirty Year Japanese Economy). *ESP* July: 17–38.

Yasui Takuma. 1979. *Keizaigaku to sono shūhen* (Economics and Its Environment). Tōkyō: Kitakusha.

Yasui Takuma. 1980. *Kindai keizaigaku to watashi* (Modern Economics and I). Tōkyō: Kitakusha.

Yatsugi Kazuo. 1971. *Shōwa dōran shishi* (The Heroes in the Showa Crisis). Tōkyō: Keizai Ōraisha.

Yatsugi Kazuo. 1981 *Shōwa seikai hiwa* (The Secret Story of Political Circles in the Showa Period). Tōkyō: Hara Shobō.

Yokoda Kisaburō. 1989. "Kyūjūnen kuraku no michi" (Ninety Years of Bitterness and Happiness). In *Arisawa Hiromi no Shōwashi* Hensan Iinkai, ed., *Kaisō*. Tōkyō: Tōkyō Daigaku Shuppankai, pp. 3–8.

Yomiuri Shinbunsha. 1971–2. *Shōwashi no tennō* (The Emperor in the Showa History). Tōkyō: Yomiuri Shinbunsha, Vols. 16, 17, 18, 19.

Yonekura Seiichirō. 1993. "Gyōkai dantai no kinō" (The Role of Trade Associations). In Okazaki Tetsuji and Okuno Masahiro, eds., *Gendai nihon keizai shisutemu no genryū*. Tōkyō: Nihon Keizai Shibunsha, pp. 183–210.

Yonezawa Yoshie. 1993. "Keizaiteki jiritsu to sangyō gōrika seisaku" (Economic Independence and the Industrial Rationalization Policy). In Kōsai Yutaka and Teranishi Jūrō, eds., *Sengo nihon no kaikaku*. Tōkyō: Tōkyō Daigaku Shuppankai, pp. 211–36.

Yoshida Shigeru. 1957. *Kaisō jūnen* (Ten Years' Recollection). Tōkyō: Shinchōsha, Vols. 1, 2, 3, 4.

Yoshikawa Hiroshi and Okazaki Tetsuji. 1990. "Keizaigaku ni okeru riron to rekishi" (Theory and History in Economics). In Yoshikawa Hiroshi and Okazaki Tetsuji, eds., *Keizai riron e no rekishiteki paasupekuterbu*. Tōkyō: Tōkyō Daigaku Shuppankai, pp. 1–12.

Yoshimura Katsumi. 1985. *Ikeda seiken: 1575 nichi* (The 1575 Days of the Ikeda Administration). Tōkyō: Gyōsei Mondai Kenkyūsho.

Yoshimura Masaharu. 1961. *Jiyūka to nihon keizai* (Liberalization and the Japanese Economy). Tokyo: Iwanami Shoten.

Yoshino Shinji. 1930. *Wagakuni kōgyō no gōrika* (The Industrial Rationalization of Our Country). Tōkyō: Nihon Hyōronsha.

Yoshino Shinji. 1966. "Sangyō gōrika" (Industrial Rationalization). In Andō Yoshio, ed., *Shōwa keizai shi e no shōgen*. Tōkyō: Mainichi Shinbunsha, Vol. 1, pp. 116–29.

Yoshino Toshihiko. 1965. *Watashi no sengo keizaishi* (My Postwar Economic History). Tōkyō: Jiseidō.

Yoshino Toshihiko. 1975. *Sengo kin'yū-shi no omoide* (The Recollection of the Postwar Monetary History). Tōkyō: Nihon Keizai Shinbunsha.

Index